Gender Pluralism

This book examines three big ideas: difference, legitimacy, and pluralism. Of chief concern is how people construe and deal with variation among fellow human beings. Why under certain circumstances do people embrace or even sanctify differences, or at least begrudgingly tolerate them, and why in other contexts are people less receptive to difference, sometimes overtly hostile to it and bent on its eradication? What are the cultural and political conditions conducive to the positive valorization and acceptance of difference? And, conversely, what conditions undermine or erode such positive views and acceptance? This book examines pluralism in gendered fields and domains in Southeast Asia since the early modern era, which historians and anthropologists of the region commonly define as the period extending roughly from the fifteenth to the eighteenth centuries.

Michael G. Peletz is Professor of Anthropology at Emory University. His specialties include social theory, gender, sexuality, Islam, and modernity, particularly in Southeast Asia. He is the author of *Islamic Modern: Religious Courts and Cultural Politics in Malaysia* (Princeton, 2002), *Reason and Passion: Representations of Gender in a Malay Society* (California, 1996), and *A Share of the Harvest: Kinship, Property, and Social History among the Malays of Rembau* (California, 1988). He is also the co-editor, with Aihwa Ong, of *Bewitching Women, Pious Men: Gender and Body Politics in Southeast Asia* (California, 1995).

Gender Pluralism

Southeast Asia Since Early
Modern Times

Michael G. Peletz

Routledge
Taylor & Francis Group

NEW YORK AND LONDON

First published 2009
by Routledge
270 Madison Ave, New York, NY 10016

Simultaneously published in the UK
by Routledge
2 Park Square, Milton Park, Abingdon, Oxon OX14 4RN

Routledge is an imprint of the Taylor & Francis Group, an informa business

© 2009 Taylor & Francis

Typeset in Goudy by Swales & Willis Ltd
Printed and bound in the United States of America
on acid-free paper by Walsworth Publishing Company, Marceline, MO

Library of Congress Cataloging in Publication Data
Peletz, Michael G.
Gender pluralism : southeast Asia since early modern times/
Michael G. Peletz.
p. cm.
Includes bibliographical references and index.
1. Gender identity—Southeast Asia. 2. Sex customs—Southeast Asia.
3. Sex role—Southeast Asia. 4. Transgender people—Southeast Asia.
I. Title.
HQ1075.5.S64P45 2008
305.30959—dc22
2008042130

ISBN 10: 0–415–93160–6 (hbk)
ISBN 10: 0–415–93161–4 (pbk)
ISBN 10: 0–203–88004–8 (ebk)

ISBN 13: 978–0–415–93160–1 (hbk)
ISBN 13: 978–0–415–93161–8 (pbk)
ISBN 13: 978–0–203–88004–3 (ebk)

Contents

vi Contents

Acknowledgments

Work on this book spanned nearly a decade, during which time I incurred many debts both institutional and personal. I conceived the idea for the book and began exploratory library research as a Fellow at the National Humanities Center (NHC) in Research Triangle Park, North Carolina, during the period 1999–2000, and continued preliminary work on the volume's basic themes at the Erasmus Institute of the University of Notre Dame the following year. In addition to acknowledging the financial and other support made available by these institutions, I would like to express my gratitude to the Institute for Advanced Study in Princeton, which awarded me a 2005–2006 residential fellowship that permitted full-time engagement with the project in a scholarly paradise free of most of life's routine distractions. Some of the funding I received from the Institute derived from the National Endowment for the Humanities, which also provided a year-long fellowship in 2007 to complete work on the book, a goal that proved largely attainable thanks to the generous leave granted by Emory University.

Conversations with Sherry Ortner at the NHC nearly ten years ago helped convince me that the project was worthwhile, as did the timely support of Ilene Kalish, then an acquisitions editor at Routledge. I also benefited from the late Clifford Geertz's interest in my work, and from conversations with others at the Institute, especially Joan W. Scott and Michael Walzer. Colleagues in the Department of Anthropology at Emory University—Joyce Flueckiger, Carla Freeman, Bruce Knauft, and David Nugent—deserve special thanks for reading early versions of chapters on rather short notice and for offering critical feedback on a then unwieldy manuscript. So too do Tony Day and Ian Mabbett who not only brought their expansive knowledge of Southeast Asian history to bear on some of my early formulations but also encouraged me to clarify a number of conceptual and other matters. At Cornell University I am deeply indebted to Tamara Loos, who organized a two-day workshop (February 22–23, 2008) on gender pluralism in Southeast Asia that focused on the penultimate draft of the manuscript. Conference participants—drawn from the fields of anthropology, art history, history, Southeast Asian studies, and women's studies—read and commented on the work in its entirety, offering many useful corrections and other suggestions. It is a rare privilege to be the beneficiary of this kind of specialist and collective insight on a work in progress. I would thus like to thank both Thak Chaloemtiarana and Wendy Treat of Cornell's George McT. Kahin Center for Advanced Research on Southeast Asia, whose administrative support and technical assistance made the workshop a reality; and the following conference participants who braved Ithaca's harsh winter on my behalf (or, in one case, endeavored to do so but was stymied by winter storms that precluded travel from afar but not the last-minute faxing of her comments): Evelyn Blackwood, Jane Ferguson, Durba Ghosh, Tom Gibson, Tyrell Haberkorn, Mark Johnson, Ward Keeler, Tamara Loos, Kathy March, Kaja McGowan, Steve Sangren, and Megan Sinnott. I am also grateful to the two anonymous readers for the press who later identified themselves to me—Tom Gibson and Ward Keeler, both of whom gave generously of their time and wisdom and helped save me from some embarrassing omissions. This list would be incomplete if I neglected to acknowledge my intellectual debts to Anthony Reid and Barbara Andaya; although neither of them read any version of the manuscript, my understanding of Southeast Asia's past owes much to their pioneering scholarship.

Thanks, finally, to the publishers who gave permission to include material adapted from previous publications (Peletz 1996, 2002, 2005, 2006, 2007); to Amaris Crawford, Shumaila Dhanani, and Stephanie Loo for their valuable research assistance; to Ellen Walker for drawing the map and designing the book's cover; to Steve Rutter, my editor at Routledge, for patience, encouragement, and perspective; to Sarah Phillips, Fiona Wade, Richard Willis, and other members of the editorial and production staff at Routledge and Swales & Willis for lending their professional skills along the way; and to Susan Henry Peletz, for all kinds of sacrifices, support, and love.

Note on Spelling, Transliteration, and Names

Throughout this book I introduce various Asian-language terms that I render in italics and spell in accordance with the most current conventions followed by scholars working in the languages in question. For ease of reading and to simplify the book's production, I have not included diacritics in my transliteration of Asian-language terms. In the languages of Southeast Asia, unlike those of South Asia and many other regions of the world, a noun typically has the same form regardless of whether or not the context implies that its number is singular or plural. As is common scholarly practice, I adhere to this convention in citing Southeast Asian-language terms (except when quoting published material that conforms to other standards), though I usually pluralize South Asian and other foreign-language nouns by adding an "s" to the singular form. Finally, following established usage, Malays, Thais, and certain ethnic Chinese (among others) are designated by that part of their name which appears first in the word order, since this is the name by which they are known to most people in both formal and informal contexts. Some other Asians are typically referred to by later portions of their names, as is the case with Westerners. Still others, such as the Burmese, have names in which all parts are of equal significance and admit of no shortening when written. Bibliographic entries are consistent with these practices (i.e., entries are alphabetized according to whichever part of the author's name is deemed of greatest importance).

1 Introduction

This book examines three big ideas: difference, legitimacy, and pluralism. My chief concern is how people construe and deal with variation among fellow human beings. Why under certain circumstances do people embrace, even sanctify differences, or at least begrudgingly tolerate them, and why in other contexts are people less receptive to difference, sometimes overtly hostile to it and bent on its eradication?[1] What are the cultural and political conditions conducive to the positive valorization and acceptance of difference? And, conversely, what conditions undermine or erode such positive views and acceptance?

The term "difference" is arguably straightforward.[2] Dictionary synonyms typically include diversity, variation, multiplicity, and heterogeneity. Scholars who write about the current state of affairs in America, Europe, the postcolonial nations and elsewhere often use one or another of these or kindred terms when discussing some of the more intractable and widespread problems facing contemporary societies, nations, and polities. In much of this writing, heterogeneity involving cultural, religious, ethnic, and racial difference is equated with or subsumed under the rubric of "multiculturalism" or "pluralism" (these terms are frequently used synonymously). The point is commonly made that tolerance, entailing at least partial (or passive) acceptance of difference, is a key condition for the proper functioning if not survival of multicultural or pluralistic societies in nations and states wracked by centrifugal and transnational forces so strong that we seem to be living in "a world in pieces."[3]

But is mere tolerance of diversity (such tolerance being an empirically variable phenomenon in any case) truly sufficient, or do those who embody, represent, or champion difference desire something more? And what might that "more" be? The short answer, in my view, is that something more than tolerance is widely sought. As political theorist William Connolly (2005:123) recently put it, "You may have noticed that people seldom enjoy being tolerated that much, since it carries the onus of being at the mercy of a putative majority that often construes its own position to be beyond question." In this view, the "more" at issue is *legitimacy* in Max Weber's (1918 [1968]) sense, which may be characterized for the time being as more or less synonymous with *validity* insofar as both concepts denote social and cultural processes

resulting in assessments—however contested and subject to historical flux—
that a given phenomenon is in general accord with one or more subsets of "the
norms, values, beliefs, [and] practices ... accepted by a group" (Zelditch
2001:33; see also Walzer 1983, 1997, 2004b, Deveaux 2000, Jost and Major
2001, Connolly 2005).[4]

The arguably commonplace if not banal realization that people seek legitimacy has important implications and does in any case receive abundant support
from the ethnographic record. Anthropologists, sociologists, and other professional sojourners the world over are commonly told by the people among whom
they work that they want others to recognize that they are human, that their
ways of being in the world are just and honorable, in a word, legitimate.[5] It is
precisely this deeply felt concern that motivates many people to allow anthropologists and like-minded practitioners into their communities and to help
them construct accounts of their ways of life which, as they often understand,
may be widely disseminated in the outside world.

If people who embody or represent one or another kind of racial, ethnic, religious, sexual, or other difference seek not merely to be tolerated by others but to
have their differences accorded legitimacy, then it behooves us to ask whether
the societies, states, or other polities in which they live their lives do in fact
grant them legitimacy. Put differently, we need to distinguish between the mere
existence of diversity in a given setting (society, nation-state, diasporic community) on the one hand, and the manner in which it is dealt with and experienced in that setting on the other. The concept of *pluralism* is quite useful here,
especially if we limit its use to conditions or settings in which diversity is
accorded legitimacy. The question then becomes: What are the material and
other conditions conducive to pluralism?

The world as a whole obviously constitutes too vast a canvas for depiction of
these processes. For this reason, I confine most of my discussion to Southeast
Asia, a region in which I have conducted over two and a half years of anthropological fieldwork and have been studying since the early 1970s. Southeast Asia
provides intriguing contexts for inquiries bearing on pluralism partly because it
has long been known for pluralistic traditions bearing on gender, sexuality, religion, and ethnicity. I hasten to add that as deeply interested as I am in this
region, I am less interested in theorizing *about* it than theorizing *from* it.

This book examines pluralism in gendered fields and domains in Southeast
Asia since the early modern era, which historians and anthropologists of the
region commonly define as the period extending roughly from the fifteenth to
the eighteenth centuries. Southeast Asia is a vast, heterogeneous region "at
once territorially porous, internally diverse, and inherently hybrid" (Steedly
1999a:13) that currently consists of 11 different nation-states and a population
of over a half billion people. Hence I should underscore that there are numerous commonalities—in linguistic structures, dietary habits, household construction and public architecture, religious beliefs and practices, patterns of
kinship/gender, sexuality, and socio-political organization—that have long
underlain the striking diversity of the region (Murdock 1960, Reid 1988,

1993b, Higham 1989, Bellwood 1997, Wolters 1999, B. Andaya 2006). Especially since the end of World War II and the beginnings of the Cold War when the US Government made funding available for scholarly research bearing on strategically defined "area studies," these commonalities encouraged scholars to approach Southeast Asia as a "culture area" or in terms of a nexus of related, overlapping "culture areas." Concepts such as "culture areas" may well have outlived their usefulness; and some scholars writing at present prefer to speak of "world areas," thus emphasizing how certain regions are situated on the world stage, in relation to global flows of capital, technology, labor, and the like that have engendered commonalities possibly overshadowing earlier similarities suggesting the relative coherence of a "culture area" (Knauft 1999, Johnson, Jackson, and Herdt 2000). Whichever of these (or other) terms one uses, it is important to bear in mind that the boundaries of Southeast Asia as a "culture (or world) area" are quite porous and contested, and are not isomorphic with the boundaries of Southeast Asia as a geopolitical region, which is usually defined as including Burma (Myanmar), Thailand, Cambodia, Laos, Vietnam, Malaysia, Singapore, Brunei, Indonesia, East Timor, and the Philippines (see Map 1). As earlier generations of scholars (e.g., Murdock 1960) have emphasized, on cultural historical grounds some indigenous peoples of Taiwan merit inclusion in the Southeast Asian "culture area," as do various groups in and around Madagascar; conversely, most inhabitants of Irian Jaya are usually

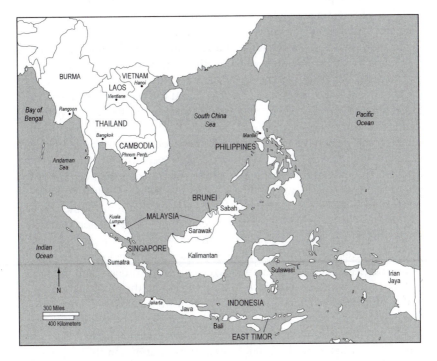

Map 1.1 Southeast Asia, showing contemporary national boundaries

classified in cultural terms as Melanesian rather than Southeast Asian. Throughout most of this book, I limit the descriptions and analyses of Southeast Asia as a "culture (or world) area" to the region that falls within Southeast Asia's modern-day geopolitical boundaries, though I also discuss Southeast Asians in the diaspora (particularly the US), and am not concerned with areas such as Irian Jaya.

My work has been inspired by discourses and controversies in a number of related disciplines, some of which bear on the hierarchy of research priorities in the scholarship on gender and sexuality in Southeast Asia and beyond that has developed over the past few decades. For mostly obvious and altogether legitimate reasons, much of the research has concerned women's experiences and voices, symbols and idioms of femininity, and, to a lesser extent, normative female heterosexualities. Far less developed—especially but not only in terms of sheer volume—is the scholarship bringing feminist and other critical perspectives to bear on understandings and representations of masculinity, and on normative male heterosexualities (Ong and Peletz 1995, Peletz 1996, Wieringa, Blackwood, and Bhaiya 2007). Needless to say, this situation is by no means unique to scholarship on Southeast Asia. What it suggests, though, is that many scholars studying Southeast Asia and other world areas still appear to regard "gender" as a synonym or shorthand for "women."[6] In a similar fashion, one could argue, as have Gayle Rubin (1984, 1994) and Afsaneh Najmabadi (2005:235–237 passim), that the dominant streams of feminist scholarship have long been primarily "about" women and to a lesser extent gender, but *not* sexuality. Analogous arguments have been advanced with respect to the social sciences in their entirety (Herdt 1993a:12, Weston 1998). One consequence, according to Rubin and others who hold these views, is that the main currents of feminist scholarship, like the social sciences generally, have shed much light on the struggles and aspirations of women faced with political, economic, and other forms of oppression but have been far less theoretically productive in analyzing the cultural politics of sexual diversity. Partly as a response to this situation, recent years have seen the development of variously defined fields of sexuality studies, such as gay and lesbian studies, queer studies, and transgender studies. These fields have gone a long way toward addressing certain of the silences and elisions highlighted by scholars like Rubin. But it is also true, as Kath Weston (1998) and others have pointed out, that some of the reigning perspectives in these fields, which are defined largely in relation to cultural studies and the humanities, suffer from an insularity that reflects their lack of serious engagement with the work of historians, anthropologists, and others concerned with analyzing sexual and gender diversity through time and space.

One of the aims of this book is to help ameliorate the problematic state of scholarship described here. I seek to do this in two ways. First, I range beyond the usual focuses (women, heterosexuality) and analyze gender pluralism in various fields, domains, and more encompassing systems in Southeast Asia since early modern times. And second, I pay particular attention to the practices, roles, and identities of transgendered persons. I use the term transgendered to refer to individuals involved in practices that transcend or transgress majoritarian gender practices, as I explain in due course. One of my basic arguments is that transgendered persons provide a powerful lens through which to view pluralism, partly because for this region and period the vicissitudes of transgenderism index processes that have occurred across a number of culturally and analytically interlocked domains. These processes include: the increased formalization and segregation of gender roles; the distancing of women from loci of power and prestige; the narrowed range of legitimacy concerning things intimate, erotic and sexual; and the constriction of pluralistic gender sensibilities as a whole, which, in recent times (since the 1980s), has gone hand in hand with a proliferation of diversity and the emergence of new loci of legitimacy. More generally, one has to start one's analysis somewhere, and I argue that transgendered persons and the sexual variability associated with them and their normatively gendered partners provide a productive point of departure for descriptions and analysis of sexual and gender diversity in the region.

An additional set of comments that will help provide context for the discussion that follows has to do with methodology, terminology, and conceptual apparatus. In terms of source material, I draw on indigenous (mostly Malay-language) manuscripts, and on the writings of Chinese, European and other explorers, European colonial officials and missionaries, as well as the research of medical personnel, archeologists, historians, and anthropologists, Asian and Western alike. Many of the published materials available to us through the end of the colonial period were produced by males, often of elite background. The potential for gender- and class-skewed accounts is compounded by factors of race, ethnicity, and religion (among others), especially during late modern times and the colonial era when outsiders had increasingly well formulated designs on the region and its resources. This period saw a profusion of writing by European (mostly Christian, heteronormatively oriented) travelers, missionaries, statesmen, and colonial officials who sought justification for their missionary and other "civilizing" projects in social and cultural difference construed as depravity, perversity, and inversion. The French, for example, typically "constructed the Vietnamese male as androgynous, effeminate, hermaphroditic, impotent, and inverted and, conversely, the Vietnamese female as virile and hypersexualized" (Proschan 2002a:436). The larger issues are that Southeast Asians, like the denizens of most other world areas, were often "represented as a limitless repository of deviance, extravagance, [and] eccentricity" (Bleys 1995:267), and that these *topoi* "served to demonstrate either the primitiveness or the degeneracy of the population concerned, and the urgent need for civilizing, Christianizing, and otherwise uplifting them" (B. Anderson 1990:277–278). Many of these accounts do not meet current standards of objectivity, are clearly socially situated (as in different ways are their successors), and deal in any case with partial truths (as also, albeit in different ways, do their successors). Some of them nonetheless contain much of value, especially when read with an historical anthropological sensibility that views them against the grain of the more stolid, straitlaced, and balanced scholarship on Southeast

Asia produced by historians, anthropologists, and others in the latter half of the twentieth century and the early years of the new millennium. The latter literature provides direct or indirect confirmation of many key observations from earlier times, while disconfirming or raising serious questions (or remaining altogether silent) about the plausibility of others.

Gyanendra Pandey (2006:31–32) has recently noted that owing partly to the nature of the written sources available to historians of South Asia, it is much easier to document the broad contours of political, economic, and religious change than to provide nuanced accounts of the lived experiences and subjectivities of variously defined social actors and their transformations through time. This is true for Southeast Asia (and most other regions of the world) as well, and is especially apparent when dealing with women and various categories of individuals involved in transgender practices and same-sex relations. For even though some of them (queens, consorts, concubines, and certain types of ritual specialists and palace functionaries) drew the attention of Chinese and Western observers armed with pen and paper, others (commoner women, the lay partners of transgendered ritualists, and those whose transgender practices and same-sex relations had no direct connection to formal ritual roles or palace activities) did not necessarily do so. Indigenous manuscripts, often produced by scribes in the employ of Southeast Asian political and/or religious elites, are informed by similar kinds of biases. Owing to factors such as these, we tend not to have access to the voices of "ordinary women (or men)" or individuals who transcended or transgressed heteronormative ideals prior to the twentieth century, even when some of their subject positions and customary practices—and the symbols and meanings associated with them—are fairly well described. This situation is in some ways analogous to that faced by scholars who have studied eunuchs in the Islamic heartlands since the twelfth century, "royal harems" in Ottoman and South Asian contexts (Peirce 1993, Lal 2005) and many other groups "without history" in Eric Wolf's (1982) sense.

I also draw on the archival research and ethnographic fieldwork that I have conducted in Malaysia since the late 1970s and on professional travel elsewhere in the region (Singapore, Indonesia, Thailand, Burma, Vietnam), mostly since the early 1990s. My research in Malaysia involved two lengthy periods of fieldwork (1978–1980, 1987–1988) totaling some 26 months and a number of shorter visits (1993, 1998, 2001, 2002, 2008). I have discussed fieldwork methods, my fluency in Malay, and my experiences in the field in detail elsewhere (Peletz 1996: Chap. 1, 2002:11–16 passim; cf. 1993b). The main periods of research were undertaken in the state of Negeri Sembilan and focused on kinship/marriage, gender, sexuality, and the cultural politics of Islam and of Islamic courts in particular. In recent times, I have worked mostly in Kuala Lumpur and have concentrated on interviews with judges, lawyers, artists, gay and lesbian activists, and individuals involved with AIDS organizations, Muslim feminist groups (e.g., Sisters in Islam), and other non-governmental organizations (NGOs). I should emphasize that I also draw extensively on anthropological and other works from earlier decades (which are of uneven quality) not to construct a timeless, heavily mythologized Other (Fabian 1983); rather, I regard such accounts as historically situated texts that can help document continuities and transformations in patterns highlighted in the earlier literature.

As for terminology and conceptual apparatus, I use the term "pluralism" to refer to social fields, cultural domains, and more encompassing systems in which two or more principles, categories, groups, sources of authority, or ways of being in the world are not only present, tolerated, and accommodated, but also *accorded legitimacy* in a Weberian sense (Deveaux 2000, Jost and Major 2001; see also Walzer 1983, 1997, 2004b, Connolly 2005). Legitimacy ("a phenomenon of the 'social order'" [Zelditch 2001:39]),[7] however much contested and in flux owing to dynamics elucidated by Gramsci (1971), is thus a sine qua non for pluralism, which means, by definition, that pluralism is a feature of fields, domains, and systems in which diversity is ascribed legitimacy, and, conversely, that diversity without legitimacy is *not* pluralism. There are important reasons, both empirical and analytic, to draw a clear distinction between diversity or difference on the one hand, and pluralism, defined succinctly as "difference accorded legitimacy," on the other. One set of reasons has to do with the fact that the differences that exist in a given milieu may be denied legitimacy and/or stigmatized (Kelly 1993). Another has to do with the fact that the proliferation of difference—defined or experienced in ethnic, racial, religious terms, or with respect to the florescence of consumer or "lifestyle" choices—can easily lead to a constriction of pluralistic sensibilities and dispositions. This is not merely a hypothetical possibility. A proliferation of social and cultural diversity (following large-scale immigration, for example) commonly brings with it new interests, standards, values, and visions. These phenomena sometimes entail not only a direct challenge to existing arrangements and the groups and interests they serve, but also repressive, monistic, or absolutist responses from the powers that be.

Scholarly and political debates involving pluralism and its discontents are rather fraught at this historical juncture. It is thus worthwhile to emphasize that pluralism is always relative, never absolute, and that a society's commitment to pluralism need not involve, as Clifford Geertz (2000:42) puts it, "the moral and intellectual consequences that are commonly supposed to flow from relativism —subjectivism, nihilism, incoherence, Machiavellianism, ethical idiocy, esthetic blindness, and so on." There are, in my view, at least three reasons for this. First, all societies delimit within certain ranges what kinds of values, norms, principles, and social practices they take to be legitimate in order to maintain a degree of social order and cultural coherence. Put differently, no society is altogether normless, although some opponents of pluralism (and of what is often referred to as "multiculturalism") obviously think so. Second, commitments to pluralism in a given society or among variously defined sectors of a society are in some ways analogous to religious faith. To quote Connolly (2005:49), they not only vary in "intensity, content, and imperiousness;" they may also be more discernible in dispositions and sensibilities than in formal creed or doctrine. And third, pluralism in a given society, like justice, equality, and hierarchy, tends to be domain specific, just as within a particular domain it tends to suffuse certain realms (arenas, offices, subjectivities) and not others. Thus, pluralistic sentiments regarding religious affiliation or ethnic identity, for instance, may not inform collective thought bearing on erotic preferences, and vice versa.

These observations have important implications. In Southeast Asian societies of the early modern period, the range of erotic activities and other bodily practices sanctioned by cosmologies, mythologies, and the ritual specialists charged with mediating relations between humans and world of the sacred was far more expansive than in late modern times. But that range was clearly bounded; it had limits. There were clear normative expectations bearing on "close mating" (incest), exogamy, and extra-marital relations, for example; and in some instances their infraction required that transgressors be exiled from the community, boiled in pitch or molten metal, or subject to other gruesome punishment. The existence of a largely implicit "heterogender matrix" is relevant here as well. For while it allowed for and in some contexts encouraged sexual relations and marriage between individuals with similar anatomies as long as they were held to be differently gendered, it made little if any provision for sexual relations or marriage involving persons viewed as identically gendered. Indeed, relations of the latter sort appear to have been beyond the pale of local thought and experience.

The always already circumscribed nature of pluralism raises other issues having to do with processes involving the cultural conceptualization and analytic marking out of domains, processes that Marilyn Strathern (1988, 1992) refers to as "domaining." These matters merit brief remark insofar as they help distinguish my use of "pluralism" from earlier terms such as "plural societies," a concept deployed in pioneering studies concerning colonial-era Indonesia undertaken by J.S. Furnivall (e.g., *Netherlands India: A Study of Plural Economy* [1939]; *Colonial Policy and Practice: A Comparative Study of Burma and Netherlands India* [1948]). Furnivall (1948:308 passim) used the term (and others like "cultural pluralism") to help him describe and analyze the existence, in the Dutch East Indies and elsewhere, of colonially engineered racialist systems characterized by a multiplicity of interdependent but sharply distinguished ethnic or racial groups, each linked to a distinctive set of ethnicized or racialized economic spheres. Analogous in some respects to India's caste system, Furnivall's plural society was predicated both on sectoral interdependence, and on principles of hierarchy, exclusion, and incommensurability that are in many ways anathema to the kinds of inclusive sensibilities and dispositions that are a defining feature of pluralism as I and like-minded scholars use the term. Readers familiar with George Orwell's *Burmese Days*, a brilliantly evocative novel grounded in Orwell's experiences as a police officer in "British Burma" during the 1930s, will immediately recognize the rigid racial segregation, animosity, and apartheid-like characteristics of Furnivall's plural societies. They will also appreciate that the British sensibilities, dispositions, and policies bearing on Burmese, Indians, Anglo-Burmese "half-castes," and the other "Orientals" that Orwell so masterfully depicted are far from pluralistic in my sense of the term.

Having drawn attention to some of the contrasts between earlier and more recent studies bearing on plural societies, pluralism, and the like, I should note an important similarity between the earlier literature on plural societies, which includes anthropological treatises such as Smith (1965), Despres (1968), Kuper and Smith (1969), and Maybury-Lewis (1982), and more recent interdisciplinary work that conceptualizes pluralism in ways that are more closely related to my usage of the term (e.g., Walzer 1983, 1997, 2004b, Deveaux 2000, Eck 2001, Oommen 2002, Connolly 2005, An-Na'im 2008). The similarity has to do with the fact that in both cases the focus tends to be on societies, nations, or states whose population includes a politically or demographically dominant ethnic or racial (or religious) majority on the one hand, and one or more ethnic or racial (or religious) minorities on the other. Such was clearly the focus of work by Furnivall and others who followed in his footsteps; and as John Bowen (2003) has noted, it is also characteristic of most of the more recent work on pluralism. Like Bowen and a few others who have dealt with some of these issues in recent years (e.g., Hefner 1998, 2000, Beatty 2002), I am less concerned with the dynamics of pluralism *across* ethnic/racial/religious divides than with the existence of pluralistic sentiments and dispositions *within* variously defined social entities, regardless of whether or not they are heterogeneous in ethnic, racial, or religious terms.

Pluralism may be viewed as a "gate-keeping" concept in Arjun Appadurai's (1986:357) sense insofar as it helps "define the quintessential and dominant questions of interest in the region" and inasmuch as some such concepts "limit anthropological [and other] theorizing about the place in question." This was the case with many indisputably important studies focusing on topic-locale icons such as "lineage in Africa, exchange in Melanesia, caste in India, ... Eskimo adaptation, Aboriginal marriage systems and so on" (Fardon 1990:26). Broadly analogous limitations are also evident in more recent scholarship concerned with topics that are iconically associated with particular places such as the sex industry in Thailand, family enterprise in Japan, the intrusiveness of the state in Singapore, and communal violence in India, Pakistan, and elsewhere in South Asia, to cite contemporary Asian examples. This need not be the case, however, especially if investigators draw comparative and theoretical inspiration from ethnographic, historical, and other sources that are widely distributed across space, time, and scholarly fields, as I and various other scholars (e.g., Strathern 1988, Pandey 2006) have tried to do.

It merits note in any event that for reasons having to do with regionally specific historical and geopolitical dynamics on the one hand and the (related) development of areal specializations in anthropology and other disciplines on the other, the concept of pluralism has dissimilar and at times highly discrepant meanings and connotations for scholars working in different parts of the world (and on different topics). Readers whose primary regional expertise lies in the Caribbean, Latin America, and/or Africa, for example, may well view the concept in a (neo)Furnivallian sense, and in the case of Caribbeanists may immediately think of the extensive genealogy of debates about creolism and creolization. Those with backgrounds in South or Southeast Asian material, Islam, Euro-America, civil religion, or civil society, on the other hand, are more likely to imagine the concept in ways that resonate (however broadly) with the conceptualization developed here.[8]

What then do I mean by "gender," "sex," and "sexuality"? For my purposes, the term "gender" designates the cultural categories, symbols, meanings, practices, and institutionalized arrangements bearing on at least five sets of phenomena: (1) females and femininity; (2) males and masculinity; (3) andro-gynes, who are partly male and partly female in appearance,[9] as well as intersexed individuals, also known as hermaphrodites, who to one or another degree may have both male and female sexual organs or characteristics; (4) the transgen-dered, who engage in practices that transcend or transgress normative bound-aries and are thus by definition "transgressively gendered;" and (5) neutered or unsexed/ungendered individuals, like some eunuchs. "Sex," by contrast, refers to physical activities associated with desire, reproduction, and the like, includ-ing but not limited to sexual intercourse of a heterosexual nature; to physical bodies that are distinguished by having genitals that are construed as "female," "male," both (as with some intersexuals), or neither (as in the case of some eunuchs); and to bodily processes associated with anatomical and physiological maturation, such as menstruation and ejaculation. "Sexuality," for its part, "may overlap with sex and gender, but ... pertains specifically" to the realm of erotic desire, passion, and pleasure (Robertson 1998:17).[10]

As for "gender pluralism," I developed this concept as a shorthand way of referring to pluralism in gendered fields or domains. It denotes pluralistic sensi-bilities and dispositions regarding bodily practices (adornment, attire, manner-isms) and embodied desires, as well as social roles, sexual relationships, and overall ways of being that bear on or are otherwise linked with local concep-tions of femininity, masculinity, androgyny, hermaphroditism, and so on. Particularly in gendered fields and domains, pluralism transcends and perforce needs to be distinguished from dualism inasmuch as more than two principles, categories, groups, etc. are usually at stake and accorded legitimacy (e.g., not simply principles constituting categories of heteronormative female-bodied individuals and their male-bodied counterparts).[11] Such principles, categories, and groups are, moreover, valorized in ways that constrain the degree to which their distinctive features are parlayed into rigid hierarchies of value that cut across and suffuse multiple fields of social practice and cultural belief.[12] By this definition, sexual pluralism, premised minimally on a concept of relatively "benign sexual variation" (Rubin 1984:283), is included under the more encompassing rubric of gender pluralism. This is in keeping with the analytic conventions subsuming sex into the category of gender (but not conflating or eliding the differences between them)—rather than vice versa—that are adopted by many scholars in the field (e.g., Strathern 1988, Butler 1990, Moore 1994, Ortner 1996, Blackwood and Wieringa 1999). It is also consistent with the empirical realities of Southeast Asia, insofar as gender difference has long encompassed sexual difference—associated with anatomy, physiology, sexual activity, and the like—rather than vice versa.

In previous publications (e.g., Peletz 2006), I have emphasized that the meanings of portmanteau concepts such as "transgender" are not clearly bounded or stable and are employed by different scholars in different ways. My reading of the prefix "trans" is informed by the work of Aihwa Ong (1999:4), who has written, "*Trans* denotes both moving through space or across lines, as well as changing the nature of something," as in transformation or transfiguration, or going beyond it—as in transcend—be it a bounded entity or process, or a relationship between two or more phenomena; Ong goes on to say that the prefix "trans" also alludes to the transactional and transgressive aspects of "behavior and imagination that are incited, enabled, and regulated" by the logics of culture and political economy. Concerning transgender, Riki Wilchins (1997:15–16) has observed, "*Transgender* began its life as a name for those folks who identified neither as crossdressers nor as transsexuals—primarily people who changed their gender but not their genitals … . The term gradually mutated to include any genderqueers who didn't actually change their genitals: [such as] crossdressers, … stone butches, [and] hermaphrodites; … [and] people began using it to refer to transsexuals [some of whom do change their genitals] as well." A similar view of the concept undergirds Joanne Meyerowitz's work: "In the popular lingo used today, … 'transgendered'" people … [is] an umbrella term used for those with various forms and degrees of crossgender practices and identifications. 'Transgendered' includes, among others, some people who identify as 'butch' or masculine lesbians, as 'fairies,' 'queens,' or feminine gay men, and as heterosexual crossdressers as well as those who identify as transsexual. The categories are not hermetically sealed, and to a certain extent the boundaries are permeable" (2002:10). Evelyn Blackwood's (1999, 2005) conceptualization of transgender, which I find helpful, builds on Wilchins's definition, though she also employs the term transgendered in its broadest sense to refer to anyone who is "transgressively gendered," to borrow Kate Bornstein's (1995:134–135) phrase (cf. Blackwood and Wieringa 1999:ix–xi et passim). Many scholars underscore that these umbrella terms sometimes have certain meanings and connotations in the West that are of questionable relevance elsewhere. Such meanings and connotations include the empirically erroneous idea that all variants of transgendering necessarily entail same-sex relations (and vice versa).[13] They also include the equally problematic notion that behavioral transgressions, even or especially in the straightforward definitional sense of practices that transcend or cross boundaries (bearing on gender or anything else), are typically stigmatized. For reasons such as these, we must utilize the terms with caution when we are labeling, grouping, and interpreting practices and identities in non-Western settings.

Even cautious and qualified usages of terms such as "transgender" have their limitations (Stryker 2006); for reasons such as these some scholars prefer to avoid them altogether. Towle and Morgan (2002:476), for example, argue that "transgender" is a trendy signifier that is too encompassing to allow for the kinds of fine-grain distinctions called for in particular "ethnographic, historical, and political contexts," and that its utilization in Western writings (especially in the semi-popular accounts of Bornstein 1995, Feinberg 1996, and Wilchins 1997) is often heavily freighted with nostalgia for a romanticized (paleoterrific) past, exemplified by contemporary non-Western Others and their forebears, that may have never existed. Mark Johnson (2006), who has used the term "transgender" in much of his (e.g., 1997) work, has also drawn attention to dilemmas of translation (transcendence and transgression are not exactly the same thing) that sometimes vex even the most carefully chosen and thoroughly qualified terminological conventions that serve our varied purposes until we settle on ones we come to consider at least marginally better.

Relevant here are the implications for our work of Roy Rappaport's (1999:10) observations concerning the role of language in human evolution: "every 'advance' sets new problems as it responds to and ameliorates earlier ones. Language was no exception." My point in invoking this observation is not to suggest that all linguistic conventions or conveniences of translation are of comparable heuristic or other value. I aim rather to encourage the humbling recognition that the last two to three decades have seen a dizzying succession of terminologies utilized in scholarly writings dealing with what Manalansan (2006) refers to as "gender insubordinate subjects" (see Peletz 2006:335), and that so too in all likelihood will the next few. This despite the existence in some scholarly quarters of wildly presentist (but usually implicit) conceits that in the years ahead certain *au courant* neologisms and terminologies will—and in the nature of things, should—attain a status that is permanently hegemonic and uncontested; and that those who deploy them are thus "present at the creation" if not actively midwifing an intellectual revolution involving one or another version of what might be termed, following Fukuyama (1992), "the end of language."

Two final sets of comments before turning to the organization of the book. The first concerns my feeling that the ample quoting (rather than paraphrasing) of other sources gives readers a sense of the tone and flavor of observations from different times and places, and also helps them distinguish between my views and the formulations of those who have preceded me. The second concerns the "engaged" nature of this work. In addition to writing as a historically oriented anthropologist committed to rigorous scholarship, I write as an advocate for the two-fold idea that the untrammeled expression of gender and sexual subjectivities and identities is in some sense a universal human right and that variation in such subjectivities and identities is in some sense a universal feature of human societies. At the same time, I am fully aware that such subjectivities and identities are socially and culturally constructed, and that they were constructed in early modern Southeast Asia in ways that accorded legitimacy to a range of variation that was unusually wide, judging either from current Southeast Asian standards or from those of the contemporary West. It is also clear that processes of modernization have led to a marked but highly uneven constriction in this range even as they have given rise to new gender and sexual subjectivities and identities. Certain of the latter subjectivities and identities are counter-hegemonic but under new conditions may be ascribed legitimacy (as among the Bugis of South Sulawesi), in which case the legitimacy accorded gender and sexual variation in early modern times is potentially a critical resource for staking contemporary claims to legitimacy that may be absent in other culture (or world) areas. Some readers may find the proposition(s) I advocate debatable; others may simply disagree. From my perspective, however, the issues are relatively straightforward. The bottom-line cross-cultural question in any case is how different cultural traditions accord legitimacy (even prestige) to or stigmatize this "natural" range of variation. Southeast Asians have long been far more flexible and pluralistic in these matters than people in most (if not all) other areas. On this score (and others) we have much to learn from them.

Organization of the Book

Chapter 2, which follows these introductory remarks, focuses on gender pluralism and transgender practices in the first half of the early modern period (roughly the fifteenth and sixteenth centuries). I begin the chapter with a discussion of gendered themes in the political cultures of pre- and early modern states, elucidating Tantric and Saivite motifs in numerous domains of society and culture (especially royal palaces) and highlighting the convergence between key features of Indic culture on the one hand and Austronesian traditions on the other. We will see that throughout the region the well-being of the ruler, symbolized by his or her royal regalia and entourage, promoted the well-being of the polity and the cosmos as a whole, and that such dynamics existed in conjunction with cosmological emphases on both the reconciliation of contrasting or opposed forces to attain harmony and liberation, and the use of the human body to achieve these ends. We will also see that religious traditions in much of the region involved the placation or "worship of ancestors and spirits, to whom offerings were made through specialist intermediaries" (Pelras 1996:47); that many of these intermediaries engaged the spirits by voyaging to other worlds in the course of shamanistic trance and possession; and that they were often involved in transgender practices grounded in a cosmology "in which the world was viewed as a polarized entity whose opposed pairs in a generalized system of symbolic equivalences were sky and earth, mountain and sea, … right and left, sun and moon, male and female, life and death" (ibid.).

Transgender practices and the same-sex relations that were often associated with them are of interest in their own right. But in the larger scheme of things they bear analytic significance for the light they shed on pluralistic sensibilities regarding gender, sexuality, and various forms of embodied experience: the legitimacy vested in different ways of being in the world. Owing partly to the legitimacy accorded diverse modalities of transgenderism and same-sex practices, and partly to the relative fluidity of gender roles and the relatively high degree of autonomy, social control, and respect enjoyed by women, I characterize the first half of the early modern period as relatively pluralistic with respect to gender and sexuality. But I also caution that this characterization should not be interpreted to mean that the reigning ethos was one of "anything goes," particularly since certain incestuous and adulterous offenses could meet with capital punishment.

The remainder of the book addresses historical trends involving the transformation and reproduction of transgender practices, same-sex relations, and gender pluralism during the second half of the early modern period (roughly the seventeenth and eighteenth centuries) and subsequently. The second half of the early modern period witnessed dramatic transformations in many domains of society and culture. These transformations occurred as entailments of a number of dialectically related processes involving the intensification of commercial activity, state building, and territorial consolidation conducive to political institutions that were "more absolutist, centralized, and bureaucratic" (Lieberman 2003:16), as well as the increased centrality, in palace realms and beyond, of Sunni Islam, Theravada Buddhism, Neo-Confucianism, and Iberian-style Catholicism. The doctrines of these World Religions provide no scriptural basis for the public ritual centrality of women or the transgendered. Due to the spread and growing appeal of broadly encompassing canonical orthodoxies, the previously sacrosanct roles of women and transgendered individuals in public ritual and religion were subject to widespread questioning and skepticism, and, ultimately, an erosion of their prestige and overall legitimacy. Also subject to a decline of prestige and legitimacy was much—but not all—of the sexual license and gender diversity long characteristic of the region, as well as bodily practices involving tattoos, amulets, ear boring, and various types of penile surgery and attendant decoration.

These trends proceeded in conjunction with a number of other dynamics that proved deleterious to women and gender pluralism alike, even though some of them might be regarded as partially offset by colonial-era developments involving the curtailment and ultimate abolition of many types of debt bondage and slavery, along with the encouragement of laws and customs that helped do away with "Oriental excess" in marriage and sexuality in favor of "Western-style" measure and monogamy. The dynamics at issue included declines in rates of female literacy; the partial exclusion of women from political office; growing poverty; and the demise of myriad forms of craft specialization and petty commodity production that enabled women to maintain the economic and social autonomy that long impressed (and frequently shocked) outside observers from China and the West. Many of these trends continued in the centuries that followed, due largely to the pronounced albeit regionally variable socio-cultural impact of colonial rule, Western (especially Protestant) missionary activity, and ever more muscular states. In most instances these states promoted one or another form of capitalism and were buttressed by ideologies of high modernity, which James Scott (1998:4) has characterized in terms of a "self confidence about scientific and technical progress, the expansion of production, … the mastery of nature …, and, above all, the rational design of social order commensurate with the scientific understanding of natural laws." The schemes of institutional and cultural rationalization thus entailed make little if any provision for the valorization of things local, be they structures of kinship or marriage, gendered divisions of labor underwriting craft specialization and petty commodity production, or locally distinctive ritual practices or forms of esoteric knowledge deemed essential for the ongoing viability of kingship or the cosmos in its entirety. Put differently, architects of institutional and cultural rationalization along with the sociocultural forces that beget them are notoriously suspicious if not overtly hostile to phenomena deemed to be ambiguous or liminal with respect to gender, sexuality, or almost anything else, unless they have folkloric or touristic value. Much the same may be said of monotheism, which is often taken to be deeply qualmish about ethical pluralism and the possibilities for diversity that it necessarily entails.

These and related developments encouraged the growth of religious nationalisms and educational reform. The latter dynamics also constricted the public, particularly religious and ritual, spaces inhabited by women and the transgendered; in addition, they undermined the continued reproduction of a good many ritual complexes that involved transgenderism just as they discouraged shamanic practices and syncretic ritual complexes generally. The strong historical bonds throughout Southeast Asia that linked politically connected ritual specialists with transgenderism and sexual variability thus almost guaranteed that radical changes in the cultural political landscape would witness attacks on transgendered ritualists and the embodied practices associated with them that were overdetermined in the most basic senses of the term. The same historical bonds helped ensure that such attacks would go a long way toward disarticulating the ties simultaneously binding these subject positions to state power and religious orthodoxy.

In this context, Chapter 3, "Temporary Marriage, Connubial Commerce, and Colonial Body Politics," explores pre- and early modern conventions of kinship, marriage, and exchange that facilitated the growth of trade networks, commerce, and urban settlement during the early modern period and thereafter. Especially in the initial sections of the chapter, I am concerned with practices and meanings associated with the "temporary marriages" involving local women and foreign traders hailing from China and the West. These relationships were in many respects symmetrical or mutualistic in the sense that they brought privileges and a degree of prestige to husband and wife alike. This soon changed, however, due partly to the monetization of economic and other social relationships and the widespread poverty following on the growth of commerce and urban centers, and partly to religious and other developments. More precisely, these relationships were restructured and redefined in ways that proved prejudicial and otherwise deleterious to temporary wives, who came to be seen as little other than prostitutes. Colonial-era dynamics exacerbated the inequities insofar as they brought about overwhelmingly male immigration, unbalanced sex ratios, the spread and deepening of poverty, and large-scale prostitution. Colonial-era prostitution involved overwhelmingly heterosexual encounters—and endemic rates of heterosexually transmitted diseases—but the colonial policies that encouraged this domain of commerce were driven by fears and anxieties that the sexual traffic in (Asian) women was far less objectionable than the most likely alternative: same-sex relations between European men, or, worse, same-sex liaisons between European and Asian men. These are some of the reasons why our descriptions and analyses of colonial body politics, which focus largely but not exclusively on the high period of colonialism (1870–1930), need to take into consideration not only heterosexual bodies and bodily engagements, but also same-sex erotics—a topic that is commonly ignored in otherwise sophisticated theoretical work on colonial sexualities (e.g., Stoler 1995, 2002).

Chapter 4, "Transgender Practices, Same-Sex Relations, and Gender Pluralism Since the 1960s," brings together material that until now has been relatively inaccessible and views that material from the perspective of an interpretive framework conducive to the analysis of historical processes entailing the widespread but regionally variable delegitimization and stigmatization of transgendered practices—and the transformation of gender pluralism generally—in the context of Southeast Asian modernity projects. These processes have not been all-encompassing, uniform, or monolithic. That said, there are striking commonalities throughout the region. Variously gendered local "priesthoods" (among the Iban, Ngaju Dayak, and Malays, for instance) have been largely discredited and most rituals associated with hermaphroditic or androgynous spirits and deities have fallen into desuetude. Transgenderism has lost much of the religious and specifically sacred significance it once had, and with a few notable exceptions (e.g., the Bugis), its cultural centrality in royal courts and the reproduction of local polities has been eroded and it has thus been delinked from religious orthodoxy and state power alike. In places such as contemporary Malaysia, transgender practices are currently most visible in the secular realms of fashion and entertainment, in increasingly scrutinized and disciplined private domains, and on the famously ungovernable Internet. More generally, we see from the perspective of the *longue durée* that many forms of transgenderism have been secularized and stigmatized, that some of them have been explicitly pathologized and criminalized as well, and that the historical processes implicated in these developments have served to redefine transgendered individuals as contaminating (rather than sacred) mediators who are perversely if not treasonously muddling and enmiring the increasingly dichotomous terms of sex/gender systems long marked by pluralism.[14]

Chapter 4 also illustrates that notwithstanding these dynamics, there was a fair degree of gender pluralism in many regions of Southeast Asia well into the twentieth century. This is particularly apparent when we look beyond ritual specialists per se and examine local attitudes and feeling-tones bearing on the "lay" majority. Moreover, in some instances (e.g., among the Bugis), radical shifts in cultural political conditions in the late 1990s saw rejuvenations of "traditional" religious practices in the context of vigorous reassertions of local (as well as diasporic) cultural identities. Owing partly to strategic alliances formed between locals and Jakarta-based Muslim feminist groups and lesbian organizations with transnational connections, the past decade has witnessed a veritable renaissance of transgendered ritualists (*bissu*) and the ("female-friendly") gendered legacies and subjectivities they are taken to represent. Cases such as these underscore the need to make analytic provision for various kinds of historical reversals, counter-flows, and openings—as albeit for different reasons does the case of Burma, the focus of the second half of Chapter 4. In Burma, transgendered ritualists (the majority of whom are male-bodied) are alive and well, but in the past few decades women have become marginalized and stigmatized by repressive state policies (heavily reliant on state-sponsored terror) that have subjected them and most of the rest of the population to serious risk and harm. In Burma, as in other contexts where hegemonic masculinities and those who champion them seek dominion over all features of the cultural political landscape, not all difference is the same.

Chapter 5, "Gender, Sexuality, and Body Politics at the Turn of the Twenty-First Century," analyzes an important range of the tensions, paradoxes, and ironies of the historical trajectories highlighted in previous chapters. I am most interested in socio-cultural dynamics associated with the paradoxical fact that an appreciable array of transformations in pluralistic sensibilities and dispositions has involved a *constriction of pluralism* whereas broadly contemporaneous transformations in myriad domains of social practice and cultural valuation has entailed a *proliferation of diversity* that ranges far beyond the pale of conventional standards of legitimacy. The two sets of movements, though at first blush seemingly disparate or opposed, are mutually constituting elements of a single dynamic process that has also involved the fragmentation of authority and attendant crises of governance stemming from the roughly concurrent emergence of competing loci of power and prestige that have helped bring into being new standards vying for legitimacy, some primarily local, others derived from or shaped in significant measure by exogenous, globalizing sources.

Chapter 5 explores these processes chiefly in the context of Malaysia, which is commonly characterized in textbooks and travel literature as "the crossroads of Asia" due to its strategic location astride the waterways of Asia and its rich ethnic and religious diversity. I begin with a consideration of mid-to-late twentieth-century discourses on "traditional" forms of Malay transgenderism, and proceed to examine narratives of "Asian values" articulated by political elites in Malaysia, Singapore, Japan, and elsewhere in the Asia Pacific region. I link the production and dissemination of these discourses in Malaysia in the early 1990s to a nexus of interrelated developments. These include: state-sponsored projects of modernity; the proliferation of sex/gender and other socio-cultural diversity that is entailed in these projects and in the state's ardent albeit ambivalent embrace of globalizing forces and neoliberalism generally; and the rise of social intolerance that went hand in hand with the production of new forms of (sexualized) criminality on the part of political and religious elites and others nurtured in a postcolonial milieu of governmentality where "states of exception" are, paradoxically, almost always the norm (Agamben 2005, Ong

2006). I continue with a description and analysis of the Pink Triangle, a Kuala Lumpur-based NGO established in 1987 to assist and empower people whose sexual proclivities and other bodily practices (e.g., intravenous drug use) put them at risk for HIV/AIDS and other types of potentially fatal harm. Brief sketches of the various communities aided by the Pink Triangle provide both the contours of the urban/sexual underground and an entrée to the struggle for sexual equality, as does the ensuing discussion, which builds on interviews with activists in the gay, lesbian, and transgendered communities to illuminate how variably situated communities of Malaysians negotiate the vicissitudes of "tolerance," open secrets, and governmentality—and how, in the process, they negotiate difference, identity, and pluralism. One of my other concerns in Chapter 5 is to sketch out possible scenarios for the future of pluralism in Malaysia and other nations in the region, and to address the comparative and theoretical implications of these scenarios and the historical and cultural political dynamics addressed in the book as a whole.

I conclude the book with an Epilogue that addresses some of the ways contemporary Southeast Asians have moved beyond the region itself. I do so for three interrelated reasons: to underscore the movement, porousness, and hybridity that have always been defining features of Southeast Asia as a "cultural area;" to draw attention to some of the dynamics of pluralism in an important diasporic context (the US), and thus to expose and undo problematic binaries that construct Southeast Asia "versus" the US as an exemplar of the West; and to point to and expand possibilities for future research involving translocal and global comparisons. The material I examine in the initial portion of the Epilogue derives from court cases involving Malaysian nationals residing in the US who have sought political asylum on the grounds that they are openly gay, lesbian, or transgendered, and that if they go back to their native Malaysia, they will face persecution owing to their publicly discernible sexual orientation(s). The narratives of asylum seekers ("asylees") and the documents produced on their behalf provide valuable perspectives on life in the homeland; they also illuminate processes of subject-making in a diasporic context as well as the associational freedoms and attendant liberatory experiences gay, lesbian, and transgendered Southeast Asians anticipate having in the US.

Asylees, as we shall see, have strongly idealized expectations of what their lives will be like in the US. This is suggested partly by the experiences of gay Cambodians living in this country (discussed in the latter part of the Epilogue), the majority of whom immigrated as refugees in the aftermath of America's war in Indochina or the resultant horrors of the Pol Pot regime—or were born to refugees already residing here. In sharp contrast to gay Malaysian asylees, gay Cambodians in the US tend to talk of paradise lost rather than gained, summing up their experiences of the differences between homeland and diaspora with remarks such as "what we did sexually [in Cambodia] is not bad like it is here" and that while we "were teased by Cambodians," we are "hated by Americans" (Quintiliani 1995:65–66). In these and other ways the perspectives of gay (and straight) Cambodian Americans challenge and otherwise trouble the linear, progressivist narratives we tell ourselves about our (pluralistic) selves, just as they raise profoundly unsettling questions about the constraints of normativity and similitude—and the possible futures of difference and its proliferation—in an increasingly borderless world.

2   Gender Pluralism and Transgender Practices in Early Modern Times

Scholars engaged in research on Southeast Asia have frequently commented on the numerous similarities—in linguistic structures, dietary habits, household design, religious beliefs and practices, and patterns of kinship/gender, sexuality, and socio-political organization—that have long underlain the striking diversity of the region (Murdock 1960, Reid 1988, 1993b, Higham 1989, Bellwood 1997, Wolters 1999, Day 2002, B. Andaya 2006), a region sometimes characterized as "at once territorially porous, internally diverse, and inherently hybrid" (Steedly 1999a:13). Some of the commonalities that underlie the porousness, diversity, and hybridity at issue may be attributed to the Austronesian ancestry shared by many inhabitants in the area.[1] Others illustrate convergent adaptations to broadly analogous constellations of climatic, geographic, and ecological features that have shaped lives and livelihoods throughout the region for many millennia. Still other commonalities attest to other variables: the geographically widespread impact of cultural and political traditions introduced into coastal communities and royal courts of Southeast Asia by merchants, religious scholars, and others from India, China, the Middle East, and elsewhere during pre- and early modern times; the commercial and other economic developments stimulated by these and attendant processes; or some combination of these dynamics (Reid 1988:1–10 et passim; cf. Johnson et al. 2000).

Among the more interesting features of Southeast Asia in comparative cultural-historical terms are the deeply entrenched and broadly institutionalized traditions of pluralism with respect to gender and sexuality. Put differently, Southeast Asians have long accorded legitimacy to numerous variants of gendered behavior. In the present context I cannot elaborate on all the reasons for these patterns or their scope, historical origins, or pre-modern transformations, though I can direct attention to a few relevant dynamics that prevailed during the first half of the early modern era (roughly the fifteenth and sixteenth centuries).[2] Perhaps most important to underscore is that during this time, and for many centuries prior to it, kinship systems throughout Southeast Asia tended to emphasize bilateralism rather than one or another variant of unilineal (e.g., patrilineal) descent and inheritance, thus valorizing relations through men and women alike as well as "looking in all directions" to forge connections and realize other social value; and that religious traditions were "profoundly dualistic, with male and female elements both needing to be present to give power and effect. Female gods of the underworld, of the earth or crops (especially rice), and of the moon balanced the male gods of the upper world, the sky, iron (that which ploughs the earth, cuts the rice-stalk), and the sun" (Reid 1993b:161–162; see also Gibson 2005: Chap. 3). Women predominated in a good many ritual contexts, associated with agriculture, birth, death, and healing, perhaps because their reproductive capacities were seen as giving them regenerative, spiritual, and other religious powers that men could not match (Reid 1988:146, Lieberman 2003:118).

Women's reproductive capacities and the powers of fertility and regeneration associated with them also raised the specter of danger (via pollution, for example) to men and variously defined moral and natural communities and were thus seen as requiring that some of the activities of women of child-bearing age be carefully regulated. Notwithstanding this regulation, the ambivalences associated with it, or the fact that men were generally accorded more prestige than women in gender ideologies throughout the region, this was a period in Southeast Asia's history that was characterized by women's active involvement in the realms of trade, diplomacy, and statecraft, by a good deal of female autonomy and social control, and by relatively egalitarian relations between males and females. Viewed from a different angle, it was a period in which, to paraphrase Barbara Andaya (2006:227), women were noticeably "less socially inferior" to men than was typically the case either in the West or in areas that neighbored Southeast Asia, such as East Asia, South Asia, Melanesia, and the Pacific. This period was also characterized by considerable fluidity and permeability in gender roles, and by relative tolerance and indulgence with respect to many things erotic and sexual, at least for the commoner majority. Portuguese observers of the sixteenth century reported that Malays were "fond of music and given to love," the broader themes being that "pre-marital sexual relations were regarded indulgently; … [that] virginity at marriage was not expected of either party" (Reid 1988:153); that divorce was rather easily initiated by women and men alike; and that women were commonly included as heirs to rights over houses and land, in some cases being favored over male heirs (Peletz 1988, 1996). Chinese and European observers emphasized similar patterns when writing about Javanese, Filipinos, Thais, Burmese, and other Southeast Asians. However, some of them also remarked on the harsh, occasionally gruesome, punishments awaiting those who transgressed prohibitions associated with incest or adultery, "the two great sexual crimes" of the early modern period (B. Andaya 2006:155); the vows of celibacy undertaken in certain religious contexts (La Loubère 1693 [1969]:119, C. Brooke 1866 [1990]:60–61, Pelras 1996:167); or the widespread institutions of debt bondage that facilitated the mobilization of labor and could involve indebtedness on the part of both males and females (see, for example, Galvao 1544 [1971]:126, Reid 1988:129–136).

In light of the patterns outlined here it should not be surprising to find that during the first half of the early modern period, and in earlier times as well, many communities of Southeast Asians accorded enormous prestige to male-bodied individuals who dressed in female attire and performed certain rituals associated with royal regalia, births, weddings, and key phases of agricultural cycles (see, for example, Van der Kroef 1956, Jacobs 1966, Reid 1988:55, Pelras 1996, Lieberman 2003:192, 196, Peletz 2006). I refer to these practitioners as transgendered ritual specialists. Such individuals, along with female ritualists who were also accorded prestige but were apparently less likely to engage in any variety of transgendered behavior (though they clearly did so in some contexts), commonly took normatively gendered male-bodied persons as their husbands and typically served as sacred mediators between males and females, and between the spheres of humans and the domains of spirits and nature. Foremost among their jobs was participation in rituals that would make manifest "the spiritual energy of the gods in the sacred world" (De Casparis and Mabbett 1992:326). A more general point is that

> in the cultures of [pre-modern] monsoon Asia, divinity was a quality of the sacred world … [which was] unseen and implicit in the things of the world …, like electromagnetic radiation or gravity, [and which] could make itself accessible and potent through ritual. Kingship was itself a kind of ritual, serving to centre the kingdom on an individual, just as a shrine could centre it on an icon; in each case, the spiritual energy of the gods in the sacred world would be manifested.
>
> (Ibid.; cf. Heine-Geldern 1956, Tambiah 1976, C. Geertz 1980)

Some Gendered Themes in the Political Cultures of Pre- and Early Modern States

I have mentioned certain gendered patterns in the broadest of terms and want to begin to sketch out their genealogies and pervasiveness; that done, I will focus more directly on the structure and content of these patterns. Particularly germane is that the gendered patterns at issue were grounded in the same frames of meaning that undergirded the cosmologies, court rituals, and architectural monuments that sanctified and enhanced the prowess of the rulers of the earliest states in Southeast Asia. These frames of meaning were built up of many autochthonous features but were also infused with myriad elements drawn from Indic cultural traditions that were introduced into Southeast Asia, beginning around the fourth or fifth century BCE (if not earlier), by seafaring merchants, scholars, and ritual specialists from India, many of whom traveled to Southeast Asia in the context of maritime trade and intellectual exchange with China.[3] Specifically, Brahmanic priests and other emissaries from India introduced Southeast Asian political elites and their retinues of ritual specialists to new forms of esoteric knowledge and statecraft, commonly expressed in the languages of Sanskrit and Pali, that were grounded in Indic templates variably informed by one or another syncretic blend of Hindu and/or Buddhist tradition. (In pre- and early modern times, the religions of Hinduism and Buddhism were not nearly as distinct as they are today, and the major sects, schools, and traditions of these religions [e.g., Mahayana and Theravada Buddhism] were likewise far less distinguishable from one another than is the case at present.) Particularly relevant here owing to its subsequent diffusion throughout the royal courts of Southeast Asia and to the provinces and hinterlands far beyond (at least in the lowlands; not necessarily in the highlands) was a nexus of foundational Indic concepts common to Hinduism and Buddhism alike. Key components of this nexus included the following notions: that a sacred peak (Mount Meru) surrounded by oceans was the abode of the principal Hindu gods: Vishnu, Brahma, and perhaps most importantly in Southeast Asian settings, Siva, the god of creation and destruction, and of fertility, harvests, yoga, and meditation; that the ruler's palace and immediate (built) environs was a replica of Mount Meru, hence a microcosm of the macrocosm as well as a *mandala* ("sacred diagram"),[4] whose studied contemplation could bring enhanced spiritual awareness, power, and merit in this life as well as better karma and a higher form of existence in the next; and that in keeping with the concept of reciprocal karmic influence, the well-being of the ruler and his or her royal regalia and entourage promoted the well-being of the polity and the cosmos as a whole. Last but not least is the cosmological emphasis on both the reconciliation of contrasting or opposed forces to achieve harmony and liberation, and the use of the human body to attain these ends.

In previous generations, scholars commonly referred to the earliest states in Southeast Asia as "Indianized" or "Indic," sometimes giving rise to or reinforcing erroneous stereotypes that these polities owed both the majority of their basic features and their very existence to dynamics of exogenous origin, that they passively received or imitated foreign culture, or both (see, for example, Coedès 1966). More recently, scholars have characterized these states either as *mandala* or as "galactic polities," the latter to emphasize their fluid boundaries and tendencies toward expansion and contraction, and, more generally, in order to distinguish them from the types of modern Western polities that have long defined scholarly discussions of states (see, for example, Tambiah 1976, C. Geertz 1980, Higham 1989, 2001, Mabbett and Chandler 1995, Wolters 1999, Day 2002). However they are glossed, such states include:

1   the kingdom of Funan, the earliest state in Southeast Asia, which emerged in the Mekong Delta area around 150 CE and to some degree controlled riverine and maritime trade in the region until its decline around 550 CE, owing apparently to "growing political powers in centres to the north" and shifting patterns of shipping and trade linking China with the West (Higham 2001:6, 34);

2   the kingdoms of Chenla, a series of agrarian successors to Funan, located further up the riverine valleys of the Mekong, nearer Tonle Sap Lake (the Great Lake of central Cambodia), which prevailed during the period

550–800 CE but were eventually eclipsed by the rise of powerful dynasties associated with the empire of Angkor;

3   the empire of Angkor (ca. 800–1430 CE), centered near Tonle Sap Lake; at its height (in the eleventh and twelfth centuries), Angkor extended throughout Cambodia, Thailand, and Laos, and boasted magnificent irrigation and engineering feats as well as Angkor Wat, the largest religious structure ever built, whose "traditions survive both in the person of the King of Cambodia and … in the court rituals of the Chakri Dynasty of Thailand" (Higham 2001:162); and

4   the kingdom of Pagan (ca. 950–1400 CE), located in central Burma, which was the first polity to bring large areas of present-day Burma under the ostensible control of a single ruler, but which declined in consequence of internal dynamics that rendered it unable to contend with invading Mongols and other centrifugal forces (Aung-Thwin 1985:28 passim).

Most relevant for our purposes is that all of the mainland Southeast Asian states at issue here (Funan, Chenla, Angkor, and Pagan), along with their insular counterparts and pre-modern successors elsewhere in the region, such as Srivijaya (seventh to fourteenth centuries CE, centered in Sumatra) and Majapahit (thirteenth to fifteenth centuries CE, in Java), have left material remains—either massive monuments, stelae, bas reliefs, inscriptions, or some combination thereof—indicating the existence of royal cults focusing on the veneration of Siva, the Hindu god of creation, destruction, and fertility (or, as in the case of Pagan, Buddhist variations on Saivite themes). As Higham (2001:10–11) has noted with respect to South and Southeast Asia generally, and Angkor specifically, Siva "may be represented in many forms, [but] the most popular … [is] as a *linga*, an erect stone phallus within a *yoni* or vulva, symbolic of the union of Shiva with *sakti*, his [consort and] dynamic energy." Motifs emphasizing the dynamic union, transcendence, and fluidity of male and female principles and creative forces have long been a hallmark of sculptures, reliefs, paintings, mythical and other narrative accounts, and dramatic performances of Siva (and of other deities in the Hindu pantheon). Not surprisingly, many scholars have long regarded them as grounds to characterize Siva (and various other Hindu deities, such as Vishnu, who though important in some Southeast Asian contexts was not generally accorded the same attention as Siva) as androgynous, hermaphroditic, bisexual, or ambiguous or ambivalent with respect to sex, gender, or both.

Scholars have spilled much ink on which of these (or other) terms either singly or in combination are appropriate as glosses for, or signposts to, Siva's gender and sexuality (see, for example, O'Flaherty 1980, White 2003). More relevant is that the multiplicity of contemporary scholarly interpretations concerning Siva's gender and sexuality may be broadly analogous to the situation that long existed in Southeast Asia. In other words, the existence of variegated iconographies of Siva in the region suggests that Southeast Asians may have long held a multiplicity of potentially contradictory views and feeling-tones concerning Siva's gender and sexuality; circumstances such as these would have been highly conducive to the florescence of diverse expressions of gender and sexuality as well as a climate of pluralism concerning sex, gender, and various other aspects of human experience, desire, and expression.[5] Such would be all the more likely in a cultural climate which placed a premium both on status rivalry and competition and on ritual innovation as a means through which to advance one's claims to status superiority. By all accounts such a climate has long existed in Southeast Asia, and still does (Leach 1954 [1965], C. Geertz 1973, 1980, Volkman 1985, Peletz 1996, Wolters 1999, Gibson 2005, Fjelstad and Nguyen Thi Huen 2006).

The construction at the behest of political elites of stone *linga*, often gilded, and their ritual consecration in temples built specifically to house them, was a sine qua non for the assertion of divinity, and of legitimacy generally, by political elites seeking to maintain or augment their control over large and small states alike. Indeed, Higham (1989, 2001) has demonstrated through masterful marshaling and interpretation of archeological and other data that these religio-political dynamics not only permeated polities in the form of states but also extended to chiefdoms existing near the boundaries or borderlands of states. There and elsewhere, chiefs who aspired to transform their polities into states or simply to expand their rule "augment[ed] their standing by self-identification with Siva" (Higham 1989:359). It is thus possible that religio-political cults focusing on Siva, *linga*, and *yoni* existed even before the emergence of the first state in Southeast Asia. It is also possible, though perhaps less likely, that such cults were ideologically implicated in the processes of political centralization that contributed to the rise of chiefdoms in areas of mainland Southeast Asia by around 500 BCE (Higham 1989), as other elements of Indic ritual and statecraft surely were. Broadly analogous processes have been described for parts of modern Southeast Asia such as highland Burma (Leach 1954 [1965]; cf. Day 2002:42–44) and for pre-contact Polynesia as well (Kirch 1984, Thomas 1994).

Inscriptions and other material dating from as early as ca. 200 CE contain a myriad of clear references to rituals focused on the consecration of royal *linga*. Unfortunately, however, there is little if any clear data on the precise content of such rituals or the multiple and potentially contradictory conceptual, moral, and other cultural guidelines, models, or messages that the social actors involved in them may have intended or otherwise conveyed. Information bearing directly on the content, scope, and force of the messages of such rituals, in other words, is largely absent both from the archeological and epigraphic record and from the written accounts left by Chinese monks and emissaries. We are fortunate, however, to have highly detailed and incisive accounts of some of these dynamics in the context of medieval India (e.g., White 2003), from which we can reasonably generalize. Relevant as well for developing a broad comparative perspective is historical and contemporary ethnographic material bearing on the caste-like groups of hermaphrodites and eunuchs known as *hijras* who are linked in popular culture with Siva and have served as ritual specialists in India for well over a thousand years.

Before turning to material bearing on medieval India and the *hijras*, brief comments on Tantric Buddhism are in order. There are two reasons for this. First, in the Southeast Asian context the beliefs and practices associated with this latter variant of (Esoteric) Buddhism were in many cases interwoven with elements of Saivism and other aspects of Hinduism, as was true in South Asia as well. The second (related) reason has to do with the convergence of Saivistic and Tantric themes emphasizing, on the one hand, the reconciliation of contrasting or opposed forces as a means to achieve harmony and liberation, and, on the other, the deployment of human bodily practices to these ends.

"Tantric Buddhism" refers to a congeries of practices and associated precepts that are codified in spiritual compendia, guidebooks, or "manuals" known as *tantras*. In the words of John Miksic (1990:22), one of the foremost scholars of Tantric Buddhism in pre-modern Southeast Asia, "*Tantras* contain practical instructions on how to accomplish a specific task. They evolved in India from popular belief in magic and spells that are even older than Buddhism [which had emerged by the end of the fifth century BCE]. They are of many kinds, but all advise devotees how to achieve quick spiritual liberation and worldly powers by taking medicines, performing rituals, and doing mental and physical exercises."

Miksic goes on to underscore that

> One of the principal characteristics of *tantras* is the attention they pay to the body. The more austere sects of Buddhism treat the body as nothing but an illusion and a hindrance. *Tantras* view the body in a more favorable light, considering it to be a reflection of divinity and arguing that mind and body cannot be separated but are merely different aspects of one all-embracing reality. On a more general level, *tantras* assume that all opposing forces are ultimately connected and that harmony can be achieved by reconciling them. Thus *tantras* argue that the body should be cultivated to help attain liberation.
>
> (Ibid.)

Noteworthy here is not only the convergence with Saivism: specifically, the cosmological emphasis on both the harmonizing of contrasting or opposed forces to attain balance, order, and liberation, and the use of the human body to achieve these ends; but also that themes such as these appear to have been prominent in Austronesian contexts as well (Gibson 2005: Chap. 3).

The evidence bearing on Tantric practices in pre-modern Indonesia is extensive. Summarizing this evidence, Miksic (1990:22) observes that "Yogic exercises began to appear in some Mahayana [Buddhist] sects by the fourth century AD;" that "Sumatran inscriptions from the late seventh century already refer to *siddhayatra* or 'pilgrimages to sacred spots to perform rituals aimed at obtaining success;'" and that "by the end of the ninth century the *Vajrayana* or 'Way of the Thunderbolt', which promised quick liberation through Tantric practices, had become very popular in Java." More generally, just as such "practices were well established in Indonesia even before Borobudur was built" (beginning in the eighth century CE), "ceremonies involving drinking, feasting, dancing on cremation grounds and ritual love-making were frequently conducted [t]here, especially during the fourteenth century in eastern Java and Sumatra" (ibid.).

The latter period (the fourteenth century) is of particular interest in light of the apparent resurgence or florescence then of Tantric cults in various parts of Indonesia, probably reflecting more direct contact between Sumatrans and Indians around this time. Not coincidentally, the fourteenth century also gave rise to King Adityavarman (r. ca. 1347–1379), who became "the spiritual father of the kingdom of Minangkabau [Sumatra]" (De Casparis and Mabbett 1992:321–322) and is thus an apical ancestor of Malays in Negeri Sembilan and the Malay Peninsula generally, who I discuss further along. Adityavarman is said to have been "always concentrated on *Hevajra*', a demonic form of the Jina Aksobhya, whose worship involved bloody and erotic rituals, the latter in conjunction with female partners" (321). One of the very few images of him to come to light is "the largest statue discovered in Indonesia: a huge, two-armed horrific Bhairava, a demonic form of Siva represented nude, and brandishing a knife, while standing on a corpse above a pedestal decorated in human skulls" (322).

It would certainly be useful to have more information on the "ceremonies involving drinking, feasting, dancing on cremation grounds and ritual love-making," alternatively glossed by De Casparis and Mabbett (1992:321) as "bloody and erotic rituals," that are said to have been frequently conducted in Indonesia and other parts of Southeast Asia that engaged Tantric themes. Unfortunately, however, as mentioned earlier, little if any reliable data bearing on such matters is available for the pre- and early modern periods, at least from Southeast Asia. A partial exception occurs in the tantalizing observations of Chinese emissary Zhou Daguan (aka Chou Ta-Kuan), who spent a year in Cambodia from 1296 to 1297 while Angkor was still in full splendor (though beginning to decline) and left a written account of his travels and observations, one of the oldest on record for Cambodia and adjacent regions.

Zhou Daguan reported that when Cambodian girls reached seven or eight years of age (or up to eleven in the case of the poor), their parents hand them over to "a Buddhist or Taoist priest for deflowering" in "a ceremony known as *chen-t'an*," and that in the context of lavish feasting, elaborate processions, and gifts to the priests of "wine, rice, fabrics, silk, areca-nuts, [and] silver plate"—all to the tune of "deafening music"—"the priest enters the maiden's pavilion and deflowers her with his hand, dropping the first fruits into a vessel of wine … . The father and mother, the relations and neighbors, [then] stain their foreheads with this wine, or even taste it," after which "some say the priest has intercourse with the girl [though] others deny this" (Chou Ta-Kuan 1297 [1993]:18–19; cf. White 2003:68 passim). These rituals were scheduled each year ("on a day of the month corresponding to the fourth Chinese moon") by "the proper authorities" who arranged to have the dates in question communicated "throughout the country." This suggests the involvement of authorities at the highest level of the kingdom. We may also infer that the ritual services were provided by "the higher class of priests," presumably from the same class(es) of specialists who advised or attended to royalty; and that the pre-nuptial ceremonies at issue included elements drawn directly from royal ritual, as has long been true of engagement and marriage ceremonies throughout Southeast Asia. We do not know whether such rituals included symbols or more encompassing complexes meant to entail emulation of royal consecration of *linga*, or whether any transgender practices (or same-sex relations) were involved. Some of the underlying logic of royal consecration of *linga* (e.g., themes of nourishment and empowerment through the transmission of sexual substances) is certainly present, however. Zhou Daguan offers only the unhelpful observation, "in the market place groups of ten or more catamites are to be seen every day, making efforts to catch the attention of the Chinese in the hope of rich presents," to which he adds, " a revolting, unworthy custom, this!" (1297 [1993]:15).

Although relevant material bearing on Southeast Asia is, as noted earlier, in short supply, material from South Asia is relatively abundant, thanks to the incisive work of David Gordon White (2003). White has underscored that far from being the marginal component of South Asian experience that much conventional scholarly wisdom suggests, "Tantric practice was—and in some cases has remained—the royal cultus, in addition to being the religion of the popular masses." This "was the case, in particular, across a wide swath of central India between the ninth and thirteenth centuries … *as well as the 'Greater India' of the Southeast Asian kingdoms of present-day Indonesia, Cambodia, and Burma*" (2003:12; emphasis added). Indeed, the *devaraja* cult described in the famous Sdok Kak Thom inscription from eleventh-century Cambodia had strong Tantric elements in the rituals that inaugurated it, as did many other ceremonial complexes that occurred in Cambodia and elsewhere in Southeast Asia around this time and subsequently (see, for example, Chandler 1974, Mabbett 1977, Eisenbruch 1992, A. Thompson 1996).

Key to these processes in South Asia during medieval times (circa the sixth to sixteenth centuries) were texts and practices focused on the transmission, between deities and the humans who sought to personify or join them (by becoming *devarajas* or "godkings"), of sexual fluids—semen, vaginal secretions, the blood of defloration and menstruation—that both nourished and empowered those who consumed them. Such nourishing and empowerment seem to have been involved in the thirteenth-century Cambodian rituals mentioned above, though the protection of the girls' future sexual partners, via priestly defusing or "dilution" of the girls' magical potency, may also have been involved (cf. O'Flaherty 1980:20, 38). In South Asia, such transmission commonly entailed oral or genital sex, or both (kissing, sucking, drinking, penetrating, etc.), often between males and females but not always. Some of the Indian inscriptions, sculptures, and reliefs from this period that White has analyzed depict ancient rituals that involved the consumption of male fluids by other males ("rituals of male-to-male transmission or initiation predate Saivism and Kaula traditions by at least two millennia" [2003:246]). Others were exclusively or predominantly female, entailing (*inter alia*) female consumption of menstrual and other uterine discharge; while still others involved mixtures of male and female emissions that were consumed by males, females, or both (cf. O'Flaherty 1980:20, 38, 52, 270). The Tantric texts, along with the precepts and practices associated with them, thus legitimized and sanctified multiple forms and combinations of gender and sexuality (at least in certain contexts) including, among many others, gender without sexuality (typified, as discussed in due course, by male and female ascetics, and by eunuchs), as well as sexuality in the absence of any unambiguous, monolithic, or immutable gender. A more general (historical) point is that legitimizing and sanctifying precepts and practices such as these occurred in the context of Southeast Asian ceremonies involving the consecration of royal *linga*, or at least "somewhere" in the royal cultus, and also figured into "the religion of the popular masses," as suggested by the material from thirteenth-century Cambodia.

Circumstances such as these recall Gayle Rubin's (1984:283) important point, made with reference to a very different context (late twentieth-century America), that a climate of sexual pluralism presumes "a concept of benign sexual variation." What we see in South and Southeast Asia, however, is much more than a concept of benign sexual (or gender) variation. In point of fact, such variation did not just exist, but was sanctified, at least or especially for the gods and the political elites, and for ritual specialists and others who were close to or personified them. This is most obvious in the case of deities such as Siva. While appearing in many myths as male (or predominantly male), Siva appears in others as female (or chiefly female), and in yet others as combining equivalently or comparably weighted elements of both male and female simultaneously (one or another form of hermaphroditism or androgyny) or over time (O'Flaherty 1980).

Hindu- and Tantric-inflected pluralistic sensibilities along these general lines existed well before medieval times, and long after them as well, as suggested by an origin myth that appears in a classic ethnography written by anthropologist Miguel Covarrubias, who conducted fieldwork among Hindu Balinese in the 1930s. One of the themes highlighted in this myth from the corpus of literature known as the *Tjatur Yoga* is Siva's nonchalance toward, even positive sanctioning of, non-heteronormative sexuality in the form of an erotic encounter involving masturbation and conception with the stump of a tree.

> After the world, the mountains, and the cardinal directions were created, and there were trees, fruits, and flowers, the gods made four human beings out of red earth, whom they provided with utensils to work with and houses to live in. Betara Siwa [Siva], the Supreme Lord, next made four mature girls for wives of the four men. The god of love, Batara Semara, made mating a pleasure so that the women would be fertilized, and eventually the four couples had many children: 117 boys and 118 girls, who grew, became adolescent, married, and had children. But there remained a girl without a husband. Broken-hearted, she went into the forest and there found the

stump of a jackfruit tree (*nangka*) which Siwa had carved, to amuse himself, into the likeness of a human being. The girl made love to the wooden figure and became pregnant. Out of pity for her, Semara gave life to the figure so that she also could have a husband, and the couple became the ancestors of the *ngatewel* clan whose totem is the *nangka* tree.

(Covarrubias 1937 [1972]:120–121)

There is much of interest here, but of most significance for our purposes is Siva's reaction to the husbandless woman pleasuring herself and conceiving with the stump of a tree: it entails no censure, rebuke or other negative sanction, only "pity" because the woman has no fully human mate or companion. What's more, Siva clearly rewards the masturbating woman by "giving life" to the magical stump, or, more precisely, by "giving it more life" (since it already had some animate and life-giving qualities). This, recall, was to provide her with a husband and thus enable her to become a fully social adult with (as we will see in due course) the capacity and desire to imitate or emulate her gods, especially Siva ("himself").

In the Balinese setting this myth is neither idiosyncratic nor unique. As Covarrubias reports, "there are endless tales like these relating the origin of the Balinese to magic or ordinary unions of the male and female principles, elements of great importance in the religion around which life revolves" (ibid., 121; cf. Boon 1977). To this he adds a series of by now familiar observations bearing on Hindu and Indic-influenced South and Southeast Asia: that the "supreme deity is Siwa, the esoteric combination of all the gods and all the forces of nature, he who is the hermaphrodite (*wandu*) in the sense that within him are the male and female creative forces, the complete perfect unity"); and that "to attain some of that divine 'completeness,'" Balinese men and women "must imitate their gods" (Covarrubias [1937] 1972:121). Balinese do this "by *uniting to form families* that worship common ancestors in the family shrine of each Balinese household" (ibid., 121; emphasis added; cf. Duff-Cooper 1985:414–415, 417–418). Here, clearly, in contrast to other examples we will discuss, identification with or embodiment of Siva entailed a relatively compulsory heteronormativity in sex and marriage—even priests married—albeit a heteronormativity that allowed for certain kinds of play.

Covarrubias does not appear to have considered the possibility that social actors among the Balinese might "imitate," emulate, identify with, embody, or immerse themselves into Siva by engaging in one or another variety of transgendered practice that symbolized the union within a single individual of the male and female creative forces, "the complete perfect unity." This could be because the theme was not especially salient in the domains of Balinese culture that Covarrubias engaged most directly during the period of his research; alternatively, it may not have occurred to Covarrubias to look into the issue in any detail. More important is the overall climate of (relative) gender pluralism that existed at the time. Such is evidenced by his observations that "the average Balinese does not attach great importance to virginity;" that "it is not difficult for a divorcee, a widow, or even a woman who has committed adultery to marry again;" and that "in general the idea of homosexuality is inconsequential to the Balinese" ([1937] 1972:137, 145), a theme also noted by Jane Belo ([1935] 1970:5) and others (Duff-Cooper 1985:415–416, Gouda 1995:182).

There is a fly in the ointment, however, for those who are hermaphrodites in the anatomical sense and assumed by Balinese to be "abnormally asexual from birth, impotent" are subject to teasing (and mild ostracism), apparently because while being a hermaphrodite is "a condition which is characteristic of gods," it is "bad and ridiculous among humans" (Covarrubias 1937 [1972]:145).[6] This latter view, that certain signs, practices, and characteristics of the gods are "bad and ridiculous among humans," contains a clear warning to scholars and others who might be inclined to overstate the significance, for the range(s) of behavior deemed acceptable for humans, of transgendered deities in Balinese Hinduism and in other religious systems as well. As I have been arguing here, the gendered characteristics of deities, like the gendering of the cosmos generally, are key variables informing gender relations and realities "on the ground." But one cannot assume, a priori, a neat, one-to-one isomorphism between the gendering of this or that deity (or the cosmos) on the one hand, and what the deities or their human guardians, interlocutors, or supplicants find acceptable for particular classes of humans in certain contexts, or humans generally, on the other (see Roscoe 1996).

To help illustrate some of the latter points as well as the ways that Siva's polyvalence helps confer legitimacy on ways of being human that are altogether different from the Balinese example just cited, we might briefly consider another Hindu context, India, and the ways that ritual specialists known as hijra identify with and emulate Siva.[7] The term hijra refers to caste-like groups of ritual specialists composed of hermaphrodites as well as males who have had their penis and testes sacrificially excised and have thus become eunuchs, the latter making up the hijra majority (Nanda 1990, 1993, L. Cohen 1995, Agrawal 1997, Reddy 2005). Hijras dress and adorn themselves as women, adopt stereotypically (often exaggerated) female hand gestures, gait, and overall demeanor, engage in female domestic activities such as cooking, sewing, sweeping, and cleaning, and behave like women in various other ways, though they also have a reputation for being louder and more verbally aggressive than ordinary women. For at least a thousand years, hijras have existed in Hindu communities in India and since the sixteenth century if not earlier among Muslims as well, performing sacred roles that have included maintaining temples devoted to deities associated with the Mother Goddess as well as dancing, playing music, and conducting various ritual services at weddings and the births of male children, events that are among the most joyous and significant ceremonial occasions for Hindus and Muslims throughout India and South Asia as a whole.

The role and social standing of hijras in contemporary India is complex and fraught, as are the quotidian negotiations of hijra identity both within their own communities and in relation to the larger society. British colonial policies bear some responsibility for this situation in that they criminalized castration, defined all eunuchs as dangerous outlaws, and otherwise denigrated the role. So, too, does the fact that many *hijras* no longer maintain the celibacy and ascet-icism that were long seen as defining features of their identities (Reddy 2005:26–28 passim). In many cases, moreover, impoverished *hijras* have turned to prostitution with (non-*hijra*, sometimes heterosexually-identified, married) males to support themselves, contributing to dissension and strife among *hijras* as to the proper ways to comport oneself and enhance or at least maintain one's honor or respect (*izzat*), and adding to the ambivalence with which they are viewed by the general public. *Hijras* are nonetheless accorded an important degree of legitimacy and sanctity by society at large. This is largely because of the valuable rituals they perform as well as their identification in India's public culture both with "Bahuchara Mata, one of the many versions of the Mother Goddess worshipped throughout India," and with a strongly androgynous if not bisexual form of "the sexually ambivalent Siva" (Nanda 1993:373, 375).

To understand how the Hindu majority conceptualize *hijras* and their spiri-tual powers, we need to bear in mind four sets of issues. First, in Hinduism "'male' and 'female' are seen as natural categories in complementary opposi-tion," each of which is "naturally" associated with "different sexual characteris-tics and reproductive organs, ... different sexual natures ..., and ... different, and complementary, roles in marriage, sexual relations and reproduction" (ibid., 374). Second, the female principle, which is "more immanent and active" than the male principle, "has a positive, creative, life-giving aspect and a destructive life-destroying aspect." In numerous contexts, "the erotic aspect of female power is dangerous unless it is controlled by the male principle," which is why many (but not all) Hindus and scholars of Hinduism believe that "pow-erful women, whether deities or humans, must be restrained by male authority. Thus the Hindu goddess subordinated to her male consort is beneficent, but when dominant the goddess" may be "aggressive, devouring and destructive" (ibid.), at least with respect to demonic enemies, in which case she may still be a savior of humans and male deities.[8] Third, just as many Hindu deities are "sex-ually ambiguous," often being depicted in myth, ritual, and iconography in androgynous or dual-gendered forms, so, too, do many of them change over time, from largely male to predominantly female, and vice versa, for instance, and/or from one to many and back again. The fourth, most general point (which follows partly from the others) is that spiritual salvation presupposes transcen-dence and change, and that Hinduism's doctrinal emphasis on rebirth, vari-ability, and multiplicity serves both to valorize mutability and transformation and to underscore their intrinsic connections with spiritual potency.

As for issues of identity and subjectivity, most individuals who become *hijras* do so through surgical removal of the penis and testes—which, in the case of effeminate boys encouraged by their parents to join the ranks of *hijras* around the time of puberty, may occur while they are in their early teens—not because they were born intersexed (hermaphroditic). It is partly for this reason that even when they view themselves as "neither man nor woman" or as "man plus woman," *hijras* sometimes consider themselves as more male than female.

Because *hijras* lack male sexual organs as well as sexual desires for women, in some contexts they think of themselves as "not male," "less than male," or as "incomplete males." Because they are not endowed with female sexual organs or the capacity to bear children but dress and adorn themselves like women and perform various female tasks, in other contexts they regard themselves as "incomplete women" rather than in terms of one or another category defined in relation to masculinity or its lack (e.g., "not male," "less than male," etc.). It is important to underscore that these identities, all of which bear on ostensibly bedrock "sexual(ized) difference," are not the only or necessarily the most personally or culturally salient identities negotiated by *hijras*. As with those of other Hindus and Muslims in modern India, *hijras*' subjectivities and senses of self are informed in complex, sometimes contradictory, ways by a panoply of factors. These include: their religious affiliations, relative piety, and place of birth; the linguistic communities to which they belong; their past and present involvement in networks of kinship, romance, and desire; the extent to which they honor one or another vow of asceticism or world renunciation (or have done so in the past); and their ritual and artistic specializations, educational attainment, occupational activities, employment status, and overall socio-economic standing (Reddy 2005:74–76 passim).

Conceptualizations of *hijras* along with the construction and entailments of the *hijra* role make clear that some Asian societies regard sexuality and gender as fluid, permeable, even hybrid categories that are contextually specific and subject to combination, flux, and change. The *hijra* example also illustrates that some Asian societies do not insist that at birth every individual be assigned a lifelong sexual designation or gender role derived from a system composed of two rigidly defined sex/gender categories; and, more generally, that not all societies operate with a binary system based on two sexes or genders. It merits note, finally, that while modern-day *hijras* tend to be viewed by normative Hindus and Muslims with ambivalence and are in some instances apparently less revered than stigmatized and feared (owing to their spiritual potency and tendencies to threaten with misfortune those who cross them), they differ from their gender-transgressive counterparts in the West in that they are accorded a meaningful and seemingly fulfilling role that is both legitimate and in some ways sanctified.

The purpose of this foray into Balinese and Indian material has been partly to underscore that emulation of Siva can and obviously does take many forms, some of which, at least from a Western perspective, are mutually contradictory or antithetical; and that Hinduism in Bali and elsewhere in Southeast Asia and beyond has long recognized "the validity of the many different ways of being human" (Nanda 1993:414). A more general point is that the validity or, as I prefer, the legitimacy of these many divergent ways or styles of being human is what pluralism, gendered or otherwise, is all about.

Throughout this discussion of the gendered political cultures of pre-modern states I have been concerned to sketch out some of the ways in which Hinduism (especially Saivism) and Buddhism (particularly its Tantric forms) converged in emphasizing the mutual accommodation of contrasting or opposed forces to attain balance, well-being, and liberation as well as the deployment of human bodily practices to achieve these ends—all of which were conducive to a climate that valorized various forms of transgendering in certain contexts. It remains to underscore that similar cosmological themes run throughout some of the Sufi-inflected forms of Islam introduced into Southeast Asia by South Asian Muslims (religious teachers, merchants, and others) beginning around the thirteenth century, and that some of these same general themes also suffused Austronesian religious systems and perhaps some of the other religious systems that pre-dated Indic influences in the area.

Aceh, in northern Sumatra, provides a good example. The mystical strains of Islam adopted by Acehnese beginning, apparently, around the thirteenth or fourteenth century, included an array of embodied performances that involved stylized dancing and chanting along with the formulaic recitation of Quranic verse and other sacred texts commemorating the life of the Prophet Muhammad. As with other genres of *dikir*, these ritualized activities facilitated the performer's direct experience of and intimate union with the Divinity (God, Allah). Some of the Acehnese performances involved competitions between teams of men from different villages, each linked with a local prayer house or mosque, and each having as its centerpiece (so to speak) a young "dancing boy" known as a *sadati* (in this context, "an accomplished one;" from the Arabic *sada* ["lord," "master"] discussed in more detail below). *Sadati* dressed in female attire and were otherwise made up to appear female; their artistic and aesthetic accomplishments, included, most notably, ideally flawless performances of youthful femininity that helped both to ensure their team's victory and to enhance the reputation of its village as a place of and for linguistic virtuosity and artistic excellence.

Dutch Islamicist Christiaan Snouck Hurgronje (1906 I:21, 63, 149 n1; II:222, 318) who observed and photographed these performances in the 1880s was struck both by the "pederastic character" of the verbal jousting that helped define these highly stylized competitions and by the same-sex relations that occurred among members of the same team. Such liaisons included, but were not limited to, relations between the older, male performers and the feminized "dancing boys." We do not know enough about the ages of those involved to ascertain whether erotic encounters with the *sadati* were or, perhaps more relevant, were held to be, intergenerational. Assuming for the moment that they were, this instance of same-sex sexuality differs from most others in Southeast Asia for which we have clear evidence, for the vast majority of the latter were *intra*generational. That said, the Acehnese example of same-sex sexuality at issue here, at least when it involved "dancing boys," is clearly heterogender and in this respect is congruent with the pervasive Southeast Asian patterns of same-sex sexuality in the early modern period. The fact that *sadati* used the term *abang*, whose meanings include both "elder brother" and "husband," to refer to and address other members of the troop, and that the latter commonly referred to and addressed the *sadati* as *adik*, a term used to refer to and address a younger sibling of either gender as well as a wife, is also revealing. This might suggest that the relations between older troop members and *sadati* were (or were construed) as intragenerational. Arguably more relevant are the symbolic resonances and other implications of these terminological conventions; namely, that in important ways the relationships in which they were deployed were informed by symbols, idioms, and metaphors associated with normative marriage, as in many other cases of ritual transgendering and same-sex sexuality that involved ritual specialists who were not only married to one or more spirits but also had earthly partners to whom they were linked via institutionalized bonds of heterogender but not necessarily heterosexual marriage.

It is not possible to specify the precise ways in which those who were involved in these unions or the activities associated with them may have construed them as specifically Sufistic or otherwise Islamic, though the recitation of canonical Islamic texts in the case of the performances at issue might suggest that participants accorded them one or another degree of Islamic legitimacy, as has long occurred with Indian-origin shadow-puppet theater (*wayang kulit*). We do know (from Snouck Hurgronje 1906 II:246, 248) that by the late 1800s Islamic religious scholars (*ulama*) viewed them with disdain, as evidence of "backward" times and pre-Islamic (animist and Hindu-Buddhist) paganism in particular. The larger, more salient issue is not whether this or that precept or practice is "essentially" or "at base" either Hindu, Buddhist, Islamic, or Austronesian (or other). It is rather that dramatic forms centered around *sadati*, which aficionados and the lay public apparently viewed as Islamic, and which seem to have been introduced into areas such as Aceh along with various aspects of mystical Islam, were broadly congruent with Saivite and Tantric themes highlighting the attainment of harmony, release, and liberation via unions of complementary or opposed principles and essences, along with reliance on human bodily practices to achieve these goals.

There is a final set of issues to address before turning to a discussion that focuses more directly on transgendered ritual specialists and the sexual practices that commonly prevailed among their ranks and in the population at large during the first half of the early modern period. It has to do with the ways that non-heteronormative sexual and gender practices in Southeast Asia and Asia as a whole have been portrayed by earlier generations of historians as well as some of their more conventionally oriented successors writing at present. Typical in some respects is Rhoads Murphey (1996:201), who writes in his encyclopedic history of Asia that "in contrast to the Judeo-Christian West," "India, Tibet, and parts of Southeast Asia had a religious tradition in which sex was used as ritual, in some ways rather like the ancient cult of Dionysus in classical Greece. Representations of sex in Indian sculpture and painting use gods and goddesses as subjects, not ordinary mortals, and celebrate the divine life force, creation. Tantric Buddhist and some Hindu temple sex rites had the same purpose." So far, so good (perhaps). But Murphey like most of his predecessors and many of his contemporaries works within a reductionist and dichotomous framework. This framework reduces gender-transgressive behavior to homosexuality, basically makes provision for only two fixed variants of sexuality (heterosexuality and homosexuality) and assumes that those who engaged in gender-transgressive behavior did so primarily if not solely "because they could," thus leaving unanswered a number of questions concerning vectors and objects of desire as well as structures of sentiment, prestige, and the like.[9] Such is suggested by his contention that "in most of Asia homosexuality was considered shameful and those who were caught at it were condemned or punished;" that it was heavily stigmatized in Confucian contexts but "more common and more *tolerated* among the samurai of Japan, many of whom remained unmarried, and periodically among rulers and the upper classes in *all* countries" (1996:202; emphases added). In some ways most revealing are Murphey's remarks, "All of this—the pleasures of the elite dallying with their concubines, sing-song girls, erotic pictures and stories, and the joys of the Islamic rulers in their harems—was far beyond the experience of most people. For the great mass of the population, sex was a brief and often furtive pleasure after dark" (1996:201–202).

Particularly conspicuous is the absence here of any reference to the fact that in a wide variety of Asian cultural contexts, gender-transgressive behavior was both legitimate and sanctified and could bring considerable religious merit and prestige to its practitioners. More generally, what is altogether lacking here is recognition of the fact that religiously informed cosmologies in the Asian region undergirded prestige hierarchies that valorized different forms and combinations of gender and sexuality and different ways of being human.

It remains to add that focusing as I do on prestige is not the same as concentrating on the political or religious elite, though it is certainly true that elite concerns with prestige were more pronounced than those of commoners and are better documented because elites, unlike commoners, enjoyed the material and symbolic wherewithal to conscript physical labor and levy taxes both for the enduring monuments they erected and to hire the artisans, scribes, and ritual specialists who sometimes left us with written records or images eulogizing their patrons and their accomplishments. Concerns with prestige and "social uplift" (to borrow White's [2003:261] terminology) were also part of the lived worlds of commoners, which means that they too would have emulated various practices of their rulers, some of which, in turn, entailed emulation of Siva and other androgynous deities. Analogous dynamics, elements of which are sometimes subsumed under the rubric of "Sanskritization" even when what is adopted from above by upwardly mobile types is not necessarily specifically Sanskrit in character, have prevailed in South Asia since medieval times, as White makes clear, though they are best documented for the nineteenth and twentieth centuries. "The low-caste, rural margins of medieval South Asian society would have adopted the Tantric practices of their rulers as a means to social uplift in much the same way that low-caste peasant communities of the nineteenth- and twentieth-century Hindu heartland of India have more recently embraced the *bhakti* cults of Rama and Krsna to assert their Hindu-ness and claim higher-caste identities and privileges" (2003:261). White draws attention to these themes in support of his argument that Tantra developed in South Asia "from on high" and "was not a grassroots 'shamanic' tradition that welled up from a non-Aryan periphery of South Asian religious society" (ibid.). I emphasize such themes for analogous reasons and to underscore that in the Southeast Asian setting an understanding of the dynamics of prestige is essential if we are to move beyond the view, as Murphey and the conventional wisdom would have it, that elites in particular engaged in gender-transgressive practices simply or primarily "because they could."

Transgender Practices and Gender Pluralism in Early Modern Times

Perhaps best known in the historical literature on transgenderism in Southeast Asia are the *bissu*.[10] This term refers to a class of ritual specialists among the Bugis of South Sulawesi that included transgendered males (as well as more or less normatively gendered females, who I gloss over for the moment). Like many Indonesians, *bissu* and other Bugis have long identified with a highly syncretic variant of Islam heavily influenced both by pre-Islamic Hindu-Buddhist beliefs and practices and by the Austronesian ritual cults that predated Indic influences in the region. The male-bodied *bissu*, observed first-hand by Antonio de Paiva and other Portuguese explorers in 1544 (Jacobs 1966), were the subject of indigenous manuscripts as well as numerous Dutch and other Western accounts in the ensuing centuries. They typically assumed female or dual-gendered attire and accoutrements, safeguarded royal regalia and the sacred "white blood" of ruling families, engaged in sexual relations and marriage with same-sex (though differently gendered, i.e., male) partners, and were apparently accorded the status of nobility, much like their more or less normatively gendered female-bodied counterparts who largely disappear from the historical record by the eighteenth century. The Ngaju Dayak and certain Iban groups of Borneo provide other well-known, albeit differently patterned, examples of ritual transgendering that have long included same-sex sexual relations in the context of ceremonies that sometimes involved "sacred prostitution." Some of the latter ceremonies, like the mythologies and overall cosmologies in which they are embedded, may be entirely Austronesian in origin but they are suggestive of both the Tantric Buddhism and the Indian cults devoted to Siva, which, as we have seen, are well documented in the monumental architecture of Java, Cambodia, and neighboring regions, and in numerous other domains of society and culture in pre- and early modern Southeast Asia.[11]

With the partial exception of some of the groups considered in due course and a few others discussed elsewhere (e.g., the Toraja, Bar'e, and Makassar, all of Sulawesi [Van der Kroef 1956, Gibson 2005], we know relatively little about the extent to which Southeast Asia's transgendered ritualists—or anyone else in the region—may have engaged in same-sex sexual relations in sacred or secular contexts, may have been inclined toward sexual relations with persons of both sexes, or may have participated in transvestism in non-ritual settings. Similarly, we do not usually know if the transvestisms at issue were eroticized in any way (and if so, how) or if we are dealing with one or more variants of transsexualism. Perhaps most crucial, in many instances we do not know if the transvestisms under consideration represent quarantined exceptions to the hegemonies bearing on sex and gender that prevailed in the societies in question, though in most societies for which there is evidence this was *not* the case. And needless to say, we have no information on the subjectivities, desires, passions, or pleasures of the individuals who were charged with orchestrating the rituals at issue or were involved in them in other capacities as participants or observers. In this regard it is well to recall a point emphasized many years ago by Edmund Leach (1954 [1965]), which has since been variously elaborated by Maurice Bloch (1989), Arjun Appadurai (1981), and others: in many instances, ritual is more a language of argument than a chorus of harmony.

Despite the gaps in our knowledge, it is important to bear in mind that with reference to the Malay-Indonesian world broadly defined—to include the Malay Peninsula, Java, Borneo, Sulawesi, other parts of Indonesia as well as the Philippines—the most knowledgable scholars of Southeast Asia's early modern history, such as Barbara Andaya (1994:105), speak of "the respect accorded bisexualism," and go on to characterize the evidence for this pattern as "particularly pronounced." Less pronounced is the evidence from mainland Southeast Asia other than Burma, but the mainland evidence nonetheless suggests broadly analogous patterns, entailing, for example, "respect accorded bisexualism." One reason for these patterns of respect may be that bisexualism, like ritual transvestism, combined elements from and simultaneously transcended the male-female duality that helped structure and animate the universe in its entirety. Another may be that in combining elements of male and female, institutionalized bisexualism and transvestism symbolized wholeness, purity, and gender totality, and thus the unfractured universe posited to exist before the advent of humanity and difference (Errington 1989, L. Andaya 2000, Gibson 2005). We have seen that in many of the cosmologies of the region, important spirits and deities were depicted as exhibiting various degrees of androgyny or as existing in male-female pairs (grandfather and grandmother, husband and wife, or brother and sister). All things being equal, then, ritual specialists exhibiting androgyny were ideally situated both to communicate and successfully negotiate with these spirits and deities, and to personify them. A somewhat analogous situation has long obtained in India, as discussed earlier.

It is also possible that the male-bodied Southeast Asians who engaged in transgendered behavior in some of the contexts at issue here were appropriating and performing potent symbols of one or another locally powerful femininity, and that it was these latter appropriations and performances, rather than a "less politically motivated" combination of male and female, that helped them establish or bolster their ritual prowess and overall spiritual potency. This would seem to have been the case in areas of the northern Philippines, where, according to sixteenth-century European observers, female ritual practitioners outnumbered their male counterparts by about fifty to one (Brewer 1999:13, 2000). Material from the northern Philippines is of further significance in light of the fact that in key ritual contexts, female ritual specialists did not dress in male attire or otherwise symbolically identify with men, masculinity, or androgyny (ibid., 12–13). This is largely true of female-bodied ritualists among the Iban, Ngaju Dayak, and Bugis, and apparently at least some Burmese, as we shall see.

However one interprets the material from the northern Philippines, there is no reason to assume that in early modern times this pattern was necessarily typical of island Southeast Asia or of Southeast Asia generally. Perhaps more common, at least among stratified societies and those that fell within their spheres of influence or sought to emulate some of their culturally salient characteristics, was the pattern represented by the Bugis *bissu*, which some modern-day scholars (e.g., Pelras 1996, L. Andaya 2000) have compared to the Two-Spirit People, formerly known as *berdache*, of Native North America, and have also described in terms of a "third gender."[12] Another possibility is the Ngaju Dayak pattern. Mircea Eliade's ([1951] 1972:353) encyclopedic ur-text on shamanism characterizes key features of this latter pattern as probably the "most autochthonous" and the least affected by other "Asiatic influences" (but see P. Graham 1987:98–99). In fact, however, we simply do not know which of these configurations—or one or another mainland variation on the theme, such as the Burmese—was the most widely distributed in the period under consideration.

I devote the remainder of this chapter to an elucidation and analysis of data pertaining to transgenderism in six ethnographic contexts. The first three cases (Iban, Ngaju Dayak, and Bugis), drawn from insular Southeast Asia, share a common Austronesian heritage along with an extensive history of involvement, via maritime commerce, with traders, ritual specialists, and others from various regions of the Indonesian archipelago as well as South Asia and areas of mainland Southeast Asia that were subject to Indic cultural influence. The fourth case, involving Malays, shares features of the first three cases, as might be expected in light of Malays' Austronesian ancestry coupled with the animist and Hindu-Buddhist traditions they followed prior to and, indeed, long after the Malay Peninsula witnessed "the coming of Islam" beginning around the fourteenth century. The remaining two cases are drawn from areas of mainland Southeast Asia that are situated beyond the orbits of Austronesian culture and Islam. The best documented of our mainland cases involves the Burmese, who have long been part of the Theravada Buddhist heartland. The case of the Siamese (Thais), who are also Theravada Buddhists, remains poorly documented but is usefully viewed in relation to neighboring Burma and other state-level examples provided by Bugis and Malays.[13]

A final set of comments before turning to the cases at hand concerns my focus in the pages that follow on transgendered ritual specialists. To select transgendered ritualists and the diversity of gender configurations and sexual practices associated with them as a point of departure for descriptions and analyses of sexual and gender variability in the region is not to conflate historical accounts of (ritual) transgenderism with accounts of same-sex sexuality (or bisexuality). One has to start one's analysis somewhere, and this seems to me a productive point of departure, especially when we bear in mind what religious rituals, particularly in the more homogeneous, face-to-face communities of the sort I focus on in this chapter, commonly "say" and "do."

I take seriously both the "work" of ritual, "the work of the gods" in Tikopian parlance (Firth 1940), as well as the scholarship of those who have endeavored to make sense of that work (e.g., V. Turner 1967, Tambiah 1970, C. Geertz 1973, Ortner 1978, Bloch 1989, Rappaport 1999). The historical prevalence, in certain categories of Southeast Asian rituals, of transgenderism, along with its conceptual and materially embodied links with same-sex relations, is usefully considered in relation to Rappaport's (1999:27) conceptualization of ritual as

> entail[ing] the establishment of convention, the sealing of social contract, the construction of the integrated conventional orders we ... call Logoi (singular: Logos ...), the investment of whatever it encodes with morality, ... the representation of a paradigm of creation, the generation of the concept of the sacred and the sanctification of conventional order, the generation of theories of the occult, the evocation of numinous experience, the awareness of the divine, the grasp of the holy, and the construction of orders of meaning transcending the semantic.

Now it is as at least logically possible that as loci of discursive (re)production the Southeast Asian rituals in question conveyed gendered messages that were, in effect, quarantined exceptions to the prevailing (society-wide) hegemonies bearing on gender and sexuality. By all accounts, however, this was *not* the case, as I have already suggested and will discuss more fully further along. Many rituals, myths, and cosmologies encouraged imaginative play conducive to implicit cultural models valorizing relativism, pluralism, and different ways of being in the world that allowed for a variety of "potential[ly] erotic enterprises" (Butler 1993:110). In another venue it would be worthwhile to offer further development of the point that what sets Southeast Asia apart from neighboring world areas (e.g., East Asia) and many others, and simultaneously renders it broadly analogous to certain regions of Native North America in former times, is not that transgenderism and same-sex sexuality existed and were accorded legitimacy in particular contexts in the early modern era and subsequently; for such phenomena have long been evident in many world areas and they continue to exist in the contemporary US, in Ivy League clubs, northern California's infamous Bohemian Grove, etc.[14] Rather, what strikes me as rather unique about Southeast Asia is that, compared to other world areas, the pluralism-friendly dynamics in question were *not* bracketed exceptions to the prevailing hegemonies. In short, the historical evidence suggests a broadly diffused gender pluralism. This pluralism, in sentiments, dispositions, etc., was variably informed by (but not limited to) sexual and gendered symbols and practices in ritual and cosmological domains; by some of the long-term historical dynamics addressed in this chapter and subsequently; and by a nexus of domestic and social structural factors that included bilateral descent and inheritance as well as variables of the general sort identified by Andrew Beatty (2002) for late twentieth-century Java (widespread fosterage and adoption, terminological usages including teknonymy, birth-order names, and the like), which engender relationality, temporal flux, and reversal and otherwise encourage conceptual and moral relativism. Put differently, these phenomena were (and in many cases remain) among the key motors of pluralism throughout the region.

Iban

Most of the early references to transgendered ritual specialists among the Iban, (Ngaju) Dayak and culturally similar groups of shifting cultivators inhabiting the highlands of south Borneo date from the mid- to late nineteenth century, but there is good reason to believe that much of what is described in these accounts is relevant to earlier centuries as well.[15] We also need to exercise caution when assuming continuities from previous times, for by the mid- to late nineteenth century, "white Rajas" and the European (mostly Protestant) missionaries who came in their wake had made significant inroads into certain areas of indigenous belief and practice. Nineteenth-century references are in any case highly uneven and at times quite inconsistent in their descriptions and interpretations, and are often suffused with thinly veiled antipathy and disgust toward ritual practitioners, the ceremonies and other activities in which they were directly or indirectly involved (e.g., headhunting), and the "sexual license" allowed unmarried males and females alike. (The more reliable and less biased reports date from the mid- to late twentieth century but these describe conditions that were much changed by the combined impact of Christianity, colonialism, and postcolonial processes involved in the building of modern-day nation-states.) Instructive in any case are the mid- and late nineteenth-century accounts bearing on Iban ritual specialists known as *manang*, a term which is perhaps best translated as shaman (earlier glosses included "medicine man," "witch doctor," and so on).

Nineteenth-century reports suggest that *manang* have long been grouped into two broad categories: the "regular" and the "irregular." Regular *manang* (*manang ngagi antiu*) were "called to ... [their] vocation by dreams" and enjoyed the revelations of spirits; irregular *manang* (*manang ngagi diri*), by contrast, were "self-created and without ... familiar spirit[s]" (H. B. Low n.d., cited in Roth 1896 [1980] I:266). Of most interest to us are the regular *manang*, who were of three types: male *manang* (*manang laki*), female *manang* (*manang indu*), and the transformed or transgendered *manang* (*manang bali*). Referring to regular *manang* as a whole, Hugh Brooke Low (1849–1887) who spent a number of years in Sarawak, many of them in close contact with Iban, explained that

> When a person conceives a call from the spirits he bids adieu for a while to his relatives, abandons his former occupation, and attaches himself to some thorough-paced *manang*, who, for a consideration, will take him in hand and instruct him until he is fully qualified to practice on his own account.

It is not enough, however, for him to simply say that he feels himself called; he must prove to his friends that he is able to commune with the spirits, and in proof of this he will occasionally abstain from food and indulge in trances from which he will awake with all the tokens of one possessed by a devil, foaming at the mouth and talking incoherently.

(H. B. Low n.d., cited in Roth 1896 [1980] I:266)

Low's use of masculine pronouns in the passage cited here should not be taken to suggest that *manang* were invariably drawn from the ranks of males. For as already noted, women could become *manang*, in which case they were known as *manang indu* unless they rose further in the *manang* hierarchy by becoming transformed or transgendered *manang* (*manang bali*), apparently an uncommon scenario (Sandin 1983:248, P. Graham 1987:118, 120–121). That the esteemed position of *manang* was open to women, and, conversely, that women not infrequently became *manang*, helps explain why outside observers have long argued that "the position of women is extremely high in Iban society" (see, for example, Pringle 1970:24). Other dynamics figuring into these assessments have included the high degree of autonomy and social control enjoyed by Iban women, the relative absence of double standards with respect to sexuality (e.g., both males and females were permitted and reportedly indulged in considerable "sexual license" prior to marriage [H. Low 1848 [1968]:195–196, Pringle 1970:24]), the respect women generally received from men, and the fact that a woman's mastery of stereotypically female occupational pursuits such as dyeing, weaving, and mat making would normally result in her being held in high regard by all members of the community. That the most highly esteemed members of the community (the *manang bali*) were typically male-bodied individuals who emulated female dress and demeanor, took normatively gendered males as their husbands, and rose in local estimation in accordance with their mastery of female appearance and persona might also be seen as a commentary on the high regard accorded females and femininity in Iban society—and on the overall climate of pluralism with respect to gender and sexuality. Conversely, the fact that *manang bali* were generally male-bodied (rarely female-bodied) suggests that male-bodied individuals were in a better position to "beat—or work—the system," and, more generally, that gender pluralism among the Iban, as elsewhere, is invariably relative.

As for the transformed or transgendered *manang*, Low observed:

The *manang bali* is a most extraordinary character, and one difficult to describe: he is a male in female costume, which he will tell you he has adopted in obedience to a supernatural command, conveyed three separate times in dreams. Had he disregarded the summons he would have paid for it with his life. *Before he can be permitted to assume female attire he is sexually disabled*. He will then prepare a feast and invite the people. He will give them *tuak* [rice wine] to drink, and he will sacrifice a pig or two to avert evil consequences to the tribe by reason of the outrage upon nature. Should he fail to do all this every subsequent calamity, failure of crops and such like, would be imputed to his conduct and he would be heavily fined. *Thenceforth he is treated in every respect like a woman and occupies himself with feminine pursuits.*

(H.B. Low n.d. I:270; emphases added)

Low tells us nothing about the procedure or entailments of "sexual disabling" or whether it was this procedure or the more general transformation that constituted the "outrage against nature" (cf. Sandin 1957, P. Graham 1987:88–89, 95–97). He avers only that

the *manang bali*'s chief aim in life is to copy female manners and habits so accurately as to be undistinguishable from other women ... [T]he more nearly he succeeds in this the more highly he is thought of, and if he induce any foolish young fellow to visit him at night and sleep with him his joy is extreme; he sends him away at daybreak with a handsome present and then, openly before the women, boasts of his conquest, as he is pleased to call it. He takes good care that his husband finds it out. The husband makes quite a fuss about it, and pays the young fellow's fine with pleasure. As episodes of this kind tend to show how successfully he has imitated the character of a woman he is highly gratified, and rises, accordingly, in the estimation of the tribe as a perfect specimen. As his services are in great request and he is well paid for his troubles, he soon grows rich, and when he is able to afford it he takes to himself a husband in order to render his assumed character more complete. But as long as he is poor he cannot even dream of marriage, as nothing but the prospect of inheriting his wealth would ever induce a man to become his husband, and thus incur the ridicule of the whole tribe. The position as husband is by no means an enviable one; the wife proves a very jealous one, and punishes every little infidelity with a fine. The women view him, the husband, with open contempt, and the men with secret dislike.

(H.B. Low n.d. I:270; emphasis added)

It is difficult to know how to interpret Low's remarks concerning the "ridicule" and "open contempt" supposedly directed toward a man who would marry a *manang bali*. The ethnographic material presented is not sufficiently detailed to provide clues concerning the specific dynamics motivating these kinds of sentiments, how widespread they might have been, and whether they were confined to particular kinship-defined categories of people, such as those who might have stood in a "joking relationship" to spouses of *manang bali*. Individuals of the latter sort would have been more or less required by the terms of such relationships to engage in disrespectful or insulting behavior toward the partners of *manang bali* or to interact with them by taking other kinds of liberties (such as helping themselves to their property). Institutionalized joking relationships are widespread in tribal societies such as the Iban. They are common in Native North America as well, having been documented in many societies for which there are reports of Two-Spirit People, which may help explain most of the ostensibly negative dimensions of the ambivalence supposedly directed toward Two-Spirits in former times (Greenberg 1988:48–56).

The existence of negative sentiments such as these in the Iban setting could reflect nineteenth-century ambivalence toward the *manang bali* "herself" and transgendering generally, due perhaps to the combined influence of heteronormative Christianity and seafaring Malay Muslims who despite their own traditions of transgendering were known to have expressed disdain and ridicule toward the Bornean variants of such institutional complexes (H.B. Low n.d. I:271). Alternatively, and perhaps more likely, we may see in these sentiments evidence of a complex dynamic of far more ancient provenance, whereby "the *manang bali* may be derided for the lack of correspondence between their natal sexual attributes and their ritually-assumed gender identity, at the same time as they are credited with powers of perception beyond the surface appearance of things and events as they are seen by ['ordinary'] Iban men and women" (P. Graham 1987:149). We do not know whether such derision stemmed from or was otherwise informed by partly displaced ambivalence (involving envy, resentment, etc.) for the *manang bali*'s having largely escaped or overcome a heavily (though obviously not exclusively or thoroughly hegemonic) dualistic prestige structure. It is telling, though, that the *manang bali*'s many accomplishments included excelling in the arts of healing, managing conflicts and resolving disputes, *and* perfectly emulating female dress and demeanor in a socio-cultural environment in which, as noted earlier, "the position of women" has long been glossed as "extremely high" (Pringle 1970:24) and "women's achievements are equally acknowledged as those of men's" (Komanyi 1972:102, cited in P. Graham 1987:104). Put simply, the *manang bali* outperformed females and males alike in gender-defined arenas of prestige and in all others as well.

In sum, the fact that other Iban may have viewed *manang bali* with one or another degree of ambivalence (the coexistence of mutually contradictory emotions toward a single object or phenomenon) does not in any way change the two-fold "bottom line": their ways of "being in the world" were viewed as altogether legitimate, and they were accorded considerable prestige both in society as a whole and in the cosmological order of things. As Low put it, "He derives his popularity [sic] not merely from the variety and diversity of his cures, but also largely from his character as a peacemaker, in which he excels. All little differences are brought to him, and he invariably manages to satisfy both parties and to restore good feeling. Then again his wealth is often at the service of his followers, and if they are in difficulty or distress he is ever ready to help" (H.B. Low n.d. I:271).[16] To this he adds that a *manang bali* "manages, not infrequently, to become the *chief of the village*" and in any case "is *always a person of great consequence*" (ibid., 271; emphasis added).

In the preceding pages I have relied heavily on the late nineteenth-century observations of Hugh Brooke Low, which to the best of my knowledge are the most detailed on record for Iban ritualists and the sexual and gender variability associated with the roles they played in Iban society prior to the twentieth century. I should thus make clear that in most key particulars the portrait Low presents of Iban ritual specialists resonates deeply not only with the accounts provided by his father (Hugh Low) nearly a half century earlier (H. Low 1848 [1968]:174–177) but also with those of subsequent observers, such as St. John (1862), Gomes (1911), Jensen (1974), Sutlive (1978 [1988], 1991), and P. Graham (1987) (discussed in Chapter 4). This despite the fact that the latter corpus provides clear evidence of historical transformations in the ritual roles and gendered ethos of Iban society that have occurred since (the younger) Low's day. I accord all the more credibility to the lion's share of Low's observations in light of the degree to which they accord with what we know of other, closely related Austronesian societies in the region (Ngaju Dayak, Bugis), especially those influenced by Malay and/or Javanese language and culture (many Malay words had been incorporated into the Iban language by Low's time [and presumably long before]; the two languages do in any event share a common ancestry), and by Hinduism. In the mid-nineteenth century, Iban ritual and cosmology clearly evinced "the remains of Hindooism," as Charles Brooke who spent more than ten years (1852–1863) in Sarawak put it, and Malays living in the vicinity of the Iban could "recollect the time when it was usually said in conversation, in reference to distant bygone dates, 'in the days of the Hindoos'" (C. Brooke 1866 [1990] I:47–48; cf. H. Low 1848 [1968]:96, 174, P. Graham 1987:62). The principal territorial referent of the latter recollection may have been Borneo, the Malay Peninsula, Java, Sumatra, or another "Indianized" region of Southeast Asia. More important is that since the beginning of the Common Era people in many parts of these lands were linked via dense networks of maritime trade. This trade saw the circulation throughout the region of myriad features of Indian-origin cosmology that resonated with Austronesian motifs emphasizing the virtues and benefits of combining and reconciling the contrasting or opposed forces constituting human bodies and societies, the spirit world, as well as nature and the cosmos as a whole.

Ngaju Dayak

Historical sources bearing on the Ngaju and other Dayak groups in Borneo are in many regards analogous to those concerning the culturally similar but more egalitarian Iban.[17] The majority of the early accounts date from the mid-to-late nineteenth century, when European influences where already evident, and they tend to focus on externals and the exotic at the expense of internal cultural and institutional dynamics that would render the exotic externals comprehensible to their intended readership. Subsequent observations (e.g., in Miles 1976 and Schiller 1997a) are far more systematic and sophisticated, but as in the case of the Iban, these refer to conditions that are in some respects much changed from those prevailing during the nineteenth century. Three themes are nonetheless clear from these sources. First, Ngaju Dayak women enjoyed many of the same prerogatives in marriage/divorce, inheritance, and extra-domestic realms that afforded them opportunities for acquiring community-wide prestige as did their Iban counterparts, and that in terms of "the division of labour between man and woman as well as reciprocal rights and duties, ... the [Ngaju] Dayak woman ... [was] better protected by the law in many respects than her European sister" (Scharer 1946 [1963]:85). Second, Ngaju Dayak and Iban shared many of the same features of kinship (e.g., bilateral descent and inheritance, teknonyms, birth-order names, and broadly classificatory terms of reference and address; along with an emphasis on siblingship and gender complementarity, and strongly sanctioned prohibitions against incest and adultery). And third, Ngaju Dayak communities have long included two analytically distinct though culturally related groups of ritual specialists, one designated as *basir*, the other as *balian*. According to dictionaries from the mid-nineteenth century, the meanings of the first of these terms (*basir*) included "barren," "sterile," and "unfruitful, as in a meager rice crop;" later reports suggest that the term was also used to refer to "impotent men" and "hermaphrodites."[18] As for the term *balian*, we know with certainty only that it referred to female ritual specialists sometimes glossed by outside observers as "sacred prostitutes" (but see Blackwood 2005:854).

Most of the early sources concur that *basir* were drawn from the ranks of male-bodied individuals, and that they dressed in women's attire and were involved in sexual relations with other males whom they commonly took as husbands. Thus Hardeland (1859) relates that "*basir* dress like women, ... are employed in idolatrous ceremonies and in sodomistic abominations, [and that] many are formally married to other men" (cited in Scharer 1946 [1963]:56). Perelaer (1870:35) observes that the "the clothes of the *basir* are in all respects similar to those of the *balian*, with the exception that he wears no headcloth. The *basir* dresses like a woman in private life also, and parts his hair in the middle of his forehead just like a woman" (cited in Scharer 1946 [1963]:57; see also Wulff 1960:127).

Basir, like *balian*, "act[ed] as mediators between men and gods and also between the two mythical groups of Maharaja Sangiang and Maharaja Buno into which the entire community is divided on the occasion of every major religious ceremony," according to Swiss ethnographer Hans Scharer (1946 [1963]:56), whose extensive fieldwork and ethnohistorical research on the Ngaju during the 1930s remains one of the best sources on this group and its past. The majority of these ceremonies, at least if associated with transition (birth, initiation, marriage, death), reenacted the drama of primal creation; during these rituals, *basir*, like *balian*, "stand between Upperworld and Underworld. More than this, they are Upperworld and Underworld together .... They are the total/ambivalent godhead whose totality they represent in the community" (ibid., 58, 81). Scharer explains that "in the special language of the priestly chants" invoked during religious ceremonies, they are termed "water-snakes which are at the same time hornbills" (ibid., 58). This is significant because "the total divinity is Watersnake and Hornbill, Upperworld and

Underworld, man and woman, sun and moon, sacred spear and sacred cloth, good and evil, life and death, war and peace, security and disaster, etc." (ibid., 18–19). In sum, *basir* and *balian* "represent and *are* the bisexual godhead and the total [divine] community" (ibid., 58; emphasis added).

Unlike the male-bodied *basir*, the ritual specialists known as *balian* were drawn from the ranks of "young and beautiful girls" and were instructed by elders in sacred chants, legends, and rites. According to nineteenth-century German missionary Charles Hupe, *balian* wore female clothing which differed from the attire of other women only by "its greater richness and a shameless exposure of the upper part of the body," which was probably not a symbolization of local masculinity (this possible exception aside, they appear not to have not engaged in transgender practices [cf. Blackwood 2005:854–855]) but more likely a gesture to local males, and

> must be present at every feast ... . [They] are more honored even than the priests [*basir*], and ... lead a fairly independent life, since they hand over to their masters only the money gained by singing, while they keep the wages of sin ["sacred prostitution"] for themselves ... . [The fact] that Dayak women, who are known for their modesty and retiring disposition likewise esteem these *bliang* [*balian*] and seek their company is due to the superior intelligence possessed by the latter, and to the knowledge of gossip and secrets which they naturally acquire by their way of life.
>
> (Hupe 1846, cited in Scharer 1946 [1963]:55–56)

Schwaner (1853–1854 [1896/1980]:clxxv) emphasizes similar themes, noting, "in spite of their sublime vocation as mediatresses between the gods and men, the Bilians [sic] also constitute a class of public women, and they know how with peculiar art to attract the attention of the men." He adds that while "many wealthy natives have lost their possessions by supporting such Bilians," the latter "*are always in great esteem and favor with the men and women, and the idea of charging them with the licentious life they lead as something bad, never occurs to anyone*" (emphasis added).[19] More generally, "The Bilans can only be dispensed with on a few solemn occasions; for, besides the above mentioned gifts with which they are endowed, they also know how to agreeably entertain the guests by their rhythmically recited songs, celebrating the exploits of the ancestors and still living heroes. On such occasions they often exercise a great influence on the men, either by exciting their imagination or urging them to wars or commercial journeys, which not infrequently have important consequences" (ibid., clxxv).

Scharer was able to clarify some of these issues on the basis of his extensive fieldwork and ethnohistorical research. I quote him at length.

> Formerly the organizer of a sacrificial feast had to spend the previous night with a *balian*, as indeed he sometimes still does ... . Sacred sexual intercourse [with *balian*] ... takes men from the present, returns them to the dawn of time and sets them in the total godhead and the Tree of Life.[20] ...

They represent as a group the totality of bisexual divinity, but also the totality of the whole community and the entire cosmos (for which reason they are also called sun and moon) .... The sacred people can only be understood, in its existence, its development, and its social structure, in relation to its idea of God. It is based upon the total godhead. It is the reflection of this ambivalent and bisexual deity. Its social, economic, ethical/religious and cosmic aspects represent the different groups, which, at a time when the tribal organization had not yet disintegrated, were probably differentially represented by moieties (Hornbill and Watersnake) and clans. In its totality the sacred people is the holy, total, and ambivalent godhead.

(Scharer 1946 [1963]:58, 59)

Scharer continues,

The sacred prostitution of the *balian* and the pederasty or homosexuality of the *basir* ... throughout the whole community at important religious occasions ... signify the unity of the individual and of the whole community with the bisexual godhead, and the return to the Tree of Life. It takes place only when the primeval sacred events of the creation are partly or completely re-enacted. The necessary condition for re-enactment is union with the godhead in sacred sexual intercourse, through which the bisexual unity is restored. It is from this that sacred prostitution derives its prominent religious significance.

(Ibid., 58)

From these and other sources we learn that "the sacred year (and with it the world-era) ends with the harvest. The two or three months between the harvest and the resumption of work in the fields are called *helat nyelo*, the time between the years," during which time, "the so-called harvest feast or new year's feast is held;" in this context, "the people return not only from their fields to the village but ... also to the primeval time of myth and the beginning of everything," a return symbolized in part by "the lifting of all secular regulations and ... the submission to the commandments of mythical antiquity and the total/ambivalent godhead" (ibid., 96).

In centuries past, as during Scharer's early twentieth-century fieldwork,

When the feast reaches its climax [and before it as well] there is sexual exchange and intercourse between the participants. This total and mass sexual intercourse is not adulterous or contrary to *hadat [adat]* and does not infringe or destroy the cosmic/divine order; it is the union of Upperworld and Underworld, Mahatala and Jata, in a personal and sexual whole and unity ... . To describe it as disorder or unchastity, or to interpret it as a survival from a former promiscuity, is to see it with European eyes and from a European point of view. It takes place strictly according to the laws governing the period "between the years," and is only to be understood in relation to the conception of God and the myth of creation. In this lies its foundation and its religious meaning.

(Ibid., 97)

All of this is highly reminiscent of the Saivite and Tantric themes noted earlier in this chapter, as might be expected in light of the Ngaju Dayak's long history of contact with Java, including Majapahit-era Java, and other parts of "Indianized Southeast Asia." Also reminiscent of Saivite and Tantric themes is Scharer's previously cited observation that "the *basir* and *balian* represent and *are* the bisexual godhead and the total [divine] community" (ibid., 58; emphasis added).

We know little about the recruitment and social origins of *balian* prior to the twentieth century and even less about the recruitment and origins of *basir*, though some of the spiritual qualifications for these offices seem fairly clear. To take the latter issue first, "divine command" was a prerequisite for becoming a ritual specialist of either variety: one had to be "called by the *sangiang*" (spirits) who singled out a person whose "soul ... [was] ... interchangeable with that of the *sangiang*" so as to "become on the one hand an instrument of the *sangiang*, and on the other an intercessor for men [humankind]" (ibid., 133). Of additional interest is that the entry of the *sangiang* spirit into the pit of the stomach of the *balian* and *basir* was called the "entry of the *bandong*-boat" ("*bandong* means someone with whom one commits or has committed fornication ... [or] adultery"), and that both types of ritual specialists were "compared with boats and ... regarded as the wives of the *sangiang*" (ibid., 134).

Of broad comparative relevance is that the deployment of symbols, idioms, and metaphors of earthly matrimony to conceptualize ritual specialists' relationships with spirits is a common theme throughout Southeast Asia both historically and at present. So too is the fact that ritual specialists' relationships with earthly partners were commonly conceptualized in terms of normative (heterogender/heterosexual) marriage, even when they involved same-sex relationships. Circumstances such as these point to the hegemonic status of (heterogender) marriage throughout the region both historically and at present, as we will discuss in more detail later on.

As for their social origins and the system of social ranking in which they and all others were embedded, early twentieth-century observers reported that both types of specialists, collectively referred to in some accounts as "the priestly group," were recruited from the ranks of the hereditarily defined "inferior or poor people." The latter, together with the also hereditarily defined "superior or rich people," sometimes referred to as "the white people" (because of their pure "white" blood)—from whom were "selected judges, military leaders, and the ... *adat*-chiefs who see that the *hadat* is followed" (Scharer 1946 [1963]:41)—comprised the "free people." The latter were distinguished from "slaves" or debt bondsmen, who might also acquire their status by birth; i.e., might inherit the debt and debtor status of a parent, along with the (mostly ritual) obligations associated with that status, but could usually free themselves through labor.[21] Some reports suggest that *balian* and *basir* came also, or instead, from this latter group ("slaves" or debt bondsmen). It is clear in any case that all of these groups were in theory endogamous, that violations of status-group endogamy or other transgressions of the divine order could result in sliding down the status hierarchy, and that *balian* and *basir* did not originate from what Scharer (ibid., 51) refers to as "the witch group," whose members "represent the evil aspect of the total godhead."

In sum, the *balian* and *basir* did not originate from the lowest of the low (the witch group) and were sharply distinguished from them in terms of the esteem in which they were held and the treatment they received, despite the fact that both groups enjoyed socially important spiritual powers. But neither did they originate from the highest of the high (the "superior" or "rich" people), although their ritual roles brought them into intimate contact with them and at least in the case of the *balian* could augment their (the "superior" or "rich" people's) material standing and overall prestige. Whether or not individuals who became *basir* and *balian* were consciously or otherwise motivated to do so in part because of the greater contact with prestigious social groups that such roles afforded them, it is clear that they served both society as a whole and those highest in the prestige hierarchy in particular.

A comparison between the Ngaju Dayak and the previously considered Iban reveals a greater separation of political and religious roles among the Ngaju Dayak. Put differently, the construction and entailments of Ngaju Dayak ritual roles diverged in important ways from the less formalized and more "multipurpose" roles of their ritualistic counterparts among the more egalitarian and less sociologically complex Iban, who lacked the particular differentiation of roles found among the Ngaju Dayak and, not surprisingly, the Ngaju Dayak's system of hereditary ranking as well. (Developmentally speaking, these two dynamics of social organization tend to go hand in hand.) Recall that the Iban's *manang bali* was something of a "jack of all trades," broadly analogous, perhaps, to a "renaissance man," albeit a Bornean transgendered one: a settler of disputes, a general peace-keeper, someone who distributed his wealth and other social goods to his supporters, a person who "managed, not infrequently to become the chief of the village" and "was always a person of great consequence." Ritual specialists among the Ngaju Dayak on the other hand were not also (by virtue of the system of ranking they could not become) political elites, though they could bask in and augment their glory.

The emergence among the Ngaju Dayak of a more complex system of social organization, evident in the system of descent-based ranking, greater role differentiation and the like, points us in the direction of the Bugis. By the twelfth or thirteenth century the Bugis had developed many features of social hierarchy, and by the fourteenth century boasted a sophisticated centralized polity in the form of a state, along with a system of formal social stratification. In this system, as we shall see, more or less full time ritual specialists, many of them transgendered, managed to acquire the status of nobility.

Bugis

The Bugis are one of the four major ethnic groups of South Sulawesi (the Mandar, Toraja, and Makassar are the others). As with other groups in South Sulawesi, they are both similar to and different from the Iban and Ngaju Dayak. Some of the similarities (in kinship, gender, cosmology, and ritual) attest to the Austronesian ancestry shared by all of these people; others reflect Indic influences that have long been pervasive in the region, as we have seen. Particularly striking are the commonalities in cosmology and ritual. In the early modern period, Bugis religion was focused on the "worship of ancestors and spirits, to whom offerings were made through specialist intermediaries" (Pelras 1996:47), many of them transgendered, who voyaged to other worlds in the course of shamanistic trance and possession. Considering what we know of Bugis past and present and of Southeast Asia past and present, scholars like Christian Pelras (ibid.) seem justified in surmising that these practices were grounded in a cosmology that depicted the world "as a polarized entity whose opposed pairs in a generalized system of symbolic equivalences were sky and earth, mountain and sea, rising sun and setting sun, right and left, sun and moon, male and female, life and death" (cf. Reid 1993b:161–162, Gibson 2005: Chap. 3).

The contrasts between the Bugis and the Borneo groups considered here are in many instances keyed to variations in socio-political organization and the dynamics with which they are linked. The Iban represent an example of a "tribal" society, where all kin groups are of roughly equal rank in terms of prestige, and all households enjoy more or less equivalent socio-economic standing. The Ngaju Dayak, as we have seen, are culturally and socio-politically similar to the Iban in many respects (their cosmologies have much in common with those of the Iban, for example, and they too are basically "tribal"), but they differ from the Iban insofar as the households and kin groups to which their members belong are associated with one or another ranked social grouping (e.g., "the rich people," "the poor people," "the witch group," etc.), membership of which is ascribed at birth. Despite the egalitarian thrust of many of their institutions, in other words, we also see evidence of the kind of hereditary inequality (or ranking) commonly associated in the literature with low-level or incipient chiefdoms. In the case of the Bugis, we have a society in which the trends toward hereditary inequality and social stratification are far more elaborated, and, more generally, at least since the fourteenth century or thereabouts, a sociopolitical system of the sort usually referred to as a state.

As with people in other states, in early modern times the Bugis boasted a degree of occupational and ritual specialization not found in stateless societies. Bugis occupational specialists included apparently full-time ritual practitioners, known as *bissu*, who were charged with safeguarding royal regalia (*arajang*) and other signs and prerogatives of royalty, including, not least, sacred texts known as *La Galigo* (described further below), and thus insuring the well-being of the polity and the cosmos in its entirety. Given the Austronesian and Indic cultural milieus out of which the first Bugis state developed, it is not surprising that the ranks of the *bissu* included both male-bodied individuals who engaged in transgender practices and same-sex relations (and were described by six-teenth-century Portuguese and subsequent generations of observers as "trans-vestites," "sodomites," and/or "homosexuals" [see, for example, Jacobs 1966]), as well as female-bodied individuals of noble birth who were apparently more or less normatively gendered (even though in some contexts they brandished ritual paraphernalia symbolizing both male and female [L. Andaya 2000:40–41, Blackwood 2005:854]).

Archeological and other evidence (from megaliths, bronzes, inscriptions, royal chronicles, myth, ritual, and linguistics) that is summarized by Pelras (1996: Chap. 2–3), Gibson (2005: Chap. 3, 6, 7), and others points to Indic reli-gious influences in the South Sulawesi region as early as the second to fifth cen-tury CE, including "Sanskrit inscriptions on seven Sivaite sacrificial columns in eastern Borneo" indicating that "an Indianized state existed just across the Makassar Straits from Mandar" around the fourth century CE (Pelras 1996:25).[22] More generally, "from the beginning of the early metal period [which in insular Southeast Asia dates from the last few centuries before the beginning of the Common Era] South Sulawesi was incorporated into a huge trading network with connections with east Borneo and presumably also with Java, Sumatra, Vietnam and perhaps indirectly Sri Lanka and India" (ibid., 26, Gibson 2005:43).

Some scholars have inferred that institution of *bissu* may have been intro-duced into South Sulawesi by Austronesian settlers coming into the area from southern China and Taiwan via the Philippines and Borneo. Whether or not such was the case, the institution was clearly informed by Indic prototypes and Bugis engagement with the Tantric Buddhist practices of Javanese and Sumatrans in particular. In support of this view, Pelras (1996:71–72), who has conducted extensive ethnographic and ethnohistorical research on Bugis, notes that a "common interpretation" of the term *bissu* "derives it from the Sanskrit … *bhiksu*, a term for Buddhist monks," adding that certain "high-rank-ing *bissu*" bore titles "bestowed on Javanese and Sumatran religious dignitaries." Circumstances such as these are consistent with what we know from Chinese and other sources of the cultural political dynamics entailed in state building and the spread of Hindu-Buddhist (especially Saivite and Tantric) motifs throughout insular Southeast Asia at the time of Srivijaya (seventh to four-teenth centuries) and Majapahit (thirteenth to fifteenth centuries) (Wolters 1970:34–35 passim, Gibson 2005: Chap. 6).

The development of the *bissu* complex in south Sulawesi is usefully viewed in relation to the emergence of social stratification in the region, for as Pelras (1996:173) puts it in discussing these matters, "from the beginning an unbreak-able bond is affirmed between the sacred, power, and wealth." Pelras believes that the origins of Bugis social stratification "coincided with the immigration in the first centuries of the Christian era, perhaps from south-east or east Borneo, of groups of migrants" oriented toward overseas trade, "each following its own leader" (ibid., 174). "Connected … [via trade] to Sumatra and the Malay

Peninsula, whose ports were ... linked to India and other places around the Indian Ocean," these communities were probably "better organized than ... the still scarce populations of Austronesian ... [and] pre-Austronesian peoples [in the area and] ... probably had a richer culture than the existing inhabitants; their religion had already received a smattering of Indic influence, and their priests were the *bissu*" (ibid., 174). "As they spread throughout the area, they progressively assumed a dominant status and imposed their social order and language" on local communities; "thus they came to constitute an aristocracy, the magnified memory of which was conveyed to following generations much later by the *La Galigo* texts, after a common culture had emerged" (ibid., 174). Similar processes probably took place in neighboring regions inhabited by Makassar, Toraja, and Mandar (ibid., 174–175; cf. Gibson 2005).

The *bissu* served as symbols and guardians of sacred boundaries, as did their transgendered ritualistic counterparts among the Iban and the Ngaju Dayak. However, the existence among the Bugis of social stratification and systems of writing, both absent among the Iban and Ngaju Dayak, meant that their roles differed in key respects from what we saw in these other two societies. Specifically, *bissu* were the stewards of sacred manuscripts that consisted of anonymous, hand-written texts inscribed on the leaves of lontar palm that provided sanctified charters for the (also sanctified) system of stratification; ipso facto, they were symbols and guardians of the system of social stratification, symbolized by the "white blood" of royalty, as well. The manuscripts served as repositories of genealogical lore and other locally important knowledge, and included, most notably, "one of the world's major epics, known as the *La Galigo* cycle, which is longer than the *Mahabharata*" and "consists of a huge corpus or cycle of versified stories, collectively referred to ... as Sure Galigo, after one of its protagonists, La Galigo" (Pelras 1996:4, 30). The *La Galigo* cycle, which has been likened to the "adventures of Ulysses in Homer's Odyssey" (Davies 2007:34) and has numerous counterparts in neighboring societies (Cummings 2002, Gibson 2005) contains "detailed genealogies of noble families, dynastic tables, ancient diaries, ... and other sundry items such as vassal lists or texts of treaties and political contracts," as well as extensive information on the origins of polities throughout the region and their various institutions, conquests, and other accomplishments (Pelras 1996:31). Significantly, most of these chronicles "state that the first rulers ... were either 'people descended from heaven' or 'people sprung up from the abyss.' Of divine origin, they were sent to humankind to put an end to the time of anarchy ... which ... followed the departure from earth of the *La Galigo* heroes, who are also described as earlier descendants of the gods" (ibid., 32). Themes of gender complementarity and androgyny involving "processes of [gender] pairing, separation, violent collision, and the production of ... new life in triadic form: male, female, and a supplementary, androgynous entity" (Gibson 2005:50) are foregrounded in many of the origin myths associated with these chronicles both among Bugis and others throughout the region, leading Gibson and other scholars (e.g., Van der

Kroef 1956, Boon 1977, Errington 1989, Hoskins 1990, 1998, Day 2002:78–89) to regard them as key symbols throughout all of Austronesia.

The "*La Galigo* texts [probably] began to take shape, at first orally, around the middle of the fourteenth century," a period of upheaval, revolution, and state formation; and they most likely provided newly emergent chiefdoms and other polities in the area with "the archetypal model of appropriate princely rituals and conduct, always to be emulated, never to be equaled, ... as they have done for Bugis nobility up to the present day" (Pelras 1996:56). If so, their status as sacred charters—or "models of" and "models for" reality in Clifford Geertz's famous (1973:93–94) phrase—would have been broadly analogous to the sacred templates enjoining *linga* worship and the emulation of Siva in areas of mainland Southeast Asia throughout the first millennium and beyond. It may be surmised further that in the case of the Bugis, "the *bissu* clergy played a major role in this process, indeed that they may have been responsible for the origin and development of the whole cycle. This would be in keeping with the status of the *La Galigo* manuscripts, until fairly recently, as holy books, and with that of the *bissu* as among the best experts in that literature" (Pelras 1996:56–57; cf. Hamonic 1975, 1977, Davies 2007: Chap. 6).

Unfortunately we know very little about the daily lives of *bissu* or their involvement in non-ritual spheres of activity. However, numerous observers have commented that in some ways the *bissu* lived "outside the social system" (Pelras 1996:82–83; L. Andaya 2000:29, 36, 46) because of their ritual roles and their attendant status as "priests to the elite." Contributing to their somewhat liminal but nonetheless sacred status is that becoming a *bissu* "was often not a matter of free choice but the result of a call by a supernatural being who became" the new *bissu*'s "mystic spouse" (Pelras 1996:83). This call was typically "marked by a psychosomatic phenomenon (sudden mutism, catalepsy) requiring a ritual cure" (ibid.; Hamonic 1975, 1977) that was followed by initiation and consecration rites, many of which are still performed by present-day *bissu*. Even in the late twentieth century, male-bodied *bissu* who cross-dressed and took a male husband tended to have one or more supernatural spouses, usually one male and one female.

Of particular significance is the existence among the Bugis in early modern times of two other transgendered roles (*calabai* and *calalai*, described below) that bore some similarities to *bissu* but seem to have been largely secular though perhaps tinged with elements of sanctity because they were conceptually linked via transgenderism with *bissu* (Pelras 1996:165–167). Consideration of these roles is important, partly because even at present "they appear to be surprisingly well accepted and integrated into a society where their status is considered by most to be completely honorable" (ibid., 165; cf. Davies 2007: Chap. 4, 5). More relevant on analytic grounds, Bugis attitudes toward the defining features of the majority of such roles (transgenderism) appear to have been positively conditioned by the exalted status of *bissu*. This is to say that *bissu* transgendering colored local views of transgendering in its entirety and perhaps of gender as a whole. Equally plausible is that all variants of transgendering were informed by the kind of "deep structural" relativism that Andrew Beatty (2002) suggests has long typified Java and, we might add, Austronesian areas and Southeast Asia as a whole.

The two roles in question were designated by the terms *calabai* and *calalai*, the first deriving etymologically from a term for "false women," the second from a term for "false men" (Pelras 1996:165). The earliest written account of *calabai* (feminine men) and *calalai* (masculine women) that I have encountered appears in the journal kept by James Brook. Brook visited the Bugis region of Wajo in 1840 in the course of travels throughout Sulawesi and Borneo, and in the following year managed to have himself proclaimed "Rajah and Governor of Sarawak," thus becoming the apical ancestor of what proved to be a long line of "white rajahs." Brooke's journal entry for February 3, 1840, begins as follows:

> The strangest custom I observed is, that some men dress like women, and some women like men; not occasionally, but all their lives, devoting themselves to the occupations and pursuits of their adopted sex. In the case of the males, it seems that the parents of a boy, upon perceiving in him certain effeminacies of habit and appearance, are induced thereby to present him to one of the rajahs, by whom he is received. These youths often acquire much influence over their masters.
>
> (J. Brooke 1848 I:82–83)

Brooke's journal entry continues with remarks comparing young *calabai*'s "influence over their masters" with "the case in Turkey, whose history abounds in instances of the rise of these young favorites to the highest honours and power." He hastens to assure his readers that "from all ... I could learn, ... the practice leads among the Bugis to none of those vices which constitute the opprobrium of Western Asia" (ibid., 83). Whatever the bases of these assessments, they are congruent with Brooke's overwhelmingly positive view of the Bugis and the treatment accorded Bugis women in particular. Brooke does not make any explicit connection between Bugis constructions bearing on transgenderism and same-sex relations (about which he probably knew very little) on the one hand and the relatively high status accorded women on the other, but some of the connections are implicit in his comments insofar as he cites additional evidence for what I would describe as a broadly diffused pluralism with respect to gender and other features of socio-political life.

> Concubinage is not common, prostitution almost unknown; and ... in these respects, as well as in the decency of the marriage condition, the Bugis are far superior to any other Eastern nation ... . All the offices of state ... are open to women; and they actually fill the important post of government, four out of the six great chiefs of Wajo being at present females ... . Amid all the nations of the East—amid all the people professing the Mahometan religion, from Turkey to China—the Bugis *alone* have

arrived at the threshold of recognized rights, and have *alone* emancipated themselves from the fetters of despotism.

(Ibid., 65–66, 74–75; emphasis in original; cf. Raffles 1817 [1830] II: Appendix F, lxxxvi; Crawfurd 1820:74)

The lives of *calabai* and *calalai* do not come into sharper focus until the mid-to late twentieth century but there is no reason to believe that the broad contours of the situations described below, based on ethnographic research begun in the early 1970s, would have been appreciably different in Brooke's time or the early modern era generally.

The *calabai* are a common sight in almost all Bugis villages: clad either completely or partially in women's clothes, they can be seen engaging in all kinds of women's tasks, such as cooking, pounding rice or washing clothes. Even though, in speaking of them, some Bugis youth smile and some strict *ulama* frown, to the Western eye they appear to be surprisingly well accepted and integrated into a society where their status is considered by most to be perfectly honorable.

(Pelras 1996:165)

The ethnographer tells us further that some *calabai* "live with their parents or with a married sister; [or] … by themselves. Others live in partnership with another young man, and although there is some restraint among the Bugis in talking about sexual matters, there seems to be no doubt that these are homosexual couples" (ibid., 165–166). This point is confirmed by Sharyn Graham Davies (2007: Chap. 5) based on 15 months of fieldwork conducted during the period 1998–2000 and a number of subsequent visits through 2005. The companions of *calabai*, for their part, "seem to be considered as sexually normal [and normatively gendered] and some of them even marry women later and have children," thus suggesting that participation in non-heteronormative relations is not an impediment to subsequent involvement in normative relations and activities; "other *calabai* who live alone are said to be impotent" though this may be because they have chosen "sexual abstinence, either in order to avoid engaging in behavior considered sinful under Islamic prescriptions, or in order to obtain enhanced magical powers through asceticism. (This latter reason for abstinence is also cited by some middle-aged heterosexual men.)" (Pelras 1996:166). In terms reminiscent both of Ngaju Dayak and of earlier discussions of Saivite and Tantric themes, most *calabai* "say that they enjoy being able to combine the masculinity with which they were born and the femininity of which they have progressively become aware during adolescence, and insist that they possess masculine strength and aggression alongside their feminine qualities" (ibid., 167; cf. Davies 2007: Chap. 5, 6).

Historical information on *calalai*, the female-bodied counterparts of *calabai*, is, unfortunately, much patchier. We know, however—and this is no small matter—that in centuries past there were "cases of *calalai* rulers" (Pelras

1996:167). Some of these individuals probably lived in same-sex couples, as they do today (see Chapter 4), perhaps engaging in sex "with the aid of dildoes made from animal guts filled with wax," as is said to occur at present (ibid.: 167, Davies 2007:57–58).

Data bearing on the existence of *calabai*, *calalai*, and their normatively gendered partners are of broad significance since they indicate that, especially in this region of Southeast Asia, individuals who participated in transgender practices and/or same-sex relations were accorded legitimacy by society at large *whether or not they assumed the roles of ritual specialists* (assuming they upheld other community norms). Many cases for which we have information are less clear on this point, partly because practices among "lay" couples are generally less visible, the data, accordingly, generally less "legible," though my view is that the Bugis situation is by no means unique. Note in any event that in the Bugis case and all others considered here, transgendered ritual specialists typically married and/or engaged in sexual relations with normatively gendered persons of the same sex *who were not themselves ritual specialists* (never, apparently, with fellow ritual specialists, with the partial exception of the furtive sexual relations that occurred in Buddhist monastic settings); and that the latter individuals did not usually incur any stigma on account of these liaisons, which, in contemporary parlance were "no big deal"—if not altogether legitimate and acceptable. This situation obtains throughout much of Southeast Asia even at present, even when the transgender practices are not associated with ritual roles, despite processes of rationalization and other normalizing trends of recent centuries. Based on what we know of Southeast Asia in early modern times and during the period since, this situation stands as a powerful reminder of the content, scope, and force of an earlier pluralism bearing on gender and sexuality that was both broadly diffused and deeply entrenched.

It remains to underscore that *calalai* and female-bodied *bissu*'s experiences of religious changes and other historical forces that contributed to social and cultural transformation throughout Sulawesi and Indonesia as a whole in the second half of the early modern period were not the same as those of *calabai* and male-bodied *bissu*. Beginning in the early seventeenth century, for example, by which time many Bugis and others in South Sulawesi had converted to Islam, we see periodic efforts by Islamic rulers committed to literal interpretations of *syariah* to discredit *bissu* and expel them from their jurisdictions (Pelras 1996:142, 188). Such moves were part and parcel of more encompassing strategies of cultural cleansing, involving temporally inflected auto-Othering, that were aimed at eradicating gambling, slavery, the consumption of opium and palm wine, ceremonials of a pre-Islamic nature, and all other evidence of "pagan times." These and analogous changes in subsequent centuries constricted earlier traditions of female involvement in what Brooke referred to as "the important post[s] of government;" they also had much greater impact on female-bodied individuals involved in transgenderism and/or same-sex relations than on their male-bodied counterparts (as discussed in Chapter 4). These dynamics bear additional significance in that they help illustrate the more general, conceptual point that just as hegemonies are invariably contested, so too are they invariably subject to temporal flux and change.

Malays

A Malay instance of ritual transgenderism that I want to mention briefly here is less well described than the cases we have examined thus far but is particularly important for some of our discussion later on. Before delving into the historiographic details and other specifics of the case, some of which lend themselves to divergent interpretation, let me note that in its overall outline, this instance of Malay transgenderism is strikingly similar to the case of the Bugis *bissu* we have just considered. Extensive historical and cultural contacts between Bugis and Malays throughout the early modern period and long before are partly responsible for these similarities; others reflect their common Austronesian ancestry and their shared state-level political organization.

The available evidence that bears most directly on this case consists chiefly of scattered references in indigenous manuscripts dating from the fifteenth to nineteenth centuries (such as the *Sejarah Melayu* or *Malay Annals*, which concerns the Melaka Sultanate and is generally believed to have been composed around 1650; and the *Misa Melayu* or *Malay Champion*, a late eighteenth-century manuscript from the state of Perak), which chronicle the mythic genealogies and real and imagined accomplishments of Malay rulers (see, for example, A. Samad Ahmad 1979, Raja Chulan bin Hamid 1991). Some of this material is summarized by Leonard Andaya (2000:31–32, 2001:56–57), who suggests that the evidence indicates the existence in the Malay Peninsula in the late premodern and early modern era of a pre-Islamic class of male-bodied priests or courtiers, referred to by the term *sida-sida* (commonly translated as "palace official" or "eunuch"), who were said to be involved in "androgynous behavior," such as wearing women's clothes and possibly performing tasks of the sort generally undertaken by women (see also Drewes 1976:279–280 passim; B. Andaya 2000a:249). A number of early observers who encountered members of this "priestly class" apparently assumed, erroneously, that they were eunuchs (thus to some degree "naturalizing" their androgyny), perhaps because seemingly similar figures were known to exist in Islamic courts and at various sacred sites in the Islamic Middle East and elsewhere. These impressions may have been reinforced by similarities between, on the one hand, the root "*sida*," which in languages cognate to Malay, such as Acehnese, "is derived from the Sanskrit *siddha*, meaning 'the learned one' or 'scholar' [or "an enlightened master"], which becomes in Acehnese, 'an initiate, aide to a religious teacher'" (L. Andaya 2000:32), and, on the other, the Arabic term *sada*, meaning "lords" or "masters," which after the twelfth century "was a common term of respect for eunuchs at the sanctuary at Madina" and perhaps elsewhere in the Muslim world as well (Marmon 1995:123 n37). It is also conceivable that the Arabic term *sada* or a version of it was adapted by Malay royalty seeking to bolster their identification with Islam during the period at issue here, as occurred with many other Arabic-origin terms bearing on sanctity, cosmology, etc. that came to be woven into or "replace" or supersede their Austronesian- or Sanskrit-origin predecessors (see Winstedt 1961, Peletz 1988, 1996). In this scenario, Malay linguistic innovation led to one or another transformation of the term *sada* (such as *sida-sida* or *sesida*) being used to refer to *bissu*-like ritual specialists attached to Malay royal courts.

Further complicating the picture is that some of the Malay manuscripts I mentioned earlier include references to "female *sida-sida*" (*sida-sida perempuan*), others to "*sida-sida* and their wives" (*sida-sida dan isterinya*). References such as these appear in *Hikayat Amir Hamzah* (*The Saga of Commander Hamzah*), for example, which was probably composed in the early sixteenth century, and *Hikayat Maharaja Marakarma* (*The Saga of Emperor Marakarma*), which dates from the 1840s (Goriaeva 1967, A. Samad Ahmad 1987).[23] Andaya makes no mention of these important references in his discussions of the term and its possible meanings, but they are consistent with his suggestion that "eunuch" is not the most appropriate gloss for *sida-sida*. While it is highly likely that the term had different meanings in different times and places, its various significations almost certainly included male- as well as female-bodied persons involved in transgender practices, some of whom may have engaged in sexual relations with individuals of the same sex, others favoring sexual relations with persons of both sexes. This would be broadly consistent with present-day meanings of the term.

In light of the foregoing, a few words on eunuchs in the Islamic heartlands are in order. Groups of eunuchs have been stationed at the Prophet Muhammad's tomb in Medina since the twelfth century, where they served as "guardians and mediators of the *baraka*, the charismatic force that infused the Prophet's tomb and the surrounding sanctuary" (Marmon 1995:ix). Subsequent years witnessed the emergence of "eunuch societies" composed mostly of individuals from non-Muslim areas of Africa and South Asia who as young boys had been captured in warfare, taken as slaves, and subsequently castrated (by having their testicles and/or penises cut off) and sold to Muslim rulers, slave traffickers, or other intermediaries who in turn handed them over to those in charge of Muslim palaces, tombs, and sacred shrines.[24] It merits note that eunuch societies "appeared at the tombs of sultans in Cairo, at the Ka'aba in Mecca, at the Dome of the Rock in Jerusalem, and at the tomb of Abraham in Hebron" [1995:ix].) As with eunuchs in Islamic courts in the Middle East and South Asia, some of the eunuch societies mentioned here existed well into modern times (e.g., the late twentieth century). The same is true of *sida-sida* in various parts of the Malay Peninsula, though to my knowledge their members never organized themselves into the societies or networks reported for the eunuchs attached to sacred sites in the Middle East.

In pre- and early modern times, *sida-sida* appear to have resided in the inner chambers of palaces. This may have been to safeguard the women of the palace and to insure order among them, especially since the unregulated spiritual powers and embodied passions of women, and of women of noble birth in particular, could wreak havoc in the domestic arenas of palaces and (because palaces were typically envisioned as microcosms of the larger universe) the world as a whole. Leonard Andaya (2000:32) considers this possibility, but discounts it (as I once did), suggesting as a more plausible explanation that *sida-sida* "were entrusted with the sacred regalia and the preservation of the ruler's spiritual powers" or potency, symbolized, as in the Bugis case, by their "white blood," hence the well being of the body politic and the cosmos in its entirety. In fact, these different interpretations need not be regarded as mutually exclusive. Both of them would have involved guarding vestibules and policing other culturally salient and symbolically charged boundaries, much like eunuchs in the Islamic heartlands.

Evidence bearing on contemporary *sida-sida* is extremely sparse but worth considering for the light it may shed on *sida-sida* in earlier times. In the mid-to-late twentieth century and even in the early years of the new millennium, the palace of the Yang diPertuan Besar in Sri Menanti, which is located in the state of Negeri Sembilan, continued to include within its retinue officials who were referred to as *sida-sida* or *sesida*, as presumably did Malay courts in Johor and elsewhere. (In the middle of the twentieth century, moreover, "the hill behind the [Sri Menanti] palace" was "still called the Mount of Holy Indra" [Winstedt 1961:33], as may also be the case at present.) Malay anthropologist Shamsul A.B. (b. 1951) recalls seeing *sida-sida* in the royal palace when he was a child. According to Shamsul, these were typically male-bodied individuals who assumed many of the mannerisms of females along with female or "mixed" (dual-gendered) attire, and were believed by the population at large to share females' normative erotic orientations toward men, or to be celibate and asexual like eunuchs. (Unlike eunuchs, however, they did not undergo castration.) Their tasks included ensuring that the food and clothing of royalty were "in order," i.e., that they had not been "tampered with" by malevolent humans or spirits, and overseeing ritual protocol such as that associated with the ceremonies of investiture that honored Shamsul in 2003 with the title of *Dato* ("Lord," "Sir").[25] More generally, *sida-sida* have long been guardians and symbols of important thresholds that include physical passageways as well as the boundaries separating ordinary mortals from embodied divinity suffused with *sakti* (a Sanskrit term referring to mystical knowledge) and *daulat* (its Arabic-origin successor, which designates royal power, sanctity, and majesty).

Two other communities of transgendered specialists that existed in the Malay Peninsula well into the twentieth century warrant brief mention here even though but also because they are now more or less defunct. The first is composed of *pawang* or shamanic specialists, who we might regard as "relatively lineal" legacies of pre-Islamic *sida-sida*, particularly in light of the heavily animist and Hindu-Buddhist complexion of their most public rituals. *Pawang* were attached to indigenously defined district-level and state polities, were seen as having "white blood" and highly potent spiritual powers vested in and symbolized by their sacred regalia, much like the Bugis *bissu*, and were described by nineteenth- and early twentieth-century British officials (e.g., Maxwell 1907

[1982]:214–22) as forming hereditarily defined groups like some of the Borneo ritual specialists mentioned earlier. In the nineteenth and twentieth centuries, certain male-bodied *pawang* were possessed by female spirits or deities, donned women's attire, wore their hair long like women, and were on occasion involved in other transgender practices (Winstedt 1961:59). Similarly, in the late nineteenth century at least some female-bodied *pawang* engaged in ritual transvestism. A case in point reported in 1895 by British resident and Orientalist par excellence Frank Swettenham (who went on to become High Commissioner of the Federated Malay States) involved a *pawang* known as Raja Ngah, "a middle-aged woman dressed like a man" who was called upon to conduct a *berhantu* (exorcism) ceremony to "relieve the torments" of the ailing Sultan of Perak and otherwise restore his failing health (Swettenham 1895 [1984]:153–159). During the ritual in question, Raja Ngah wore "a short-sleeved jacket, trousers, a *sarong*, and a scarf fashioned tightly round her waist" and was possessed by a male spirit (*jinn*) by the name of Israng with whom she conversed in an unknown tongue (said to be "the spirit language"). Of her attire and comportment in everyday life we know little, although Swettenham describes her as "a scion of the reigning house on the female side and a member of a family skilled in all matters pertaining to occultism" (ibid., 154). That Raja Ngah apparently had at least one child (Swettenham mentions "the daughter of Raja Ngah" leading the orchestra of "five or six girls holding native drums" whose music accompanied the ritual exorcism Raja Ngah oversaw) might suggest that she was or had once been partner to a conventional (heterosexual) marriage. Of arguably broader relevance is that after the Sultan regained consciousness—in the course of the exorcism he, too, experienced possession by spirits and went into trance—he explained to Swettenham that he "took part in this ceremony to please his people and because *it was a very old custom*" (ibid., 159; emphasis added).

The second community of transgendered ritualists I want to mention here consists of performers of *mak yong* theater and related dramatic and musical genres, many of whom enjoyed royal patronage, were linked to palaces in other ways, and engaged in same-sex relations. The most detailed information bearing on this community and local attitudes concerning the kinds of diversity it embodied derives from mid-twentieth-century research in the state of Kelantan, long considered by Malays and others a bastion of "traditional" Malay culture. Anthropologist Douglas Raybeck found that in the late 1960s Malays in Kelantan "regard[ed] homosexuality as peculiar, different, and even somewhat humorous, but they ... [did] *not* view it as an illness or as a serious sin" (1986:65; emphasis added). In some ways more revealing, there were several "specialized homosexual villages in or near the state capital," Kota Baru, the best known of which adjoined the palace of the Sultan, who in better times enjoyed the wherewithal to maintain troupes of performing artists and all varieties of ritual specialists and retainers. These villages were made up entirely of male-bodied couples engaged in same-sex sexuality whose primary breadwinners earned their living as transvestite performers of a dramatic genre of Thai origin known as *mak yong*. The latter performers were highly regarded for their artistic and professional skills and could outearn other (heteronormative) villagers, who comprised the bulk of their audience. In former times (e.g., the mid-nineteenth century) the young males involved in these performances "disguise[d] themselves as women so successfully that Malay youths have been known to fall in love with them, forsake their campongs [villages] and wander for days in the train of the actors" (Vaughan 1857:134). Whether this continued into the following century is unclear, though we do know that the "specialized villages" in which *mak yong* artists resided in the 1960s were not segregated ghettos to which gender transgressors known to be involved in same-sex relations were banished. Nor is there any evidence to suggest anyone raiding these communities—which were more or less identical to normative communities except that they included no children—or bothering their members.[26] The fact that these communities came to the attention of the visiting anthropologist means that they were certainly known as well to other villagers, to local as well as regional and state-level religious and secular authorities at all levels, including of course the Sultan of Kelantan, who was their royal patron, and to Malay (and Malaysian) society at large, especially in the case of the community that abutted the Sultan's palace. More to the point is that Sultan in particular didn't simply "know about" these communities, he actively helped constitute them.

We are left with important questions that cannot be answered conclusively with presently available evidence. One such question has to do with how normatively oriented Malays viewed the sexual partners of *sida-sida*, *pawang*, and *mak yong* performers during the early modern period. If male-bodied *sida-sida*, *pawang*, and *mak yong* performers were in certain respects feminized in locally meaningful ways (or masculinized in the case of their female-bodied counterparts), which seems to have occurred, then both their sexual partners as well as their spouses (when they were married) were probably regarded as more or less normatively gendered males (or normatively gendered females, in the case of female-bodied ritualists), as is true in all of the Southeast Asian examples we have considered thus far as well as virtually all others for which we have evidence. It is also quite likely, given the hegemonic status of marriage in Malay culture and throughout the entire Southeast Asian region both historically and at present, that most sexual relations between Malays at this time occurred in the context of marriage, which was invariably heterogender although not necessarily heterosexual. This despite the fact (noted at the outset of this chapter) that in the sixteenth century Malays were said to be "fond of music and given to love" and that throughout the first half of the early modern period there was relatively little emphasis placed on pre-marital virginity for either males or females.

Same-sex relations probably occurred as well among individuals who were not ritual specialists, as we saw in the case of Bugis *calabai* (feminine men), *calalai* (masculine women), and their normatively gendered partners; and such relations, rather than incurring stigma, may have partaken of (or involved efforts to "piggy-back" off) the aura associated with sanctified god-kings. Such would help explain the Reverend John Gottfried Haensel's less than flattering remarks, based on his observations of Malays living in and around the royal palace of Kedah in the year 1786, that "they are exceedingly addicted to the vilest lusts, and have no sense of shame in gratifying their passions" (Haensel 1812:16). Although the good reverend does not make explicit reference to what others of his time sometimes euphemistically referred to as "the abominable sin," his arguably oblique wording would have left very little to the reader's imagination. The precise links (in terms of symbols, meanings, experiences, and the like) between the facts alluded to here and Indic cultural patterns of the sort discussed at the beginning of this chapter are, unfortunately, impossible to specify. Suffice it to note that "Wang Ta-Yuan reported human sacrifice in Trengganu in 1349 before images of fragrant wood apparently by Tantric worshipers of Kali, the dread Hindu goddess of death," that "Fei Hsin claims to have seen it in Pahang in 1436," and that in Kelantan through the 1950s invocations in "state séance[s] still call[ed] upon Siva as Kali the Destroyer" (Winstedt 1961:31).

I turn finally to comparative perspectives from neighboring Java since Tantric and Saivite (and Austronesian) themes are also well documented for Java in premodern times and throughout the early (and late) modern era, and, more generally, since evidence from Java is broadly relevant to our understanding of Malay society and culture during the early modern period (and beyond), and vice versa. One important Javanese source—"one of that culture's most touted classics"—is the *Serat Centhini*, an encyclopedic poem the oldest known version of which originates from a manuscript of 1616 (B. Anderson 1990:277). According to Benedict Anderson (ibid., 278), the *Serat Centhini* "shows, by the many examples it offers and its unconditionally Javanese technical vocabulary, that male homosexuality at least was an unproblematic, everyday part of a highly varied traditional Javanese sexual culture. (It includes, *inter alia*, detailed descriptions of sodomy, fellatio, mutual masturbation, multiple-partner intercourse, and transvestitism.) Heterosexual sex is described in exactly analogous ways; the *Centhini* is quite catholic—or should one say encyclopedic?—in its coverage" (cf. Keeler 1990:148–150).[27] This material is consistent with what we know of the Malay case, though we have seen that Malay data from this period are rather sparse.

Not coincidentally, broad commonalities are also evident in the status of women, with both Javanese and Malay women playing active roles in trade, diplomacy, and statecraft; exercising considerable autonomy and social control both within the domestic realm and beyond (e.g., in marriage, divorce, inheritance, and the marketplace); and enjoying freedom of movement and a degree of respect and overall social significance not usually accorded their counterparts either in South Asia or East Asia or in Melanesia or the Pacific as a whole (Raffles 1817 [1830]:394, H. Geertz 1961:46, Brenner 1995:23 passim; see also Keeler 1987, 1990, Smith-Hefner 1988, Hatley 1990, Sears 1996). Dynamics in the state of Negeri Sembilan on the west coast of the Malay Peninsula are particularly telling in this regard. Similar in many ways to the Minangkabau of Sumatra, from whom they traced their descent, Malay women residing in

Negeri Sembilan owned and inherited most rights over houses, homestead plots, rice land, and other cultivable acreage (males received rights to livestock, weapons, cash, and most political titles) and served as the de facto heads of households and localized kin groups. These arrangements were keyed to ideologies of matrilineal descent and inheritance, and the notions of gender linked with them. The latter portrayed men as formally endowed with more "reason" (*akal*) and less "passion" (*nafsu*) than women but, in practice, more prone than women to squander resources and ignore important social and moral obligations (see Peletz 1988, 1995, 1996; cf. Brenner 1995, 1998). The formal system of matrilineal clans and lineages characteristic of Negeri Sembilan and a few other regions in the Peninsula is not typical of Malays, or Javanese. But a great many features of Negeri Sembilan Malay kinship, gender, and sexuality outlined here (and in Chapters 4 and 5) and discussed in detail elsewhere (Peletz 1988, 1994, 1996) clearly are.

Burmese

Much of the discussion thus far has focused on insular (Austronesian) Southeast Asia. It is also crucial to examine data from areas of mainland Southeast Asia since I have suggested that many of the patterns at issue here also existed in lowland regions of mainland Southeast Asia, at least in a "theme and variation" sense, and were thus more or less pan-Southeast Asian. I focus first on Burma, which, as mentioned earlier, was not part of the Austronesian world linguistically or culturally. Rather, during the early modern period, most Burmese spoke one or another language either in the Tibeto-Burmese or Mon-Khmer language family and, in cultural (religious) terms, partook of the syncretic, Tantric- (and Saivite-) inflected Theravada Buddhist traditions found in most of mainland Southeast Asia, e.g., Thailand, Laos, and Cambodia (but not in the more "sinicized" Vietnam, whose religious traditions included a syncretic blend of Mahayana Buddhism, Confucianism, Taoism, and animism).

I begin with a consideration of Burmese bodily practices of the early modern era that were conceptually and materially linked both to same-sex relations and to heterosexuality. These practices were of widespread provenance in Southeast Asia—they are also documented for Thailand, the Philippines, Java, Bali, Sulawesi (including Bugis areas), and parts of Borneo and beyond—and thus index the geographically and culturally expansive scope of an important range of gendered patterns throughout the region as a whole (D. Brown, Edwards, and Moore 1988). A key component of these bodily practices involved the surgical implantation of metal pins, balls, bells, and spurs in men's penises. Many sixteenth-century European accounts report that "the men of Pegu [southern Burma], according to their wealth and social position, ... insert little round balls into their sexual organ in the flesh of the foreskin. These bells, which are ... the size of acorns or small plums, are made of gold, silver, or lead and the more expensive golden ones are said to 'have delightful treble, contralto, and tenor tones'" (Lach 1965:553). In 1515 Portuguese apothecary and explorer Tomé Pires recounted not only that the men in Pegu undergo such surgery but also that Malay women "are very fond of them" and "rejoice greatly when ... [they] come to their country." As he famously put it, "the reason for this must be their sweet harmony" (1515 [1944]:103; see also Fitch 1592 [1811]:421–422).

Burmese myths widely disseminated in Western sources from the sixteenth and seventeenth centuries suggest the balls and bells were invented by an ancient Burmese queen for two reasons (Lach 1965:553–554). She wanted to enlarge men's penises for the greater gratification of women (see also Pelras 1996:124), and more directly relevant here, she hoped to break Burmese men of what many European sources phrased as an "addiction to sodomy" (Fitch 1592 [1811]:421–422; see also Hamilton 1727 [1930] II:27–28, Sangermano 1818 [1893]:158–159).[28] It was allegedly with an eye toward enticing men and keeping them from male-to-male sexuality that the women of Burma reputedly went about with very little clothing.

All such "nefarious abuses" were shocking to European sensibilities because they bespoke far more pluralism—specifically, a much broader range of legitimized variation with respect to the adornment and deployment of bodies and the pursuit of pleasure and desire—than the moral doctrines prevailing in their mother countries led them to expect. They were in any event "examples of what can happen in the absence of Christian belief," which, by definition, entailed being "under the influence of the devil" (Lach 1965:554).

Also shocking to Europeans were Burmese traditions of transgenderism and same-sex relations, which are documented in historical accounts dating back to the early sixteenth century (see, for example, Fitch 1592 [1811]:421–422). One of the more detailed of the early accounts derives from Englishman Alexander Hamilton, writing in the early 1700s. After describing the annual "Rocket Festival," Hamilton reported that

> A little While after the Rockets flying they have another Feast, called the Collock, and some Women are chosen out of the People assembled, to dance a Dance to the Gods of the Earth. *Hermophradites* [sic] who are numerous in this Country, are generally chosen, if there are enow present to make a Set for the Dance. I saw nine dance like mad Folks, for above half an Hour, and then some of them fell in Fits, foaming at the Mouth for the Space of half an Hour; and, when their Senses are restored, they pretend to foretel Plenty or Scarcity of Corn for that Year, if the Year will prove sickly or salutary to the People, and several other Things of Moment, and all by that half Hour's Conversation that the furious Dancer had with the Gods while she was in a Trance.
>
> (Hamilton 1727 [1930]:31; emphasis added)

Hamilton's reference to "hermophradites" most likely pertains to individuals involved in sexual relations with persons of both sexes, who, in eighteenth-, nineteenth-, and early twentieth-century European discourses, both medical/

scientific and popular alike, were often characterized as suffering from "psychic hermaphroditism," sometimes abbreviated as "hermaphroditism" (Herdt 1993a:74–76, Trumbach 1993:115–116 passim, Bleys 1995). Since Hamilton makes more than one mention of women in this passage and suggests that the "hermophradites" were selected from the ranks of women, he is apparently referring to female-bodied ritual specialists (known as *nat kadaw*, "wives" or "spouses" of the spirit[s] or *nat*) involved to one or another degree in bisexuality. I might mention that Burma specialists with extensive knowledge of the region (e.g., Spiro 1967:220) have interpreted passages such as these in the same way.

Roughly a century later the highly prolific British envoy John Crawfurd wrote of these same *nat kadaw*, though the context of his observations was quite different since by this time the Crown was bent on annexing Burmese territories to its holdings in "British India" and had only recently emerged from the costly military campaigns that came to be known as the First Anglo-Burmese War (1824–1826). Considering these ritual specialists to be "a curious specimen of the superstition, credulity, and folly of the Burmese and their Government," Crawfurd described the role they played against British forces in "the action at Simbike."

> Finding that all their ordinary efforts to make head against the invaders were unavailing, they had recourse to magic; and among other projects of this nature, sent down to their army before Prome, all the women at Ava who had the reputation of having a familiar spirit, in order to put a spell on the foreigners, and it was said, unman them. These females, who rather labour under some mental derangement than are imposters, are called by the Burmans Nat-kadau, or female nats. They profess to hold an intercourse with the demigods of that name, and to be inspired by them with supernatural powers. The presence of such persons was known to the British army; and among the wounded, after the action at Simbike, there was found a young girl of fifteen or sixteen years of age, dressed in male attire, believed to be one of them. Her sex was recognised and attention was paid to her; but she expired in half an hour after being taken prisoner … [due apparently to having] received wounds in the neck and head.
>
> (Crawfurd 1834 I:74–75)

The available sources do not specify how these or other female-bodied *nat kadaw* could "unman" their male adversaries, though presumably this occurred through the intercession of the *nat* to whom they were married. It merits mention in any event that not all female-bodied *nat kadaw* were transgendered, as is also true at present, and that in Southeast Asia as a whole, female-bodied ritual specialists were apparently less likely than their male-bodied counterparts to engage in cross-dressing or transgender practices of other kinds. The description of *nat kadaw* provided by Italian missionary Vicentius Sangermano, who resided in Ava and Rangoon from 1783 to 1808, makes no mention of transgender practices but merits consideration in light of its similarities with some of the Austronesian cases discussed earlier. According to Sangermano, in cases of illness,

> the physician ... will prescribe some superstitious observance, and administer what he calls the medicine of the witches; or if it be the Natzo [sic] that has caused the evil, he will set before him rice and cooked meats, roasted fowls, fruit., etc, ... or else he will make the devil or Natzo dance. For this purpose a middle-aged woman to whom they give the name of wife of the Natzo, must dance, and go through a number of contortions, to the sound of a drum or some other musical instrument, in a tent erected for the occasion, in which is placed a quantity of fruits and other things as an offering, but which turn to the account of the dancing girl. By degrees she feigns to become infuriated and utters some incoherent words which are regarded as the answer of the Nat, who has been thus consulted with regard to the conclusion of the malady.
>
> (Sangermano 1818 [1893]:172)

The relationship between *nat* and *nat kadaw* on the one hand and royal courts (and the states that succeeded them) on the other is rather complicated, certainly far more so than the Bugis *bissu*, who were far less ambivalently linked to sources of royal power in the first few centuries of their existence. This is partly because while localized *nat* cults have existed throughout Burma for approximately 2 to 3,000 years (perhaps longer), the relatively recent emergence of states in the region saw only partly successful efforts on the part of powerful political elites to exercise control over the cults and place them under state jurisdiction. Put differently, the pantheon of the "37 *nat*" (the main *nat* in Burmese cosmology) has long symbolized both the autonomy of local entities, especially villages and the kin groups and households comprising them, and their incorporation as subordinate units into a Burmese system of monarchy that promoted and ostensibly governed in accordance with Theravada Buddhism as the state religion (Brac de la Perrière 1996:45–46 passim). The much revered culture hero Anawratha (r. 1044–1077), the first king to establish Burmese dominance over the entire Irrawaddy valley, waged an extensive struggle to convince his subjects to abandon pre-Buddhist beliefs and practices, associated with *nat*, for example, and to convert to Buddhism. The *nat* were not abandoned, but they were "placed under the authority of Thi'dja, the Burmese version of Indra," the king of the Vedic gods, "who is asserted to be the protector of Theravada in Burma" (ibid., 46). Arguably more germane is that "by the intermediary of Thi'dja, the king made clear the subordination of the former cults to the new state religion, Theravadan Buddhism" (ibid.), even though *nat* continued to be regarded as sovereign and as rebels and potential rivals of the monarch and his successors. This situation differs in key particulars from what we have seen in Austronesian examples considered earlier, such as the Bugis and Malay cases.

Nat kadaw were not the only transgendered ritual specialists in Burma in the early modern period; there were two other categories of transgendered special-ists we know about, hence at least three in all, much like the Malay case and per-haps that of Siam as well. Both of the latter categories included individuals attached to royal courts who were or had once been male-bodied. The first involved male-bodied individuals who donned female attire in the course of theatrical and/or musical performances sponsored by the king, who were said to hail from Siam (Cox 1821 [1971]:9). The second involved individuals who were described by the late eighteenth- and early nineteenth-century Western observers as "eunuchs" (Symes 1827 II:69, Cox 1821 [1971]:88). British envoy Michael Symes notes in his pioneering account of Burma at the end of the eigh-teenth century that the eunuchs were Muslims who had been taken as prisoners in military campaigns against neighboring Arakan, and that they were kept at the royal court primarily as tokens of military prowess rather than for any other symbolic or other function they might have served, such as safeguarding royal regalia or palace women (1827 II:69). Captain Hiram Cox, a rough contempo-rary, offers only a brief description of their attire and the position of symbolic importance accorded eunuchs next to the king when he sat in state: "To the right and left of the throne, ... just within the arcade of the tent, were ranged twenty of the King's bodyguard, in satin gowns trimmed with gold lace, with tre-ble scalloped capes and cuffs, and gilt hats like Mambrino's helmet. Nearer the throne, to the right or west side, were seated in a line with the body-guards, six eunuchs of the palace, native Mahomedans, in white jammas and coloured silk lungees, with white handkerchiefs round their heads" (Cox 1821 [1971]:88).

We know nothing about the sexual orientation of the cross-dressing per-formers mentioned above, though based on what has been reported for other parts of Southeast Asia, it is highly likely that many of them engaged in same-sex relations with males considered to be normatively oriented who incurred little if any stigma from their participation in these relations and may have derived a measure of prestige from them. Nor do we have any information on the sexual and other activities of those described as "eunuchs"; we do not even know if they were in fact eunuchs.

The case of the *nat kadaw*, on the other hand, is more clear-cut. Like their Austronesian ritualistic counterparts, these specialists included among their ranks many individuals who engaged in cross-dressing and other transgender practices as well as same-sex sexual relations, as is true today. The fact the majority of *nat kadaw* were phenotypically female—and continued to be so even through the mid-twentieth century (see Chapter 4, below)—is a significant point of contrast with the Austronesian examples discussed here, though clearly in keeping with situation of the northern Philippines referenced earlier.

More germane is a commonality that the Burmese material shares with Austronesian cases such as the Bugis: a long-term acceptance of—and accord-ing of legitimacy to—same-sex sexual relations among couples of "lay people" (not just ritual specialists and their partners), male and female alike. We see clear evidence of this even in the twentieth century. Based on extensive fieldwork undertaken in the 1960s, Spiro (1977:229) reported on Burmese atti-tudes toward the sexual practices of ritual specialists *and* others; referring pri-marily to their occurrence in the general population, he wrote that Burmese viewed same-sex sexual practices with a "relatively tolerant attitude" and that urban-dwelling "lesbians (*yaukkyasha*) ... also ... meet with the same relative toleration." Spiro's latter point concerning same-sex erotics among females is confirmed by well-known Burmese writer and social scientist Mi Mi Khaing (1919–1990) who wrote a definitive account of Burmese family life in the mid-twentieth century as well as a subsequent study of Burmese women based partly on her experiences growing up in Burma and partly on research conducted through the 1970s. She observed that same-sex intimacy often occurred among unmarried women, "particularly among young girls in dormitories," going on to claim that such women "are not ostracised" even in the apparently rare cases where they forge life-long attachments (Mi Mi Khaing 1984:114–115). The extent to which the women involved in such relations may have endeavored to garner a measure of legitimacy for their unions by cloaking them in the symbols and idioms associated with ritual specialists (e.g., *nat kadaw*) is not clear, though we know this occurs in the Bugis case (among *calabai* and *calalai* alike), and that broadly analogous dynamics have been reported for Chinese women involved in same-sex erotics in Singapore in the mid-twentieth century (Chapter 3).

Most important is the illustration that the legitimacy accorded transgen-dered ritual specialists involved in same-sex intimacy does not constitute a quarantined exception to the prevailing hegemony bearing on gender and sexuality. Rather, it indexes a broadly diffuse pluralism with respect to gender and sexuality that is also readily apparent in the autonomy and social control enjoyed by Burmese women, their active participation in small-scale peddling, large-scale trade, and other economic arenas, and their rights with respect to marriage, divorce, inheritance, and the like. Spiro (1997:11) summarizes these dynamics in his remarks, "Burmese women probably occupy a higher social sta-tus than any other women in Asia. Indeed, until the dramatic changes in the status of women in the West in the past fifty years, Burmese women enjoyed a degree of economic, legal, and social equality that arguably was unsurpassed either in Asia or in Europe and North America." Mi Mi Khaing (1984) concurs, devoting much of her book to the subject.

The legitimacy accorded females and femininity in Burma is by no means limited to the mid-twentieth century. During the latter part of the Pyu era (ca. 200–840 CE), for example, young boys and girls alike entered the monastery for potentially extended periods of religious study and moral training, with girl novices and nuns apparently having their own facilities and initiation cere-monies, just like—and on a rough cultural par with those of—their male coun-terparts (Maung Htin Aung 1962:135; cf. Mi Mi Khaing 1984:1). According to Chinese texts written around 800 CE, "When they come to the age of seven, both boys and girls drop their hair and stop in a monastery, where they take refuge in the Sangha [community of monks]. On reaching the age of twenty, if they have not awoken to the principles of the Buddha, they let their hair grow again and become ordinary townsfolk" (cited in Maung Htin Aung 1962:135). Burmese historian and folklorist Maung Htin Aung points out that "the passage does not [explicitly] say whether the nuns and girl-novices had their own monasteries," but like many others who have considered the relevant data, he concludes that they did. Centuries later, the legacies of these women continued to be recounted. Thus British envoy Michael Symes who traveled about Burma in the late 1790s, writes of being "told that formerly there were nunneries of virgin priestesses, who, like the Rhahaans [monks], wore yellow garments, cut off their hair, and devoted themselves to chastity and religion" (1827 I:249). Especially when one factors into the picture the importance during this time of spirit mediums (*nat kadaw*), the majority of whom have long been phenotypically female, it seems clear that during the Pyu era the religious activities of females were the subject of as much cultural elaboration and cultural interest as those of males, and that males and females may have enjoyed comparable if not equivalent access to the sacred and comparable if not equivalent prestige.

Women's options to participate in monastic institutions were constricted and in some cases terminated during the succeeding Pagan period (c. 950–1300), which was characterized by extensive state-building, on a scale that was previously unknown in Burma and adjacent regions, along with territorial and ethnic consolidation conducive to a political system that was more centralized, bureaucratic, and absolutist. In an apparent reference to this period, Symes (1827 I:249) writes that "nunneries of virgin priestesses ... were long ago abolished" and that this occurred because they were "injurious to the population of the state." We should be clear that Symes did encounter "a few" unordained "old women" who evidently after having married and raised families "shave their heads, wear a white dress, follow funerals, and carry water to the convents;" these were "venerable dames," according to Symes, who had "some portion of respect paid to them" (ibid.). As to what might have been "injurious to the population of the state," and to the creation of the ideological apparatuses undergirding the state, I would thus suggest that it was the life-long celibacy of nuns and all that it signified. This celibacy precluded realization of these women's politically valuable reproductive potential and also symbolized the high degree of autonomy and independence enjoyed by such women. All of this flew in the face of increasingly salient Buddhist precepts that authorized male control over females and also emphasized male-female contrasts of the sort that were muted if males and females alike renounced sexuality for their entire lives. The imperatives of state building are of key significance here. For as in many other contexts these imperatives entailed creating and maintaining a large, ethnically diverse, and otherwise status-differentiated population of loyal subjects who were ultimately united under the sacred canopy of state-sponsored religion (in this case, Theravada Buddhism), and who could provide labor power, taxes, and tribute to the monarch as well as an audience for his or her displays of grandeur. More to the point, these imperatives took precedence over the continued existence of institutions that enabled women to renounce all worldly attachments so as to devote full time to the study of sacred texts and perform rituals that (in popular understanding) would help them to gain one or another degree of enlightenment.

The early modern era and the centuries leading up to it thus witnessed the exclusion of women as ordained nuns from monasteries along with state efforts to delegitimize spirit cults under women's charge, all of which contributed to a partial distancing of women from important loci of spiritual power and prestige. Analogous developments occurred in specifically political arenas, even though we have seen that Burmese women continued to "enjoy a degree of economic, legal, and social equality that arguably was unsurpassed either in Asia or in Europe and North America" (Spiro 1997:11). During the Pyu period, for example, and in the centuries after the collapse of Pagan (but, significantly, not during the Pagan period itself), a number of Burmese queens including the famous Mon queen, Shin Saw Bu, ruled in their own names not simply as the wives or consorts of Burmese kings (Mi Mi Khaing 1984:6). Thereafter, however, traditions of Burmese queenship all but disappear, despite the fact that women continued to serve as heads or *thugyis* of more territorially limited politico-administrative units, such as villages (ibid., 8), at least until the nineteenth century.

The existence of these latter traditions helps explain why Chinese and Europeans who traveled to Burma in the eighteenth and nineteenth centuries frequently commented on the high status of Burmese women (see, for example, Symes 1827 I:255, Bowring 1856 [1969] I:309, Jardine 1893:xviii). Other factors that help account for these characterizations include Burmese women's predominance as diplomats, traders, and ritual specialists (e.g., *nat kadaw*), and the previously commented-upon legal rights (in the realms of marriage, divorce, inheritance, etc.) enjoyed by Burmese women in most walks of life. Factors such as these are also relevant to my characterization of early modern Burma as relatively pluralistic with respect to gender and sexuality, just as they support my view that despite important differences, early modern Burma shares broad commonalities with Austronesian cases involving Iban, Ngaju Dyak, Bugis, and Malays.

Thais

The histories and cultures of many regions of mainland Southeast Asia are deeply intertwined. It is thus not surprising that politico-religious structures and patterns of symbolism in Siam (renamed Thailand in 1939) have long had much in common with traditions of neighboring Burma and Cambodia. We have seen that the dominant religious and ritual orientation in all three areas has long been informed by a variant of Theravada Buddhism that remains heavily inflected with Saivite and Tantric elements as well as the animistic features that predated Indic influences in the region. Burma's *nat*, for instance, are strikingly similar to Thai and Cambodian spirits (*phii* and *nak ta*, respectively)—as well as their counterparts in the Malay Peninsula (*jinn*) and throughout Indonesia, the Philippines, and the Austronesian world as a whole. Extensive similitude is evident in the spirits' mythological origins, their cosmologically enshrined relationships to the world of nature and humankind, the scope and force of their mystical or occult powers, the specifics of their comportment and appearance, and what they expect or demand of humans by way of appeasement or the repayment of vows. Many other commonalities (bearing on Mount Meru as the *axis mundi*, the built environment as a replica of the cosmos, etc.) can be observed in the symbolism and overall design of stupas, pagodas, and monumental architecture dating from the pre-modern period and from early modern times as well. Noteworthy too is that Angkorian motifs continue to be conspicuously present in the rituals of Thai royalty and were likewise evident in circles of Burmese kings prior to the dismantling of the Burmese monarchy by the British in the final months of 1885.

There are, moreover, myriad similarities throughout this broad swath of mainland Southeast Asia in kinship, gender, and sexuality. The majority of my generalizations about women, gender, and sexuality in Burma in early modern times (and before and since) could easily be transposed—with appropriate qualification—to Siam/Thailand (and to a lesser extent, Khmer-speaking Cambodia), especially my generalizations concerning women's predominance in various public arenas, Buddhist-inflected gender ideologies, and the manner in which key features of these ideologies depict women's alleged spiritual, intellectual and overall moral inferiority (addressed in Chapter 4). Additionally, many findings drawn from historical and contemporary ethnographic research on kinship and marriage among Burmese would serve as a useful point of departure for understanding lowland-dwelling Thais (and Khmer speakers as well), particularly the importance of (1) nuclear family households, (2) bilateral kinship, (3) matrifocality, (4) fosterage and informal adoption, (5) one or another degree of matrilocal post-marital residence, and (6) terminological practices involving birth-order names, teknonyms, and broadly classificatory terms of reference and address.

In light of convergences in these areas (kinship, gender, religion, cosmology) it is curious that historical sources bearing on the early modern period in Siam contain few if any conclusive references to transgendered ritual specialists other than "royal eunuchs." I should be clear that many aspects of the ethos, world view, ritual, and symbolism that are elsewhere associated with specialists such as Burmese *nat kadaw*, Malay *sida-sida* and *pawang*, Bugis *bissu*, and the like have been well documented for the Siamese case (e.g., Tambiah 1970), but with the exception (of eunuchs) noted earlier, the evidence presently available does not allow us to substantiate the existence in early modern times of transgendered ritualists per se (but see Wood 1935:109, Totman 2003:71–72, and opposite p. 86; see also below).

Concerning "royal eunuchs," French envoy Simon de La Loubère, one of the first Europeans to visit the court of Siam and leave a detailed account of his experiences, reported in 1693 that these officials were accorded a critically important role, stationed as they were in the inner chambers of the royal palace. La Loubère (1693 [1969]:32) writes, "Tis said that no person enters further, not the King's Domesticks themselves, excepting his Wives and Eunuch." The "true Officers" of the king's chambers "are Women, 'tis they only that have a Priviledge of entering therein. They make his Bed, and dress his Meat; they cloath him, and wait on him at Table: but none but himself touches his Head when he is attir'd, not puts any thing over his Head. The Pourveyors carry the Provisions to the Eunuchs, and they give them to the Women [one of which] plays the Cook" (ibid., 100).

Not surprisingly, the eunuchs attached to Siamese courts were similar to their Burmese counterparts in many respects. Areas of commonality included not only their privileged physical and symbolic proximity to the king, but also their attire and general appearance, the roles accorded them with regard to mediating relations between the monarch and the inner chambers of the palace on the one hand and the outside world on the other, and last but not least, the fact that they were typically "Musselmen," "Moormen," or Chinese, hence ethnic and religious "outsiders." (In the Thai case, Muslim eunuchs apparently originated from the Coromandel Coast, not from Arakan, the source of Burma's eunuchs.) The Chinese eunuchs who served the king of Siam at various points in Siamese history apparently did so at the request of the king, who held them in great esteem, especially during the period that Siam paid tribute to China in recognition of its sovereignty over Siam (see, among others, Bowring 1856 [1969]). The dual, arguably ambiguous status of eunuchs in Siamese courts as palace "insiders" who were simultaneously ethnic/religious "outsiders" is reminiscent of foreign-born eunuchs in the Islamic heartlands since the twelfth century and may have given rise to the same feelings of fear and awe said to have been inspired by eunuchs in the latter contexts (Marmon 1995). Their interstitial gender status as neither man nor woman may well have contributed to these kinds of sentiments as well, as presumably did their physical and symbolic proximity to the king, who claimed divinity and oversaw rituals predicated on the proper maintenance of relations between the microcosm and macrocosm, a more or less pan-Southeast Asian theme.

In any given setting, eunuchs evince (at least) one way of being (trans)gendered, sexed, and otherwise human. But in most historical and ethnographic cases for which we have evidence such as Ming China and the Ottoman Empire, eunuchs are *not* associated with a broadly diffused (society-wide) pluralism with respect to gender and sexuality. Even though eunuchs symbolized and literally embodied one or more kinds of difference in these settings (Ming China, the Ottoman empire), they are more appropriately viewed as quarantined exceptions to the prevailing gender hegemonies, which tended to be quite strict, except for elite males, and generally not very friendly to women. More to the point is that the presence of eunuchs in Siam's (and Burma's) royal palaces during early modern times is, at best, weak evidence for a society-wide pluralism, particularly since they were ethnic outsiders, were apparently asexual (much like Buddhist monks), and may well have been perceived by the populace at large as less "about" mixing or transcending boundaries, bearing on sex and gender, for example, than zealously guarding them and ensuring their strict maintenance and reproduction. Historical evidence bearing on nineteenth-century Siam's royal place (The Inner City), which in its heyday included nearly 3,000 royal wives and concubines, makes clear that one of the eunuchs' main jobs was to police the king's wives and concubines (*caocom*), who were subject to extremely strict regulations concerning both their sexual comportment and their loyalty to the king (the two were inextricably bound) and severely punished should they evince any behavior hinting of disloyalty (Bowring 1856 [1969] I:435–436, Loos 2005).

I am thus suggesting that from an analytic point of view, "classical" eunuchs do not have much in common with transgendered ritual specialists of the sort found among Iban, Ngaju Dayak, Bugis, Malays, and Burmese. More generally, not all differences (embodied in "thirdness") are the same, to paraphrase a comment made by Lawrence Cohen (1995:277) and perhaps Yogi Berra before him—and neither are their implication for gender pluralism in the societies in which they exist. I want to turn now to why there is no clear evidence of transgendered ritualists of an Austronesian or Burmese sort in Siam's early modern history and what we might make of this situation.

The dearth of explicit references to transgendered ritualists in the historical record bearing on Siam lends itself to (at least) two different interpretations. One interpretation, the less compelling in my view, is that with the exception of "royal eunuchs," no such specialists existed. The other, more plausible, interpretation is that while some such specialists provided ritual services in royal courts, others in the countryside, conclusive evidence of their existence has not yet been found and may never surface.

To support this position I cite four sets of dynamics. The first has to do with the technologies of writing and record keeping in pre- and early modern Siam (and beyond), specifically that manuscripts and other written documents were fashioned from highly perishable materials such as palm leaf, bark, and bamboo, which are highly vulnerable to moisture, rot, and fire. It does not help matters that when the Burmese sacked the Siamese royal capital of Ayutthaya in April 1767, they burned all manuscripts and other documents that they could get their hands on, thereby destroying nearly all historical records that the kingdom had produced or maintained.

The second relevant factor is that historical research on gender and sexuality both globally and in Southeast Asia and Siam/Thailand in particular is still in its infancy.[29] For the most part, earlier generations of historians dealing with Siam/Thailand (e.g., Wyatt 1994, 2003, Thongchai 1994) paid very little attention to gender and even less to sexuality. With some noteworthy exceptions, moreover, historians have generally been loath to write about aspects of sexuality construed as beyond the heteronormative pale. This problem has plagued the overwhelmingly ahistorical anthropology of Thailand as well, at least through the mid-1980s. The problem is so acute that prior to that time, few if any anthropologists or other academics were willing to deal with the hugely conspicuous sex industry that has flourished in Bangkok and elsewhere in Thailand since roughly midway through the American war in Vietnam

(1950–1975) (Bishop and Robinson 1998: Chap. 2), or to address issues bearing on same-sex sexuality among Thais, except in a passing comment or two relegated to a footnote (see, for example Keyes 1986:96 n 47). There are, more generally, (at least) two realms of academic discourses on Thailand, as on many other regions, one more established and "mainstream"—which is relatively ungendered and disembodied (work by Tambiah 1970, Wyatt 1994, 2003 and Thongchai 1994 being good examples)—the other more recent and more inclined to focus on gender and sexuality, especially transgenderism and same-sex erotics (e.g., Morris 1994, Jackson and Sullivan 1999, Sinnott 2004, and Loos 2005). These discourses do not always succeed in engaging one another or communicating across the de facto boundaries that separate them (Loos 2005:906). Because issues of concern to one set of scholars are not necessarily of interest to the others, references and insights gleaned from indigenous manuscripts and other primary sources that might be widely shared among colleagues (or otherwise more broadly disseminated) are not.

The third set of dynamics relevant to the paucity of conclusive references to transgendered ritualists concerns the relationship between China and Siam throughout the early modern period and into the nineteenth century. Historical accounts bearing on Siam underscore the long history of diplomatic and commercial ties between envoys from China and representatives of Siamese monarchs, and contain frequent references to Chinese eunuchs visiting the Siamese court (in 1388, for example [Bowring 1856 (1969) I:73]) and advising Siamese officials on ceremonies of investiture and various other matters deemed crucial for the ritually efficacious conduct of statecraft. Thomas Bowring, who later served as Governor of Hong Kong and successfully prevailed upon the Siamese (partly via well articulated threats of military action) to grant trade and other concessions to the British, notes in his 1856 account, *The Kingdom and People of Siam*, that Siamese officials held Chinese eunuchs in such great esteem that they requested their presence in Siamese courts at various points (in 1753, for instance [1856 (1969) I:78–79]). Evidence suggests that by the nineteenth century, if not earlier, the cultural salience in palace circles of Chinese eunuchs and other assorted functionaries from China outweighed the importance of Indian officials, Muslims, and others who had previously enjoyed privileged access to the monarch. Thus in the mid-1850s Bowring observed, "There seem to have been a greater proportion of Moors, Mahometans and Indians occupying high places at the court than are now to be found. Their influence has been superseded by the great influx of the Chinese races," who were part of a "vast emigration of … men from China, … brought down by every north-east monsoon," who he estimated to number some 1,500,000 in the kingdom at the time (1856 [1969] I: 81, 84, 100; cf. Finlayson 1826 [1988]:223).[30] The "sea change" at issue here might be implicated in the dearth of historical records bearing on transgendered ritualists (other than eunuchs) in the courts of Siam. Indeed, it could well be that one or more groups of such ritualists went the way of the "Moors, Mahometans and Indians occupying high places at the court" and that this is one reason why we have little conclusive evidence of their existence.

The fourth set of dynamics that helps explain the relative absence of conclusive evidence concerning transgendered ritualists during the early modern period has to do with processes of cultural and institutional rationalization. Such processes were well under way in Siam during the early 1800s (and before). Indeed, many scholars have made note of the "rewriting of Thai religious and legal texts" that occurred under Rama I (r. 1782–1800), the founder of the Chakri dynasty (B. Andaya 2006:180; see also Wyatt 2002:51–56). The more encompassing processes involved the delegitimization and erosion of numerous traditions that from the points of view of increasingly significant canonical orthodoxies of Theravada Buddhism and Western rationalism alike had come to be seen by Siamese elites as "backward," "superstitious," or both. Travelers who visited Siam during the late eighteenth and early to mid-nineteenth century (and subsequently) frequently commented on the king's efforts to eradicate "excess," "superstition," and "folly." In the mid-nineteenth century, for example, "the King ... [was] reported to profess a modified or reformed Buddhism, and once said to the missionaries, that his religion was, as contrasted with the religion of the vulgar, what Protestantism is to Catholicism, for he only wished to retain the pure text of the sacred books, and to get rid of superfluous and superstitious ceremonies" (Bowring 1856 [1969] II:302; cf. p. 85). Such efforts could well have entailed or otherwise contributed to the sanitizing of indigenous manuscripts (as probably occurred with Malay manuscripts as well), which may be why scholarly investigations of such documents have thus far yielded relatively little evidence of sort with which we are concerned (Jackson 2003, 2004). The larger dynamic—the morally and politically laden encounter between Southeast Asian religions and Protestantism—helps explain why custodians of Southeast Asian Buddhism and Islam emphasized heightened (hetero)normativity, particularly in the late nineteenth century, which saw the onset of "high colonialism" in most of the region, and subsequently (see El Rouayheb 2005:9, 153–161 and Najmabadi 2005 for elucidation of analogous developments in the Muslim Middle East). This dynamic should also serve as a reminder of a conceptual point of far-reaching significance emphasized in connection with (but by no means limited to) the case of the Bugis: just as hegemonies are invariably contested, so too are they invariably subject to historical flux and change.

The historiographic situation at issue here is all the more striking in light of the diverse sexual practices and gender identities that anthropologists have documented in Thailand since the 1980s, especially in and around Bangkok and Chiang Mai. Relevant here are *kathoey*, the subject of important work by Peter Jackson (1997, 2003), Rosalind Morris (1994), Richard Totman (2003) and others. *Kathoey* is a polysemic term, possibly of Khmer origin. Its various meanings include hermaphrodites as well as male-bodied individuals who either cross-dress or engage in stereotypical female occupations or pastimes linked to fashion or entertainment, or practice any other form of transgenderism that simultaneously feminizes them and distances them from normative masculinity. Additionally, the term is sometimes used to refer to female-bodied individuals who transcend or transgress heteronormative ideals bearing on femininity, but this is much less common.

Among contemporary Thais, "it is frequently remarked that ... the vast majority of male [spirit] mediums are *kathoeys*" (Morris 2000:132; cf. Totman 2003:76, Sinnott 2004:57–58).[31] The existence of conceptual links between *kathoey* and ritual practices undertaken by spirit mediums may point to an earlier (early modern) ritual role for *kathoey*, one that is perhaps analogous to Burmese *nat kadaw*, Malay *sida-sida* and/or *pawang*, Bugis *bissu*, and/or others we have considered in this chapter. Additional support for this interpretation comes from *kathoey* themselves. The self-described *kathoey* cabaret dancer who narrates the BBC documentary film *Lady Boys* (Marre 1992) for example, makes clear that in former times *kathoey* were attached to the palaces of the king. Late nineteenth-century photographs showing troupes of "*kathoey* dancers" (see Totman 2003, opposite p. 86; and p. 72) might be cited to help substantiate this view insofar as such troupes would have normally been maintained by the palace, much like their transgendered counterparts in neighboring regions of northern Malaya, who practiced a dramatic genre (*mak yong*) that is of clear Thai provenance. Additional support for my view that *kathoey* involvement in ritual long predates the twentieth century derives from the well-established fact that dance in Thailand and elsewhere in Southeast Asia is widely seen as a key medium through which to summon the spirits and has "long been used as a conduit to the supernatural" (B. Andaya 2006:188; cf. Brandon 1967:61 passim, Totman 2003:71–72).[32]

References to "hermaphrodites" or "true *kathoey*" in Pali Buddhist scriptures (the *Tipitaka*) whose written forms date from the first century BCE point to the antiquity of a "third sex" (or "third gender") in the Thai context, although they do not link such persons with any ritual roles (Jackson 1998, Totman 2003:50–52). So too do Mon (central Thai) origin myths that have been widely discussed by scholars debating assertions that Thais have long recognized the existence of at least three (anatomical) sexes and four sexualities (see, for example, Morris 1994, Jackson 1997:169, L. Andaya 2000:32–33). These scriptural and mythic sources accord a degree of legitimacy to *kathoey* but this is not to say that they necessarily depict them in an altogether flattering light. Buddhist doctrinal emphases on reincarnation and karma underscore themes of transformation and multiplicity in a larger (philosophical and epistemological) context of conceptual and moral relativism and compassion. But Buddhist doctrine also maintains that those who are born (or come to consider themselves) *kathoey* have fallen short and incurred bad karma in past incarnations—because of one or another misdeed such as "adultery, being a female prostitute, sexually abusing one's children or failing to fulfill an expected role in the reproductive process, such as a man's not caring for a woman who is pregnant by him" (Totman 2003:57)—for which reason they are *kathoey* in their current lives. According to Buddhist doctrine, *kathoey*ness is an unfortunate state not only for the suffering associated with one or another variation on the theme of "gender dysphoria" but also because it allows for fewer opportunities to practice spiritual cultivation as compared with those available to normatively gendered males (Jackson 1998).[33]

Canonical texts and myths are clearly significant, but they should not be confused with popular understandings, which in the case of Siam/Thailand have typically been more favorably disposed toward various types of transgression involving gender and sexuality. This is suggested by the observations of W.A.R. Wood, who was born and raised in England but spent 69 years working (as clerk, factotum, British Consul, judge, etc.) in Siam/Thailand beginning in 1896. In good Thai fashion, Wood casually and non-judgmentally describes "a young fellow of good family living near ... Lampang who sometimes dressed as a man and sometimes as a woman" about whom "it was popularly believed that during the early part of each month he actually was a male and during the latter half of the month became a female;" he also offers the following generalizations:

> In Siam, especially in the North, there are a certain number of men who habitually wear female clothing and grow their hair long. *It does not seem to be thought that there is anything morally wrong about this*, and so far as I have been able to make out, these *Pu-Mia* (men-women), as they are called, really possess, as a rule, no moral eccentricities. Physically also, I am told, there is nothing peculiar about them. *They prefer to dress as women, and that is all that there is to say about it.*
>
> (Wood 1935:111; emphasis added)

Most relevant about Wood's remarks are the Thai attitudes and feeling-tones he conveys, which involve both lack of censure and "nonchalance." Wood does not specifically claim that "men-women" were accorded legitimacy. But in maintaining that Thais saw nothing morally wrong with their behavior and felt there was really nothing to say about it—and that "nobody worries about them or interferes with them" (ibid., 112)—that seems to be his point. Wood's other point, a culturally comparative one, is also worthy of our consideration, especially since pluralism is by definition always relative: "In England, if a man goes about dressed as a women he is *arrested*;" moreover, any "tendency in a man to assume female dress is [taken as] a sign of some sort of *moral perversion*" (ibid., 111; emphasis added; see also Van der Meer 1991, 1993, Blackwood 2005:864).

The apparent absence in Wood's day of any sense among Thais that there was something "morally wrong" with "men-women," ritual specialists or otherwise, is highly revealing. For by this time, monarchs in the Chakri dynasty along with other Thai elites had long been involved in projects of modernity that targeted a broad range of pluralistic and other practices, and the sensibilities and dispositions associated with them, in the name of curtailing "excess," "folly," and "superstition," and thus fending off American and other Western imperial designs on their kingdom. Equally revealing is that the vast majority of Wood's "men-women," like the nineteenth-century "*kathoey* dancers" mentioned earlier, were male- rather than female-bodied (though he does recount the case of a female-bodied dependent of the prince of Lampang who always dressed as a male, "did all sorts of heavy work about the Prince's palace, utterly despising every kind of female accomplishment," and proceeded, with royal blessing, "to marry one of ... [the prince's] female servants" [1935:112]). This situation underscores the importance of recognizing that even a broadly diffused pluralism has limits and is thus by definition always relative. The considerable autonomy, social control, and freedom of movement long enjoyed by Thai women and the fact that Thai women served in many instances as powerful rulers, diplomats, and traders in their own right, not simply as the wives, sisters, or daughters of powerful men (La Loubère 1693 [1969] I:73, Hamilton 1727 [1930]:96, Bowring 1856 [1969] I:119–120, 309–310, Napat and Gordon 1999), did *not* go hand-in-hand (at least in the nineteenth century) with a "laissez-faire" approach to female sexual practices or women's decisions concerning whether or nor they would assume stereotypical female kinship and gender roles—a situation that existed to some degree among the Bugis, and even, albeit to a lesser extent, among Burmese. In all of these cases phenotypic males enjoyed far more privileges and prerogatives and were subject to fewer constraints than phenotypic females, though considerations of status rank (e.g., descent) could easily trump gender, such that a high-ranking woman would typically enjoy more privileges and prerogatives than a low-born male.

Presently available evidence does not allow for a conclusive explanation for these contrasts. One productive line of argument worthy of further research suggests that a key factor driving these dynamics may have been the highly elaborated system of status ranking that prevailed in Siam (as compared, for example, with neighboring Burma), coupled with the more elaborated concerns among Thai (as distinct from Burmese and other Southeast Asian) elite with advancing or at least maintaining their status in a system that was ultimately rather flexible in the sense that it allowed for a fair degree of social mobility. In this system, the actions taken during one's lifetime could result in movement a considerable distance up the hierarchy, or in sliding way down it (much like the more encompassing karmic cycle). Royal and other elite polygyny loomed large in these dynamics. (Significantly, polyandry did not exist, even though female monarchs were by no means unheard of in Siamese history.) This is not only because polygynous practices enabled a king to forge strategic alliances, via "gifts" of virtuous sisters and daughters, with well-placed supporters among officials in his ministries and in outlying provinces (and vice versa), but also because amassing large numbers of women and siring many children was a sign of male prowess and spiritual potency (Loos 2005). All things being equal, the more (virtuous) wives, concubines, and children a king had, the higher his status and the more likely he was to prevail over rivals and detractors.

Relevant in this regard are the *caocom* or "concubines" of Siam's Inner City, who numbered nearly 3,000 under King Chulalongkorn in the mid-nineteenth century, a number, which, as Loos (2005:883) notes, is more than three times the number of women in the much discussed "harems" of Ottoman rulers during their heyday in the seventeenth century. The sexual comportment of *caocom* was subject to intense surveillance and control, bound up as it was with issues of loyalty to the king (all such fidelity being an index of the king's ability to amass and command followers beyond the palace walls), and violations of palatine laws bearing on a *caocom*'s erotic activities could result in swift death. The more general points are that the constructions of elite masculine power at issue here were relevant "not just to the king but also to other royal men and noblemen;" and, arguably, that "the form of masculinity expressed though the [king's] ability to attract numerous women applied to and was practiced when possible by lower-class men as well" (Loos 2005:896 n15), at least by the nineteenth century. Evidence bearing on the "trickledown" to commoners—or commoner appropriation of—elite notions of masculine prowess are broadly analogous to processes of Sanskritization discussed at the beginning of this chapter. A key difference is that the content of the nineteenth-century appropriations bore relatively little resemblance to the polymorphous sexualities and ambiguous gender positionings characteristic of Hindu deities such as Siva, and had more in common—but were clearly not isomorphic—with present-day Thai heteronormativity.

Loos (2005) shows that virtually all of the nineteenth-century palatine laws that have been discovered concerned a *caocom*'s relations with men, and that with the notable exception of a limited number of legal proscriptions and "oaths" bearing on relations among palace women, there were no laws on the books in nineteenth-century Siam that prohibited same-sex intimacy among females (or males), although Buddhist scriptures portray such intimacy (along with the male versions) as sinful and therefore to be avoided. This is not to suggest that same-sex relations among *caocom* or other Thai women (or men) were common in the nineteenth century, though clearly they did exist (Wood 1935:112, Jackson 1998, Sinnott 2004:49–53, Loos 2005). It is mainly to point out that with respect to gender and sexuality, what mattered most at this time was that one conduct oneself in accordance with the basics of an internally stratified heterogender matrix. In the case of women this entailed (heterosexually) faithful and reproductive (fertile) marriage or concubinage with someone of the "opposite" gender and appropriate rank. It did not necessarily mean refraining from acting on same-sex desire, even though the public venues for female-bodied individuals to engage in transgender practices, commonly associated in Siam/Thailand and elsewhere in the region with same-sex relations, appear to have been more limited than those available to their male-bodied counterparts. In these regards, the situation in Thailand during the nineteenth century is reminiscent of late imperial China, which is not surprising given the contact between China and Siam and the influence of Chinese models of virtue and statecraft in the Siamese context. Tze-Ian Sang has noted that late imperial Chinese representations in literary works and other contexts are "little concerned with a woman's natural inclinations or fulfillment; rather ... [they depict] marriage as simply a woman's duty. Women must marry to fulfill their roles as obedient daughters, wives, and mothers. Such obedience to men throughout one's life defines virtuous womanhood, according to Confucian teachings. Therefore, it may be that *compulsory marriage, compulsory sexual service, compulsory reproduction,* and *compulsory chastity* are more apt than *compulsory heterosexuality* as descriptions of women's fate at the hands of traditional Chinese patriarchy" (2003:92; emphasis in original).

Elaborating on the theme that during this time, "intimacies with women" are ultimately "inconsequential," Sang advances a compelling argument that is relevant far beyond late imperial China and may be a general characteristic across Southeast Asia and Asia as a whole: "What determines a woman's gender conformity or non-conformity is first and foremost her relations with men, *not* her relations with women. Female-female desire does not render a woman defective or make her a gender outcast as long as it cooperates with the imperative of cross-sex marriage. *In sum, female-female desire by itself is not taboo; marriage resistance is*" (ibid., 93; emphases added).

Conclusion

I began this chapter with a discussion of gendered themes in the political cultures of pre- and early modern states, elucidating Tantric and Saivite motifs in numerous domains of society and culture (especially royal palaces) and emphasizing the convergence between key features of Indic culture on the one hand and Austronesian traditions on the other. We saw that throughout the region the well-being of the ruler, symbolized by his or her royal regalia and entourage, promoted the well-being of the polity and the cosmos as a whole, and that such themes existed in conjunction with cosmological emphases on both the harmonizing of contrasting or opposed forces to achieve balance, orderliness, and liberation, and the use of the human body to attain these ends. We also saw that religious traditions throughout the region involved the placation and worship of ancestral beings and local spirits to whom prayers and other offerings were made through ritual specialists who served as intermediaries; that many of these intermediaries engaged the spirits by voyaging to other worlds in the course of shamanistic trance and possession; and that many of them were also involved in transgender practices grounded in cosmological templates that configured the universe "as a polarized entity whose opposed pairs in a generalized system of symbolic equivalences were sky and earth, mountain and sea, ... right and left, sun and moon, male and female, life and death" (Pelras 1996:47).

Transgender practices and the same-sex relations that were commonly associated with them are of interest in their own right. But in the broader scheme of things they bear analytic significance for the light they shed on pluralistic sensibilities regarding gender, sexuality, and various forms of embodied experience: the legitimacy vested in different ways of being in the world. Owing partly to the legitimacy accorded diverse modalities of transgenderism and same-sex practices, and partly to the relative fluidity of gender roles and the relatively high degree of autonomy, social control, and respect enjoyed by women, I have characterized the period with which we have been concerned in this chapter as relatively pluralistic with respect to gender and sexuality. But I also cautioned that this characterization should not be interpreted to mean that the reigning ethos was one of "anything goes." There are many reasons to reject the "anything goes" gloss on gender pluralism in Southeast Asia during the early modern period, three of which merit brief recapitulation. The first has to do with the implicit heterogender matrix compelling the directionality of and otherwise informing marital relations (both earthly and spiritual) along with the sex/gender system in its entirety. This matrix encompassed both the realm of the mystical or occult, insofar as ritual specialists' relations with spirits were often conceptualized in terms of normative/heterogender marriage (and inasmuch as many ancestral spirits and other deities existed in heterogender pairs: brother and sister, husband and wife, grandfather and grandmother, etc.), as well as ritual specialists' unions with their same-bodied earthly counterparts. More generally, this matrix valorized certain forms of same-sex sexuality as long as—but apparently only if—they entailed unions of divergently gendered individuals (who might or might not be anatomically different). A second reason to reject the idea that the early modern period was resolutely laissez-faire with respect to gender and sexuality has to do with the fact that incest prohibitions, in conjunction with conceptualizations of monogamy, polygyny, status endogamy, hypergamy, and adultery, clearly constrained people's choices and experiences (failure to heed these constraints could result in swift—or long drawn-out, torturous—death). A third reason is that, regardless of how they were gendered, female-bodied individuals had fewer options available to them than did their male-bodied counterparts. This was true especially during the second half of the early modern period (roughly the seventeenth and eighteenth centuries) when, as we have seen, various hegemonies (e.g., among Iban, Bugis, and Thais) came to be more strongly contested than was the case during immediately preceding centuries.

In sum, the systems with which we are dealing are clearly not characterized by one or another philosophy of "anything goes." It is more appropriate to view them in terms of systems of "graduated pluralism," a concept I develop based partly on Ong's (1999, 2003) work on "graduated sovereignty." The term "graduated pluralism" draws attention to the differential distribution throughout societies, polities, and diasporic as well as other transnational spaces of certain kinds of sentiments, dispositions, and institutionalized arrangements conducive to or inhibiting pluralism, many of which are keyed to systems of stratified reproduction defined as encompassing systems of power relations that encourage certain groups' nurturance and reproduction while discouraging or precluding those of others (Foucault 1978, S. Cohen 1995).

The following chapter clarifies many of these issues by focusing on various forms of marriage in the first half of the early modern period, especially what has come to be referred to as "temporary marriage." One of my major concerns is to elucidate the transformation of this once positively valorized institution during the second half of the early modern period and to show how it evolved into concubinage and prostitution during that era and subsequently. This was a time characterized by the constriction of pluralistic sensibilities, and we shall see that while many forms of transgenderism and same-sex sexuality continued to exist, they were in many cases both delegitimized and otherwise transformed. The onset of such processes clearly predated the colonial encounter as I have shown, but forces of colonialism definitely exacerbated the trends.

3 Temporary Marriage, Connubial Commerce, and Colonial Body Politics

In Southeast Asia, the second half of the early modern period—roughly the seventeenth and eighteenth centuries—witnessed dramatic transformations in many realms of society and culture that we examined in the previous chapter. These transformations came about due to a number of dialectically related processes involving the intensification of commerce, state building, and territorial consolidation conducive to political systems that were "more absolutist, centralized, and bureaucratic" (Lieberman 2003:16), as well as the heightened centrality, in courtly realms and beyond, of Sunni Islam, Theravada Buddhism, Neo-Confucianism, and Iberian-style Catholicism. The doctrines of these World Religions, described by some as "male oriented, legalistic and hierarchical" (B. Andaya 1994:106) make no scriptural provision for the public ritual centrality of women or the transgendered. The spread and enhanced appeal of broadly encompassing canonical orthodoxies—many of which came to be rationalized in ways that reflected their morally and politically laden encounter with the Protestantism of Western missionaries and colonial elites—helped ensure that in many contexts the previously sacrosanct roles of women and transgendered individuals in public ritual and religion were subject to processes of questioning and, ultimately, to declines in prestige and overall legitimacy, as, indeed, were countless "purely local sources of sanctity" (Lieberman 2003:58, 192, 196, Reid 1993b:149–150, 162, Blackwood 2005).[1] Such processes were especially clear in the Philippines. "The Spaniards always linked the female shaman with Satanism, and explained the identification of the 'male' with the 'feminine' with reference to either a supposed anatomical deficiency or what they labeled 'the abominable sin against nature,' or sodomy" (Brewer 1999:4). They also tailored their policies accordingly: "With the arrival of the Spaniards the privilege and social status that accrued to shaman men from actively identifying with the feminine in animist society was stripped away" (ibid., 16). Also questioned and subject to an erosion of prestige and legitimacy in many areas of Southeast Asia was *linga*-worship and much—but not all—of the sexual license and gender diversity that had long characterized the region, as well as tattoos, amulets, ear boring, and various other bodily practices, such as the use of penis balls (and attendant bells, pins, etc.) and the wearing of long hair by men (Lach 1965:553, n298, Reid 1988:76, 77, 81–3, 150; 1993b:161–4 passim, Lieberman 2003:320, 355 passim).

These trends went hand in hand with a number of other dynamics that proved detrimental to women and gender pluralism alike, even though some of them might be seen as partially offset by colonial-era developments involving the reduced scope and ultimate elimination of many forms of debt bondage and slavery, along with increased pressure on the region's mostly male monarchs to curtail the size of (and improve conditions in) their royal "harems" and encourage laws and customs that would do away with "Oriental excess" in marriage and sexuality in favor of "Western-style" measure and monogamy (Loos 2006). The dynamics to which I refer included: declines in rates of female literacy;[2] the relative exclusion of women from political office; an increase in poverty; and the demise of various forms of craft specialization and petty commodity production that helped women maintain the economic and social autonomy that long struck sojourners from China and the West (Reid 1993b, B. Andaya 1998, 2006). Many of these trends continued in subsequent centuries, much as they did in other parts of the world as diverse as Tonga and the Andes (see Gailey [1987] and Silverblatt [1987], respectively). This was due in no small measure to the pronounced albeit regionally variable socio-cultural impact of colonial rule, Western missionary activity, and increasingly muscular states. These states typically promoted one or another form of capitalism and were undergirded by ideologies of high modernity, which James Scott (1998:4) has characterized in terms of a "self confidence about scientific and technical progress, the expansion of production, ... the mastery of nature ..., and, above all, the rational design of social order commensurate with the scientific understanding of natural laws." There was—and remains—little space in such schemes of institutional and cultural rationalization for the valorization of things local, be they kinship structures, gendered divisions of labor underwriting craft specialization and petty commodity production, regional polities, or locally distinctive ritual practices or forms of esoteric knowledge deemed necessary for the reproduction of kinship, kingship, or the cosmos as a whole. Perhaps more to the point, architects of institutional and cultural rationalization along with the socio-cultural forces that spawn them are notoriously unfriendly to all phenomena deemed to be ambiguous or liminal with respect to gender, sexuality, or most anything else, unless they have folkloric, touristic, or other market value. The same may be said of monotheism (even though the adoption of Christianity is sometimes said to improve the status of women), which is often (and for good reason) taken to be deeply suspicious of ethical pluralism and the kinds of diversity that it logically entails.

These and attendant developments stimulated the growth of religious nationalisms and educational reform, which also constricted the public, especially religious and ritual, spaces accorded women and the transgendered. More generally, just as they worked against the continued reproduction of a good many ritual complexes that involved transgenderism and same-sex relations, so too did they discourage shamanic practices and syncretic ritual complexes (particularly spirit possession and spirit mediumship) as a whole. This is to say that the strong historical bonds throughout Southeast Asia between politically connected ritual specialists on the one hand and transgenderism and sexual variability on the other almost guaranteed that radically changed cultural political contexts would result in attacks on transgendered ritual practitioners and their sexualities that were overdetermined in the most basic senses of the term, and that such attacks would go a long way toward severing the ties linking these practitioners with religious orthodoxy and state power alike.

The dynamics that I have outlined here are the subject of this chapter and the next. This chapter examines pre- and early modern features of kinship, marriage, and exchange that facilitated the expansion of trade networks, commerce, and urban settlement during the early modern period and subsequently, focusing on practices and meanings associated with the temporary marriages arranged between local women and foreign traders from China and the West. These relationships were in many respects relatively egalitarian, or at least symmetrical or mutualistic in the sense that they entailed privileges and a degree of prestige for both parties. This changed, however, due partly to the monetization of economic relationships and the spread of poverty that resulted from the growth of commerce and urban centers, and partly to religious and other transformations. Specifically, these relationships came to be restructured and redefined in ways that proved disadvantageous to temporary wives, who came to be regarded as little other than prostitutes. Colonial-era developments exacerbated the inequities inasmuch as they gave rise to predominantly male immigration, unbalanced sex ratios, deepening poverty, and large-scale prostitution—dynamics that paved the way for the modern-day sex trade, addressed in subsequent chapters.

Colonial-era prostitution involved overwhelmingly heterosexual liaisons (and endemic rates of heterosexually transmitted venereal diseases). But the colonial policies that encouraged and regulated this variant of commerce were driven by fears and anxieties that it was far less objectionable than the most likely alternative: same-sex relations among European men, or, worse, same-sex liaisons between European and local men, who were typically represented in colonial discourse as "androgynous, effeminate, hermaphroditic, impotent, and inverted" (Proschan 2002a:436)—and thus, along with their kith and kin, in dire need of redemptive "civilization." For these and other reasons our discussion of colonial body politics and the transformative impact of Western intrusions into Southeast Asia needs to consider not only heterosexual bodies and bodily engagements, but also same-sex relations—a topic that is well documented historically and ethnographically but is curiously ignored in otherwise sophisticated and influential theoretical work on colonial-era erotics (e.g., Stoler 1995, 2002)—and other, non-sexual dimensions of embodied experience.

Temporary Marriage

Among the more important customs facilitating the growth of trade networks, commerce, urbanism, and attendant phenomena during the early modern era were institutionalized arrangements involving "temporary wives". The latter phrase refers to girls and young women, usually the daughters of elite families, who entered into temporary sexual relationships or more formalized marriages —"be it [for] a few days or months or even years" (B. Andaya 1998:13)—with foreign men from China, Europe, and elsewhere whose pursuit of trade opportunities led them to the shores and capitals of Southeast Asian polities in increasing numbers in the seventeenth and eighteenth centuries. These unions not only helped create the networks of kinship and alliance that were vital to the expansion of commerce and the growth of multiethnic cities throughout the region during this period and subsequently (ibid., 11). They also provided some of the structural precedents for the colonial-era development of concubinage and prostitution, which came to involve large numbers of women in urban areas. The latter phenomena in turn set the stage for the late twentieth-century sex trade, for which certain parts of Southeast Asia (e.g., Bangkok, Manila, Jakarta) have become world renowned. Both for these reasons and because the trajectory "from temporary wife to prostitute" (to borrow from the title of Barbara Andaya's insightful [1998] essay on the subject) provides a valuable optic on transformations in the status of women during this period, the entailments and historical fate of temporary wives deserves careful consideration.

Some of the broader context for understanding the relationships at issue is suggested by Alexander Hamilton's experience in the Malay state of Kedah in 1694. Remarking on local rulers' direct involvement in exchange relations with high status or potentially influential foreigners, Hamilton wrote,

> The King ... never fails of visiting stranger Merchants at their coming to his Port, and then, according to Custom, he must have a present. When the Stranger returns the Visit or, or has any Business with him, he must make him a Present, otherwise he thinks due Respect is not paid to him, and in Return of these Presents his Majesty will honour the Stranger with a Seat near his sacred Person, and will chew a little Betel, and put it out of his royal Mouth on a little gold Saucer, and sends it by his Page to the Stranger, who must take it with all Signs of Humility and Satisfaction and chew it after him.
> (Hamilton 1727 [1930] II:73; cited in Bowrey 1680 [1905]: 273, n2)

Hamilton followed these remarks with the comment that "it is very dangerous to refuse the royal Morsel," the larger point being that Malays, like other Southeast Asians, "have a high sense of personal honour ... [and that] Europeans, particularly sailors, not aware of this sensitiveness, were formerly in the habit of trespassing upon it by practical jokes, but soon found that inexperienced persons playing with edged tools are liable to have their fingers cut" (Newbold 1839 II:185).

One of the earliest references to practices involving temporary marriage comes from Zhou Daguan (aka Chou Ta-Kuan), the Chinese emissary to Cambodia who traveled about the empire of Angkor from 1296 to 1297: "In

Cambodia it is the women who take charge of trade. For this reason a Chinese, arriving in the country, loses no time in getting himself a mate, for he will find her commercial instincts a great asset" (Chou 1297 [1993]:43). More generally, "Chinese sailors coming to the country note with pleasure that it is not necessary to wear clothes, and … [that] rice is easily had, women easily persuaded, houses easily run, furniture easily come by, and trade easily carried on" (ibid., 69). The bad but perhaps not altogether surprising news for those in charge of these men and the ships on which they labored was that, as a consequence, "a great many sailors desert to take up permanent residence" (ibid.).

We do not know as much as we would like about the actual arrangements that were made by or on behalf of the young women who became temporary wives during this period, though Barbara Andaya (1998:13) suggests that the institution could not have been as widespread or as long-lived without the "compliance, cooperation, and active involvement" of the women concerned. This suggestion makes sense in light of the region's long history of female predominance in arranging marriages as well as the prevalence of Southeast Asian women both in—and in control of—retail trade throughout the early modern period and subsequently. The conspicuous presence of women at all levels of commerce and the relative autonomy and social control that such involvement afforded them were in any case among the features of the gendered landscape that consistently struck travelers from China and the West, partly because they were so dissonant with their own experiences of gender, and of "women's place" and female autonomy in particular.

We are fortunate that we have detailed descriptions of many aspects of these relationships as they existed in the late 1600s and early 1700s. Two of these accounts are worth quoting at length. The first, penned by William Dampier in 1697, concerns temporary marriage in Mindanao (southern Philippines).

> The Women are very desirous of the company of Strangers, especially of White Men; and doubtless would be very familiar, if the custom of the Country did not debar them from that freedom which seems coveted by them. Yet from the highest to the lowest they are allowed liberty to converse with, or treat Strangers in the sight of their Husbands.
>
> When Strangers arrive here, the Mindanao Men will come aboard, and invite them to their Houses, and inquire who has a Comrade (which word I believe they have from the Spaniards) or a Pagally, and who has not. A Comrade is a familiar Male-friend; a Pagally is an Innocent Platonick friend of the other Sex. All Strangers are in a manner oblig'd to accept of this Acquaintance and Familiarity, which must be first purchased with a small Present, and afterwards confirmed with some Gift or other to continue the Acquaintance: and as often as the Stranger goes ashore, he is welcome to his Comrade or Pagally's House, where he may be entertained for his Money, to Eat, Drink, or Sleep; and complimented, as often as he comes ashore, with Tobacco and Betel-Nut, which is all the Entertainment he must expect gratis. The richest Men's Wives, are allow'd the freedom to

converse with her Pagally in publick, and she may give or receive presents from him. Even the Sultans and the Generals' Wives, who are always coopt up, will yet look out of their Cages when a Stranger passeth by, and demand of him if he wants a Pagally: and to invite him to their Friendship, will send a Present of Tobacco and Betel-nut to him by their Servants.

(Dampier 1697 [1717/1906] I:335)

They are so free of their Women, that they would bring them aboard and offer them to us; and many of our Men hired them for a small matter. This is a Custom used by Several Nations in the East Indies, as at Pegu, Siam, Cochin-China, and Cambodia, as I have been told. It is used at Tunquin also to my knowledge; for I did afterwards make a Voyage thither, and most of our Men had Women aboard all the time of our abode there ... . It is accounted a piece of Policy to do it; for the chief Factors and Captains of Ships have the great Men's Daughters offered them, the Mandarins or Noblemens at Tunquin ... . And by this sort of Alliance the Country people are engaged to a greater Friendship: And if there should arise any difference about Trade, or any thing else, which might provoke the Natives to seek some treacherous Revenge (to which all these Heathen Nations are very prone), then these Dalilahs would certainly declare it to their White Friends, and so hinder their Country-mens Designs.

(Ibid., 393)

Alexander Hamilton's roughly contemporaneous (1727) account of practices associated with temporary marriage in Burma sheds light on aspects of this complex that are not addressed in Dampier's remarks; equally important is that Hamilton's comments indicate the extensive similarities in the institution throughout Southeast Asia.

The Women are very courteous and kind to Strangers, and are very fond of marrying with *Europeans*, and most Part of the Strangers who trade thither, marry a Wife for the Term they stay. The Ceremony is (after the Parties are agreed) for the Bride's Parents or nearest Friends or Relations, to make a Feast, and invite her Friends and the Bridegroom's, and at the End of the Feast the Parent or Bride-man, asketh them both before the Company, if they are content to cohabit together as Man and Wife, and both declaring their Consent they are declared by the Parent or Friend to be lawfully married, and if the Bridegroom has an House, he carries her thither, but if not, they have a Bed provided in the House where they are married, and are left to their own Discretion how to pass away the Night.

They prove obedient and obliging Wives, and take the Management of Affairs within Doors wholly in their own hands. She goes to Market for Food, and acts the Cook in dressing his Victuals, takes Care of his Clothes, in washing and mending them; if their Husbands have any Goods to sell, they set up a Shop and sell them by Retail, to a much better Account than they could be sold for by Wholesale, and some of them carry a Cargo of Goods to the inland Towns, and barter for Goods proper for the foreign Markets that their Husbands are bound to, and generally bring fair Accounts of their Negotiations. If she proves false to her Husband's Bed, and on fair Proof convicted, her Husband may carry her to the *Rounday*, and have her Hair cut, and sold for a Slave, and he may have the Money; but if the Husband goes astray, she'll be apt to give him a gentle Dose, to send him into the other World a Sacrifice to her Resentment.

If she proves Prolifick, the Children cannot be carried out of the Kingdom without the King's permission, but that may be purchased for 40 or 50 *L. Sterl.* and if an irreconcilable Quarrel happen where there are Children, the Father is obliged to take Care of the Boys, and the Mother of the Girls. If a Husband is content to continue the Marriage, whilst he goes to foreign Countries about his Affairs, he must leave some Fund to pay her about six Shillings eight Pence *per* Month, otherwise at the Year's End she may marry again, but if that sum is paid on his Account, she is obliged to stay the Term of three Years, and she is never the worse, but rather the better lookt on, that she has been married to several *European* Husbands.

(Hamilton 1727 [1930]:28; emphases in original)

Hamilton's remarks, along with those of Dampier and Zhou Daguan cited earlier, make clear that foreign traders and their backers were motivated to enter such unions for a variety of reasons. They sought access to local trade and those who were centrally involved in it. They needed the services of cultural intermediaries (or brokers) both for purposes of trade and so as to better enable them to understand and negotiate with political and other elites who established the ground rules for their residence in, travels about, and overall comportment in local polities generally and in urban areas and royal palaces especially. And since they usually traveled to Southeast Asia without their wives or other females, they, or at least the majority who were primarily or exclusively heterosexually oriented, were desirous of female companionship and female sexual partners.

Local women and their networks of kin, for their part, were motivated to enter such relationships for a variety of reasons as well, though some of their reasons differed from those just outlined for Chinese and European men. Perhaps most obviously, they sought to enhance their positions in trade through access to the commercial goods and outlets that the Chinese and European men offered them. At the same time, they were eager to ally themselves with foreigners whose wealth and origins in distant countries endowed them with high status and a reputation for sexual potency, for as A.M. Hocart (1927), Marshall Sahlins (1981), Barbara Andaya (1998), and others (e.g., Gibson 2005) have noted, throughout Austronesia and Southeast Asia, "things"—especially men—"from outside" were commonly invested with *mana* or *mana*-like power.

The institution of temporary marriage that I have outlined here is of interest not only because of the ways it facilitated the development of trade networks, commerce, and urban growth during the early modern period and subsequently. It bears additional significance in light of the pluralistic ethos informing certain aspects of the institution. An institution such as this may seem an unlikely site of pluralism, predicated as it was on exchange relations involving transactions in rights over female sexuality which in subsequent centuries provided a key structural precedent for the development of a highly exploitive industry of prostitution focusing on the traffic in Southeast Asian (as well as Japanese and Chinese) women. There is nonetheless evidence that an ethos of pluralism suffused some domains of the institution of temporary marriage insofar as Burmese and other Southeast Asian women were permitted, indeed encouraged, to enjoy what British envoy Lieutenant-Colonel Michael Symes famously referred to as the "comforts of connubial commerce" with, as he put it, men "of whatever climate or complexion" (Symes 1827 I:91). Since some readers may see opportunism rather (or more) than pluralism in the embracing as temporary husbands men "of whatever climate or complexion," I should perhaps emphasize that pluralistic sensibilities were also evident in the domestic policies of many of Southeast Asia's early modern states, which allowed "every sect freely to exercise its religious rites" (ibid.), the larger point being the relatively pronounced degree of legitimacy accorded to individuals and groups embodying ethnic and religious diversity (as we would now term it). In his *Account of an Embassy to the Kingdom of Ava* (1827), which was based on his travels in the region during the final years of the eighteenth century, Symes makes clear that sentiments we might describe as pluralistic informed state policies bearing on all of these seemingly disparate domains (i.e., temporary marriage, which by Symes' time had given way to prostitution, as well as ethnicity and religion). In good social scientific fashion, Symes prefaces his remarks with comments to the effect that pluralism is always relative; this by noting that the situation in Southeast Asia differed from that of China and India:

> It is well known, that even the public prostitutes of China are strictly prohibited from having intercourse with any other than a Chinese; nor is any foreign woman permitted to enter the territories, or visit the parts of that jealous nation. The Hindoo women of rank are no less inaccessible; and admission into a respectable cast is not attainable by money.
>
> To such narrow prejudices the Birmans are superior. With a Lacedemonian liberality, they deny not the comforts of connubial commerce to men of whatever climate or complexion. They are sensible, that the strength of an empire consists in its population, and that a prince is great and powerful, more from the number of his subjects, than from the extent of his territory. Hence the politic indulgence that the Birman government grants to every sect freely to exercise its religious rites. They tolerate alike the Pagan and the Jew, the Mussulman or Christian, the disciples of Confucius, or the worshipers of Fire; the children of whom, born

of a Birman woman, equally become subjects of the state, and are entitled to the same protection and privileges, as if they had spring from a line of Birman ancestry.

(Symes 1827 I:90–91; cf. Finlayson 1826 [1988]:310, 384)

To more adequately convey some of the flavor of ethnic and religious plural-ism in Burma, Symes provides readers a description of the city of Rangoon. Said to have about 5,000 registered taxable houses at the time of Symes' travels, thus around 30,000 residents, it was a city

crowded with foreigners … who find from the Birmans a friendly reception, … a motley assemblage of merchants, such as few towns of much greater magnitude can produce: Malabars, Moguls, Persians, Parsees, Armenians, Portuguese, French and English, all mingle here, and are engaged in vari-ous branches of commerce. The members of this discordant multitude are not only permitted to reside under the protection of government, but like-wise enjoy the most liberal toleration in matters of religion. They celebrate their several rites and festivals, totally disregarded by the Birmans, who have no inclination to make proselytes. In the same street may be heard the solemn voice of the Muezzin, calling pious Islamites to early prayers, and the bell of the Portuguese chapel tinkling a summons to Romish Christians. Processions meet and pass each other, without giving or receiv-ing cause of offence. The Birmans never trouble themselves about the reli-gious opinions of any sect, nor disturb their ritual ceremonies, provided they do not break the peace, or meddle with their own divinity Gaudma; but if any person commit any outrage, which the Musselman in their zeal for the true faith, will sometimes do, the offender is sure to be put into the stocks; and if that does not calm his turbulent enthusiasm, they bastinado him into tranquility.

(Symes 1827 I:251)

Symes was correct in his assessment that especially in Southeast Asia a ruler's control over his or her subjects exceeded in importance the ruler's dominion over territory per se. However, he erred in assuming that the religious tolerance at issue was merely a "politic indulgence" driven by demographic imperatives— in this case, relatively low population densities and relatively plentiful resources such as land that allowed subjects the option of flight and resettle-ment elsewhere if they felt oppressed by the sovereign. Such a reductionist explanation cannot account for the scope and force of pluralistic sensibilities at all levels of society, from royal courts to urban thoroughfares, back alleys, and the domestic spaces adjoining them in town and village alike. Nor do such per-spectives help us to understand why variations on the themes described by Symes are alive and well in many parts of contemporary Southeast Asia, including late twentieth-century Java (Beatty 2002), one of the most densely populated regions on earth.

The relatively pluralistic sentiments and dispositions conducive to this climate of "live and let live" have been well documented for the thriving entrepôt
of Melaka during the fifteenth, sixteenth and seventeenth centuries (Sandhu
and Wheatley 1983; cf. Hefner 2000:29–31). Indeed, they seem to have been
characteristic of much of Southeast Asia during the early modern era (Reid 1988,
1993b). They were nonetheless notably absent or greatly constricted under conditions of warfare and civil strife, and during "scripturalist peaks" such as those
that occurred in Aceh and Sulawesi during parts of the seventeenth century, for
example (Reid 1993b, Pelras 1996), some of which saw calls for an end to female
secession to political office on the grounds that Islamic doctrine depicts women
as intellectually, spiritually, and morally inferior to men. Periods of "religious
(and political) fervor" such as these underscore that the prevailing hegemonies
were at times strongly contested if not sharply redefined, and (if less directly) that
cultural-political contestation and flux of one sort or another were most likely
the usual state of affairs. One clear example from the Buddhist heartlands of
mainland Southeast Asia is the 1782 law promulgated by the newly ascendant
king and founder of Siam's Chakri dynasty, Phra Phutthayotfa (Rama I;
r. 1782–1809), mandating "that all the phallic representations of the god Shiva
should be gathered together and burned (ignoring the fact that many were of
stone)" (Wyatt 2002:52). According to Wyatt, Rama I passed laws such as these

> in order that the people of Siam should follow what he considered the
> "true" Way of Buddhism. This was necessary in order that a revived Siam
> might avoid the calamities that had beset the kingdom of Ayutthaya a gen-
> eration earlier [April 1767], when Siam had been attacked and utterly
> sacked by armies from Burma, … and to avoid the ridicule of foreign [espe-
> cially Western] visitors.
>
> (Ibid., 52)

In some areas of Vietnam, Burma, and the Malay Peninsula, developments
along these general lines entailed critiques of transgendered ritualists, whose
practices were said to be offensive to religion and nature alike (Drewes
1976:279–280, B. Andaya 2006:84, 89). Whether they also did so in Siam
remains unclear (for reasons addressed in Chapter 2), though it is highly likely.
The more encompassing dynamic to bear in mind concerns the ways in which
Southeast Asian political and religious elites endeavored to rationalize
Buddhism, Islam, and other religions in the course of their morally and politically laden encounter with Western Christianity and Protestantism in particular, and how these rationalizing endeavors sought (and in some instances
clearly entailed) reformulations of Southeast Asian religions in ways that would
render them more compatible with both the puritanical ethos and the sex/gen-
der binaries and hierarchies associated with the Christian, especially
Protestant, traditions of Western colonial powers.

Despite challenges such as these (and others discussed in due course), sentiments and dispositions bearing on gender and sexuality remained relatively

pluralistic throughout most of the period discussed in this chapter, and well into the twentieth century. This is partly because the scope and force of these sentiments and dispositions were variably informed by (but not limited to) sexual and gendered symbols, idioms, and metaphors in domains of myth, ritual, and cosmology; by "long-standing modes of 'globalization' in which substantial areas of Southeast Asia have been engaged since at least the first century CE" (E. Thompson 2006:332); and by a nexus of domestic and social structural variables of the general sort identified by Beatty (2002) for late twentieth-century Java, which are especially important since pluralism obviously begins at home. The latter variables include: widespread fosterage and adoption; high rates of separation and divorce; terminological usages involving teknonymy, birth-order names, and classificatory terms of reference and address; and a host of other practices that engender relationality, temporal flux, and reversal, and otherwise encourage conceptual and moral relativism. Far from being confined to modern Java or the more encompassing Malay-Indonesian archipelago, many of these variables have been a feature of the broader Austronesian region for at least two millennia, if not longer, and are also found in non-Austronesian areas of Southeast Asia such as Burma and Siam/Thailand (see, for example, Bowring 1856 [1969] I:183–184, Mi Mi Khaing 1984:10). Hindu-Buddhist emphases on rebirth, transcendence, transformation, and multiplicity are clearly relevant as well. So too are animist and other religious traditions that valorize similar (or analogous) themes, shaping social actors' embodied experiences of—and conceptual models "of" and "for"—self, other, similitude, commonality, and difference beginning at a very early age, and toning them up and otherwise bolstering and reinforcing them throughout the life course.

Also directly relevant to the theme "pluralism begins at home" were the gendered symbolics of architectural designs and ritual practices (involving the proper disposal of the afterbirth, for example) long associated with residential spaces throughout Southeast Asia. Specifically, houses (like boats and other built objects) included clearly marked masculine and feminine elements and more encompassing spatial domains—and were thus (if only implicitly) dual-gendered or androgynous; and proper proportionality and relations among these elements and more encompassing domains were necessary if the current or former inhabitants of a house were to enjoy the protection (or at least not attract the wrath) of deceased ancestors and local spirits and otherwise lead (spiritually and morally) balanced and sustaining lives (Waterson 1990, Carsten and Hugh-Jones 1995, Peletz 1996, Gibson 2005).We know from cross-cultural research that the mere existence of such gendered spaces and practices could conceivably give rise to or intensify gender antagonism and female subordination of the sort characteristic of Highland New Guinea and Amazonian societies—well known in former times for exclusivistic men's houses (whose "cult secrets" were kept from women partly via well-advertised threats of gang rape and the like) as well as menstrual huts and other feminized spaces that men approached at considerable risk to their masculinity and in some instances their very lives (Gregor 1985, Herdt 1993c). But these macho and misogynistic dynamics were largely absent from Southeast Asian societies of the early modern period, which tended to be characterized instead by one or another gender(ed) ethos emphasizing complementary and relative equality between males and females, and by the idea that houses, like persons, were composed of male and female elements (e.g., "reason" and "passion," respectively, in the case of humans) both of which needed to be present "to give power and effect" (Reid 1988:146). In sum, being born into and raised in dual-gendered or androgynous houses, and being brought up in social and cultural milieus in which one important (gendered) Other was always already present within oneself, provided important templates for the development of a habitus conducive to the florescence of pluralistic sentiments and dispositions bearing on gender, sexuality, and the body (Bourdieu 1977).

From Temporary Wives to Concubines and Prostitutes

In the latter part of the early modern period, the relative mutualism characteristic of the relationships entailed in temporary marriage gave way to arrangements that were far less beneficial to women inasmuch as they came to include one or more features of concubinage or prostitution and were ultimately redefined in terms of these latter institutions. At least three sets of dynamics contributed to these changes. The first dynamic, noted earlier and discussed in more detail in due course, involved the spread and more extensive incorporation, into courtly realms and daily life beyond the palace, of key features of World Religions (especially Islam, Buddhism, and Christianity), all of which placed great emphasis both on male control of female sexuality and on women's virginity at marriage. The canonical orthodoxies of these religions, along with the political and religious elites centrally involved in their dissemination throughout courtly realms and beyond, stigmatized women who enjoyed one or another degree of sexual autonomy, especially if such women entered into one or more temporary relationships with foreigners and later sought to marry men belonging to the circles of native elite. These stigmas effectively discouraged elite women from involvement in temporary unions not only because elite men and women were the most likely to internalize and advocate key features of "new" religious ideologies, but also because elites were more concerned than commoners with, or at least had a more narrow definition of, unions defined as appropriate in mutually constitutive terms of morality and status.

The developments outlined here did not have the same effect on those outside the circles of the elite. One result was that by the early eighteenth century, temporary wives were drawn more or less entirely from the ranks of commoners (B. Andaya 1998:16). As Symes observed during the latter part of the eighteenth century, "The lower class of Birmans make no scruple of selling their daughters, and even their wives, to foreigners who come to pass a temporary residence amongst them" (Symes 1827 I:253); lest there be any confusion as to which segments of the Burmese population were involved in such practices, he added that "the custom of selling their women to strangers ... is *confined to the lowest classes of society*" (ibid. II:68; emphasis added). Of particular interest here is not only the status divide at issue but also the fact that the transactions adverted to are now characterized in terms of "sale" rather than "exchange." *Inter alia*, the sexual futures of commoner women diverged increasingly from those of elite women. Changes such as these had critically important implications for relations between elites and commoners as well as relations between locals ("natives") and outsiders (especially Europeans).

A second dynamic that undermined the institution of temporary marriage and contributed to its recasting as prostitution was the increasing monetization of economic relationships characteristic of much of the early modern period, which resulted in the growing indebtedness of rural and urban populations alike (B. Andaya 1998:24; Reid 1993b: Chap. 5). The problem was by no means confined to Southeast Asia, as suggested by Thomas Bowrey's accounts of his travels in "countries round the Bay of Bengal" during the period 1669–1679. Bowrey reports that by this time the monetization of rural economic relations had led to much prostitution throughout Asia:

> Moneys is nowadays soe much coveted, that by many people it is not much prick of conscience how it is acquired, and hath soe corrupted good laws that most Governours in Asia (for theire owne interest's sake) doe allow that any woman (Moore, Gentue, or Ouria) unmarried may lawfully turne common Whore, and leave her relations, and take her habitation among Other Whores in Small Villages Separated from any married folkes houses, paying soe much per mensem to the Governour of that part of the Countrie, and Every thursday night repaire to the Governours and Cattwalls, i.e. the Justice of Peace his house, before whom they doe and must dance and Singe, and make many Salams. Then the handsomest of them must Stay all night to Suppresse the Leachery of him and his Punes.
> (Bowrey 1680 [1905]:206–207)

In the Southeast Asian context (as elsewhere), these dynamics, along with the heightened demand for local women that resulted from the massive influx of foreign men who were single or unaccompanied by their wives, entailed a monetization and subsequent commodification of relationships involving sex; these processes were highly detrimental to women, as discussed in more detail below.

The third dynamic that undermined and otherwise transformed temporary marriage involved European and Chinese efforts to emulate indigenous elites, whose assertions of status and prestige presupposed conspicuous displays of attendants, courtiers, and other retainers that included large numbers of female domestics and slaves (B. Andaya 1998:17). The increasingly burdensome expense of maintaining the females at issue encouraged their owners to devise means through which they could help cover some of the costs associated with their upkeep. One solution that was soon seized upon, due partly perhaps to its capacity to generate immediate payment, was the sale of their sexual services. As Barbara Andaya notes, while "slave women could ... contribute to the household income by spinning and weaving, and by hawking such items as food or cloth in the streets or markets," the "sale of sex was quickly seen as another means by which [female] slaves could help maintain a household critical to the status of the master and his wives or favored consorts" (ibid.). Chinese and other foreign men thus found it advantageous in terms of status considerations, as well as expedient both economically and in light of the emotional labor and social obligations at stake, to forgo relationships of the temporary marriage variety in favor of relationships that were more narrowly and more instrumentally defined. The latter relationships typically involved one or another variant of concubinage or prostitution, both of which flourished in the context of European colonialism, indeed, as a direct result of colonial policies, even though they originated in earlier centuries.

European and other foreign perceptions of the essential(ized) features of local "character" (variably defined in ethnic, racial, or national terms) as sub-human or at least given to "barbarous custom" helped justify further monetization of the economy through colonial adventures and missionary enterprise. I quote Symes on Burma again, here at length, both to help convey some of these points and because toward the end of his remarks we see some of the increased emphasis on women's reproductive capacities that occurred during this period and subsequently. "In their treatment of the softer sex the Birmans are destitute both of delicacy and humanity, considering women as little superior to the brute stock of their farms. *The lower class* of Birmans make no scruple of *selling* their daughters, and even their wives, to foreigners who come to pass a temporary residence amongst them. It reflects no disgrace on any of the parties, and the woman is not dishonoured by the connexion" (Symes 1827 I:253; emphasis added).

> The custom of selling their women to strangers ... is perhaps oftener the consequence of heavy pecuniary embarrassment, than an act of inclination. It is not, however, considered as shameful, nor is the female dishonoured. Partly, perhaps from this cause, and partly from their habits of education, women surrender themselves the victims of this barbarous custom with apparent resignation. It is also said, that they are seldom unfaithful to their foreign masters; indeed, they are often essentially useful, particularly to those who trade, by keeping their accounts and transacting their business.
>
> But when a man departs from the country, he is not suffered to carry his temporary wife along with him. On that point the law is exceedingly rigorous. Every ship, before she receives her clearance, is diligently searched by the officers of the custom-house. Even if their vigilance were to be eluded, the woman would be quickly missed, and it would soon be discovered in what vessel she had gone; nor could that ship ever return to a Birman port but under penalty of confiscation of the property, and the infliction of a heavy fine and imprisonment on the master. Female children also, born of a Birman mother, are not suffered to be taken away. Men are permitted to

emigrate, but they ["Birmans"] think that the expatriation of women would impoverish the state, by diminishing the sources of its population.

(Symes 1827 II:68–69)

Observations such as these suggest, among other shifts, a revalorization of— if not an increased emphasis on—female sexuality and reproductive capacity in constructions of female kinship roles (wife, daughter, sister, etc.) and in conceptualizations of femininity as a whole. Cross-cultural research bearing on Polynesian and other societies indicates that developments along these lines commonly have negative implications for constructions of femininity and the prestige of women insofar as they highlight the ways that females and their bodies and bodily processes diverge from males and male embodiment, which typically, and in the scenarios outlined here, increasingly constitute the implicit standards for assessments of humanity and cultural value (Ortner 1996, Ortner and Whitehead 1981, Gailey 1987, Peletz 1996). In short, heightened concerns with "manpower," which is always already of strategic importance in state contexts, often translate into pro-natalist cultural imperatives that reduce female life options and are otherwise detrimental to constructions of femininity and the overall standing of women alike. This seems to have been the case in many parts of Southeast Asia during the second half of the early modern period.

The more encompassing dynamic at issue here—the constriction of pluralism—was by no means confined to cultural assessments of contrasts with respect to gender and sexuality. Similar constrictions are evident in sentiments and dispositions bearing on ethnic and racial variation as well as dissimilar religious orientation. Such was the case at various points in the second half of the modern period due in no small measure to regional and transnational dynamics associated with shifting patterns of maritime commerce involving networks of goods and traders from the Middle East as well as South Asia, China, and Europe. Shifting trade patterns along with other dynamics mentioned earlier (the greater centrality in courtly realms and beyond of World Religions; the monetization of economic relationships; the growing indebtedness of rural and urban populations alike; and the intrusion into the area of increasing numbers of Chinese, European, and other foreigners) entailed the creation of new loci of power and prestige, thus undercutting political leaders' abilities to command the labor services and other tribute and respect to which they were accustomed. These developments gave rise to policies that saw local states becoming, on the one hand, more centralized, bureaucratic, and autocratic, and, on the other, less involved in trade and the promotion of urban commerce and urban expansion in particular. The latter trends are noteworthy in that they halted and reversed growth in urban areas and occurred at a time when Europeans were gearing up for increased involvement in the region's economic and political affairs. Anthony Reid (1993b:264) puts his finger on the central dynamics of concern to us—why the constriction of pluralism occurred and why some elites promoted policies with this outcome or at least saw it as a positive development—when he notes that during the second half of the early modern period and, we might add, the ensuing colonial (and postcolonial) era, "institutions of pluralism … inhibited progress toward the bureaucratic institutionalization of state authority."

Colonial Body Politics and the Constriction of Pluralism

The permanent settlement of Europeans in Southeast Asia for the purpose of gaining control of the spice trade and obtaining other economic benefits along with glory for Crown and God began with the Portuguese conquest of the port-city of Melaka in 1511 and continued with Magellan's 1521 arrival on the island of Samar and the subsequent establishment of Spanish outposts in the Philippines. The Dutch planted their flag in communities in coastal Java and other parts of the Indonesian archipelago beginning in the early seventeenth century (and in 1641 succeeded in wresting control of Melaka from the Portuguese), just as the British were to do later both in Penang (1786), Singapore (1819), and Melaka (which they obtained from the Dutch in 1824), and throughout the Malay Peninsula, most of Borneo, and Burma (chiefly in the second half of the nineteenth century). The French subjugation of territories comprising present-day Vietnam, Cambodia, and Laos was roughly contemporaneous, occurring primarily during the period 1859–1893, as were some of the early European and American concessions forced upon Siam, which was never formally colonized but experienced nonetheless some of the same erosions of sovereignty and other imperial intrusions as its neighbors. Textbooks sometimes give the impression that colonial rule in Southeast Asia, which was largely a European project (even though Americans won control of the Philippines from Spain in 1898 and maintained a formal colonial presence there through 1946), extended over a period of some five hundred years, or refer, for example, to "three and a half centuries" of Dutch colonialism in Indonesia. Impressions and statements such as these are highly misleading inasmuch as they exaggerate the impact of the European colonial presence, which through the late eighteenth century tended to be felt mainly in coastal areas and only some of them at that. The high period of colonialism in any case was 1870–1930. The ensuing discussion focuses largely (but not exclusively) on this latter period and the half-century or so preceding it, paying particular attention to three interrelated themes: the colonial-era development of institutions of concubinage and prostitution; the ways that some women resisted these institutions (and/or conventional heterosexual marriage) through participation in same-sex relations; and why it is essential that our accounts of transformations in gender, sexuality, and pluralism during the colonial period not only engage heteronormativity but also make full provision for diverse modalities of same-sex erotics and transgender practices alike.

Concubinage, Prostitution, and "Sworn Sisterhood"

Our understanding of the dynamics involved in the development of concubinage and prostitution in different localities of Southeast Asia is highly uneven but we have a fairly clear sense of how they played out in certain areas.[3] Regions that are well documented include the Netherlands Indies (also known as the Netherlands East Indies, the Dutch Indies, and the Indies), now Indonesia (thanks to Hanneke Ming's pioneering [1983] study and the incisive work of Ann Stoler [1995, 2002]); and the British colonies of Singapore, Malaya, and Burma (owing to James Warren's important [1993] research on prostitution in Singapore and work by Ballhatchet [1980], Hyam [1990], Manderson [1996], and others on Malaya and Burma). Ming's mostly empirical analysis of archival sources and other Dutch colonial records illustrates how discourses of gender, sexuality, race, class, and nation informed Dutch attitudes and policies in the Netherlands Indies, particularly interactions between Dutch men and local women both during the period that is the main focus of the study (1887–1920) and in the half century or so leading up to it. Unlike Stoler's more theoretically oriented discussion of colonial-era sexuality in the Indies, which, curiously, focuses entirely on heterosexuality, Ming makes clear from the outset that Dutch officials' fears and anxieties concerning same-sex relations both among Dutch men and between Dutch men and native men are of considerable analytic significance. There are at least two reasons for this. First, they gave rise to many of the policies that helped ensure a steady supply of Asian women to European men and Chinese laborers; and second, in doing so, they contributed directly to epidemics of venereal disease that for many Asian women entailed a decidedly early and painful death. Dealing substantively with European fears and anxieties—as well as involvement in—same-sex relations is thus essential. For additional reasons discussed later in this chapter, failure to do so gives rise to many conceptual and analytic problems, including the erroneous impression that the only kinds of sexuality that entered into imperial discourses of gender, class, race, and nation were those that fit comfortably within a heterosexual matrix of connection and desire.

The architects of Dutch colonial policy along with the officers charged with implementing such policy tended to view the men who made up the bulk of the Dutch forces in the Indies as "the dregs of society, as social irredeemables of low birth and trifling value, fit only to serve as cannon fodder" (Ming 1983:66). It was also widely assumed that like their British counterparts in India, these men "lack[ed] the intellectual and moral resources required for continence" (Ballhatchet 1980:2) and therefore needed "solace," lest they protest their living conditions and desert their posts—or worse, engage in "unnatural behavior," which, as elsewhere, was "despised as unmanly, and ... dreaded as a threat to military discipline" (ibid., 10). Equally widespread was the view, often hedged with one or another degree of moral ambivalence, that the main source for such solace was "drink and concubinage" (Ming 1983:67).

Dutch officials' ambivalent acceptance of concubinage involving soldiers from the Netherlands and local women derived partly from a sense that the expenses involved in maintaining European women and the children that might be born to them and their husbands would siphon money from Dutch coffers that might be better spent elsewhere. Some Dutch officials were also both aware and enamored of the traditions of temporary marriage that provided a structural precedent for colonial-era concubinage. Closer to home in a temporal sense were customary arrangements that involved the employment of "native auxiliaries" who traveled with European troops accompanied by their wives and children. "The European took over this custom, and, and although not every European lived with a native woman, at least by 1836 his right to do so was acknowledged" (ibid.).

The other relevant factor motivating Dutch acceptance of concubinage had to do with the previously mentioned fears and anxieties among colonial officialdom and civic and religious leaders in Holland that soldiers deprived of sexual "outlets" with members of the "fair sex" would necessarily resort to sexual relations with one another or, worse, would succumb to sexual temptations involving native men. This occurred in at least one barracks in Gombong. As noted in a postscript to an 1893 report, "Several years ago, it transpired that *far more than half* of the young men quartered there were guilty of practicing unnatural vice," which in this context clearly refers to same-sex sexuality (ibid., 69; cf. 81; emphasis in original). More generally, when concubinage came under attack on moral and specifically religious grounds, both the Army High Command and Roman Catholic authorities condoned and defended it because it prevented more heinous sins in the form of homosexual activity (ibid., 83; cf. Manderson 1996:166–167). Some officials who defended the institution offered concrete examples of its clear benefits, in the form of cautionary tales such as those involving the Gombong Barracks cited earlier. Another remarked, "It has to be noted that an NCO [Non-Commissioned Officer] who previously lived in concubinage, and was then transferred to a garrison where he had no chance of contacts with local women, was *caught in the act of pederasty*. I would not be prepared to wager that this is an isolated case" (Ming 1983:85).[4]

The institution of concubinage was in any case exceedingly widespread. In the Indies in the early to mid-nineteenth century, according to Retired Lt. Col. de Rochemont, "Not only the soldiers in the barracks, but also most of the generals, field and other officers, governors of territories, residents, senior and other officials, have a *nyai* [in this context, a concubine][5] if they are not married" (cited in ibid., 69). Even in the final quarter of the nineteenth century, by which time attitudes had begun to change due to the successful lobbying efforts of increasingly numerous and vociferous missionaries, fully "half the European men in the Netherlands Indies were still living with concubines. *A decline in this number is only perceptible after 1890, and it occurred along with an increase in prostitution*" (ibid., 70; emphasis added).

The entailments of plantation and barracks concubinage for the women involved were exceedingly grim. According to some observers, the barracks in Batavia were "virtually indistinguishable from brothels," constituting "an outrage, an immorality of indescribable horror and bestiality, nay it goes far below the animal level" (ibid., 79). Some men "enjoyed … animal rather than … human relationship[s] with [their concubines];" others, according to reports at the time, "regard the concubine simply as part of the household furniture, no less than spoon and clock, knife and cooking range, sustaining the master's health and happiness" (ibid., 82, 89). In most cases, *nyai* had no legal rights and were heavily stigmatized by members of their natal communities. As one General Boetje put it in a letter to the Governor-General: a native woman who has "followed a European soldier" has

> sunk very low in the eyes of her fellow-countrymen. If such a woman is expelled from the barracks, owning nothing, and usually in no position to work to support her children, it ... [is] very doubtful that there will be a place for her or her children in the kampong, that is, in native society. None of the men will be eager to take her as his mate, and in most cases it can be predicted that, in dire need, she will be forced to turn to prostitution for her livelihood.
>
> (Ibid., 72)

Concerns with the welfare of these women were, at best, of marginal relevance to the Dutch officials and clergy who sought to reform or restrict barracks concubinage, or to eliminate it altogether. The issues, rather, were the "undue" influence on Dutch men of native women, "the embodiment of every kind of dark and sinister force" (ibid., 82), and the implications, for the maintenance of the class and racial hierarchies that were so important to the Dutch, of the existence of "half-caste" offspring born of these unions (Stoler 1995, 2002). One critic of the institution spoke to the first of these concerns in remarks made around 1905: "Whatever the abominable means employed— whether they mingle their spittle or blood or some other filth in his food; or whether they know how to invoke and use secret powers unknown to us to make him a supine tool in their hands—they dominate him completely, still more fatally than the hypnotist dominates his subjects" (Ming 1983:82). For these and other reasons, some critics proposed that Dutch men living with concubines should be housed among the natives, thus discouraging other Europeans from following suit. Others, who saw "disguised prostitution" in these relationships made clear that Dutch soldiers' involvement in concubinage would have deleterious effects on their careers (ibid., 82, 83).

By most accounts, the emergence and growth of "mixed race" populations in the late nineteenth and early twentieth centuries served to catalyze moral and other opposition to barracks concubinage and to shift the weight of public and official opinion from broad approval (tinged with ambivalence) to disapproval. Lacking recognition in the Netherlands and thus falling outside the purview of welfare policies there and simultaneously stigmatized by local populations in the Indies, this pauperized community threatened racial hierarchies, particularly the racial superiority claimed by Europeans. This resulted ultimately in the abolition of concubinage in the early decades of the twentieth century, and, with its abolition, a rise in prostitution.

The dynamics sketched out here bear on the previous "flexibility" of European ideas regarding extra-marital sexual intercourse: whereas in earlier times a European man living with a concubine "would not conceal his situation," "by the end of the last [nineteenth] century this era had passed" (ibid., 92). In these trends we see a clear constriction of sensibilities concerning what was right and proper for overseas Dutch and other Europeans in the bedrooms, the barracks, and beyond. Although we lack conclusive evidence that the same, relatively brief period (the last few decades of the nineteenth century and the first few decades of the twentieth) witnessed a comparable transformation of sexual mores on the part of local elites, such a constriction seems almost certain in light of the Western education and religious instruction made available to local elites and the related fact that the prestige hierarchies of Dutch and native elites were closely intertwined and, in important ways, mutually constituting. It is telling in any event that by the late nineteenth century, "marriages [between Dutch men and] …the daughters of the Javanese aristocracy practically *never* occurred;" that "the native [here "the native in general," not just the native elite] was averse to permitting his daughter to have *any* social intercourse with a European, at least if the latter fulfilled a military function;" and that, "evidently there was no real change in this attitude thereafter," partly because by this time "Indonesian nationalism had already taken root" (ibid., 88, 89; emphases added). These observations, along with the fact that "well-do-do Javanese … looked down on the concubine" and that such marriages as did occur between Javanese and Dutch involved "Javanese girls form the *popular* classes" (ibid., 88; emphasis added), point to a situation that was a far cry from that of earlier centuries, when Southeast Asian women's involvement with foreign men as temporary wives brought neither shame nor dishonor, but, rather, potentially considerable wealth and prestige.

These changes bespeak a dramatic transformation of women's relations with foreigners and a constriction of pluralistic sensibilities and dispositions bearing on women and their comportment. The transformations concerned both the content of these relationships and local views bearing on their intrinsic good or lack thereof insofar as women involved with foreigners were no longer seen as linked to sources of *mana*-like sacred power but as contaminating and polluting. More generally, owing partly to the class-inflected disdain with which local elites viewed concubines and prostitutes, particularly if they gave birth to "half-castes," and partly to elite concerns to distance themselves from women of ill-repute in their ranks, these dynamics appear to have encouraged pre-marital chastity and fidelity in marriage, at least or especially for women, who thus experienced (*inter alia*) a constriction of pluralism. It was certainly no longer true in any event that males and females alike "were given to love" and that pre-marital chastity was not expected of either party to a marriage. For reasons such as these Ronald Hyam's (1990) study of empire and sexuality in British colonies in Asia, Africa, and the Pacific concludes with a summary discussion of British officers' and civilians' sexual involvements with women belonging to the colonized populations, emphasizing that while such relationships were often exploitative, there was a more pernicious legacy of the colonial experience in the realms of gender and sexuality. To wit, the introduction and subsequent institutionalization throughout numerous domains of culture and practice of rigid, puritanical notions of sex and gender, coupled with the subsequent "willingness of Third World governments to adopt the peculiar Purity Laws and conventions of Britain in the 1880s as if they represented ultimate truths about human civilisation" (1990:215). I will return to this theme in due course.

Having focused on the Netherlands Indies, I want to make clear that the situation was similar elsewhere in Southeast Asia, including areas under British control, such as Burma, Malaya, and Singapore. In Burma in the 1860s, "many [British] officials had Burmese mistresses" (Ballhatchet 1980:145–146), some of whom did double duty as housekeepers (cf. Hyam 1990:108). The designation "housekeeper" often entailed European expectations that had little to do with "keeping house," partly because of the "greater attractiveness and perfect freedom" of Burmese women as compared with their Indian counterparts (Ballhatchet 1980:147). As Lord George Hamilton put it around 1900, "The Burmese women, I have always understood, are most admirable housekeepers: they are busy engaging females, with a natural aptitude for the society of men, and I am afraid there always will be sexual relations existing between a certain number of Englishmen and their housekeepers in Burma" (cited in Ballhatchet 1980:150). Dynamics of housekeeping aside, there was also the draw of learning difficult vernaculars in appealing circumstances, especially if the rigors of language instruction offered by "sleeping dictionaries" were appropriately rewarded: "In the old days," according to numerous sources, "many officials were said to owe their fluent command of the vernacular to intensive instruction in such intimate circumstances" (ibid., 153). This despite the long-standing view, expressed by Colonel Fytche, the Chief Commissioner, in a confidential circular of 1867, that "With a race like the Burmese, accustomed under their former Native Government to bribery and chicane, it is probable that in no case is a Burmese mistress altogether free from evil influences" (ibid., 146).

In Malaya too concubinage and other forms of sexual exploitation involving British men and local women—or prostitutes imported from China or Japan—were extremely common (Manderson 1996: Chap. 6). Such was only natural for the "white exile," according to school inspector, director of education, and Orientalist par excellence Richard Winstedt. With "No home life, no women friends, no libraries, no theatres or cinemas, not always big enough community for bridge or tennis, no motor-cars, no long walks on account of that labyrinth of trackless jungle: was it any wonder that the white exile took to himself one of the complaisant, amusing, good-tempered, and good-mannered daughters of the East?" (Winstedt 1969:18). Clearly informing Winstedt's views as to what was natural were his personal experiences in Malaya, which led him to the view that those who refrained from taking up with one or more "daughters of the East" ended up being prone to "mental troubles. In thirty-two years in Malaya, he personally knew fourteen Europeans who shot themselves: all had been of sound mind when they went out" (Hyam 1990:90; Winstedt 1969:103–105).

The more general dis-ease that engaging the company and sexual services of one or more "daughters of the East" helped prevent, even though it might also contribute to the affliction, was "tropicalization," a much-feared degenerative process involving the synergistic effects of unhealthy and monotonous climate, contact with lethargic, indolent locals, and deprivations of various kinds that was widely believed to render Europeans susceptible to emotional instability, insanity, and suicide (Bleys 1995:148–149, Manderson 1996:74–75, W. Anderson 1997). "Gin, more gin, always gin" also helped ameliorate or at least mask "the noxious stimuli of the tropics" that were believed to "cause amnesia, irritability, loss of self-control, and an unduly high percentage of suicides" (Winstedt 1969:101, 176). The bottom line, opined pioneering sexologist Magnus Hirschfeld (1935:93) after his 500-day tour of "the East" in 1931–1932, is that "In the long run the tropics are no place for a white man .... The longer a white man lives in the tropics the lazier he feels, both physically and mentally, the duller and stupider he becomes."

Also "natural," perhaps, at least to Europeans, were the liberties they took with female plantation workers. "In 1914 Tamils went on strike in Malaya, demanding, among other things, an end to the molestation of female labourers" (Hyam 1990:94). Things remained "fairly free-and-easy" through the 1930s, according to Hyam, as evidenced by cases of British administrators creating and maintaining harems, some staffed by young girls raided or otherwise procured from local orphanages. Describing the more general situation, Hyam writes

> Every village in the Federated Malay States [Perak, Selangor, Negeri Sembilan, and Pahang], if it was big enough to have a post office, had its brothel, in which most of the girls were Japanese. In very small towns without a rest house, the brothel doubled as a hotel for Europeans, and these brothels were in regular use. Sir Malcolm Watson, who was well-placed to know ..., estimated that ninety percent of Europeans in outstations had Asian mistresses in the 1890s .... [Even in the early 1920s,] the young journalist R. H. Bruce Lockhart ... had no difficulty ... in living with a well-born Malayan girl for several months while working on a rubber plantation. It was still a recognized custom.
>
> (Ibid., 109; cf. Manderson 1996:195–196)

My comments thus far have concerned concubinage more than prostitution, though the distinction between the two forms of sexual commerce is in many instances difficult to maintain. I want to proceed to a discussion focused more squarely on colonial-era prostitution, analyses of which reveal a great deal about the diverse sexualities and body politics that flourished under colonialism as well as the myriad interests served by the practices and relations of the different groups of actors involved in the industry: prostitutes; those who recruited, transported, and managed them; their clients and their clients' employers; and last but not least, those who benefited from their clients' labor and overall presence in the colonies. This is nowhere more apparent than in Singapore during the period 1870–1940. Warren's incisive (1993) study of brothel prostitution in Singapore during its heyday as a British colony reveals the critical role that Chinese and Japanese prostitutes played in the economic development of the colony, and at least in the case of the Japanese prostitutes (generally known as *karayuki-san*, "those who travel to China" or go abroad, especially as sex workers), how their remittances contributed to the economic development of Japan during a critical period in that island nation's modern history.

An appreciation of demography, as we have seen, is key to an understanding of sexual commerce. Prior to Singapore's official "founding" by Sir Thomas Stamford Raffles in 1819, the permanent population of the island included only a small community of Malay fisherman and their families, perhaps 200 to 300 inhabitants in all. In subsequent decades, British and Chinese capital helped transform the island into a major colonial entrepôt, as did the influx and toil of large numbers of laborers and merchants from southern China, the overwhelming majority of whom were male. By the early 1870s, over 76,000 Chinese had migrated to Singapore and taken up residence there. The early 1880s saw this number increase to over 230,000; and by the early years of the 1900s, it had risen to over 653,000 (Warren 1993:33). "This massive influx of migrants altered the character of Singapore, building roads, railroads, and government buildings, loading and unloading cargo and supplies, and working in godowns and factories. The labour market could absorb them, but such an unprecedented increase created a serious social problem, as nearly all the immigrants were bachelors. These coolies crowded into working-class tenements in Chinatown and the density rates soared. As more and more *singkeh* (newcomers) moved in, the need for prostitutes climbed proportionately" (ibid., 9).

The male migrants were drawn out of southeastern China, especially Fujian and Guangdong provinces, by many of the same dynamics that insured the successful recruitment of the women whose sexual services they sought out in their new "homeland:" hunger, poverty, harsh and exploitative taxation, and other calamities and injustices resulting from floods, famines, poor harvests, overpopulation, and oppressive landlords. The "choices" available to the laboring classes for recreation, solace, and the like were in many respects similar to those available to the lower-class Europeans who made up the bulk of the colonial military forces, though they also included opium, generally discouraged for Europeans, steady supplies of which were widely available for Chinese to purchase as a matter of government policy; the government's monopoly on the sale of opium to Chinese was in fact a major source of colonial revenue (Trocki 1990). Concerning sexual matters, these "choices" boiled down to: enforced celibacy, which colonial authorities saw as an unlikely outcome for Chinese men; sexual relations with other men, which the authorities greatly feared; or prostitution, which as elsewhere was far and away the most desirable solution in colonial eyes, particularly since the men

> live for the most part herded in cubicle lodging-houses, rickshaw-puller 'Kongsi' houses, and coolie lines erected close to the factories. These

people are literally packed together at night, and sleep in quarters which contain the minimum amount of air space allowed by municipal regulation ... . In these circumstances, ... cut off from any of his own womenfolk and with no inducement to stay inside his cramped sleeping quarters, the Chinese workman and coolie is inevitably drawn to the brothels to seek not only gratification of his most powerful natural instinct, but also the single change possible from the drab circle of his everyday life.

(Cited in Warren 1993:33–34)

Whatever the relevance (if any) of "natural instincts," Singapore's two main brothel districts came to include large numbers of girls and young women from China and Japan, as well as small numbers of mostly female prostitutes from Malaya, Siam/Thailand, France, central and eastern Europe, and Russia. Some men and boys worked as prostitutes as well, but information on their numbers and national origins is difficult to come by since "not all sexual behavior [for this period] is documented" (ibid., 37 n36; cf. Manderson 1996:167, 178, 179, 276 n10; Aldrich 2003:10). Significantly, however, Singapore's brothels included no women from Britain, despite the fact that London and other areas in the British Isles boasted teeming red-light districts that had developed symbiotically with "thriving subculture[s] of prostitution and pornography" (Warren 1993:40, 144). The laws explicitly prohibiting British prostitutes from plying their trade in Singapore were zealously maintained out of fear and anxiety that a blurring of racial and class lines would occur due to the presence in brothels of white women who were both poor and diseased; for some of them would no doubt end up beneath Asian men, thus doubly eroding the racial privilege undergirding empire. Not surprisingly, the brothels in which prostitutes worked were sharply differentiated by race and class, as were the women within them. This differentiation obtained both in the case of registered brothels, of which there were approximately 212 in 1877 and about 353 in 1905, and in the case of the unregistered or "sly brothels" (as they were known), whose numbers, though unreported, probably greatly exceeded those of their registered counterparts (ibid., 45).

The history of brothel registration and management reveals that in the case of Singapore and other colonial port-towns in Asia and the Pacific, such as San Francisco, the traffic in women was a multi-million dollar industry. In Singapore, "running brothels ... was considered one of the easiest ways to accumulate capital before the turn of the century;" more generally, "brothel prostitution played an important economic role in providing the capital for the growth of Chinese and Japanese enterprise in Singapore at that time," for example, in retail shops, business, and foreign exchange sent back to Japan, and "for economic diversification both within Singapore and Japan" (ibid., 59, 61, 62). In this connection we might note that by 1888 the city's population included over 2,500 prostitutes and by 1915 perhaps more than 1,500 women of the night from Japan alone (ibid., 87, 113).

As elsewhere in Southeast Asia, colonial policies promoting prostitution, concubinage and related arrangements generated broadly ramifying debates—

some overwhelmingly moralistic, others couched more in pragmatic and utilitarian terms—both in the colonies and back home. One result was legislation,
such as the Contagious Diseases Ordinance (CDO) of 1870 and The Women
and Girls Protection Ordinance(s) of the 1880s, which was intended, via more
careful state regulation, disciplining, and mandatory medical inspections of
prostitutes—but never their clients—both to put a lid on moral and other
objections to the industry, and to curtail the spread of venereal and other diseases (tuberculosis, typhoid fever, pneumonia, and gastro-intestinal disorders
[ibid., 344]) to which sex workers were especially susceptible. Unfortunately,
however, British authorities in Singapore like their counterparts elsewhere
"found it impossible to suppress traffic in women and children and the abuses
connected with it. Nor was it considered feasible to declare brothels illegal"
(ibid., 100). Hence key provisions of the CDO were repealed in 1887, and the
enforcement of related measures was inconsistent at best. Note in any case that
in the prevailing discourses of "deviant sex"

> all oppression was directed at women as, a priori, any woman infected [or
> seen as likely to become infected] with a venereal disease was treated as a
> criminal. The failure of the Victorian sexual system to explicitly apply the
> same standard and law to upper-class gentlemen, soldiers, and sailors, in
> order to protect the privacy of male individuals as carriers, defeated the
> [Contagious Disease] Acts' purpose, exposing the double standard of the
> age, and sexual prejudice among the 'respectable' classes toward prostitu-
> tion and the poor.
>
> (Ibid., 112)

The repeal of the CDO gave rise to massive epidemics of venereal disease over
the next decade. Worst hit were the waterfront brothels and the sailors and other
laboring-class men who frequented them. In the case of some European vessels,
"more than half ... [the] ship's company had been in hospital with VD during the
year [1890]" (ibid., 132). More generally, due to the collapse of containment
policies and related measures, Singapore "became infamous within the space of
several years as one of the unhealthiest spots in the Empire" (ibid., 130).

The formal abolition of brothel prostitution in Singapore during the period
1919–1927 was not the panacea that some naively expected. For the most part,
it led instead to more clandestine prostitution and to the spread of venereal diseases that wreaked havoc on the Chinese population (ibid., 177). Ironically,
the formal abolition of prostitution also increased the dangers that had long
faced women involved in sex work. Such risks included pregnancy, life-threatening abortion procedures, problems stemming from the ravages and abuse of
alcohol and opium, and violence from clients, coolies, mamasan, and others,
the frequency and gravity of such was that "the spectre of violent death always
haunted" Singapore's prostitutes (ibid., 290).

Before turning to an examination of the ways that some Chinese women in
Singapore resisted the conditions of sexual commerce discussed here along with

the institutions of kinship and marriage that helped spawn them, I want to draw attention to the target population and overall raison d'être of the red-light district surrounding Malay Street, near the iconic Raffles Hotel, which aimed at the high end of the European market. In the late nineteenth and early twentieth century, European men in Singapore could not be seen publicly with Asian women without threatening the racialized hierarchies of privilege undergirding empire; hence this district existed to cater to those well-heeled European men who wanted to "taste something of the local flavours" (ibid., 269–273). In these facts and in various other aspects of late nineteenth- and early twentieth-century prostitution we see some of the ways in which colonial-era prostitution differed from its early modern predecessor, the institution of temporary marriage.

I have mentioned some of the better documented living arrangements (e.g., "cubicle lodging houses," "rickshaw-puller 'Kongsi' houses") and monetized forms of heterosexual congress that prevailed in Singapore during the colonial era, but I have yet to comment on other modalities of domesticity and sexuality that developed among Chinese living in Singapore as well as in Chinese enclaves in Melaka, Penang, Kuala Lumpur, and "throughout Malaya, Borneo, Sarawak, Siam, Indo-China and Indonesia" (Topley 1956:90) during the early and middle decades of the twentieth century. These included associations of single women and young girls who had emigrated from silk-producing regions of southern China during the worldwide economic slump associated with the Great Depression in search of livelihoods in places like Singapore that seemed from afar to promise a better standard of living. By this time, restrictions on Chinese females immigrating to Singapore and other parts of Malaya had been greatly relaxed; between 1934 and 1938 alone, "there was a migrational gain of 190,000 Chinese female deck passengers, the majority of whom were peasant women" (Topley 1954:55).

Like many of their forebears in areas of southern China that were home to silk factories reliant on female labor, significant numbers of these women were part of a "marriage resistance movement" (Topley 1975, Sankar 1986). Either renouncing marriage in its entirety or simply refusing cohabitation with the husbands who had been chosen for them by their families, the women in this movement formed associations that involved living together, often in paired relationships informed by "vows of sworn sisterhood" that entailed same-sex relations (Topley 1959:214). In China the members of these associations lived "at home, in the home of one of their members or in houses called [appropriately] ... 'spinster houses'" (koo p'oh uk [in Cantonese]) (ibid.). In Singapore, however, they were more likely to live in hostels, dormitory-like settings, or run-down tenements. The other residents of these dwellings included a revealing mix of Chinese women with few other options in the colony: former prostitutes who had contracted debilitating diseases or had passed their prime and had no families to support or care for them; "lonely widows ..., actresses ..., and dancing girls who, unable to marry while young, f[ou]nd themselves alone in their old age" (Topley 1954:51); as well as women who had no direct knowledge or experience of circumstances in southern China but refused or opted out of heterosexual marriage for one or another reason such as mistrust or disdain of husbands or potential mates who were likely to be involved in prostitution or concubinage without their knowledge or might be inclined to trick them into becoming prostitutes or concubines themselves.

Sometimes referred to in Singapore as "vegetarian houses," these residences served vegetarian food in accordance with Buddhist prohibitions on the killing of animals. They often had altars or shrines that included statues or images of Guanyin, the Boddhisattva commonly glossed by Westerners as the Goddess of Mercy, who, according to frequently cited legends, "successfully repelled all efforts on her father's part to get her married off and became a Buddhist nun in spite of great opposition from her family" (ibid., 59). In Singapore at mid-century, many of the women who lived in these houses worked as cooks or maids, returning after a day's work to eat, socialize, and retire for the evening with other women, some of whom shaved their heads and adopted the clothing and other outward appearance of Buddhist nuns.

Typical replies to questions posed by anthropologist Marjorie Topley concerning why they joined vegetarian houses included comments such as the following: "My husband is dead and I cannot burden friends and relatives with the trouble and expense of keeping an old woman and providing her with a funeral"; "Men are bad. Why marry? If one does not marry one can save up for one's old age and join a vegetarian house or live with a friend. Or one can buy a child and have everything that marriage has to offer and one's own money too;" "It is easier to get to the happy land if one does not marry"; "If I get married and my husband becomes rich, he takes a concubine; if he becomes poor, I have to go out to work. Better to work for myself and when I am old come here and live permanently"; "Marriage is no good, men cannot be trusted. If I got married, how would I know that the man would not have a wife already in China; that happened to a friend of mine" (ibid., 60–61).

These forms of association were flourishing at the time of Topley's research in the immediate post-World War II period and are thus important for a variety of reasons, though many of their basic features, pertaining to the realms of the erotic and the explicitly sexual, for example, remain poorly documented if not altogether unknown outside the ranks of the initiated. These relationships provide clear evidence that some women who came of age during colonial times resisted heterosexual marriage and male-female intimacy altogether, preferring both female camaraderie and homosocial, homoerotic, if not explicitly homosexual, bonding (Topley 1959:214) and co-residence with other women, to participation in one or another set of erotic or domestic arrangements defined in relation to a patriarchal male or a male-female pair. Insofar as some women participated in these unions in lieu of entering into marriage with a man who was likely to maintain a concubine or engage in prostitution on the side (or to pressure or trick them into selling their sexual favors to others), these associations and the partnerships or cells comprising them can also be read as critiques of colonial labor policies and racial discourses that constructed Chinese masculinity in relation to concubinage and prostitution.[6]

This excursus on the ways some Chinese women in Singapore exercised agency to resist colonial-era conditions of sexual commerce along with the institutions of kinship and marriage (both Chinese and European) that helped spawn them raises broader issues bearing on resistance to European intrusions into Southeast Asia and how such resistance may have tempered the effects of forces conducing toward a constriction (or other transformation) of pluralism. Suffice it to note two points (taken up in more expansive context in Chapter 4). First, both female-bodied persons and the transgendered, to focus for the moment on two broadly defined (overlapping) categories of social actors that were strongly affected by European influences, did in many instances actively resist imperial intrusions and the normalizing discourses associated with them. And second, in many cases such resistance did much to ensure that European efforts to recreate Southeast Asians in their own moral image(s)—or at least according to their own moral calculus—were never fully realized. This situation is perhaps best documented for the Philippines (Brewer 2004), where we see an extensive genealogy of resistance, especially on the part of female shamans, to Spanish-inflected Catholicism and the heavily androcentric forces of imperial governance in which it was imbricated, though we should be clear that not all of this entailed resistance on the basis or gender or sexuality per se (see also Ileto 1979, Rafael 1988). Evidence bearing on Sulawesi's past suggests, more generally, that throughout (written) history, the Bugis *bissu*, aided by the nobility whose "white blood" and prerogatives they both symbolized and safeguarded, actively resisted efforts to undercut their prestige and succeeded in convincing many people of the righteousness of their cause (Harvey 1974, L. Andaya 1981, 1993, Pelras 1996, Gibson 2005: Chaps. 8–9). Similarly, in Burma in 1824–1826, transgendered ritualists (*nat kadaw*) assumed a prominent role in military charges against the British, in what came to be known as the First Anglo-Burmese War (Crawfurd 1834 I:74–75; cf. Ritchie and Evans 1894:113–114). The Burmese and European sources I have consulted do not provide much useful information on the battles in which *nat kadaw* or other ritual specialists were involved. Nor do they shed much light on circumstances surrounding the unfortunate demise of the cross-dressed female-bodied adolescent, armed with spirit familiars and reportedly intent on "unmanning" her adversaries, who died from fatal head wounds inflicted by British weapons in what Crawfurd euphemistically refers to as the "action at Simbike." We know, however, that ritually bolstered resistance of this sort was more or less routine both in Burma and in Borneo (e.g. among the Iban), Bali, and elsewhere in the region (see, for example, J.C. Scott 1976, Pringle 1970, Wiener 1995, Day 2002: Chap. 3); and that it typically enhanced the reputations and occult repositories of ritual practitioners and all that they signified in cosmogenic terms, even when the ritualists and their charges experienced resounding military defeat by advancing imperial forces.

A more general point is that Southeast Asians have a long and venerable history of fortifying themselves through ritual and religion in order to render themselves invulnerable to enemy weapons and otherwise increase the likelihood that their military and political campaigns—as well as their more personal endeavors (Peletz 1988, 1993a; cf. Wikan 1990, Watson and Ellen 1993)—meet with success. Even at this writing (2008), these traditions are alive and well, as illustrated by the degree to which young militants born and raised in the predominantly Muslim provinces of southern Thailand are concerned to fortify themselves ritually (with spells, amulets, and passages from the Quran inscribed on bits of paper) before engaging in actions against the Thai state (McCargo 2008). The larger issue is that despite important changes, the religious cosmologies informing these practices continue to be relatively pluralistic with respect to gender and sexuality; in conjunction with active resistance on the part of those targeted for elimination or "domestication", they are among the key variables that have helped reproduce a good measure of pluralism in Southeast Asia despite colonial-era and other forces conducing to its constriction and overall transformation.

Desires That Dare Not Speak Their Names

With the notable exception of the discussion of relationships involving "sworn sisterhood," the material presented thus far in this chapter has focused largely on erotic encounters and body politics of a heterosexual variety. That said, I have emphasized that in British and Dutch colonies especially, official policies promoting large-scale industries oriented toward satisfying the sexual needs, desires, and fantasies of European soldiers, Chinese laborers, and other males were predicated on colonial officials' fears and anxieties that failure to provide men with adequate heterosexual "outlets" would lead to these men's involvement in reprobate and otherwise unchristian activities that were far more debilitating than any of the moral evils or health threats of heterosexual concubinage or prostitution. The spread of same-sex desires and practices among the ranks of Europeans and between Europeans and Asians, it was feared, would entail the sapping of masculinity undergirding empire, just as it would pose a problem of potentially enormous proportions once feminized European men returned to their mother countries. Colonial-era discourses concerning heterosexuality on the one hand and homosexuality (and bisexuality) on the other were obviously deeply intertwined if not mutually constituting; all such varieties of sexuality were also deeply imbricated in colonial-era taxonomies and more encompassing discourses of gender, class, race, and nation.

Ann Stoler's (1995, 2002) contributions to our understandings of some of these dynamics have been exemplary. But they are also emblematic of a still pervasive tendency in certain quarters, even among otherwise theoretically sophisticated scholars, to marginalize or altogether exclude same-sex practices and desires from analyses of sexuality—even when abundant evidence of such practices and desires exists and has long been prominent in the historical and ethnographic record (part of a larger dilemma noted in Chapter 1). Brief consideration of Stoler's influential scholarship in relation to some of Foucault's writings is instructive here, especially if we seek to develop analytic perspectives that simultaneously build on their strengths and transcend their limitations. In this spirit, my critical engagement with Stoler's work aims at a reading of the relevant data that is "post-Stoler" rather than "anti-Stoler." I should also make clear that I engage Stoler's work primarily as an exemplar of certain variants of anthropological, historical, and feminist scholarship that provide highly incisive analyses of gender, race, and class (and other axes of difference and inequality) but nonetheless ignore sexual diversity—much as I did in the first of the three books that I wrote on kinship, gender/sexuality, law, and related themes in Malaysia (see Peletz 1988 "vs" Peletz 1996, 2002). Among the main questions that follow are: What are the implications of thus narrowing our purview? And what types of methodological and attendant research strategies might inadvertently lead to such a narrowing?

Stoler offers a provocative (re)reading of Michel Foucault's *History of Sexuality*, Volume 1 (1978; hereafter *History of Sexuality*). Her (re)reading is informed on the one hand by her extensive study of Dutch colonial records and other archival resources bearing on the Netherlands East Indies in addition to secondary sources such as Ballhatchet (1980), Ming (1983), and Hyam (1990); and on the other by developments in feminist, subaltern, and postcolonial scholarship as well as a careful analysis of a series of lectures on race that Foucault presented at the Collège de France after he completed work on the *History of Sexuality*. Stoler demonstrates the marginalization of imperial discourses of race in Foucault's descriptions and analyses of nineteenth-century constructions of "bourgeois selves," illustrating not only how the heavily sexualized "racial thinking in the past has shaped racial discourse today," but also, *contra* Foucault, that "a history of nineteenth-century European sexuality must also be a history of race" (1995, back cover).

Readers familiar with Foucault's corpus will recall that the *History of Sexuality* deals at length with what Foucault contends was the relatively abrupt appearance in Europe in the eighteenth and nineteenth centuries of juridical and other discourses concerning "the homosexual" as a unique species or subspecies of person. Foucault is not at great pains to clarify why these or attendant discourses "suddenly" appeared at this historical juncture, but he does insist that this focus on the homosexual as a type of "species being" superseded earlier narratives centered on sexual practices, normative and otherwise, and was part of a larger epistemic shift that gave rise to a variety of normalizing discourses. These discourses not only targeted and problematized childhood and adolescent sexualities; they also harnessed pedagogical institutions to the task of better supervising and regulating "the problem" of childhood and adolescent sex (Foucault 1978:104).

To provide larger context for these claims, Foucault explains that in sixteenth- and seventeenth-century France, the moral categories of "excess" and "debauchery" were of considerable cultural elaboration and of broad sociopolitical concern. This is largely because they were seen as cause and effect of "heredity" and were thus always already implicated in potentially anxious discourses on "the health of the race," and, by implication, "the health of the nation." By the eighteenth and nineteenth century, however, the moral category of "perversion" had superseded that of "excess/debauchery." Anxious concerns with "perversion" as cause as well as effect (symptom or sign) of racial and/or national "degeneration" thus permeated discourses in a number of different fields in eighteenth- and nineteenth-century France, as elsewhere in Europe as well. Moreover, according to Foucault (1978:101) the appearance in the nineteenth century of an extensive series of psychiatric, jurisprudential, and literary "discourses on the species and subspecies of homosexuality, inversion, pederasty, and 'psychic hermaphrodism' made possible a strong advance of social controls into this area of 'perversity.'" It simultaneously "made possible the formation of a 'reverse' discourse: homosexuality began to speak in its own behalf, to demand that its legitimacy or 'naturality' be acknowledged" (ibid.).[7]

These brief comments do not do justice to the scope or force of Foucault's arguments concerning the historical emergence of French or other Western discourses bearing on same-sex sexuality and "perversion;" but they should suffice to highlight some of his major concerns. Given these concerns as well as the task that Stoler has set for herself—a critical reassessment of the *History of Sexuality* in light of the colonial experience—it is curious that for all intents and purposes Stoler never engages the subjects of same-sex sexuality or transgenderism. One of three partial exceptions is a sentence-long passage that appears roughly two-thirds of the way through the text, following her remark, "In the Indies, more than half of the European male population were cohabiting out of wedlock with native women in the late nineteenth century" (Stoler 1995:129). The passage reads: "Among subaltern soldiers, concubinage was the 'necessary evil' that would ward off venereal disease and, more importantly, homosexuality within the lower ranks." A single footnote, keyed to this latter sentence, constitutes the second of the partial exceptions mentioned earlier. The first part of this footnote reads as follows: "The absent presence of the dangers of homosexuality in these debates is striking. What is more, in the Dutch archives, the threat of homosexual desire among stolid Dutch agents of empire, of the colonial *middenstand*, is rarely if ever mentioned. When homosexuality is broached, it is always in the form of a deflected discourse, one about sodomizing Chinese plantation coolies, about degenerate subaltern soldiers, never about respectable Dutch men" (ibid., 129 n93[sic; 97]). The footnote continues with remarks proffered as an explanation of Stoler's "silence on this issue" (homosexuality) and "the prominent place" that she "give[s] to heterosexuality." These omissions and the attendant privileging of heterosexuality, Stoler writes, "reflect my long-term and failed efforts to identify any sources that do more than assume or obliquely allude to this 'evil' [homosexuality], thereby making the other 'lesser' evils of concubinage and prostitution acceptable .... As such, *my colonial treatment of Foucault's fourth 'strategic unity', constituting the 'perverse adult', is only minimally explored*" [emphasis added].

But Stoler does not "minimally explore" Foucault's "fourth 'strategic unity', constituting the perverse adult;" she never really broaches the subject (although she mentions homosexuality again, in passing, on pp. 180 and 181, this being the third of the three partial exceptions I noted). Moreover, much of her discussion of these matters is relegated to footnotes. And, as discussed earlier, the key footnote in question does not appear until fully two-thirds of the way through the book, when in fact, given the subject matter and title Stoler selected for her project, it would seem far more appropriate to forecast its contents at the book's outset. The extremely limited scope of her purview—what she takes to be relevant sources, relevant voices, and, ultimately, relevant issues—precludes description and analysis of some of the most revealing material to emerge from this period. (The pre-colonial period in its entirety, moreover, is altogether ignored, a curious move in any study of colonial-era discourses and their entailments.) Some readers may feel that this narrow purview results in her being inadvertently complicit in reinscribing many of the very silences, elisions, and heteronormative biases that were central to the civilizing mission undergirding and animating the imperial project in the first place, though I would not go that far (and could conceivably be subject to similar critiques in light of omissions in Peletz 1988). Be that as it may, colonial regimes of gender and sexuality, their local counterparts, and the intertwining of colonial and local genealogies were far more interesting, complex, and fraught with ambivalence and contestation than Stoler suggests in the context of her privileging of heterosexuality and her deafening silences on the subjects of same-sex erotics and transgenderism.

The issue is not really one of sources, as Stoler claims in the passage cited above. (See, for starters: the myriad historical and ethnographic sources bearing on colonial-era Indonesia [Aceh, Bali, Borneo, Celebes, Java, etc.] as well as colonial-era Malaya, Singapore, Burma, Vietnam, and the Philippines that I cite in Chapter 2 and elsewhere in this book; Bleys' [1995:273–319] 47-page bibliography of sources relevant to "male-to-male sexual behavior outside the West and the ethnographic imagination" during the period 1750–1918; and the numerous texts cited in Robert Aldrich's 436-page *Colonialism and Homosexuality* [2003].)[8] It is, however, partly a matter of methodology insofar as one's choice of methodologies is to a significant degree a function of where one expects to find relevant data and how one defines relevance and data in the first place. Like some other historians and historical anthropologists, Stoler accords highest priority to the archival resources and other written records left behind by colonial officials, their families, and the bevies of professional and popular "experts" who guided their moral development, and tends to regard the matrices informing their output as more or less isomorphic with the ideological apparatuses underlying colonial governmentality. The latter in turn are viewed as more or less synonymous with "colonial culture."[9] But what of other products of—or windows onto—colonial culture, such as the voluminous writings of travelers, missionaries, colonial-era ethnographers, and modern-day anthropologists who began conducting fieldwork in the early part of the twentieth century, or colonial-era literary and artistic representations bearing on homoerotics, homosexuality, and transgender practices involving Southeast Asians,

Europeans, or both? If these sources are ignored, as is more or less the case in Stoler's scholarship, we are likely to be presented with highly sanitized, "flattened," and otherwise "culturally thin" accounts of colonial sexualities and indigenous sexualities alike, to borrow the terminology Ortner (1995) deploys in her critique of certain trends in the study of domination and resistance. *Inter alia*, these accounts make little if any provision for the same-sex fantasies, liaisons, and scandals that involved colonial and "native" and that were perforce multiply transgressive, at least from hegemonic European perspectives, in ways that go far beyond anything their authors convey to their readership.

My plea here is thus for more broadly cast descriptions and analyses of colonial-era regimes of gender and sexuality that do not arbitrarily privilege certain modalities of sexuality and gender (such as heterosexuality) and completely ignore others (e.g., same-sex sexuality, transgenderism). I hasten to add that my position is not motivated primarily by concerns with historical or ethnographic holism, a goal which however admirable it once seemed is altogether unrealistic and otherwise doomed to failure, though I do consider it important to try to avoid providing perspectives that are unjustifiably or inexplicably partial. My position is motivated instead by analytic considerations. More broadly cast accounts of the sort offered here, which build on the insights of scholars like Stoler but endeavor to transcend their limitations, are essential if one seeks an analytic understanding of the implications of colonial-era policies with respect to local systems of gender and sexuality during either colonial times or the subsequent, postcolonial era.

We know, for example, that many of the Dutch, British, and others who were involved in colonizing, policing, and/or writing about the region saw their assignments in Southeast Asia, if not from the outset, at least as time wore on, as ripe with opportunities to engage in sexual experimentation and indulgence of a variety that would not be feasible, because it would be far more seriously stigmatized, in the mother country (Said 1978:190, Hyam 1990: Chap. 4, Aldrich 2003: Chap. 2). Such experimentation and indulgence sometimes involved liaisons with fellow European soldiers; recall the previously cited case of the Gombong barracks in late nineteenth-century Java (which Stoler mentions on a footnote on p. 181), where "far more than half of the young [Dutch] men quartered there were guilty of practicing unnatural vice," in this context clearly a reference to "sodomy" (Ming 1983:69). Others involved boys and men belonging to local societies, some of whom worked in (or out of) houses of prostitution of the sort made famous by Richard Burton's (1886 [1973]:15–16) accounts of "boy brothels" in Karachi, a half dozen or so of which were reported to exist in colonial-era Singapore (Aldrich 2003:10; see also Manderson 1996:167, 178, 179, 276 n10). Some of these liaisons drew unwanted because largely negative publicity, resulting in broadly ramifying crises that transgressed boundaries of race, class, and empire. A "social upheaval" occurred in "British Malaya" in the 1930s, for instance, when, in the words of a high-ranking, career civil servant stationed there at the time, "the diary of a professional Chinese catamite fell into the hands of the police, resulting in an official inquiry, the disgrace of several prominent persons, and the suicides of two of those who were implicated in the matter" (Purcell 1965:250). A broadly analogous "homosexual scandal ... producing numerous arrests and dismissals, and several suicides" also broke out then in Dutch-administered Bali (Aldrich 2003:163; cf. 198–202). Margaret Mead, who was living there at the peak of the crisis (1938–1939), wrote that "many of our friends and associates in Bali were under attack," and proceeded to characterize the period as involving a colonially inspired "witch hunt against [European] homosexuals" and their white- and brown-skinned partners that "echoed from Los Angeles to Singapore" (Mead 1977:155; cf. Gouda 1995:181–182). Most such incidents were of course hushed up before they became scandals and "homosexual witch hunts." And in many instances, including Bali and Sarawak throughout the 1930s and subsequently, same-sex relations between well placed European men including "white rajas" and disaffected artists seeking refuge from the rising tide of fascism in Europe on the one hand and locals on the other were "open secrets" that did not necessarily give rise to public outcries but were nonetheless widely known in European and local circles alike (Aldrich 2003:161–165; cf. Walker 1998).

Probably well known to locals as well were other kinds of practices involving "sexual indulgence" and "excess" on the part of European officials and others of their countrymen who were occupied as soldiers, planters, or traders. Some of this behavior has been described in the memoirs of former colonial agents such as Victor Purcell (1965:249–251), who served in the Malayan Civil Service from 1921 to 1946, maintained a Chinese mistress and acknowledged that he was "never ... able to distinguish between the sexual urge and the urge to live" (ibid., 251). Purcell recounts a number of relevant cases, some of which apparently involved adultery and "wife swapping," another a British officer posted to a remote outstation who was believed to have been "living incestuously" with his sister. Hyam (1990:109), moreover, estimates that as many as two-thirds of the European men living in colonial Malaya in the early twentieth century had at least some sexual experience with local men (cf. Manderson 1996:178, Aldrich 2003:195 passim).

I cite this material not to convey the impression that the British and other Europeans in Southeast Asia were driven to "indulgence," "excess," or "perversion" either by "constitutional" factors or by "tropicalization," the much-dreaded degenerative process mentioned earlier, which involved the synergistic effects of unhealthy and monotonous climate, contact with lethargic, indolent locals, and deprivations of various kinds that were widely believed to render Europeans susceptible to emotional instability, insanity, and suicide. The relevance of such material lies, rather, in the substance (both real and imagined) that it offered local narratives concerning the "sexual habits" and overall moral codes of the ruling Europeans ("the European natives"). The fact that it provided such substance—and that it did so in much the same ways as scandals and non-scandalous "open secrets" involving same-sex relations between European men and local males as well as European men's unmistakable proclivity for heterosexual concubinage and prostitution with local women or women imported from China or Japan—is clear from the explicitly contrastive ("anti-European") politics of virtue that developed among Southeast Asians during the high period of colonialism and in postcolonial times in particular, as discussed further along.

I have yet to emphasize that colonial understandings of local practices and desires that were taken to be transgressive with respect to gender and sexuality were central components of the "differentiating mythologies" utilized to construct the taxonomies of race and cultural Otherness that were increasingly prevalent in Western scientific circles and beyond in the second half of the nineteenth century both in Europe and its overseas colonies (Bleys 1995:137 passim). As Benedict Anderson (1990:277) has put it, "One of the characteristic *topoi* in the 'anthropological' writings of nineteenth- and twentieth-century colonial officials and missionaries [stationed in the Dutch East Indies is] gloomily pleasurable reference to the natives' incorrigible addiction to pederasty and homosexual sodomy. Dayaks, Acehnese, Balinese, Buginese, Javanese, Batak, Minangkabau, or Chinese—however much these peoples might differ in other ways, they were all said to share a passionate addiction to such vices."

> For example, the noted ethnologist George Alexander Wilken observed that "pederasty [is] a vice universal among the Dayaks" ... [1912] ... ; the celebrated Islamicist Christiaan Snouck Hurgronje wrote of "the general prevalence of immorality of the worst kind in Acheh," symbolized by the popular *seudati* shows, where the poetry sung was "paederastic in character" ... [1906] .... The sharp-tongued physician Julius Jacobs, after visiting Bali in the early 1880s, observed many dance performances by young boys dressed up like women, and commented: "One knows that they are boys, and it is sickening to see men from all strata of Balinese society proffering their *kepengs* (Chinese coins) to have the chance to dance with these children, sometimes in the queerest postures; one is still more revolted to discover that these children, sometimes after exercising for hours in a *perpendicular* position, are compelled, utterly exhausted though they may be, to carry out *horizontal* maneuvers with the highest bidders, after being fondled by this man and kissed by that" ... [1883].
> (B. Anderson 1990:277–278 n15; emphasis in original; cf. Gouda 1995:181)

As in Vietnam, where "French colonial observers constructed the Vietnamese male as androgynous, effeminate, hermaphroditic, impotent, and inverted and, conversely, the Vietnamese female as virile and hypersexualized" (Proschan 2002a:436), these *topoi* "served to demonstrate either the primitiveness or the degeneracy of the population concerned, and the urgent need for civilizing, Christianizing, and otherwise uplifting them. Pederasty and sodomy also served to draw a drastic moral contrast between 'abandoned' natives [on the one hand] and good Dutchmen [and other Europeans on the other], who naturally regarded such unnatural practices with practised horror" (B. Anderson 1990:277–278).

Theories of evolution promoted by Lamarck, Darwin, and others are clearly relevant here, especially since they conduced toward a constriction of Southeast Asian pluralism with respect to gender and sexuality. Many evolutionary schemes circulating in the nineteenth century (and earlier) seized on institutionalized patterns of transgenderism and same-sex sexuality as indices or signs of a society, "race," or "racial type" (as various societies were commonly designated) that was "inherently" "feminine" or "feminized" or—because of climate, other environmental factors, or ill-advised practices contributing to "racial degeneration," including "excessive" masturbation, miscegenation, and the like—had somehow become so. Signs of the "feminine" were held to be all the more prevalent in societies and races in which same-sex practices occurred in the context of "gender-structured" (heterogender) roles, as was and remains typical of much of Southeast Asia, rather than being "age-structured" or "egalitarian," as in various other world areas, such as Melanesia and the West, respectively. In such cases (Iban, Ngaju Dayak, Bugis, Burmese, Malay, etc.), as we have seen, one of the (typically male-bodied) partners assumed the attire, comportment, and various aspects of the role of the "opposite" sex. Since same-sex practices in Southeast Asia were usually of this variety, Europeans were particularly struck by—and apparently especially anxious about—the ways in which non-normative sexual and other bodily practices involving phenotypically male Europeans could result in the feminization not only of the individuals involved, but also, through one or another form of intimacy and contagion, the larger European community.

A number of factors augmented European anxieties about same-sex sexuality and transgenderism, including political and military resistance threatening imperial hegemony. One such factor was lack of consensus within the scientific community as to whether same-sex praxis and transgenderism of the sort widely reported for Southeast Asia represented "traces," "residues," or "survivals" of an early evolutionary stage from which many societies or races had successfully evolved. Might they instead index a later, more advanced stage of societal evolution characterized by subsequent degeneration and decline, which could, alas, be the fate of the "European race," as suggested by what Stepan (1986) and Bleys (1995:145) describe as a developing "anthropology of degeneracy and morbidity?" According to this prototype of a broadly cast forensic anthropology, it was not merely, as Stoler argues, heterosexual "race mixture" with the potential consequence of "half-caste" progeny that threatened the boundaries and integrity of colonizing races and the prestige structures undergirding them. Intimacies with same-sex bodies, whether fellow colonial or native, could also threaten the manhood of white soldiers and colonial officials alike. Such contact could easily render them unfit for imperial service. In some ways far worse, it could interfere with the "proper sexual functioning" expected of them once they completed their tours of duty and returned to Europe. The specter of failed reproduction (both biological and social) posed disquieting threats to the reproduction of European class and racial hierarchies, as in different ways did the overtly political challenges to British authority in the colonies that occurred in the second half of the nineteenth century, such as the Sepoy Rebellion ("Indian Mutiny") of 1857 and the Morant Bay Rebellion ("Jamaica Uprising") of 1865.

Debates among medical personnel, ethicists, and guardians of public morality concerning what to make of—and how best to police—the increasingly visible communities of mollies, sapphists, and "third sexes" that emerged in urban areas of Europe in the eighteenth and nineteenth centuries fueled controversies among the colonizers concerning sex, gender, and nearly all things intimate (Trumbach 1993, van der Meer 1993, Hekma 1993). Conversely, clinicians, scholars, and others in the developing field of sexology drew extensively on the accounts of colonial officials, missionaries, and others (of the sort cited in Chapter 2 and elsewhere in this book) who wrote about same-sex praxis and transgenderism in the colonies and other areas outside the West. The political and economic prominence of Western nations, especially Britain, Holland, and France, including, in particular, their sophisticated technologies and weaponry, helped guarantee that Western science, including sexology, psychiatry, and allied fields, would be accorded considerable prestige by Asians, Africans, and others who sought to modernize their institutions and thus either "catch up with the West" or surpass it and throw off its yoke. Put differently, the development of print capitalism coupled with the fact that Western scientists and medical experts, including physicians, psychiatrists, and sexologists, traveled, lectured, and spread their gospel widely in Asia and far beyond helped insure that modernizing elites in Asia and elsewhere would become familiar with many of the basics of their doctrines. As discussed in more detail in due course, these and attendant dynamics also helped insure that modernizing elites would themselves come to espouse key elements of these Western discourses in the context of developing the "rational," "scientific" views of the world that were held to be the sine qua non for joining the ranks of the "modern."

In light of the foregoing, a few words on the development of the Western scientific discourses that congealed in the field that came to be known as "sexual science" or "sexology" are in order. During the late nineteenth and early twentieth centuries in particular, European and American scholars such as Sigmund Freud, Richard von Krafft-Ebing, Havelock Ellis, and Magnus Hirschfeld developed a corpus of scholarship on the anatomy, physiology, psychology, genetics, evolution, sociology, and folklore of sexuality that was widely disseminated throughout the world. Much of this scholarship defined transgender practices and same-sex relations as "pathological," requiring "cure" via medical or psychiatric treatment, although some of the literature promoted more positive views of these phenomena. Of arguably broader relevance than the fact that the pathology view prevailed is that transgender practices and same-sex relations were for the first time subject to intense scientific and public scrutiny, having been effectively created as a legitimate object of scientific study and public debate, as Foucault (1978) has discussed.

As noted earlier, the military prowess enjoyed by Western nations in the early twentieth century, when most of Africa, Asia, and the Pacific, and much of the New World as well was subject to Western colonial rule, helped insure that Western scientific discourses, including sexology, were accorded tremendous prestige throughout Asia and the rest of the world. In China, for example, the rise of nationalist sentiments and soul-searching among intellectuals who sought to break with their feudal past and derived one or another degree of inspiration from Western models of modernity and "progress" led them to embrace Western notions of race and evolution, along with attendant concepts of racial hierarchies and racial degeneration, some of which were yoked to sexology. "The scientism of ... May Fourth [early twentieth-century] intellectuals was assisted by their anxiety over the weakness and regression of the Chinese race, which made them susceptible to the sway of late nineteenth- and early twentieth-century European sexology, which claimed to discover hereditary degeneracy, male effeminacy, and female masculinity in homosexuality" (Sang 2003:16). Both in China and Japan and in Southeast Asia and other regions of "the East," these developments were linked to objective reductions in the power and autonomy of overwhelmingly male elites and to the masculinization of leadership generally; they did in any case give birth to binary notions of sexuality, sexual "essences," and sexual types ("heterosexuality" vs. "homosexuality;" "the heterosexual," "the homosexual") and a host of other Western-origin concepts which had no local counterparts. More generally, they contributed to "the sexological abnormalization of same-sex intimacy ... in many Asian societies" as occurred as well "in Europe and America since the early twentieth century" (ibid., 7; cf. Pflugfelder 1999, El-Rouayheb 2005, Najmabadi 2005).

Instructive in this regard is the life work and transnational influence of pioneering sexologist Magnus Hirschfeld (1868–1935), whose ascendancy to international prominence might be said to have begun with the publication in 1896 of a volume on male and female homosexuality that quickly became a key text in the burgeoning field of sexology. Over the next few decades Hirschfeld published a number of other ground-breaking studies. While many of them advocated "homosexual emancipation" and might thus be seen as highly progressive for their time, they shared with the work of his more conservative colleagues a grounding in then current notions of race and evolution along with attendant concepts of racial hierarchies and racial degeneration, all of which were firmly yoked to his sexology.

On March 1, 1931 Hirschfeld set sail from San Francisco for a 500-day tour of "the East." His travels took him to Hawaii, Japan, Hong Kong, mainland China (Beijing and beyond), the Philippines, Celebes, Bali, Java, Singapore, and Sumatra (he had intended to visit Cambodia and other parts of mainland Southeast Asia but earthquakes and inclement weather prevented him from doing so) as well as Ceylon, India (Bombay, Calcutta, Delhi, Benares), Egypt, and Palestine. In the course of this trip he gave 176 lectures based on his research in the field of "sex ethnology," many of which were translated into vernacular languages as he delivered them in his native German or in English. The auditoriums reserved for his lectures overflowed with enthusiastic scholars, medical faculty, students, social reformers, and others eager to hear his insights and wisdom on "Sex and Love Customs of Mankind," "Love, Marriage, and Sex," "Love, Art, and Sex," as well as topics ranging from infant betrothal, birth control, polygyny, prostitution, widow burning, purdah, sterility, coeducation, mixed-race marriage, and female equality, to matriarchies, phallic cults, sexual differentiation, homosexuality, transvestitism, and "mystic sex customs which … often degenerate into absolutely superfluous self-torture" (Hirschfeld 1935:140). Newspaper and other media coverage of his lectures, some of which were delivered over the radio, was extensive, as were his meetings with local nobility and other political leaders. *Inter alia*, he met with the Sultan of Jogjakarta, the King of Siam, Jawaharlal Nehru, and the American governor of the Philippines, as well as fellow sexologists, dermatologists, psychiatrists, professors of anatomy, medical students, leaders of women's groups and other social activists, and last but not least, prostitutes, geisha, "ordinary" housewives, and "female impersonators." His account of his travels, translated into English and published as *Men and Women: The World Journey of a Sexologist* (1935) is a fascinating text, if only for its documentation of Hirschfeld's encounters with students and others throughout Asia who were already thoroughly familiar both with his work and with the writings of Freud, Ellis, and other important figures in the fields of sexological research.

The consequences of these kinds of cultural flows merit careful consideration, not least because they were mutually contradictory—as might be said of Southeast Asians' engagements with colonialism as a whole (Rafael 1988, 2000, Peletz 1988, 1996, 2002, Day 2002). On the one hand, the work of Hirschfeld and similarly oriented sexologists provided hope and ammunition to local reformers throughout Asia seeking an end to child betrothal, arranged marriage, *purdah*, widow burning, and the like. More generally Hirschfeld's feminist sensibilities, anti-colonial sentiments, and deep humanism came as welcome news to those involved in nationalist struggles and other emancipatory movements. On the other hand, some of his exoticized portrayals and gross distortions of local customs bearing on matters sexual and erotic undoubtedly gave many the impression that "the East" was a land characterized by all varieties of excess, indulgence, and deviance. In this regard some of his writing unwittingly shares a deep resonance with the less sympathetic accounts penned in earlier times by colonial scholars, missionaries, and the European explorers and other travelers who preceded them in the region. It also resonates, albeit in a slightly different way, with late twentieth-century discourses on "Asian values" articulated by Asian leaders who, inverting the signs and signifiers, simplistically portray the West—not the East—as the realm (*fons et origo*) of indulgent excess and deviance (discussed in Chapter 5).

The Janus-faced nature of these types of cultural products and their heterogeneous local impacts warrants emphasis since one of our major concerns in this chapter is the ways in which the dynamics of colonial culture informed local regimes of gender and sexuality and how, in the process, they contributed to the constriction of pluralism in these domains. Colonial culture (and "its" analysis, assuming for the moment one can speak in the singular) cannot be reduced to colonial governmentality (and its analysis), however sophisticated our discussions of colonial policies or governmentality may be. Sources bearing on the interactions between colonizer and colonized, which were of course always culturally mediated, are likewise far more extensive and variegated than the sources that have been deposited in colonial archives or left behind by civil servants, colonial military figures, and their families. It is particularly important, finally, that we not confine the study of "sexuality" to heterosexuality and that we not reduce the study of gender to the "woman question." To fall prey to either type of reductionism amounts to seriously impoverishing the data and precluding recognition let alone analysis of some of the most significant dynamics of the colonial period, many of which have proven to be of enduring relevance in the post-colonial era as well.

One such long-term dynamic involved the partial silencing of "desires that dare not speak their names." This dynamic occurred in the context of more encompassing trends entailing a constriction and overall transformation of pluralistic sensibilities concerning transgenderism and gender and sexuality as a whole (the focus of the following chapter), even though broadly defined counter-trends were also evident in the increasing delegitimization (and in some instances the gradual elimination) of traditions involving royal concubinage and polygyny, child betrothal, debt bondage, slavery, and the like. In his incisive analysis of an important range of these matters historical anthropologist Rudi Bleys (1995:266–267) notes that the exceedingly common "repression of homosexuality in post-colonial discourse on ethnic, cultural, and/or national identity ... can be noticed on many levels, from some forms of popular music to official policies defining male-to-male sexuality as 'alien' to one's own culture." Bleys observes that such repression "has gained particular urgency in the wake of decolonization ..., modernization ..., communism ..., and fundamentalism" (ibid., 267). In accounting for this development, he argues that "to some extent such intolerance may be explained as the expression of a desire to eliminate 'unwanted' indigenous practices at the threshold of ethnic, cultural or national emancipation, and *to some extent it is a reaction against some side effects of colonial sexual exchange between European and indigenous men*" (ibid., 267; emphasis added). This latter point underscores the necessity of factoring same-sex sexuality into descriptions and analyses of "colonial sexualities" and their long-term, post-colonial consequences.

On a more abstract level, the tropes of homophobia in postcolonial politics also reveal the way in which "European constructions of sexuality ... coincided with the epoch of imperialism and... were mutually intertwined" (K. Mercer). Homophobia constitutes a reply against the way in which non-western sexualities were read, interpreted, and represented as a *limitless repository of deviance, extravagance, eccentricity* and integrated in the European enterprise of cognitive *bricolage* and eclecticism, aiming simultaneously at the marginalization of cultural and sexual minorities.

(Ibid., 267; emphasis added)

Nineteenth- and twentieth-century discourses of Western (e.g., colonial) origin that portrayed Southeast Asian men, particularly elite men, as feminine are clearly relevant here; for these discourses often highlighted Southeast Asian men's (real or imagined) involvement in same-sex relations and transgender practices as unmistakable signs of their femininity *cum* degeneracy. All things considered it is not surprising that Southeast Asian men's assertions of masculinity during the colonial period and the postcolonial era in particular assumed a more (hetero)normative cast and were otherwise more in keeping with Victorian binaries, as also occurred in other regions subject to European colonialism such as the Muslim Middle East (El-Rouayheb 2005:9, 156, 160, Najmabadi 2005).

Conclusion

The first sections of this chapter concerned the institution of temporary marriage and the ways it came to be redefined in terms of concubinage and prostitution owing to a nexus of interrelated dynamics involving the growth of commercial networks and urban centers, the monetization of rural economic relations, and the spread of an endemic poverty that went hand in hand with these trends. My descriptions and interpretations of the trajectory from temporary wife to concubine and prostitute did not entail an exhaustive consideration of the transformations that occurred during this period with respect to female sexuality, the prestige accorded women, or their social standing as a whole. But we saw that the second half of the early modern period witnessed declines in rates of female literacy, the relative exclusion of women from political office and ritual domains, and the partial demise of various forms of craft specialization and petty commodity production that helped women maintain the economic and social autonomy that long struck outside observers from China and the West.

Broad generalizations such as these are in keeping with the (also broad) temporal and regional scope of this chapter, which focuses on long-term, regionally widespread trends, rather than on short-term shifts (e.g., "scripturalist peaks") characteristic of one or another society or polity (or group of such)—or developments that were arguably dissonant or incongruous with respect to the larger thrust of historical change. Such a focus may—but is not intended to—suggest more linearity and uniformity than is warranted by the data, which is one reason why some anthropologists and historians rightly caution against unilineal and "evolutionary narrative[s] of women's degradation with the rise of the state" (à la Engels [1884 (1972)] or some of his contemporary interlocutors) or as a consequence of broadly analogous dynamics, even when their analyses of the *longue durée* (particularly if divested of qualifications and caveats) provide compelling support both for transformations of the sort at issue in this chapter and for their centrality with respect to women's lived experiences (Silverblatt 1991:141; B. Andaya 2000a:232, 2006:102–103; cf. Gailey 1987, Silverblatt 1987, Ortner 1996: Chap. 3, Merry 2000). Another reason to reject the idea that what we see in this chapter are Southeast Asian variations on the theme of "the world historical defeat of the female sex" (Engels 1884 [1972]:120) is that gender relations in many regions of Southeast Asia (e.g., Burma, the Malay Peninsula, Borneo, Sulawesi, Java) continued to be relatively egalitarian well into the twentieth century, the larger point being that even at present one can discern a good measure of pluralism with respect to gender and sexuality (albeit decidedly less than in times past). Chapter 4, which deals substantively with four case studies and includes data relevant to the expanse of time addressed in this chapter (though it is chiefly concerned with the period since the 1960s), does in any event complicate the narrative presented here, partly by emphasizing the historical counter-flows, openings, and reversals that are strikingly evident when we examine particular cases through an optic that permits a more fine-grained view of local realities and their transformations through time. So too in different ways does Chapter 5.

I have also argued for the importance of dealing squarely with colonizers' views, fears, and anxieties of same-sex sexuality involving Europeans, "natives," as well as "interracial" unions between Europeans and Asians. There are many reasons for this, three of which merit brief reiteration. First, colonial discourses concerning same-sex sexuality (and transgenderism) among the natives provided much of the bedrock justification for the civilizing missions necessitating a colonial presence in the first place. Second, colonial fears and anxieties about same-sex sexuality within their own ranks and beyond were heavily suffused with class and racial angst and were of critical significance in shaping colonial policy bearing on Europeans and natives alike, including, not least, policies that subjected large numbers of Asian (especially Southeast Asian, Chinese, and Japanese) women to sexual exploitation and brutal objectification. And third, official colonial prudery with respect to some of these issues, which was typically cast in heavily binary discourses extolling the virtues of monogamous heteronormativity, while often wildly inconsistent with (and profoundly hypocritical vis-à-vis) actual colonial practice as well as conditions "on the ground" in the mother country, gave shape and form to the discourses and practices of local elites both during colonial times and in the postcolonial era as well. No small matter here is the relevance of this legacy—*inter alia*, a hardening of the categories—for Southeast Asians' experience of state-sanctioned biopolitics in the postcolonial present, the subject of the following chapter and much of the remainder of the book.

4 Transgender Practices, Same-Sex Relations, and Gender Pluralism Since the 1960s

Long-term cultural-political developments bearing on transgender practices, same-sex relations, and gender pluralism in Southeast Asia have not been uniform or all-encompassing but the overall trends, like the dynamics that helped bring them about, are clear. The latter dynamics include forces of political centralization (involving, *inter alia*, the consolidation and expansion of state power at the expense of local polities); the development of nationalist/modernist discourses emphasizing rationalized religion, science, technology, economic progress, secular education, and mass literacy; processes of urbanization, bureaucratization, and industrialization; and the rise of (mostly capitalist) market economies. These dynamics not only entailed widely ramifying institutional and cultural rationalization that undercut the moral bases of agrarian communities and the cosmologies in which they were embedded; they also contributed to increased social differentiation and stratification and new forms of surveillance, discipline, and control geared toward producing heightened normativity in domains of kinship, gender, and sexuality, and, indeed, in all areas of social life. In the process, many local "priesthoods," however gendered, have been largely discredited, just as many rituals associated with androgynous spirits and deities have fallen by the wayside. In addition, in many (perhaps most) contexts transgendering and the sexual variability linked with it has been stripped of its positive associations with religion and the sacred. With a few notable exceptions (e.g., the Bugis) the long-standing centrality of gender and sexual variability in state cults, royal courts, and the reproduction of local polities exists primarily in scattered memories and archives. In places like contemporary Malaysia, such variability tends to be most visible in secular venues of fashion and entertainment, in the increasingly scrutinized and disciplined private domain, and on the notoriously ungovernable Internet. When viewed from a long-term perspective, we see that many variants of transgendering and same-sex relations have been subject to processes of secularization and stigmatization, and that some of them have been heavily criminalized as well; and that most transgendered individuals have been redefined as contaminating rather than sacred mediators who are perversely muddling and enmiring the increasingly dichotomous terms of sex/gender systems long characterized by pluralism. Southeast Asia thus has much in common with other parts of the world that have been or are currently involved in transitions to (late) modernity, for generally speaking these transitions entail processes whereby once sacred mediating and liminal figures come to be redefined as contaminating, perverse, pathological, and categorically criminal if not explicitly treasonous.

There is of course more to gender pluralism than bestowing legitimacy on the transgendered, however much the prestige accorded the latter may be a rough barometer of pluralistic sensibilities for certain regions during certain historical periods. Hence it is well to recall that female-bodied ritual specialists (heteronormative and otherwise) saw their prestige eroded by many of the same processes that denied legitimacy to the (usually male-bodied) transgendered. The fate of female-bodied ritual specialists, like that of the transgendered, is also (albeit in different ways) indexical for this region and period—though not necessarily each and every specific case—of the greater formalization and segregation of gender roles, the distancing of women from sources of power and prestige, the narrowed range of legitimacy concerning things erotic and sexual, and the constriction of pluralistic gender sensibilities as a whole.

Despite the overall (delegitimizing and stigmatizing) thrust of the long-term historical processes outlined here, a fair amount of gender pluralism existed in many (perhaps most) areas of Southeast Asia well into the twentieth century. This is especially evident when we look beyond ritual specialists per se and examine the "lay" majority's basic attitudes and feeling-tones toward gender and sexual diversity. Thus, Jane Belo, writing about Bali in the 1930s, noted a pervasive nonchalance concerning sexual relations between persons of the same sex (whether or not they held formal ritual roles), a pattern widely reported for twentieth-century Java as well (see, e.g., Peacock 1968, Keeler 1990:148–150, Oetomo 1996, Boellstorff 1999, 2004a, Wieringa 1999, Beatty 2002). According to Belo (1935 [1970]:5), such relations, whether they involved men or women, were regarded by Balinese as a form of play activity—main-main in local parlance—and were not to be taken all that seriously, in sharp contrast to other variants of non-normative behavior, such as incest or failure to bear children. "Women who have no children are believed to go to hell, and lurid paintings and drawings abound which depict the barren women in hell with enormous hairy caterpillars sucking at their dry breasts" but "no such fate awaits the homosexual, either male or female" (ibid.; cf. Covarrubias 1937 [1972]:137, 145, Duff-Cooper 1985:415–416, Gouda 1995:182). Similarly, M.A. Jaspan (1969:22–23), referring to Sumatra and Southeast Asia generally in the 1960s, could still relate that "homosexuals and transvestites are treated with kindness and an amused tolerance; ... are seldom considered a menace to society, blamed for being what they are, or made to feel that they must be kept in separate places from other people, ostracised or confined to institutions." Significantly, however, Jaspan makes no mention of the same-sex practices associated with sadati performances that Snouck Hurgronje (1906 I:21, 63, 149 n1; II:222, 318) documented among the Acehnese in the 1890s, presumably because they had been delegitimized and were no longer as common, public, or visible.

Observations of the sort registered by Belo and Jaspan are in keeping with ethnographic accounts from the Philippines and Thailand based on research during the middle half of the twentieth century (see Hart [1968] and Yengoyan [1983], and Keyes [1986:96 n47], respectively). These observations also resonate with the sparse information bearing on rural Vietnam from the late 1960s, most of which concerns ritual specialists and is phrased in ways that reflect the clinical backgrounds and epidemiological interests of the researchers. Heiman and Le (1975) report the existence in southern Vietnam of high status and powerful "hermaphroditic witches," a phrase they set off in quotes throughout their essay (implying that it is a rough gloss for a Vietnamese term, probably *ong dong* [Proschan 1998:2]), who they also refer to as cross-dressing (male-bodied) "witch doctors." "Trained in their careers as healers from childhood" and "inhabited by female [and sometimes male] spirits" during which time they experience trance, these ritual specialists "have the power of communicating with evil spirits and curing diseases by complicated rituals." In some ways most telling, the authors describe these ritual practitioners as continuing to enjoy "high status and power" in their rural communities but *not* in "westernized Vietnam" (Heiman and Le 1975:91, 93–4).

More recent fieldwork from socialist Vietnam since Doi Moi (Renovation) in the late 1980s confirms these historical trends inasmuch as it points to society's deeply ambivalent attitudes toward still popular spirit mediums, many of whom, like both the ritual specialists who dress them and others involved in maintaining and guarding temples (devoted to the Mother Goddess, for example), participate in transgender practices and same-sex relations. Such attitudes are shaped partly by "neo-Confucian conceptions and practices of ancestral veneration and filial responsibility (*hieu*), in which a man's most important duty is to reproduce a male child to carry on the ancestral line" (Proschan 1998:1), and partly by the modernist disdain suffusing the discourses of government critics and state-controlled media that characterize the rituals of shamanic mediums, especially Len Dong ceremonies, as "superstitious, … frivolous and wasteful" (Nguyen 2003:1).

More generally, while "Vietnamese society today offers little space within the public sphere of sociopolitical discourse even to discuss homosexuality" (Aronson 1999:215), gender and sexual nonconformity have long flourished—and continue to do so—particularly in certain conventional roles and spaces associated with genres of popular drama and ritual mediumship, and in temple complexes and Buddhist monasteries as a whole (Proschan 1998, 2002b:633 n92). There is, moreover, growing awareness and tacit acceptance among urban Vietnamese that certain venues within large cities (e.g., the park surrounding Hanoi's Hoan Kiem Lake and countless nightclubs and other gathering spots in Ho Chi Minh City), along with myriad virtual locales in cyberspace, serve as meeting places (cruising spots) for males seeking to meet other males with whom they might engage in sexual encounters. Some of these relationships do not conform to traditional patterns of same-sex unions insofar as both partners are of outwardly masculine appearance and demeanor, which is to say that the

relationships are not heterogender, at least as far as the larger society is concerned. Both in Vietnam and elsewhere in Southeast Asia, relationships of this
sort pose considerable challenges to the systems of classification that are
enshrined in long-established regimes of sex/gender, for these systems appear
always to have been predicated on hierarchically coded male-female differen-
tials. Going a long way toward mitigating such challenges and endowing them
with at least a modicum of legitimacy is the fact that both in Vietnam and in
Southeast Asia generally, many of the males who participate in these relationship are also involved in (or planning to enter into) heterosexual marriage
entailing procreation, thus fulfilling normative expectations that are in
many ways far more weighty than those specifying that sexuality be confined to
heterosexual relationships. They do, in short, fashion identities and strategies
for survival that entail "drawing variously on endogenous traditions and identities as well as exogenous concepts and practices, combining and recombining
them, and at the same time contesting both cultural conventions that would
condemn homosexuality as incompatible with filial piety and metropolitan
notions that would insist there is only one way to be authentically gay"
(Proschan 1998:3).[1]

Of broader concern is that even though some of the observations bearing on
Bali, Java, Sumatra, the Philippines, Thailand, and Vietnam contained in the
accounts cited here suggest a certain dismissiveness, ambivalence, and
(arguably) a euphemized violence of exclusion, they are in many respects relatively positive, albeit decidedly less so than in earlier times, and largely consistent in a "theme and variation" sense with what we know for Southeast Asia as
a whole during this period. The remainder of this chapter, which focuses largely
but not exclusively on the period since the 1960s—a period that witnessed cultural, political, and economic changes whose pace, force, scope, and overall
intensity greatly surpassed changes in earlier times—will further substantiate
these points. It will also facilitate a more nuanced analytic understanding of
similarities and differences in the dynamics of transgender practices and same-
sex relations in late twentieth-century Southeast Asia as well as the challenges
that contemporary projects of modernity can pose to transgenderism, same-sex
sexuality, and gender pluralism generally.

As in preceding parts of this book, the discussions in this chapter vary a good
deal in terms of scale, scope, and detail. Some of my remarks encompass a broad
range of Southeast Asian societies; others deal with a single society, doing so
with a fair degree of specificity in order to facilitate description and analysis of
some of the significant detail and texture of a case that is in one or more ways
illustrative of the larger region or an important range of societies or globally
inflected trends within it. I begin the chapter by returning to three of the insular Southeast Asian cases discussed in Chapter 2. In the first two of these cases,
the Iban and the Ngaju Dayak, I address downward shifts in the status of transgendered ritual specialists, the constriction of pluralistic sensibilities and dispositions bearing on the gender and sexual variability long associated with these
practitioners and their partners, and the rise of female prostitution (at least

among the Iban). The third case, the Bugis, which is much better documented, allows for a discussion that is both more expansive and more nuanced, one that encompasses not only the current vicissitudes of transgenderism associated with ritual domains but also an array of gendered subjectivities and same-sex relations that are not linked to ritual practices. The Bugis case reveals the proliferation of new subject positions and subjectivities along with the emergence of new sources of legitimacy, some of which are keyed to processes of religious reenchantment since the late 1990s that help bestow respectability on a broad range of gender and sexual variability.

The remainder of the chapter addresses data bearing on the Burmese, the case I deal with most substantively, partly because it is among the least well known in all of Southeast Asia. The Burmese case differs in major ways from the others considered here insofar as transgendered ritualists who are commonly involved in same-sex relations, though viewed with ambivalence, are still accorded great esteem and critically important roles both in rural communities *and* in urban settings; their "lay" partners, moreover, incur no stigma on account of their involvement in these relationships. (This situation has obtained since the 1960s and long before, and thus differs from its Bugis counterpart insofar as the recent "*bissu* renaissance" followed a period of sharp decline over much of the twentieth century.) One reason for this is that state policies pursued during the past four decades have isolated Burma from much of the world; consequently, much of Burma's population is still committed to agricultural endeavors and the ritual practices and more encompassing moral and cosmological precepts long associated with them. While Burma might therefore be considered a glaring exception to many of the generalizations offered earlier, concerning the historic delegitimization and reduced status of transgendered ritual practitioners, and the constriction of gender pluralism generally, I have emphasized that processes of delegitimization and stigmatization have not been uniform, all-encompassing, or monolithic. More to the point, Burma is most appropriately viewed as exemplifying a space where state strategies aimed at distancing the nation from certain aspects of modernity, especially the capitalist-driven world economy and global flows of people, ideas, and technologies, has allowed for if not encouraged the reproduction and continued vitality of long-established roles of transgendered ritualists and some (but certainly not all) of the social patterns and cultural sensibilities conventionally associated with them.

My examination of the Burmese case also considers sociolinguistic data bearing on various referents of terms commonly used for spirit mediums and shamans, along with the links and disjunctions between these references and other Burmese terms utilized to denote gender and sexual transgression, some of which reveal efforts to create new, masculinized space for males involved in same-sex relations. We turn finally to a discussion of women and femininity in Burma at the turn of the twenty-first century. The material considered here serves as an important reminder that while transgenderism provides a powerful optic on gender as a whole, the status of transgendered ritualists in a particular milieu at any given point in time is not necessarily a clear index of the status of women (one can be "high," the other "low;" this is everywhere an empirical question); and, more generally, that with respect to these and attendant matters, much depends on the practices and policies of political (and religious) elites. Burma's political elites have impoverished their charges and have sought to scale down the pluralistic sentiments and dispositions that have long characterized rural culture; in the process they have forced many women into prostitution and have otherwise marginalized them and subjected them to multiple forms of stigma, risk, and harm.

In the concluding section of the chapter I summarize the historical and cultural-political dynamics conducive to the transformation and erosion of gender pluralism over the long term as well as countervailing forces that help explain why gender pluralism remains relatively robust in many Southeast Asian societies despite pressures long arrayed against it. I also consider some problems with the ways that the term "heteronormative" is commonly employed, in addition to issues having to do with the proliferation of gender and sexual diversity in the postcolonial era and the last few decades in particular. Of chief interest is the relevance of the ethnographic cases considered here for scholarly debates concerning the globalization of sex/gender regimes in Southeast Asia (and beyond), many of which have to do with variable scholarly understandings of the relationship between "traditional" and (late) "modern" identities and discourses associated with globalization, and whether (and if so how) identities and discourses of the latter sort have colonized or supplanted sex/gender identities and arrangements of earlier times or have instead been creatively incorporated into (or otherwise melded with) them.

Some Insular Southeast Asian Cases

Iban

The case of the Iban, who currently number around 600,000, is productively approached by focusing first on transformations and continuities in the office of the transgendered ritual specialist known as *manang bali*. Long the most important of the Iban's ritual practitioners, the typically male-bodied *manang bali* dressed in women's attire and behaved in other ways like women, commonly marrying men as husbands. It will be recalled from Chapter 2 that even through the mid-nineteenth century, the *manang bali* was, to mix metaphors, a jack of all trades, a "renaissance man," albeit a Bornean transgendered one, someone who settled disputes, distributed his property, wealth, and other social goods to his followers, and not infrequently became the chief of the village. Arguably most germane is that, according to observers such as Hugh Brooke Low (n.d., cited in Roth 1896 [1980] I:271), the *manang bali* was "always a person of great consequence." We also know that the second half of the nineteenth century was a period that saw countless encroachments into Iban territory on the part of British colonial agents, Christian (mostly Protestant) missionaries, and Chinese and Malay traders (trafficking in beads, salt, iron, earthenware jars, etc.), among others. Significantly, seafaring groups of Malay Muslims who had their own traditions of ritual transgendering but nonetheless held Iban traditions in contempt had succeeded in dissuading some coastal Iban groups from observing local traditions of transgendering as early as 1896 (ibid.)

Based on extensive field research among the Iban, anthropologist Erik Jensen (1974) delineates the changes that occurred from the mid- to late nineteenth century through the late 1950s and mid-1960s, the period of his research. As of the mid-1960s, by which time Iban territory and Sarawak as a whole had been fully incorporated into the newly independent state of Malaysia, most Iban had abandoned slash-and-burn horticulture along with their semi-nomadic ways of life and key features of their *adat* ("tradition," "custom," "customary law"), in favor of settled agriculture, cash cropping, and (syncretic) Christianity, which has been embraced by increasing numbers of Iban as a statement of opposition to Islam and all that it signifies (see also Sutlive 1978 [1988]). Similarly, by this time Iban had attained considerable familiarity with European *ars medica* and were in many instances highly enamored of it. Iban romance with European medicine undermined key features of the indigenous medical system, which was inextricably linked to (because thoroughly grounded in) their religious systems and cosmology alike. In the face of these challenges, Iban retained selected elements of their "customary" religion and tradition (jettisoning others, as noted), but their meanings were in many instances radically transformed. So too in the process was the social standing of the various ritual practitioners (including, but not limited to, *manang bali*) who had long served the Iban by overseeing the curing ceremonies and other rituals that insured mutually beneficial and otherwise proper relations between the living and the dead, the past and the present, the sacred and the profane, and the realms of the upperworld and underworld.

Two sets of changes associated with the office of the *manang bali* are particularly noteworthy. The first has to do with the social standing of the individual who assumed this office on the one hand, and the overall status of the office on the other. In the mid-nineteenth century, the individual who rose to this office was described as enjoying great "popularity" due to the many kinds of social goods he provided his followers and the community at large; for these same reasons, as already noted, he was said to be "always a person of great consequence." The current situation is dramatically different. "At present," according to Jensen (1974:63), the occupant of this office "is commonly a person who in the ordinary Iban context counts for little." Part of the reason for this is the restructuring of what counts as success: people who become *manang bali* are commonly afflicted with poor eyesight if not one or another degree of blindness. This may be "interpreted as an asset in dealings with the spirit world," since "spirits move mainly at night and ... see in the dark, when the Iban cannot normally see; conversely blindness may be taken to imply spirit sight" (ibid., 63). On the other hand, such visual impairment can be a "handicap so severe as to make a man almost totally dependent on his *bilek* [longhouse apartment] family" (ibid.). More generally, "The *manang*, as someone capable of intercourse with the spirit world may be a person of some power in the locality where he operates," but "usually his influence is confined to a limited area" and "although known for his achievements when effective, the *manang* is not otherwise a man of consequence or status in the community" (ibid., 142–143; emphasis added). "On the contrary, the expression 'to be like a *manang*' (*baka manang*) is derogatory since it implies that a man grows insufficient rice for his *bilek*" (ibid., 143). Hence children poke fun at them, and they are not held to be successful in local schemes of valuation because "success is measured largely in plentiful harvests, and [because] the *manang* ... is frequently ... absent from his farm [and] is rarely a successful farmer" (ibid., 143).

A more general problem is the encroachment of a market logic entailing the constriction and demise of rituals of many varieties that encapsulate "Iban cosmology and eschatology, uniting time and eternity, the living and the dead, earth and non-earth" (Sutlive 1978 [1988]:196). In 1984, when ethnographer Vinson Sutlive inquired about the truncated fate of the pageantry he had observed in previous decades, he was told that "they had not hired bards 'because they are too expensive' and [that] more pageantry was not included because 'we can't afford the time'" (ibid., 197).

The second set of changes bearing on the *manang bali* has to do with the declining significance of transgenderism and same-sex relations as constituent features of this role. In Hugh Low's time (the 1840s), transgenderism that commonly entailed same-sex relations was said to be a usual if not necessary part of the role [H. Low 1848 [1968]:174–177; cited in Jensen 1974:144)]. "St John (1862 I: 73) mentions it also; Gomes (1911:180), on the other hand, encountered it only once in seventeen years among the Iban. The tendency apparent in Gomes's experience ... [in the early twentieth century] is borne out by recent enquiries" and it "is now [in the 1960s] virtually unknown," at least according to some observers (e.g., Jensen 1974:144; but see Sutlive 1978 [1988]:56, who suggests that some of Jensen's observations cannot be generalized to all Iban).

Sutlive may well be correct in suggesting that for most Iban a conceptual link still exists between *manang bali* and same-sex sexuality. (He notes, for example, that the *manang*'s "homosexual tendencies are commonly acknowledged by the Iban" [ibid., 56].) Even so, there is little disagreement that the variability in gender practices and sexual relations long linked with *manang bali* declined more quickly than other aspects of the role—or, put differently, that such variability was more sensitive to forces of change than other features of the role. This suggests that a necessary condition for the reproduction of the (transformed) role into the present was that it be stripped of its more "exotic," transgressive elements, much as the Ngaju Dayak and Bugis cases considered in due course.

What then of the larger question as to whether the declining fortunes of transgendered ritualists index a constriction of pluralism-friendly dynamics bearing on gender and sexuality throughout Iban society as a whole? The short answer is that the signs are not at all encouraging. Here it is important to recall the earlier traditions of female ritual specialists who like their male-bodied counterparts enjoyed access to the sacred and were as a consequence accorded tremendous power and prestige. This tradition has long since disappeared; and in the increasingly urban enclaves in which Iban find themselves, it would have little meaning in any case unless circumstances gave rise to an efflorescence of spirit mediumship, as has occurred in recent decades in urban areas of Thailand, Burma, and Vietnam. The relative autonomy, social control, and respect that Iban women long enjoyed in their rural communities has been threatened and undermined by the same general dynamics undercutting the roles of *manang bali*. Put differently, the declining viability of rural (especially economic) institutions and the erosion of the cosmologies in which they were embedded have encouraged migration to urban areas and the resultant proletarianization of the Iban, a trend that has gone hand in hand with the rise among the Iban of (female) prostitution. We should be clear that unlike temporary wives of previous centuries, contemporary Iban sex workers garner little if any prestige in their communities and are in fact heavily stigmatized.

The prevalence of prostitution among Iban women living in cities such as Sibu has been linked to desires for urban living, themselves testimonies both to the decline of rural livelihoods and to the emergence of the "two paycheck family" (Sutlive 1978 [1988]:197). Iban settlement in Sibu increased from fewer than 500 in 1950 to upwards of 10,000 in 1984 (Sutlive 1991:496). There and in other urban settings, Iban women find that "traditional prescriptions and opportunities for achievement ... have given way to economic and political systems with uneven advantages for males" (ibid., 497); that the "control exercised by state and federal governments over land, forests, oil, and other resources [are] all in the hands of men;" and that "access to top level posts in ministries and departments is restricted almost exclusively to men" (ibid.). In sum, gender egalitarianism "is becoming increasingly uncharacteristic of contemporary Iban society" (ibid., 493).

Sutlive (1978 [1988]:186) observes that employment as a domestic servant, like that involving prostitution, provides economic options "not available otherwise to Iban women," submitting, more controversially, that "the role of the prostitute ... does not conflict with the relaxed attitudes of Iban toward sex" (ibid., 186). According to Sutlive, many of the 400 to 800 prostitutes working in Sibu in 1984 "came from economically depressed areas and claimed there was no work or economic opportunities for them in their longhouses" (ibid., 198). And while "many were generally happy, pleasant, and confident," in "their interviews [with Sutlive] a majority indicated that they had been abused or abandoned, and that prostitution was a way by which they could get what they wanted with no obligation to anyone else" (ibid., 199). On closer inspection then things are not as rosy as they seem. It is nonetheless significant that for some Iban women joining the ranks of sex workers is viewed and experienced as a (largely economic "lifestyle") "choice" (Sutlive 1991:504–506), albeit a choice exercised in a cultural-political environment in which extremely limited educational and economic resources conduce toward few other meaningful alternatives (cf. Law 1997).

We need also consider the discourses of development and "damaged goods"—and of dishonor, dirt, and disease—that help define sex work in the Iban context. A female government worker in the Social Welfare Department spoke of Iban prostitution in terms of "immoral behavior" but qualified her critique of sex workers by saying that they were casualties of development. She seemed relatively sympathetic to their plight, especially the emotional costs they bore, but it is clear from her comments on development that they were in need of moral transformation.

> We talk of development and development, but I'm not sure it's development at all, because the psychological and emotional costs are so high, and needs are not being met. I feel angry that all this development is taking place and we in the Welfare Department are not being given enough staff and enough mandate and enough facilities to assist in this development. It seems as if we are here just to take care of all the casualties [e.g., prostitutes] and to do the bandage work. And actually the casualties are so many that we can't cope with them.
>
> (Cited in Sutlive 1991:519)

Medical anthropologist Winny Koster documents far less charitable views of Sibu's prostitutes, based on a study conducted from March to May 1986: "Respectable people, and in particular women, generally look down on prostitutes. Prostitutes are supposed to have no sense of honour, to be rude, to want to earn cheap money easily, to be dirty and to carry diseases. Also women find them dangerous because prostitutes are seducing husbands and boyfriends. Respectable women think of prostitutes as belonging to another category of women than themselves with whom they do not want to mix" (cited in ibid., 521). Significantly, Koster found that most prostitutes disliked the work they were doing, that many were formerly married, and that "the life of a prostitute is troublesome and sometimes dangerous. The women ... complain[ed] about men being aggressive and using force, not wanting to pay, not wanting to use condoms if they asked them to .... Many of the prostitutes have often felt threatened and afraid" (ibid., 527, 528).

Both Koster's material and some of Sutlive's findings indicate that Iban attitudes toward sex are somewhat less "relaxed" than Sutlive suggests, and that present-day prostitution is likewise less compatible with current Iban sensibilities than Sutlive submits. Perhaps the best explanation for the disjuncture at issue is that Sutlive's careful attention to social change among the Iban is not matched by sufficient attentiveness on his part to the historically contingent nature of Iban pluralism, which is clearly less robust than in times past.

I have already cited numerous dynamics that have contributed to a constriction of gender pluralism among the Iban and would thus underscore that many of these same dynamics are likely to inform the future of Iban pluralism as well. One additional variable that merits brief mention is the reduced frequency of adoption, which is part of a nexus of change that also involves shifts in post-marital residence (e.g., the heightened prevalence of uxorilocality and neolocality), and the decreased popularity both of arranged marriage and of longhouse and community endogamy [Sutlive 1978 [1988]:172–173]). I attach particular significance to the decline in adoption, coupled, I assume, with declines in informal arrangements involving temporary fosterage, because these practices occur at a very young age and help set the stage for the kind of "trading places" that promotes both conceptual and moral relativism. These changes are dialectically related to (i.e., both cause and consequence of) transformations in pluralistic sentiments and dispositions bearing on other domains of embodied experience and fields of social relations, and because of their generative capacity are likely to have widely redounding implications in the years ahead.

Viewed from a long-term perspective, we might say that Iban women have been subject to processes that have distanced them from the public sphere, and, when not distancing them from it, have marginalized and degraded them within it. It is certainly relevant that once highly regarded female shamans have all but disappeared, and that, at present, Iban women act in the public domain primarily as dishonored, potentially disease-bearing prostitutes. Put differently, the public domain has been masculinized both by dynamics that have operated to the detriment of women and by attendant processes that have delegitimized transgendered ritual specialists and seen their replacement by more or less normatively gendered individuals with unambiguously male bodies and overwhelmingly secular, bureaucratic sources of authority.

This is not to suggest that Iban women or the transgendered, or normatively gendered males, for that matter, have been passive subjects or victims of history; far from it. There is a rich literature documenting Iban resistance both to the White Rajahs—the Brooke dynasty that ruled much of Sarawak from the 1840s until 1941—and to Christianity and various policies of the postcolonial Malaysian state (see, for example, Pringle 1970, Sutlive 1991, and the sources cited in these texts). An estimated 6,000 Iban joined forces with about 500 Malays to repel British forces in a battle of June 11, 1843, and took untold numbers of European heads, spurred on, as is usually the case among Iban, by women and ritual specialists, to cite but one of many early examples (Pringle 1970:74). More generally, the literature makes clear that the resistance to which I refer has involved ritual specialists and "laymen" alike, and all varieties of gendered bodies.

The fact remains however that despite short-term victories and historical reversals that appeared to promise a largely unfettered reproduction of core values and relations, Iban cosmologies, status hierarchies, and systems of social relations have been radically transformed in recent centuries, largely because—through treaty, trickery, and sheer force on the part of external actors with superior fire power—they have come to be embedded within more encompassing systems of non-Iban design, such as those associated with local Christian churches and the strongly "pro development" (and "Malay first") policies of the Muslim-majority Malaysian state. Contemporary Iban live in a milieu that is heavily inflected by state-sponsored discourses of capitalist development and Christian and Muslim normativity, including medicalized narratives on AIDS that encourage practices of pre-marital chastity and monogamy and simultaneously eschew all varieties of non-heteronormativity. Building (most likely) on nineteenth-century structural precedents and ambivalences of the sort that reportedly entailed derision of men married to *manang bali*, discursive regimes such as these make little space for unauthorized Otherness, as will be abundantly clear when we examine the Malaysian case in more detail (Chapter 5).

Ngaju Dayak

Another Austronesian group discussed in Chapter 2, the Ngaju Dayak, has much in common with the Iban and resides only a few hundred miles away but lives in the portion of Borneo (Kalimantan) that is claimed by Indonesia rather than Malaysia. The Ngaju Dayak, who numbered between 500,000 and 800,000 in 1994 (Schiller 1997a:14), have engaged Protestant missionary influences (mostly German and Swiss) since the 1830s as well as the effects of mid-nineteenth-century (and subsequent) Islamic revivalism, Dutch colonialism, and state-sponsored capitalism. In addition, along with their neighbors, many educated Ngaju Dayak were involved in a guerrilla movement in the 1950s that sought to reduce the cultural-political influence of nearby (Banjarese-Malay) Muslims and resulted in the creation (in 1957) of the province of Central Kalimantan. More generally, Ngaju Dayak have had to contend with the postcolonial policies of the Javacentric Indonesian state, which has encouraged the formation of modern political parties and has promoted massive transmigration of Muslims, Hindu Balinese, and others into their ancestral homelands. One result of these dynamics has been the large-scale (though not total) abandonment of traditional religious practices and conversion to World Religions. In the province of Central Kalimantan, home to most Ngaju Dayak, "the majority of the indigenous inhabitants ... embrace Christianity [at least nominally], and a growing number have converted to Islam .... At best, only about 30 percent of the Ngaju continue to embrace the traditional religion openly, though it is rumored that many more than that ... observe it surreptitiously" (Schiller 1997a:23). Extensive rationalization processes, both institutional and cultural, have occurred among the Ngaju Dayak in the same general ways as they have taken place among the Iban, the Meratus of Kalimantan (Tsing 1993), the Toraja, Wana, and "headwater peoples" of Sulawesi (Volkman 1985, Atkinson 1989, George 1996), the Tengger of East Java (Hefner 1985), as well as Balinese (C. Geertz 1973), Malays (Peletz 2002), and others in the region. Formerly encompassing concepts of *adat* (*hadat*; "tradition," "custom," "customary law") have been objectified and fragmented, and many of the more "flamboyant" features of Ngaju practices that occurred in connection with fertility cults, death ritual, and periods of ceremonial license have been eliminated or else dramatically toned down. Some such practices have been "reduced" to ritual displays involving adornment with "enormous wooden phalluses or halved coconut shells representing female genitalia" and dancers "gesticulating obscenely and mimicking coitus" (Schiller 1997a:66). Equally telling, female ritual specialists (*balian*) who in former times engaged in "sacred prostitution" have all but disappeared;[2] very few of their male counter-parts (*basir*) are involved in cross-dressing or transgender practices of other kinds; and, as in most other parts of Southeast Asia, styles of clothing—especially for women—are decidedly more modest than in times past.

In light of the circumstances outlined here it should not be surprising to find that, as one anthropologist (Schiller 1997a:26, 40 passim) has reported, some Ngaju Dayak ritual specialists living at present are at pains to distance themselves from certain of the more "catholic" traditions of their ancestors. The prevalence of transgendered ritualists and ceremonial sexual license in earlier time offends the ethical sensibilities of these largely Christian Dayak. It is deeply embarrassing and politically inconvenient as well, further complicating their already fraught efforts to garner the respect, legitimacy, material resources, and political representation to which they feel entitled in Muslim-majority Indonesia. All such problems are compounded by the fact that state and local policies have not only marginalized Ngaju Dayak communities but have also resulted in an upsurge of both sectarian and criminal violence directed at Christians, including Dayak groups, and others who embody one or more kind of difference. The distancing at issue, which simultaneously involves a kind of temporally inflected auto-"Othering," occurs partly through explicit denials of the veracity of key particulars of earlier accounts bearing on their community, such as Scharer's (1946 [1963]:57) contention that all *basir* used to be involved in cross-dressing and other transgender practices. These denials surface in con-versations with contemporary anthropologists (such as Schiller); they are also manifest in silences, discursive elisions, and somewhat nervous laughter in response to questions on some of the more sensitive issues (see, for example, Schiller 1997a:40; cf. Miles 1976:76, Jay 1993:164).

This situation is broadly reminiscent of many other sensitive encounters involving anthropologists and members of the communities in which we work. One is reminded, for instance, of Samoans, who for some decades now have prided themselves on being deeply and thoroughly Christian. Some contempo-rary Samoans are not at all pleased with Margaret Mead's (1928 [1968]) account of patterns of gender and sexual diversity in the 1920s and have in some instances adamantly denied much of what Mead reported, claiming she was led astray, duped, toyed with, and so on, as Derek Freeman (1983), who conducted fieldwork in a very different part of Samoa decades after Mead left the islands, was quite happy to underscore. Bruce Knauft (2005:133–137) describes an analogous but more temporally compressed scenario, involving the Gebusi of Papua New Guinea. The Gebusi's large-scale conversion to Christianity begin-ning in the 1980s (the vast majority are now Catholics, Evangelicals, or Seventh Day Adventists) brought about the complete disappearance, within a single generation, of thoroughly institutionalized practices of same-sex sexual-ity involving young boys and senior males, which Knauft observed first-hand in the late 1970s. At least equally striking is that no knowledge of these features of their abandoned past have been imparted to contemporary youth, who were genuinely incredulous and deeply shocked when Knauft inadvertently broached the subject with them in the late 1990s, thus implicating all of their fathers, uncles, and other senior males.

The point here is not that anthropologists, who are often outsiders, get it right, and that "the natives" (insiders) often do not; far from it. Rather, my point has to do with the ways we interpret the constructions of the past that are offered to us, through explicit comments, elisions, silences, laughter, and the like, by those among whom we work. Ngaju Dayak clearly have very mixed feelings about their past as well as certain contours of their present. So too do Iban, Bugis, Malays, and many other groups discussed in this book. Rather than interpret the negative dimensions of these kinds of mixed feelings as unqualified corrections to previous accounts, we should consider the possibility that they are an index of present-day ambivalences about the past (and the present). This seems all the more worthwhile since Schiller (1997a:26, 134) observes, "many Christian families emphasize their ancestors' barbarity prior to conversion," while others "decried the backwardness of the ancestral rituals, declaring them unworthy of the name 'religion'" (cf. Jay 1993:164–165).

These ambivalences are worthy of further consideration. So too are twentieth-century shifts in the domestic and social structural arrangements that contributed to them, some of which are implicated in the emergence of new subjectivities and systems of status relations that have eclipsed earlier sociopolitical distinctions among "free people" (a category composed of "superior [or rich] people" and "inferior [or poor] people," as discussed in Chapter 2) as distinct from "slaves" or debt bondsmen (see Miles 1964, 1966, 1971, 1976 for an overview of some of these dynamics). But I want to turn to commonalities between Ngaju Dayak and Iban with respect to the constriction of pluralistic sensibilities bearing on gender and sexuality in the latter half of the twentieth century. A prominent feature of change in this area, in my view, is the delegitimization of non-heteronormative practices. We should be clear that, as with other cases considered earlier, the frequency of these practices is less at issue than the symbols and meanings associated with them, including whether and why they are accorded one or another degree of prestige or stigma. We should also be careful to avoid the conceptually and empirically unwarranted assumption of commonalities "across the board," particularly with regard to the position of women (in the sense of the esteem in which women are held), which is generally much higher among Ngaju Dayak than among Iban (not all constrictions of pluralism are the same), even though in both cases women have been squeezed out of key ritual roles and thus distanced from important loci of power and prestige. How much of this contrast has to do with the ongoing salience among Ngaju Dayak, even among those who have converted to Christianity or Islam, of key elements of indigenous ritual and cosmology, some of which continue to prominently feature dual-gendered themes and women (Miles 1976:47–48, Schiller 1991, Jay 1993), or much lower rates of out-migration and urban residence—these dynamics are dialectically related—is not clear. It is relevant, though, that the continued viability of the Ngaju Dayak's "traditional" economic institutions (based on the shifting cultivation of rice and on hunting, fishing, and the collection of forest produce) renders permanent out-migration and urban residence and the female prostitution that often accompanies it less likely. Also less likely as a consequence is the emergence of discourses such as we see among the Iban and elsewhere in Sarawak and far beyond that construct female prostitutes, and by extension, potentially all women, as dirty, disease-bearing, and dishonorable.

It remains to note that, as in many other areas of Indonesia—but, significantly, not Sarawak or elsewhere in Malaysia—the 1990s saw a renewed interest in many locally distinctive religious practices, including those of Ngaju Dayak. Some of this renewed interest on the part of Ngaju Dayak and others entails a reassertion of local autonomy and cultural identity in the face of decades of heavy-handed Javacentric state policies that marginalized or punished those at the geopolitical periphery. Some however is promoted by the state to build tourism and the revenue conducive to "development" (*pembangunan*) (Schiller 1997b). This renewed interest has not gone hand in hand with a relegitimization (or reenchantment) of transgendered ritual specialists or the gender and sexual variability iconically associated with them, as has occurred among the Bugis. By the late twentieth century, the Ngaju Dayak's transgendered specialists and much that they symbolized had apparently been irrevocably stigmatized, situated as they were between a (mostly Protestant) Christian rock and a Muslim hard place, and were thus too far gone to meaningfully resurrect. The situation among the Bugis is quite different, as we shall see.

Bugis

The extensive (but highly uneven) literature on the Bugis since the sixteenth century allows for a description and analysis of gender pluralism that is more nuanced and expansive than is possible for the Iban and Ngaju Dayak. This literature makes clear that the adoption by 1611 of various features of Islam by Bugis rulers, their charges, and most others in South Sulawesi posed serious dilemmas for the highly esteemed ritual specialists known as *bissu*, dilemmas that were simultaneously moral, existential, personal, and political. This is partly because the mostly male-bodied *bissu* (I will return to their female-bodied counterparts in due course) claimed "heavenly beings [one male, one female] as mystic spouses" as well as more earth-bound same-sex spouses (Pelras 1996:83). The other part of the problem was the local orthodoxy that *bissu* descended from the gods and perforce partook in the gods' divinity—a major heresy in Islam, especially the reformist or "scripturalist" Islam circulating in and around South Sulawesi at this time. Hence beginning in the early seventeenth century we see periodic (but not consistent or sustained) efforts by Islamic rulers committed to literal interpretations of *syariah* to discredit *bissu* and expel them from their jurisdictions (ibid., 142, 188). Such moves were part

and parcel of more encompassing strategies of cultural cleansing aimed at eradicating gambling, slavery, the consumption of opium and palm wine, ceremonials of a pre-Islamic nature, and all other evidence of "pagan times."

The imposition of Dutch colonial rule in South Sulawesi in 1905 resulted in
additional challenges to the prestige and roles of *bissu*, as did Indonesia's independence in 1949. The two sets of developments were of course quite different
but both contributed to the emergence of new sets of status relations (if not new
status hierarchies) and new groups of elites, and otherwise foreshadowed the
elimination in Sulawesi and elsewhere of long-sovereign kingdoms. In doing so
they "deprived the *bissu* of their royal patrons and their principal *raison d'être*":
guarding royal regalia and enhancing the sacred potency of local rulers (L.
Andaya 2000:44). Another, related factor relevant to the transformation and
decline of the *bissu* role is that the sacred texts (e.g., *La Galigo*) that served as the
bases of their legitimacy and sanctity have become somewhat (arguably largely)
irrelevant due to the spread throughout Indonesia of modern-day science, education, and transnational media, coupled with the increased importance of
Islamic institutions and pan-Islamic discourses and the attendant creation of
new forms and loci of power and prestige. It did not help the cause of the *bissu*
that by the mid-twentieth century many Bugis regarded them as remnants of
feudal times, a view which sheds light on why *bissu* were tortured and killed by
some groups of reformers during the South Sulawesi Rebellion (1950–1965)
and why for most of the rest of the century "bissu activities were officially out-
lawed" (Davies 2007:92, 98; Pelras 1996:286). Nor does it help that, since the
1960s, good numbers of Bugis have felt that all remnants of feudalism should be
eradicated in the name of forging authentic Bugis identities that are simultaneously modern, Islamic, and Indonesian. This is not to suggest that *bissu*, transgendering, and same-sex sexuality have ceased to exist in South Sulawesi or
have lost all meaningful ties to their early modern predecessors; for they have
not. It is revealing though that Susan Millar's book-length (1989) study of
Bugis weddings, based on 21 months of field research from 1975 to 1976, barely
mentions *bissu*, a silence that resonates with Pelras' (1996:167) observation,
from fieldwork undertaken around the same time, that "genuine *bissu* have
nearly disappeared."

Historians, anthropologists, and others who are concerned with the *longue
durée* are well advised to emphasize, as I have done at various points in this book,
that the pace, scope, force, direction, and overall intensity of change in the
cases with which we are concerned are rarely if ever uniform or linear. This is
certainly true in the case of the Bugis. Among the Bugis, and in other societies
throughout the region, the legitimacy of female-bodied ritualists, the majority
of whom appear not to have been transgendered, was undermined more quickly
and more thoroughly than the legitimacy of their male-bodied counterparts
(Blackwood 2005). Indeed, whereas after the eighteenth century there are few
references in the literature to female-bodied *bissu*, male-bodied (and intersexed) *bissu* continued to ply their trade. We have seen, too, that in the mid-
twentieth century, *bissu* were intentionally hunted down, tortured, and

murdered by Indonesian reformers, whereas in earlier times they were subject to less extreme and more diffuse sanctions—gossip, ostracism, and the like probably being the most common, though social "excommunication" and forced exile also occurred. Circumstances such as these indicate that the intensity of opposition to *bissu* roles, along with the stigma attached to such roles, has varied a great deal over time, as, conversely, has the prestige that *bissu* have been accorded. In sum, as with other cases discussed in this book, the twentieth century tended to bring "deep change" that was typically more profound, in terms of its pace, scope, force, and overall intensity than transformations that occurred in earlier times. This having been said, among the Bugis and in South Sulawesi generally, the turmoil and upheavals of the fourteenth and to a lesser extent the seventeenth century, might be seen as giving the disruptions of the twentieth century a good run for their money (Pelras 1996:174 passim).

The final years of the twentieth century and the first few years of the new millennium provide additional evidence of the importance of making analytic provision for non-linear transformations, including historical reversals and other kinds of counter-flows and openings. Suharto's fall in 1998 created a power vacuum that brought with it a broad range of opportunities for political maneuvering and local advocacy, along with crises of legitimacy of all kinds. These dynamics helped pave the way for reassertions of local cultural identities that had long been marginalized or suppressed, as we saw among the Ngaju Dayak (cf. Boon 1979). The reflowering of Bugis identity has entailed a revival of interest in *bissu* and the gendered legacies, subjectivities, and experiential spaces they are taken to represent. The chief reason for this "*bissu* renaissance" is that *bissu* are seen—and strive to position themselves—as guardians of sacred texts and traditions that help define Bugis *adat*, which is central to Bugis identity, as Sharyn Graham Davies (whose publications on the Bugis prior to 2005 appear under the name Sharyn Graham) demonstrates, based on 15 months of fieldwork she conducted among Bugis during the period 1998–2000 and a number of subsequent visits through 2005 (Davies 2007:98 passim). In some quarters of Sulawesi and among certain groups of Indonesian activists in Jakarta and elsewhere in the archipelago, the turn of the twenty-first century has seen the formation of modern-day NGOs devoted to revitalizing or reactualizing *bissu* roles, as recently noted by Indonesian scholar and activist Dede Oetomo (2006:331; cf. Tsing 2005). This is highly significant, as are the strategic alliances these NGOs have forged with Muslim feminists in organizations such as Fahmina, Rahima, and the women's wing of the *Perhimpunan Pengembangan Pesantren dan Masyarakat* (Society for Islamic Boarding Schools and Community Development), commonly known as P3M. As with other dynamics we have considered, these developments underscore that historical vicissitudes of gender and sexuality in South Sulawesi and elsewhere in the archipelago and beyond are rarely if ever unilinear, and that struggles for the hearts and minds of ritual specialists and non-specialists alike involve myriad forces and multiple sources of legitimacy.

It remains to be seen whether organizations committed to *bissu* revitalization will be co-opted by institutions promoting cultural tourism and whether the *bissu* destiny in the years to come will be largely confined to the realm of the folkloric, involving a transformation "from priests into clowns," as one early twentieth-century observer (Holt 1939:35) assumed. Judging from the past decade, though this is not always a reliable way to proceed in the case of Indonesia, this is not likely, for during this time *bissu* specialists have been avidly sought out to conduct rituals associated with birth, death, and marriage, and to perform ceremonies geared toward restoring health and well being and insuring safe journeys, including the pilgrimage to Mecca (Davies 2007:94). Of the 60 or so weddings Davies attended during her fieldwork, fully 45 involved *bissu* (or *calabai* "proxies"). Contemporary demand for *bissu* occurs not only in Sulawesi but also in places like Jakarta, home to large numbers of people who identify as Bugis. When the mayor of East Jakarta, who is of Bugis ancestry, organized the lavish, well attended festivities for his daughter's wedding in 1999—guests included then President B.J. Habibie, among many other notables—he made certain that *bissu* were centrally involved both in overseeing preparations for the relevant rituals and in insuring, through their participation, that the rituals were appropriately orchestrated, sanctified, and efficacious (Davies 2007:104–118). It is not only the high-born or relatively wealthy who seek out *bissu* services. Commoners of relatively humble means also endeavor to engage *bissu* for the ceremonies they sponsor as a means of asserting their self-worth and challenging the privileges claimed by nobility. Whether they are able to afford the services of *bissu* or must settle instead for those of less costly and less prestigious *calabai*, it is clear that *bissu* are centrally involved in contests over democratization in present-day Indonesia.

Much of the immediate and long-term future of the *bissu* may depend on how struggles for democracy and justice unfold in Indonesia, and on whether Indonesia follows Thailand and Singapore's regionally unique efforts to market gay and lesbian chic and all things seen as related to sexual and gender diversity in an effort to capture a lucrative market share of "pink dollars." As I write, however, paroxysms of violence, some largely sectarian, others more squarely criminal, are still painfully recalled in parts of Sulawesi and neighboring regions, such as the provinces of Maluku and North Maluku, where some 10,000 people died in Muslim-Christian violence in the 1999–2003 period alone (Aragon 2001, Hefner 2009:55). One is reminded of the ostensibly unrelated attack by Islamists in 2001 on the nearby headquarters of one of Indonesia's better-known *gay* organizations, GAYa Makassar (Davies 2007:76; cf. Boellstorff 2004b). Incidents of this sort are spawned by many of the same dynamics that in other contexts (e.g., Thailand, Singapore, Taiwan, the USA, Canada) give rise to market campaigns for pink dollars. They are, at the same time, statements of rejection and resistance to these kinds of openings and are in many ways mutually contradictory in terms of their basic implications for pluralism.

A final set of comments bearing on present-day *bissu* has to do with an apparent change in *bissu* sexuality that has occurred in the past few decades. I remarked earlier that contemporary *bissu* are mostly phenotypically male and transgendered, and want to add here that they commonly don attire that includes elements of men's and women's clothing, along with gendered accessories and female jewelry and make-up, like their predecessors. But unlike the majority of their predecessors, who engaged in same-sex relations with the normatively gendered men they took as husbands, present-day *bissu* are regarded by normatively oriented Bugis as celibate and largely asexual. Whether they are in fact celibate or largely asexual is another matter, but Davies (2007:89–90) suggests that this is the case (or at least the ideal). If this is true, it would indicate an important change in relation to previous generations, when most *bissu* (like *calabai*) exhibited one or another of two distinct and more or less mutually exclusive sexual orientations, one of which involved same-sex relations, the other celibacy (Pelras 1996:165–167, L. Andaya 2000:44–45). The fact that celibacy is apparently the only legitimate sexual orientation found among present-day *bissu* might conceivably be seen as a constriction of pluralistic sensibilities and dispositions among Bugis. On the other hand, insofar as Bugis celibacy is a personal, domestic, and overall "life option" accorded legitimacy, one seen, moreover, as conducive to the attainment of exalted spiritual powers that are still widely valued, we need to recognize it as a locally viable and respectable way of being in the world, one with sanctified roots in the broader Southeast Asian region that extend back some 2,000 years.

Having focused thus far on *bissu*, we need to recall that in earlier centuries there were also other categories of transgendered individuals among the Bugis, such as the *calabai* (feminine men) and *calalai* (masculine women), who were not involved in ritual transgendering unless they became *bissu* but did on at least some occasions succeed in becoming heads of state. In Pelras' day, *calabai* continued to enjoy a fair degree of legitimacy, though this was not the case, he claimed, for *calalai*, who were said to be disliked even (or especially) by *calabai* (Pelras 1996:167). The legitimacy that the former enjoyed may be explained in part by the fact that as far as the larger society was concerned, they were conceptually linked with the sanctity of the mostly male-bodied *bissu* by virtue of the transgenderism and same-sex sexuality associated with all such roles and subject positions—multifaceted commonalities that Pelras summarizes through invocation of the highly condensed symbol of "ambivalence" (ibid., 167). Especially in recent years, the conceptual link with *bissu* has been consciously cultivated by *calabai* (but apparently not by *calalai*), who seek to enhance their prestige both in local society and in the more encompassing social and cultural spheres in which they move (S. Graham 2003; cf. Millar 1989:83 n17). Efforts to broaden or deepen this conceptual link have entailed *calabai* movement into ritual domains formerly restricted to *bissu*. As Pelras (1996:167) puts it, "now that genuine *bissu* have nearly disappeared, many of the ordinary *calabai* have taken on aspects of their former role in the organization and celebration of weddings," e.g., in cooking, decoration of the house, make-up, dress of bride and groom, and so on. Circumstances such as these are of considerable analytic interest. They make clear that even if they are largely if not entirely secular, certain key features or expressions of contemporary transgenderism and same-sex sexuality, including, not least, the subject positions and subjectivities associated with them, derive a portion of the legitimacy accorded them by "piggy-backing" off the sanctified prestige formerly and to some degree still enjoyed by transgendered ritualists and, if only by implication, the gender-transgressive and sexually diverse practices long associated with them. This dynamic, which is of course historically and culturally specific, cuts both ways: the intense demonization of *bissu* that occurred during certain periods of Bugis history most likely entailed intense stigmatization of the gender and sexual diversity associated with *bissu*, variations on the theme being common throughout Southeast Asia, as we have seen.

The "shame" or *siri* that attaches especially to *calalai* calls for further comment, as do aspects of their subjectivities. In the Bugis context and indeed throughout most of Southeast Asia, failure to marry and produce children through birth or adoption is a source of embarrassment and shame, and if one is not yet married, it is universally assumed one will eventually do so, unless one has a seriously disfiguring skin disease or is held to be insane or otherwise patently disqualified for marriage on medical or other grounds (see Millar 1989, Peletz 1988, 1996). It is nonetheless true that being attached to a community and generally upholding basic social norms helps mitigate the stigma and shame at issue. Thus Graham reports that many *calalai* lead lives that are more or less "normal" and even, as some *calalai* claim, "charmed," since they do not feel the need to adhere to local prohibitions or prescriptions bearing on normatively defined femininity and can interact with their love interests much more freely than if these individuals were male (S. Graham 2001, Davies 2007).

The variegated reasons why female-born individuals come to regard themselves as *calalai* are instructive. Graham discussed these issues with five *calalai*, one of whom (Rani) regarded herself as a "tomboy" since she was a young child. "It was not something I was taught, or that I had to discover. It was always just who I was. Since I was little I have always been like a boy" (Graham 2001:6). For another (Maman), "it was more environmental: 'I have eight sisters. I was treated like a son since I was born. For me, becoming *calalai* was because of parental influence and the X-factor [factor-X].'" For Ance' a more aesthetic reason was revealed: "You know the real decider for me? It was clothes. I hate women's clothing, they are so hot and tight and uncomfortable. I never wear *baju bodo* [traditional dress], *kebaya*, or even a *duster* [a loose house-dress made from cotton]. Yuck!" (ibid., 6–7). For others, such as Eri, "a feeling of being *cocok* [suitable] with someone is central to hir gender identification":

> You know, the most important factor was influence from a *linas* [a term referring to the sexual partner of a *calalai*]. You see, I was chosen and seduced by a *linas* over a long time, and this is what made me become ill [*sakit*; about which more below]. Before, I wasn't ill, I used to just act like a man… Then there was a *linas* who always approached me and wanted to be *pacaran* [partners]. At first, when we became friends, I didn't think about

sex. The *linas* kept paying me lots of attention but I was still scared because I still had feelings like a woman. I was still 16 then. But I was from a broken home and I really enjoyed all the attention I was getting. So finally I too became ill [... *sakit*] and became a *hunter*.

(Ibid., 7)

The fact that *calalai* often refer to themselves as "hunters" suggests that at least on some level they accord themselves an appreciable degree of agency, even when their narratives as to how they came to regard themselves as *calalai* do not. "Fate" and "destiny" (*kodrat, nasib*), which are in God's hands and are thus largely beyond control, are in fact recurring themes in the originary accounts that Graham presents. Another recurring motif in these accounts, including Eris' (considered above), is the idea that same-sex desire signals, or is itself, an illness (*sakit, kesakitan*), unlike gender transgression that does not entail same-sex desire. Transgression of the latter sort (e.g., wearing men's clothes) apparently falls within the domain of the more or less healthy or normal, even though it is often construed as sinful in Islam.

For a variety of reasons I attach considerable significance to the Bugis idea of same-sex desire as illness, a theme involving the medicalization of sin. One such reason has to do with the fact that it is apparently quite widespread if not thoroughly pervasive and hegemonic, reflecting, as Graham puts it, "public discourse" which is heavily inflected by Islam, and "which states that same-sex sexual desire is sinful" (2001:7). Another noteworthy feature of the public discourse is that it is evidently internalized by *calalai*, and judging from Graham's accounts, is internalized rather unproblematically in the sense that it appears not to give rise to serious misgivings or ambivalences on the part of the *calalai* (though arguably we would need more detailed information of a psychological sort to make such assessments).

It is well to bear in mind that Graham encountered only a half dozen or so *calalai* in the course of her two years of fieldwork—and clearly, she was looking for them—but over a hundred *calabai*. This is to say that male-bodied individuals involved in transgender practices and same-sex relations outnumber their female-bodied counterparts by about twenty to one. Non- or potential *calalai*'s perceptions of the real and imagined psychological stigma, social costs, and divine retribution involved in (or resulting from) adopting the role undoubtedly help explain why it is of such limited occurrence, especially in relation to its male-bodied (*calabai*) counterparts.

A number of questions present themselves. Do notions of same-sex desire as illness and sin apply equally to males and females, or are they more likely to be invoked or mobilized against women? Are *calabai* as likely as *calalai* to internalize notions of same-sex desire as illness and sin? And more generally, why do *calabai* outnumber *calalai* twenty to one? Since these latter kinds of patterns, involving male-bodied predominance in gender transgression and same-sex relations, are quite widespread if not more or less universal throughout Southeast Asia and other world areas, interpretations bearing on why they exist are not unique to the Bugis though they still need to be framed in terms appropriate to this case.

In Bugis society and in most other cases for which we have relevant information, males tend to enjoy more power and prestige than females (although considerations of social class and related variables may trump gender in any given context). They do, moreover, typically display their power and prestige in gendered arenas and in specifically sexual contexts, the latter being among the quintessential settings in which we see displays of power and prestige in any society. Displays of male power and prestige are frequently manifested not only in the socially recognized ability to transgress and transcend gender norms with relative impunity (albeit within limits), and to define the terms of and otherwise control female transgression and transcendence in these areas. A second, related set of dynamics has to do with the fact that female transgression is more often noticed, regulated, and disciplined (through gossip, ostracism, explicit censure, and, in some contexts, more focused, physical sanctions) because the relative status honor of families and more encompassing kin groups is often heavily dependent on or otherwise keyed to the perceived moral purity and overall comportment of sisters, daughters, and other female relatives, as is certainly true among the Bugis. These dynamic go a long way toward explaining why, in terms of gender and sexuality, male-bodied individuals are allowed more "play" than their female-bodied counterparts, and why, as a consequence, they are more likely to outnumber them in terms of involvement in transgender practices and same-sex relations. These dynamics also suggest that even when notions of same-sex desire as illness and sin apply equally to males and females, they are more likely to be mobilized against women than men and thus more likely to be internalized by them.

A penultimate set of comments bearing on the Bugis has to do with the new sources of legitimacy that *calalai* (and *calabai*) are able to draw upon to fashion their subjectivities in positive terms and thus counter some of the stigmatizing effects of certain Islamic and other public discourses that portray them in a largely negative way. In the case of the *calalai*, these new sources of legitimacy derive partly from the quarters of Jakarta- and other urban-based Muslim feminists who support their cause, and partly from cosmopolitan discourses of a more secular bent that are keyed to civil society advocacy, transnational feminism and lesbianism, or both. Judging from Davies' accounts (including those published prior to 2005 under the name Graham), however, the processes of relegitimization at issue here may be more potential than actual. There is, in any case, no discursive or practical support for homogender relations of any variety, which are aesthetically and morally offensive to the majority of—but not all—*calalai* and to most others, and are largely beyond the pale of local sensibilities and dispositions (Davies 2007:26–28, 68).

As of this writing, the new discourses at issue appear not to have entirely supplanted the more established sources of legitimacy, such as "mainstream" (Bugis) Islam and the congeries of state-sponsored discourses known as *"ibuism"* (from the Indonesian term for mother [*ibu*]) that define a woman's role primarily in terms of heterosexual marriage and mothering and also help frame more general understandings of what is right and proper for Bugis and Indonesians as a whole. That said, it is clear that *calalai* creatively negotiate and manipulate a number of local and exogenous symbols and idioms of gender and sexuality in order to fashion meaningful lives and otherwise carve out viable spaces for themselves and their partners. In making this point I seek not to romanticize *calalai* as heroic champions in the trenches of gender struggle who are toiling on behalf of gender outlaws worldwide. But neither do I want to suggest that they are sad victims of multiple marginalization who lack agency and find little if any meaning in their lives.

By way of concluding this discussion of Bugis, I want to comment more explicitly on the ways in which the relatively robust pluralism that we see in local attitudes toward *bissu*, *calabai*, and *calalai* are also evident in Bugis attitudes toward normatively gendered women and female-bodied persons in general, a theme addressed by James Brooke (1848 I:65–66, 75) in the 1840s and by a number of other nineteenth-century European observers (e.g., Raffles 1817 [1830] II: Appendix F, lxxxvi; Crawfurd 1820:74). Suffice it to say first that from the perspective of many Bugis, female-bodied individuals are accorded a number of respectable life-options or, put differently, that they are born and socialized in a cultural-political environment in which diverse "ways of being in the world" are construed as legitimate. In the case of those who are in their twenties or thirties or older, these include: being normatively gendered and married (or once married); being normatively gendered and never married, with no intention of getting married (assuming that considerations of high rank and hypergamy effectively preclude marriage, or that one assumes the subject position of *linas* [partner of a *calalai*]); and being *calalai*, with—or without—a life-partner. This range of options owes something to the circulation throughout Bugis society of discourses promoted by Muslim feminist organizations and lesbian groups in Jakarta and elsewhere in the archipelago. But it would be a mistake to see all this as entirely (late) modern. The gendered division of labor among Bugis has long been relatively flexible, as have female dress codes, at least for commoners. So too has Bugis Islam, which, notwithstanding scripturalist peaks and polarizing political developments of the past, is understood and practiced by most present-day Bugis in ways that embrace symbols, idioms, and human embodiments of femininity, masculinity, and androgyny alike (Davies 2007:58–60, 76–80, 99–101 et passim, Gibson 2007)—and otherwise encourage compassionate engagement with difference—much like Islam in Java and many other areas of the archipelago (C. Geertz 1960, Woodward 1989, Bowen 1993, 2003, Sears 1996, Hefner and Horvatich 1997, Beatty 1999, Hefner 2000). The bottom line is that symbols, idioms, and physical embodiments of femininity appear always to have been highly valued throughout society, not only when they have been appropriated by male-bodied persons (or the intersexed). This despite the fact that female-bodied *bissu* largely disappear from the historical records by the eighteenth century, just as variously gendered female bodies tended to be squeezed out of specifically political arenas at various points in Bugis history (though one or two elderly women continue to exercise some of the ritual and symbolic prerogatives of earlier queens [Davies 2007:9, 105]).

Pluralism among the Bugis may well have always been more pronounced than among groups such as the Iban and Ngaju Dayak. But it certainly helps Bugis who seek to maintain or enhance pluralistic traditions and the sentiments and dispositions associated with them that in engaging the discourses, political projects, and military forces of the Indonesian state they do so from a position of considerable strength, unlike the Iban and Ngaju Dayak, one based on having well developed (state-level) political institutions in place, and a large, politically powerful population, estimated as around 3,500,000 in Sulawesi and perhaps as many in the diaspora.[3] Access to strategic material resources, along with viable economic institutions, is also of crucial importance, partly because they render large-scale female prostitution unlikely (because unnecessary) and thus help prevent the emergence of discourses that link femininity with dishonor, disease, and contagion and that otherwise entail an increasingly strict and "reactive" heteronormativity of the sort we see among the Iban. That Bugis have long enjoyed a reputation for being among the most devout Muslims in the archipelago, as opposed to wild "tribal" pagans (turned Christian) such as the Iban and Ngaju Dayak, also helps in their dealings with the Muslim-majority state, as does the more or less serendipitous fact that B.J. Habibie, who served as Indonesia's president from 1998 to 1999, was of Bugis ancestry. All of this is to say that with respect to the conditions of the possibility for pluralism, the specific ways in which a society or polity is encompassed within a modern state is critical, as are the cultural resources, including, most notably, the practices and symbols of pluralism, that its members bring to bear on their encompassment. Many of the same dynamics are relevant to the manner in which members of a society or polity are able to draw upon their pluralistic traditions to negotiate shifting political conditions within a state—the virtual disappearance of the center, to take one (extreme) example—and to reproduce and ideally enhance their relative autonomy, ethnic identity, and cultural patrimony in the process. The flip side of the coin is of course the culture of the state, which for most of Indonesia's history has embraced many kinds of difference.

The Case of Burma

Like almost all the rest of Southeast Asia, Burma was subject to processes of colonialism and all that came with it, but throughout most of the postcolonial era, which began in 1948, Burma's leaders pursued state strategies geared toward isolating their country from the rest of the world. The military coup of 1962, for instance, saw not only the installation as head of state of General Ne Win, described by many as "superstitious and xenophobic, ruthless and maniacal" (Clements 1992:19), but also the onset of an era of extreme geopolitical isolation, political repression, economic stagnation and decline, and attendant hardship and misery that continues to this day. Particularly in terms of its geopolitical isolation and economic decline, Burma is a far cry from nation-states like Thailand, Malaysia, and Singapore, which have embraced capitalism, modernity, and globalization with a vengeance.

One result of policies pursued during the past four decades is that much of Burma's population of 51 million people (some 68 percent of whom are ethnic Burmans)[4] is still heavily committed to agricultural pursuits, and to the animistic beliefs, ritual practices, and more encompassing moral and cosmological precepts long associated with them. Partly for this reason it should not be surprising to find that during the 1980s and 1990s, transgendered ritual specialists who are commonly involved in same-sex relations (and are generally known as *nat kadaw* and/or *acault*), though viewed with ambivalence, were still accorded great esteem and critically important roles both in rural communities and in urban settings. Burma might thus be considered an exception to many of my generalizations bearing on the historic delegitimization and reduced status of transgendered ritual practitioners, and the constriction of gender pluralism generally. But I have stressed that processes entailing delegitimization and stigmatization have been neither uniform nor monolithic. This is to say that Burma is more appropriately regarded as a space where state strategies seeking to distance the nation from certain aspects of modernity, particularly the capitalist-driven world economy and global flows of people, ideas, and technologies, have permitted if not encouraged the reproduction and continued vitality of long-established roles of transgendered ritualists and a significant range of the social patterns and cultural sensibilities conventionally linked with them—even while these same strategies have given rise to a national economy governed primarily by black-market forces (many of which are clearly transnational) and thus some of the most intense, unregulated forms of capitalism ever known.

Before turning to material bearing on the 1980s and 1990s, it is worth mentioning that the available accounts concerning the late 1950s and early 1960s vary a good deal in the extent of their treatment of relevant issues. At one extreme lies Manning Nash's classic (1965) ethnography, which devotes over 300 pages to "village life in contemporary Burma" (the book's subtitle) but provides readers with a single sentence on the subject of non-heteronormative genders and sexualities: "Deviations like homosexuality, sodomy, or transvestism seem to be known to villagers chiefly through stories and not through village examples" (Nash 1965:256). All the more frustrating for scholars seeking to discern what Burmese cultures of gender and sexuality were like during the 1960s is that having registered this observation, Nash does not even add a parenthetical aside to inform his readers about the most general contours of villagers' attitudes or feeling-tones toward such phenomena.

The roughly contemporaneous and ethnographically rich work of Melford Spiro (1967, 1970, 1977, 1997) is far more helpful, particularly since Spiro is attuned to the *longue durée*. Spiro (1977:229) reports that forms of same-sex or "unisexual intimacy—sometimes associated with latent homosexuality in the West—are frequent. Thus, one often sees two young men occupying the same mat with one lying against the other, or lying on the other's buttocks, or holding the other in his arms." Overt same-sex practices, on the other hand, were said to be relatively rare (or absent) in villages in the early 1960s, except among shamans and their spouses or partners, though Spiro adds that "homosexuality is found to some extent ... in the cities, as is male prostitution" (ibid.). In Mandalay, for instance, "the haunts of homosexuals (*meinmasha*) are known to everyone, and they, as well as male transvestites (*gandu*), are viewed with a relatively tolerant attitude .... Lesbians (*yaukkyasha*) are also found in the cities, and they too meet with the same relative toleration" (ibid.). Spiro's latter point concerning same-sex relations among females is confirmed by Mi Mi Khaing (1984:114–115), as noted earlier; she reports that same-sex intimacy often occurs among unmarried urban women, and that women involved in such intimacy "are not ostracised," even in the apparently rare cases where they forge life-long attachments.

Referring to the long haul, Spiro (1977:229) avers, "If the older literature on Burma is credible, the infrequency of homosexuality [in rural contexts, except among shamans and their spouses and partners] in contemporary Burma represents an important historical change, for some of the older sources specifically mention the high incidence of homosexuality." Gone too, he might have added, are the days of penis bells, penis pins, and the like. Concerning the sexuality of shamans, Spiro (1967:220) writes

> With few exceptions male shamans seem to be either homosexual (manifest or latent), transvestite, or effeminate (and sometimes all three). Their *nat* [spirit], of course, is always female. If the male shaman, either in possession or in a dream, perceives himself as a female or identifies with his female *nat*, his sexual satisfaction [in "real life"?] acquires explicit homosexual overtones ... . The reverse, of course, is true of female shamans ... . Some shamans ... are possessed by ... brother and ... sister ... nats, a type of possession which has even more obvious homosexual possibilities. This is all the more plausible in the light of the *apparent bisexuality of some shamans*, a characteristic already remarked upon as early as the eighteenth century [e.g., Hamilton 1727 (1930) II:31] (emphasis added).

The political climate in Burma from 1962 through the mid-1990s allowed for little social science research by the Burmese or by outsiders; hence substantive ethnographic material from this time is relatively meager. One of the better known accounts from this period, co-authored by two psychologists and an endocrinologist (Eli Coleman, Philip Colgan, and Louis Gooren), was based on a brief stint of research conducted in the late 1980s that apparently focused on the Mandalay region, like Spiro's (see also Brac de la Perrière 1989). Coleman et al. report that during the 1980s it was still the case that the transgendered shamans and seers they refer to as *acault*, the majority of whom engaged in same-sex sexuality, were accorded great respect and extremely prominent roles in certain community rituals. Many aspects of these rituals continue to be motivated, defined, and validated by animistic beliefs and underlying moral precepts associated with the worship of the 37 *nat* comprising the Burmese pantheon.

> One of the *nats* is the female spirit called Manguedon, ... who can bestow fortune or success. Manguedon intercedes in the lives of the Burmese through certain males whom she decides to possess, evidenced by their cross-gender traits. These males are spiritually drawn to Manguedon and eventually go through a ceremony in which they become married to her ... [thus] formaliz[ing] ... their status ... as 'acault'. Once married to the spirit the boy or man is married for life; he ... takes on the characteristics of the female spirit and will always be an *acault* in his behavior and feelings.
>
> (Coleman et al. 1992:315)

This entails relinquishing the gender identity of a male and assuming an identity that is "neither male nor female, or mainly female, despite a male body" (ibid., 317).

More significant, "the acault ... have an important and revered place in Burmese society":

> Prominent businessmen frequently invite acault to their homes ... [and] offer money and gifts to ... [them] on behalf of Manguedon to insure their good fortune .... When good fortune comes true, the businessman holds a 3-day celebration honoring Mangudeon in an especially built pavilion .... All the people in the village or city are invited to celebrate and to watch the acault dance in ceremonial fashion to give homage and pay thanks to Manguedon ... . On these occasions, the acault ceremonially dress in female-type clothing and cosmetics. They dance in a ritualized manner until they go into trances .... As they dance, they go into close communication with Manguedon and can grant requests.
>
> (Ibid., 316)

In addition to these "community events," "the acault celebrate a 7-day festival of dancing in honor of the *nats*" on the occasion of the full moon in August. "At this festival, all the acault of Burma gather at Mount Popa ... [near Mandalay] to dance in their finest ceremonial clothes and feminine appearance. Much food and a great deal of liquor insure the success of the celebration. Many non-acault Burmese attend these celebrations to also participate in honoring the *nats*" (ibid.).

Despite their "important and revered place in Burmese society," there is a downside to joining the ranks of *acault*, including an inability to reach nirvana, which in the orthodoxy of (Theravada) Buddhism is reserved for males. Additionally, since "becoming an acault reflects on the merits of one's family," some Burmese "believe that to have a son become an acault is evidence of a disreputable life in the parents' previous incarnation, ... may be embarrassed by their son['s] ... cross-gender behavior, and subsequently try to prevent further influence by Manguedon" (ibid., 315–6).

As for the gender identities and erotic preferences of *acault* and their sexual partners, "some [*acault*] live their lives in the role of a female and express the wish to have the body of a woman. All acault engage in occasional cross-dressing during ceremonial activities..., [and] most ... restrict their sexual activities to other males" (ibid., 317). Burmese men who are not *acault* "may partake in sexual encounters with the acault without stigmatization of homosexuality because of the connotation of a connection to Manguedon as well as not seeing the acault as male.[5] In Burmese culture, the thought of a male having sex with another male is socially and morally repugnant" (ibid.) and sex between males is in fact illegal. "Having sex with an acault, however, is not viewed as homosexual behavior," which is to say that "the concept of two biological men coupling *is* accepted in Burma ... as long as it ... [is] defined as a 'heterosexual' man living with an acault" (ibid.), thus indicating that in local culture the *acault* are feminized. In such cases "the acault is usually responsible for taking care of 'his/her husband' financially as well as sexually" (ibid.). Such husbands "are somewhat frowned upon in Burmese society ... [and] considered lazy, in that they are not working to be meritorious in this lifetime. What is notable is that this sanction is *not* about the sexual behavior; it is about laziness" (ibid.; emphasis added).

The material presented by Coleman et al. that I have cited extensively differs in some key particulars from Spiro's earlier findings; for instance, according to Coleman et al., the majority of the ritual specialists in question are male-bodied, whereas according to Spiro (and earlier accounts [e.g., Hamilton 1727 (1930) II:31, Sangermano 1818 (1893):172, Crawfurd 1834 I:74–75, R. Brown 1915: 358]) they are mostly female-bodied. Overall, however, the material is broadly congruent with Spiro's data and, more importantly, it indicates a great deal of continuity in relation to the past, as is also true of Spiro's research. So too does the critically acclaimed documentary film, *Friends in High Places: The Art of Survival in Modern Day Burma*, directed and produced by Lindsey Merrison (2001), which was shot in the capital city of Rangoon in 1998 and 1999. This film also gives the clear impression that most of the ritual specialists (*nat kadaw*) are phenotypically male, as does the work of Bénédicte Brac de la Perrière (1989, 1998:173 passim) who reported that male-bodied individuals accounted for 61.5 percent (99/161) of the ritual specialists about whom she obtained information. When viewed in the context of other historical and ethnographic research, this might suggest another instance of the historical pattern, widespread throughout Southeast Asia, whereby male-bodied practitioners usurped ritual roles formerly held by female-bodied individuals. Most striking about the ethnographic film and literature cited here, though, is their demonstration that even or especially in highly urban locales such as Rangoon (whose population exceeds five million people) and Mandalay (the country's second largest city), there is great demand for the services of transgendered ritual specialists who can provide intellectually and emotionally satisfying meanings and solutions to dilemmas associated with illness, faltering marriages, uncertain economic ventures, indebtedness, and the imprisonment or fatal "disappearance" of loved ones.

Burmese data on transgendering are productively viewed, to rephrase a point made earlier, as broadly characteristic of those regions of Southeast Asia that are in some ways relatively unaffected by state-sponsored modernity. But this is not to suggest that all such regions are the same, that the state in Burma or anywhere else in Southeast Asia rules with a light hand, or that Burma's State Law and Order Restoration Council (established in 1988 as the official face of the junta) or its successor (the State Peace and Development Council) has dealt with *acault* and *nat kadaw* as national treasures, like Sumo wrestlers in Japan. It may well be that the generally austere, puritanical regime, which has sought to purge Burmese Buddhism of "fringe elements" incorporated into "popular religious and folk traditions that are deemed open to scorn and ridicule by 'outsiders'" (Sadan 2005:105) and has otherwise endeavored to promote scripturally based forms of Buddhism favored by colonial-era reformers and civil servants and subsequent generations of Burmese with modern education and experience of urban centers, has consciously refrained from promulgating policies that would curtail the practices of transgendered ritualists or otherwise undermine beliefs and activities associated with *nat* cults—even while it has cracked down on and in some cases tortured and killed Buddhist monks (as well as students, ethnic minorities, and others) suspected of pro-democracy leanings. The junta may even be inclined to tolerate if not tacitly encourage the propitiation of *nat* in light of its concerns to shore up its much contested legitimacy (it cannot afford to be seen as overtly hostile to religion in its entirety) and its related desire to position itself as heir to a long line of Burmese sovereigns who promoted *nat* cults, partly with a view toward enhancing local prosperity.

Regardless of what other dynamics have contributed to the reproduction into the present of beliefs and practices associated with *nat*, and obviously many other dynamics are involved, the propitiation of *nat* is alive and well in Burma, as are the transgendered ritual specialists who have long afforded the populace privileged and unparalleled access to them. Indeed, recent decades have seen a marked revitalization of Burmese spirit mediumship, especially in urban areas, much like Thailand, Cambodia, and Vietnam. Thailand in particular has witnessed an efflorescence of spirit mediumship, "a veritable explosion of magical practices" performed by transgendered *kathoey* and women (Morris 2000:132 passim, 236, cf. Jackson 2003, 2004).

Deeper into the Labyrinth(s)

At this juncture I would like to attend to certain of the other referents of the terms commonly used for spirit mediums and shamans (*nat kadaw, acault*) along with some of the links and disjunctions between these referents and other Burmese terms utilized to denote gender and sexual transgression. My larger concern is with the symbols, meanings, and overall status of transgenderism and same-sex relations in contemporary Burma, especially Rangoon, including those forms of transgenderism and same-sex sexuality that are not construed by the Burmese as linked to the world of spirits or the sacred. One important caveat here is that this discussion focuses almost entirely on phenotypic males since there is no comparably detailed sociolinguistic research of which I am aware that deals with their female-bodied counterparts.

I noted earlier that in some contexts the terms *nat kadaw* and *acault* are used more or less synonymously. Here I want to clarify that while the semantic domains of these two terms overlap, they are nonetheless quite distinct and that according to sociolinguistic research undertaken in the mid-1980s by George van Driem (1996), they constituted two of the four terms commonly deployed in Burma at the time to refer to certain forms of male-bodied transgenderism and same-sex erotics. Let us consider these terms one at a time.

Acault (sometimes transliterated as *achauk*) or "*nat*-possessed one" may derive from a verb that means "frighten, scare, haunt," "terrorized," or "visited by spirits" (at least according to van Driem [1996:96]; others dispute this derivation),[6] and, as van Driem (ibid.) puts it, "traditionally [refers to] a male homosexual who functions as a spiritual medium in the worship of *nats*." But "in modern usage … [it] denotes *any* male homosexual whose sexual orientation is either intentionally or inadvertently conspicuous or *any* male homosexual who is generally candid about his sexual orientation" (96–97; emphasis added). More generally, *acault* "denotes individuals ranging from effeminate long-haired men, provided they are not transvestites, to short-haired homosexual men who exhibit no pronounced cross-gender behavior." *Acault* "are not necessarily prostitutes, but any 'male prostitute', whether manly or effeminate, is, due to the disrepute of his profession, classified as an … [*acault*], unless he is a transvestite. (Transvestite prostitutes [like transvestites generally] are categorized as … [*meinmasha*]," discussed below [ibid.].) In sum, the term *acault* is heavily moored in semantic domains of spirit mediumship and ritual transgenderism but is also used to refer to any male whose appearance or behavior suggests a predilection for gender transgression—or simply gives the impression that he is a "sissy" (because, for instance, he is unable to change the oil in a car)—or a preference for or interest in same-sex relations.

The term *nat kadaw* (wife [*kadaw*] or spouse of a *nat*) may be used to refer to an *acault* (or at least certain types of *acault*) though technically speaking it designates someone who has undergone a ceremony entailing formal marriage to a *nat*, not simply someone who is possessed by a *nat*. "Spiro (1967:219) reports that 'in most, but not all, cases, the *nat* is believed to love the shaman [*nat kadaw*] sexually'. Alternatively, the … [*nat kadaw*] may effectively become the *nat* and, as such, acquire the sexual orientation of the *nat*" (van Driem 1996:98).

Meinmasha is perhaps best translated as "cross-dresser," "transvestite," "sissy," or "pansy." (Van Driem offers the archaic and obscure "gynaecopath," Spiro prefers "homosexual."). This term

originally denoted palace transvestites who fulfilled a function similar to that of the Indian *hijada* [*hijra*] at the Moghul courts. In present-day usage, too, the meaning of the term ... hinges upon the idea that a homosexual orientation is associated with effeminate or transsexual [sic; transgendered?] behaviour. Today the term is used ... [both] ... as a generalized, deprecatory term for male homosexuals, and ... in a strict sense to denote effeminate homosexual men who wear their hair long and exhibit transvestism.

(Van Driem, ibid., 96)

More generally, while *meinmasha* are sometimes centrally involved in *nat* festivals (ibid., 97–98; see also Brac de la Perrière 2005), the term "designates the most outspokenly cross-gender of male homosexual behavioural categories differentiated in the Burmese lexicon" (van Driem 1996:96).

The fourth term van Driem encountered in his research is *dzibou* (alternatively transliterated as *gyibon*), which according to van Driem's possibly fanciful interpretation derives from the morpheme for a small species of deer known as the muntjac or "barking deer" and the verb "to hide oneself" or "conceal oneself;" van Driem thus translates it as "hiding muntjack deer." A *dzibou* "does not advertise ... his sexual orientation" and to some degree "actively conceals it" from family members and others so as to maintain his "social respectability." Unlike individuals in the three categories noted earlier, *dzibou* do not appear in public with *thanaka* powder on their faces, a common practice among women and children, and are *"not considered effeminate by Burmese standards"* (van Driem 1996:100; emphasis added). Some *dzibou* are bachelors, others are married with children. They participate fully in most domains of life, something that the other groups, which are stigmatized according to van Driem (98–99) and are generally viewed as lacking social respectability, cannot do. In some ways most revealing is that "this role is less well defined than the others" considered here (ibid.). This may indicate the relatively recent emergence of the role. It might also be taken as evidence of the relative fluidity of the Burmese system of gender and sexuality, which has seen additional changes since the period of van Driem's research in the 1980s. (As discussed below, these involve the emergence in the 1990s of gay and lesbian identities that appear to have been largely absent in earlier decades.)[7]

The four terms considered here do not encompass all phenotypic males who participate in same-sex relations but it is noteworthy that according to von Driem there is little if any discrepancy between self-labeling and the ways the larger society (including those "in the know" in the case of *dzibou*) label the persons in question. Someone who has relations with an individual in one of these categories may not consider himself—or be regarded by others—as a *dzibou* or inclined toward same-sex sexuality. The relationship in question may be seen as one of the prerogatives of (male) youth or bachelorhood, a temporary "aberration," due partly perhaps to the fact that women are "so hard to get" (ibid., 102). Recall in any event that it is not unusual, as Coleman et al. (1992:317) reported, for a male to have sexual relations with an *acault* or, presumably, with someone in one of the other lexically marked subject positions, and that pursuing erotic encounters with someone in one or another of these subject positions does *not* involve forfeiting either one's social respectability or one's claims to heteronormative masculinity (ibid.).

To better appreciate recent historical trends we might consider case studies provided by Coleman et al., based on their research on *acault* in the Mandalay area in the late 1980s, in relation to case studies presented by van Driem, which are derived from research conducted at the same general time (the mid-1980s), albeit in Rangoon. Although the samples involved are exceedingly small, parents' reactions to their son taking on roles like that of *acault* are far more positive in Mandalay, the last royal capital, than in Rangoon, a much larger city which was not only the national capital through November 2005 but is also showcased by the current military government as the main locus of its "huts to high-rises" development strategies as well as the wave of the future (Skidmore 2004). More generally, we shall see that *acault* and other male-bodied individuals involved in transgenderism and same-sex relations enjoy far more legitimacy and far more life options in Mandalay than in Rangoon.

Case 1

Kothan, age 30, whose "gender identity was apparently male" (Coleman et al. 1992:319), married Manguedon when he was 27. "He had some desire to marry the spirit … at age 20, but tried to resist that desire" until he was 27, by which time "the spirit possessed his thinking" and he married her. Kothan "had many pictures of himself at the marriage ceremony, and was proud to display them. His family appeared to be at ease with his social status, as he was still living with them." ("His cross-gender behavior appeared to be restricted to ceremonial activity and status; otherwise, he lived in the male role;" Coleman et al. provide no information about Kothan's sexual practices, which Kothan "seemed reluctant to discuss" with them.) Kothan enjoyed "a thriving career as a fortune teller, telling businessmen how to please Manguedon. He seemed to be happy and content with his life. When asked if he would like to be reincarnated as a man, woman, or acault, he responded that he would like to be an acault" (ibid., 319).

Case 2

Maaye, age 38, "claimed he was like other boys" until the age of 17, around which time his "feelings changed and he married Manguedon" (318). "From that time on, he has only wanted to act like a woman" in dress and manners (he tied his *longyi* as women do and "sometimes wore makeup") and in terms of having a male sexual partner, though he considered himself a male (318–319). "Maaye had no desire to have a female body" and, moreover, had a husband with whom he had regular sexual relations; he supported the husband (but did not live with him), doing so by engaging in paid sex work with other men who were typically over 30 years of age (ibid.). There was no indication that Maaye or "his family felt embarrassed about his social status and/or sexual behavior. He led a comfortable life in the community, regularly participating at weddings and ceremonies honoring Manguedon" (319).

Case 3

Toto, 28, who "had lived, acted, and dressed as a woman for the past 5 years," exhibited cross-gender behavior from an early age, and at age 17 "began to cross-dress full time and engage in sexual activities with males." Toto was living with her sister at the time of the interview because her family disapproved of her and were apparently ashamed of her. "Although she was completely comfortable with her female role and her status as an acault" (318), she was frustrated because her boyfriends wanted only sex with her; she wanted to get married to a man and to have a female body "but ... had no knowledge of sex-reassignment surgery" (ibid).

Van Driem's material from Rangoon suggests a less happy situation than that encountered by Coleman et al. around Mandalay, including as it does numerous references to homeless *acault* (as well as homelessness among other male-bodied individuals involved in transgenderism and same-sex relations) who congregate around Sule Pagoda and nearby Mahabandula Park, both in central Rangoon, and are subject to harassment and extortion from the police. Partly because many of these individuals have been disowned by their parents and evicted from their homes, they seek refuge in temples and pagodas that afford them food, shelter, and protection from the authorities. The relationships these *acault* have with agents of the state and official Buddhism is a far cry from that of the pre- and early modern periods, notwithstanding the long-term commonality in these relations suggested by King Anawratha's early eleventh-century insistence that certain prominent *nat* shrines be placed within the confines of the Shwezigon Pagoda as a symbolic statement of the ostensible submission of *nat* and the ritual cultus in its entirety to state authority and orthodox Buddhism alike.

Case 4

An *acault* in his early 20s who wears his hair long, sports *thanaka* powder and eyeliner, and tends to sleep in pagodas or on the streets. "He is not accepted by his family"—"Only his sister ... will have anything to do with him"—owing to the fact that he is a prostitute, not, according to van Driem, because he is an *acault*. He earns part of his living "at a men's toilet situated underground" and part from "clientele at a transport depot for long-distance lorry drivers," and "has often been a victim of police extortion" (106).

Case 5

Twenty-seven years old, a "manly *acault*," who "wears his hair short and shuns feminine attributes" and is of low-caste Nepalese (cum Burmese) ancestry.

Van Driem describes him as an "attractive and successful" prostitute but notes that he contracted venereal diseases from his clients, for which he undergoes regular treatment. "His first wife died shortly after their marriage;" he subsequently remarried and fathered a daughter, and later became a sex worker. His second wife evicted him from their home because of his involvement in prostitution. He has also been disowned by his father (his mother died when he was a child) who works driving a truck for the government. The fact that his son is an *acault* is, according to van Driem, "sufficient grounds for disowning" him, as is his (the son's) involvement in the sex trade, and he is severely beaten by his father when he returns home. Like the *acault* considered in the preceding paragraph, with whom he is close friends, "he sleeps on the streets and, if possible, in pagodas" (107).

Case 6

A 41-year-old *dzibou*, "known for his promiscuity and flirtatious behavior" who is "married to a devoted wife and is the proud father of a young son." He has a desk job in a government office and "enjoys a sexual relationship with a young bachelor who works in one of the canteens on the slope of ... Shwedagon Pagoda." His "visits to his lover at the pagoda do not embarrass the lover because" he (the lover) is out to his many co-workers (i.e., the lover is not a *dzibou*), some of whom "make jocular and ribald references to the length and thickness of their ... [co-worker's] penis, averring that that is "what lures ... [him] to the pagoda." However, the lover does not visit him at his place of employment because "this would constitute a grave indiscretion" inasmuch as "it would expose ... [his] status as a ... *dzibou*, even though some of ... [his] friends at work are both aware of and indifferent toward his orientation" (104).

Case 7

This 40-year-old *dzibou* has a permanent stall in one of Rangoon's large covered markets where he sells imported Indonesian textiles. He is "a successful merchant and makes small donations to needy ... [*acault*] on a regular basis," unless they are good-looking, in which case he often gives them a cold shoulder. According to van Driem, this is because he is not considered handsome, is "seldom the object of anyone's sincere sexual attraction" and is thus envious and somewhat uncharitable toward *acault* who are attractive. He has been "greatly embarrassed" by an *acault* who has approached him at his workplace seeking money and has been embroiled in an ongoing feud with him because he suggests that the *acault* repay any money offered with sexual favors, which the *acault* declines. "For fear of stigmatization, ... [he], like most Rangoonese ... [*dzibou*], does not frequent Mahabandula Park or other places" where men seeking male sex partners "are known to congregate" (104–105).

Case 8

This *dzibou* is in his mid-20s; he has some Chinese ancestry, makes a living driving a taxi, and is very concerned about his social respectability. "He consorts with ... *acault* in the evenings" and "is always said to be on the lookout when he is in Mahabandula Park, for fear of being spotted." His parents are unaware that he is a *dzibou* and "he has no intention of informing them because he anticipates that the idea would not be well received" (105–106).

Case 9

A middle-aged, unmarried *dzibou*, formerly a biology professor at a university who was well liked by students but was pressured into giving up his job for political and other reasons. Prior to independence, his family were wealthy jewelers. He speaks English and French as well as Burmese, and has a large group of *dzibou* friends who travel to the beach together each year for a vacation. He lives in the suburbs in a large house shared with his parents and his siblings and their spouses and children. "All his relatives are aware of his and his friends' sexual orientation." His *dzibou* friends have all been introduced to his family and are well received in his home. "His young to middle-aged ... *dzibou* friends likewise live with their respective families," are accepted by them as *dzibou*, and also feel free to bring their friends home with them. He "claims to be indifferent to others' attitudes toward his sexual orientation. Although his self-acceptance is undoubtedly a factor contributing to his overall well-being, he believes that his nonchalance in this regard may have been a factor in bringing about his expulsion from the university where he worked" (108). One of his colleagues at the university committed suicide, apparently "because of problems of self-acceptance in connexion with his homosexual identity" (ibid.).

The six (uneven) case studies from Rangoon presented here raise a number of interesting issues but I will confine my remarks to a few of the most salient themes. Perhaps most obvious, just as this material suggests the existence (at least in Rangoon) of an empirical and conceptual link between *acault* and male prostitution, so too does it imply that perceptions of *acault* are dragged down by negative attitudes toward prostitution. The case studies also make clear that of the four lexically marked subject positions considered here, *dzibou* enjoy the most social respectability, and that this is largely because they tend to (but do not always) conceal their involvement in same-sex relations from family members and others, doing so partly through participation in heteronormative forms of masculinity that involve marriage to a woman and fathering (or adopting) children, and/or holding down a prestigious or at least respectable job. To some degree, holding down a prestigious or respectable job substitutes for other signs or markers of heteronormative masculinity or renders them less critical or compelling. This means (among other things) that landing a prestigious or respectable job and, by implication, climbing up the ladders of social class allows for a broader range of options with respect to gender, sexuality, and domesticity, and, conversely, that sliding down class ladders entails a constriction of options in these and other areas.

Recall in any case that *dzibou* are not considered effeminate by Burmese standards, and that their subject position is the least well defined of the four considered here. This indicates that through the 1980s there was relatively little space in urban Burmese schemes of gender and sexuality for males who simultaneously identified as masculine, were erotically drawn to other males, and evinced no appreciable interest either in marrying the spirit Manguedon (or a ritual specialist wed to her), or in performing those elements of heteronormative masculinity that involve marrying heterosexually and fathering (or adopting) children.

This situation began to change in the 1990s. One of the defining features of the burgeoning *gay* movement in Burma at the turn of the twenty-first century is its emphasis on the creation of *gay* identities and discursive spaces for men who are attracted to other males but who identify as masculine and thus eschew not only female attire and other accoutrements of femininity long associated with male-bodied individuals drawn to other men, but also heteronormative marriage. Before turning to a more in-depth discussion of these matters I might note that the emergence of *gay* male identities in Burma in the 1990s, roughly two decades after they are first reported for neighboring Thailand (Jackson 1997), indicates the temporary "successes" of Burmese rulers who since the military coup of 1962 have sought to block the flows of countless global discourses seen as detrimental to both the Burmese Way to Socialism and (with the abandonment in 1988 of some aspects of centralized state planning in favor of a new openness to capitalist markets) the state's subsequent commitment to forced capitalist development. That said, the fact that a movement involving gays—as well as lesbians and transgendered people—emerged at all indicates the ultimate futility of the regime's efforts to micro-manage the Burmese people's involvement in modernity and the diverse modalities of gender and sexuality with which it is iconically associated. So too of course does the emergence in 1988 of the National League for Democracy (NLD). The NLD carried the 1990 general elections (whose results were immediately nullified by the junta) and for some years now has been headed by Nobel Laureate Aung San Suu Kyi who, as a consequence of her involvement in oppositional politics, has spent 12 of the past 18 years under house arrest in her family home in Rangoon. The junta's heavily gendered attacks on Aung San Suu Kyi reveal a great deal about constructions of and contests over femininity in contemporary Burma and will be considered further along.

Some of the changes afoot in realms of masculinity in present-day Burma are clear from the experiences and autobiographical remarks of Aung Myo Min (born ca. 1966), the founding director of the Human Rights Education Institute of Burma and the Campaign for Lesbigay Rights in Burma. The recipient of a number of international awards for his work on behalf of human rights (and gay and lesbian rights in particular), Aung Myo Min was interviewed by Burmese journalist Than Win Htut for an article dated February 20, 2005, which was posted on the Internet bearing the title, "Aung Myo Min: A Burmese gay with a human rights cause."[8]

Aung Myo Min describes himself as *gay* and says that he has been aware of his attraction to other males since he was a teenager. He was a college student (majoring in English) at Rangoon University in 1988 when authorities initiated a nation-wide crackdown on student demonstrators and others involved in a general strike in protest of the government's economic and political policies. Like thousands of other students in the wake of the August 8, 1988 massacre, which saw upwards of three thousand protesters mowed down by authorities, Aung Myo Min fled to a remote jungle area along the Thai-Burma border that served as headquarters for various ethnic groups and others who sought to overthrow the junta. He soon joined the All Burma Students' Democratic Front but he was initially reluctant to tell his fellow freedom fighters and others in the opposition movement that he was *gay*, for fear of their reaction. For as interviewer Than Win Htut expressed it, "misunderstandings about, and phobia of, gay life and homosexuality are very common in Burma." Than Win Htut went on to observe that in Burma, "people [usually] think gay men think like women and want to have women's bodies. Therefore, gay men were not regarded as capable of being reliable in armed struggle."

Says Aung Myo Min, "I worried that I would be assigned lighter duties in my army base rather than being allowed to fight Burmese government forces in the frontline if they knew my sexual orientation." Even though he initially hid his sexual identity, some of his close friends gradually learned his secret and he thus began sharing it with others. "It was a difficult decision to open up. I asked myself, 'why ... should [I] be so scared to reveal my real identity?'" Than Win Htut's article continues as follows:

> Although many suffer greatly when they "come out" to their parents, Aung Myo Min ... was lucky. His mother was accepting of him when he told her over the phone after he had left for exile .... His father had already passed away and others in the family responded well. "My mother told me that she already knew," Aung Myo Min said with a brighter smile on his face. "But ... if my father had known, it would have been a serious problem," for ... [he] had been a high official in the Burma Army and held strong feelings against gays.

Aung Myo Min refers to this period "in the liberated area, ... [among] democracy activists along the Thai-Burma border," as his "difficult time." Than Win Htut reports:

> Some comrades said they didn't dare sleep in the same hut with him. Some, "just kidding," joked ..., "we are more afraid of something behind us than shooting in the frontline." This kind of talk caused Aung Myo Min much suffering. It was only after time had passed and he had nothing left to hide that he began to feel lighter and enjoy his freedom from pretending. This

in turn gave him more confidence which drove him to struggle increasingly harder in his work.

Aung Myo Min eventually traveled to the US where he obtained a masters degree in human rights. Since returning to Burma, he has "played an active role in human rights education and the gay rights movement. There were still many challenges as a gay activist to lead human rights documentation and training along … Burma's borders with Thailand, China, India and Bangladesh." One such challenge is opening his countrymen's eyes to the fact that some gay males in Burma consider themselves to be masculine men and have no interest in cross-dressing or in any aspects of feminine roles. For example, whenever he travels in the course of his work, "everybody is initially surprised" by his "handsome appearance," including the fact that he is a "tall strongly-built man" who is open about his gay life. (According to Than Win Htut, he "had an image of being a bit of a 'rocker' with his passionate voice, pretty, long, dyed hair down to his strong shoulders and a plump face with small, round glasses.") Aung Myo Min told the reporter that "most gay men from Burma also hope when they meet him that he might be a cross-dresser and not the masculine, perspiration-covered face they see," to which he added, "One thing I hate most is stereotypes among the Burmese community—… they think a gay man might be dressed in women's clothes."

"While some gay men want to marry their partners, Aung Myo Min doesn't believe in marriage on paper. Instead, living together and understanding each other is more important than to be recognized as legally married in order to have legal rights to property, social welfare and other benefits." As is also the case among Thais, "most Burmese believe being gay is a result of reincarnation and due to sexual misconduct with a woman or man in a previous life. Moreover, it is sin and a serious taboo to talk openly in public about being gay, though there is no legal restriction on being gay."[9]

Although "the majority" of Burmese, according to Than Win Htut, "are still far from understanding homosexuality, cross-dressing," transsexualism, gay marriage, and the like, Aung Myo Min retains his strong belief in "the naturalness of being gay" since he feels that he was gay from birth, "was born this way:" "Nobody made me gay, so nobody can change that about me." And despite his trials and tribulations among fellow freedom-fighters (and others) as well as canonical Buddhist views that same-sex sexuality incurs negative karma and postpones the attainment of nirvana, he maintains, "if I were to be born gay in my next life, I would happily accept this life again." Most relevant for our purposes though is Aung Myo Min's rejection of the traditional Burmese subject-positions and attendant subjectivities available to males inclined toward same-sex relations. Such rejection is clear not only from his previously cited comments concerning his frustrations with fellow gay men and heteronormative Burmese who expect that he cross-dresses and otherwise identifies as a woman, but also from his insistence, "I don't want to have a wife and I don't want to have a woman's body. I want to be a man and … to have a boy friend who loves me as a gay man."

Aung Myo Min's struggle to carve out a new space for Burmese masculinity is fraught with countless obstacles, two of which merit brief mention. First, as his comments and other material considered here suggest, gay and transgendered communities in Burma are quite diverse, and many Burmese males who identify as *gay* (or are otherwise erotically inclined toward relations with other males) or transgendered continue to be oriented in accordance with more conventional Burmese notions (such as *acault*, *nat kadaw*, and *meinmasha*) that feminize male-bodied individuals desirous of relations with other males. Second, in recent years members of the heteronormative majority have increasingly utilized the term "*gay*" to designate *all* phenotypic males involved in same-sex relations or transgender practices, the majority of whom are feminized to one or another degree. The tendency to use the term "*gay*" to refer to feminized male-bodied ritual specialists such as *acault* and *nat kadaw* is evident in the language of Burma's youth (among others). Burmese youth make distinctions between what they take to be canonically acceptable and meritorious forms of Buddhist spirit worship on the one hand, and "cheap," suspect, and backward activities involving the honoring and propitiation of *nat* on the other, such distinctions attesting in any case to the modernist (some would say Protestant) tenor of various strands of contemporary Burmese Buddhism.[10] Many educated youth, for instance, balk at the idea that the worship of spirits such as Bo Bo Gyi (Great or Respected Grandfather or Elder/Ancestor) and Medaw (an esteemed female spirit, "like the Chinese Kwanyin, ... the goddess of mercy") has anything to do with *nat*, arguing that "a nat is a very cheap thing," whose worship involves "all ... [that] silly dancing and alcohol and cigarettes and *all those gay guys* .... A Bo Bo Gyi is very pure and sublime. There's no Bo Bo Gyi-*pwe* (festival). You don't get alcohol and *gays* around a Bo Bo Gyi" (Sadan 2005:91–92; emphasis added).

On both counts then there are strong links in Burma between male-male sexuality and femininity that pose serious challenges to Aung Myo Min's efforts to create a gay masculinity. At the risk of oversimplifying some of the sociolinguistic processes involved, we might say that the semantic domain of the concept *gay* seems to be informed by the semantic domain of the umbrella term *acault*, which encompasses, and does not distinguish among, transvestism, homosexuality, transsexualism, and effeminacy; and that in local parlance the term *gay* may be superseding earlier umbrella terms such as *acault*, albeit in ways that emphasize both gender *and* sexual transgression rather than gender transgression alone, which was the defining feature of *acault*hood. Similar processes are underway in Thailand and elsewhere in Southeast Asia, and among Cambodian Americans and other Southeast Asians living in the diaspora (see, e.g., Jackson 1997, Sinnott 2004, and the Epilogue, below).

Burmese masculinity is being redefined in other ways as well, as indicated by Ward Keeler's incisive analyses of the contemporary and classical genres of theatrical and musical performance he observed in and around Mandalay in the 1990s and in the early years of the new millennium. The male stars of traditional Burmese theater troupes are known as "princes" (*min-tha*), and at certain points during their night-long performances they typically assume the roles of Burmese male aristocrats. The sartorial splendor and overall demeanor of the stylized aristocrat is such that "it is difficult for an American [or other Western] observer to look at images of a Burmese theatre troupe's star in his princely mode" without, "to put it bluntly," thinking he is "a drag queen" and thus on some level gay (Keeler 2005:206). This impression "is not simply due to the yards and yards of brightly colored fabrics, multiple necklaces, diamond stud earrings, and brilliant red lipstick and nail polish that they wear … . There is in addition the matter of style: hand gestures (delicate, mannered) and even facial expressions (fey and dreamy) that in the princely mode take on what might be seen as an effeminate cast" (ibid.). The Burmese, however, do not regard princely attire or demeanor as effeminate or indicative of "a transvestite impulse" but rather as "a masculine refinement." While such refinement is still accorded prestige in many Burmese circles, it has come to be "supplement[ed] or largely supplant[ed] … [by other] conception[s] of masculine behavior … formulated largely in the mass media" (ibid., 207, 219). These include performances considered to be "modern," involving new dance styles and Burmese pop songs.

In these productions,

> each prince performs a solo while a semicircle of women, the 'princesses', sit or stand behind him. These women may sing a chorus to his singing, or one of them may take the microphone and sing when he puts it down to dance a few steps. The princesses … often clap in time to the music as well, and … may dance simple movements. But they are a backdrop to the prince, rather than the other half of a duet … [as they were in former times]. …They have been demoted from costars to the status of extras, a group of modestly dressed chorus girls.
>
> (Ibid., 217)

The older theatrical style, "one shared in many respects by the marionette tradition … appears to have lost its currency" (ibid., 220). More to the point,

> the allure that used to attach to the aristocratic male has largely disappeared. It has been replaced by the romantic, lovelorn crooner, who is … [analogous in some respects] to the West's 'sensitive New Age male'. The affinities with the older convention are real: refinement of feeling and gesture grounded the princely demeanor, just as they do the crooner's. The difference lies in the fact that the crooning pop star provides another image of a *modern* masculinity, not a classically aristocratic one: his status stems not from his mastery of a specifically Burmese version of refinement but rather on his mastery of an internationally promoted style—smooth, ingratiating —and as seen in Hollywood movies. So the distinction between the prince and the rock star is maintained, in the contrast between refinement and aggressiveness. But both partake of a modernity that places the star apart

from everything old fashioned, everyday and familiar—and therefore little worthy of attention.

(Ibid., 220; emphasis in original)

One component of the modernity staged by contemporary Burmese troupes involves the performance of Burmese rap music. Commenting on one show he observed, Keeler writes,

Many of the singers were very effective: they imitated the angry, aggressive, macho style of rappers brilliantly. Ko Naw We's performance was especially noteworthy ... . He dipped forward and straightened up frenetically while screaming into the microphone ... [and striding] around the stage looking fierce ... . This highly aggressive style has come to stand, in the West as in Burma, for a particular understanding of masculinity. What it means to be male in this version is to be assertive, ferocious, and strong— an absolutely autonomous agent ... . An angry, aggressive individual unconstrained in gesture or appearance by the dictates of everyday social life or government fiat, constitutes a version of masculinity with great appeal in contemporary Burma—as it does in much of the rest of the world.

(Ibid., 221)

But

the simple truth about most males in Burma today, especially the young men who attend theatre performances in large numbers, is that they are humiliatingly powerless ... . In the early to mid-1990s the regime liberalized the economy sufficiently to bring about a sudden upsurge in foreign investment. But continued political stalemate, along with graft, corruption, bureaucratic ineptitude, and arbitrary and byzantine procedures, have all brought general disaffection [both] among potential investors ... [and among many committed investors] ... who have cut their losses and left.

(Ibid., 221–222)

The growing likelihood of widespread civil unrest that Keeler and others with first-hand knowledge of Burma foresaw in the early years of the new millennium became reality in September and October 2007 when hundreds of thousands of monks and other protesters in Rangoon and elsewhere took to the streets in protest of government policies, only to meet with brutal repression from the junta.

Massive unemployment in a political-economic climate characterized by endemic graft and corruption, untold thousands of government informers, Kafkaesque bureaucratic nightmares, shuttered universities, and galloping inflation so severe that even driving taxis is no longer a viable outlet for university graduates, due to the price of gasoline on the black market (ibid., 222), is only part of the problem. Processes involving the impoverishment and repression of the majority and the escalation of state-sponsored terrorism waged against the populace have gone hand in hand with trends that have seen conspicuous concentrations of wealth and privilege among the chosen few favored by authorities—high-ranking members of the military and a handful of Chinese and other merchants who deal in illicit drugs or other contraband or have cornered one or another sector of the more "above-ground" black market. The glaring inequities have exacerbated the resentment felt by those without work (or underemployed), who are relegated to passing their time in Burma's ubiquitous teashops since, as one of Keeler's 30-year-old friends expressed it, "Every day's a holiday for us" (ibid.).

Burma's contemporary youth have few meaningful educational or employment opportunities, no freedom of expression, and very little freedom of movement. Not surprisingly, they feel they have little if any political agency. One of the few arenas available for the expression of any agency is "stylistic: how one dresses, how one carries oneself, how one presents oneself in public." Here lies much of the appeal to the Burmese of "the rock star [who is both] ... in charge, in a fashion—and out of control," and of predominantly male theater performances more generally, which are usefully viewed both as "covert expression of a fantasized modern masculinity, and a covert expression of many people's rage at its denial to them" (ibid., 222, 223).

Keeler deploys the expression "disappearing females" to underscore that one of the striking contrasts between earlier dramatic genres and their contemporary counterparts is the relegation of females in the modern to a subsidiary, back-up role. "If performances focus on modernity, they do so almost exclusively with reference to males, not females. If performances suggest alternative masculinities, the subject of femininities seems to elude them altogether—and modernity thereby becomes a version of masculinity alone" (ibid., 223). Why should this be so? According to Keeler, it is "because the question of how to represent a Burmese woman as both modern and feminine admits of no clear answer. If a woman takes on the demeanor and dress of foreign women, particularly as seen in the movies, few Burmese, male or female, could see her as anything but a prostitute" (ibid., 224). This situation is reminiscent of the Iban case and of Malaysia as a whole.[11] The only alternative, of depicting women in contemporary performances as "the refined, modest, graceful princess[es] of the classical tradition, would presumably hold no more allure than representing the prince in a purely classical mode. The solution for the prince has been to turn into a pop singer." Princesses, in contrast "simply fade into the background" (ibid., 224–225).

One fly in the ointment (there are many) is that "in Burma, as elsewhere, to idealize masculinity as consisting above all in a radical autonomy means deemphasizing sexual connectedness." But the potency of a rock star in Burma and beyond is a highly sexualized potency and that "implies something like interdependence." Hence the symbolic denial of the interdependence by means of misogynistic (Western) verse, or in the Burmese case, by women being more or less written out of the picture (ibid., 226).

There are, more generally, diverse modalities of masculinity in contemporary Burma. An important range of these modalities is exemplified by: (1) modern rappers; (2) monks in the all-male monastery; (3) gay activists like Aung Myo Min; and (4) the all-male junta. The defining features of these masculinities clearly differ, but those who embody and champion them share a pronounced concern to distance themselves from if not denigrate certain symbols and idioms of femininity (e.g., women's dress and demeanor and the interdependence and relationality associated with them) if not variably defined femininities in their entirety.

Monks are of course heavily dependent on women for gifts of rice and other food, as is readily apparent to anyone out and about in Burma during the early morning hours. But what is culturally salient about this relationship is not the interdependence at issue but rather the distance that in virtually all other contexts monks assiduously maintain from women and females of all ages, and their lack of sexual and other physical contact with them in particular. Formal distancing from women also occurs among members of the junta, all of whom are of course "born of women." It may thus seem somewhat paradoxical that feminized male-bodied ritualists (*acault, nat kadaw*) are alive and well. I would argue that the paradox is more apparent than real, especially when we consider three additional sets of issues. The first, as noted earlier, is the continued salience of the cosmologies in which transgendered ritualists are embedded, which prominently feature variously gendered—and divergently sexed—*nat* and which continue, albeit differentially, to be intellectually and emotionally meaningful to political and military elites, rank and file military personnel, non-military commoners, and religious devotees alike. The second is the rather unforgiving nature of Buddhist soteriology, which, as many observers (e.g., Spiro 1967, Tambiah 1970, Ortner 1978, Gombrich and Obeyesekere 1988) have argued, tends to encourage popular engagement both with *nat* (and their counterparts in other Buddhist contexts: *phii* in Thailand, *nat ka* in Cambodia, and so on), astrology, and alchemy, and with the ritual specialists long associated with these domains of the occult. The third involves domestic practices and social structural arrangements that include birth-order names, classificatory terms of reference and address, teknonymous usages, adoption, and the like, all of which encourage both "trading places" and conceptual and moral relativism, much like Buddhist (and Hindu) doctrinal emphases on rebirth, transcendence, and mutability.

There is nothing inevitable and in this particular sense "transhistorical" in the masculinizing developments at issue here. They are firmly grounded in the culture and political economy of Burma's history. One can discern structural precedents for them in earlier dynamics associated with processes of state building and religious standardization and centralization that occurred during the Pyu and Pagan periods and subsequently, for example (aspects of which were outlined in Chapter 2). They do in any case entail a further working out of cultural-political scenarios addressed in more detail elsewhere (e.g., Spiro 1967, Lieberman 1984, Aung-Thwin 1985; cf. Ortner 1989, Peletz 1996). A small but interesting subset of these dynamics, keyed to ritual and religion, therapy, and the care of the self, has been identified by Spiro (1967:240 passim), whose schematic position I present here in highly telegraphic terms (thus further schematizing it). Distinguishing between shamans (who propitiate harmful supernatural spirits) and exorcists (who control them), Spiro speculates that while exorcism in Burma was originally practiced by female shamans (he makes no provision in this scheme for transgendered persons or mediating categories of any kind), historical forces brought about a nexus of transformations that entailed a shift from shamanism to exorcism, "a change in the sex of the therapist from female to male," and a reorientation "from self-induced trance in, and thereby possession of, the therapist, to a therapist-induced trance in, and thereby possession of, the patient." These transformations went hand-in-hand with shifts in "the cultural content and meaning of therapy—from expulsion of the offending spirit by the power of the therapist, to exorcism of the spirit by the power of 'Buddhism'" (Spiro 1967:240). Originally the domain of the (female) shaman, "the treatment of supernatural possession has," in this view, "become the exclusive monopoly of the (male) exorcist," the more encompassing processes involving a number of "triumphs," including the "triumph of magical Buddhism over magical animism" and the "triumph of verbal over ecstatic" (ibid., 241). This model, pertaining as it does to the longue durée, necessarily ignores short-term reversals, counter-flows, and the like, such as we see among the Bugis. It also has something of the misplaced concreteness and finality not only of Engels' pronouncement, in a very different context, of "the world historical defeat of the female sex" but also of Weber's claims about the rise of rationalized religion and the attendant "disenchantment of the world." It does however resonate with changes in specifically political arenas and domains of popular culture, including but not limited to contemporary theater and music. For these and other reasons, the basic features of Spiro's model merit future historical and ethnographic research both in the Burmese context and elsewhere in Southeast Asia and beyond.

Women and Femininity at the Turn of the Twenty-First Century

The sidelining of women in Burmese theatrical productions has occurred, according to Keeler, because of ambiguities, ambivalences, and other dilemmas in how to represent Burmese women as simultaneously modern and feminine. The question thus arises as to the subject positions and subjectivities of contemporary Burmese women, the life options currently available to them, and the extent to which they may still enjoy the relatively high status said to be accorded them from early modern times through the colonial era and well into the twentieth century. In the latter connection we might recall Spiro's (1997:11) assessment, based mostly on research in the 1960s: "Burmese women probably occupy a higher social status than any other women in Asia" even though they have been squeezed out of most ritual roles and thus distanced from important sources of power and prestige. "Indeed, until the dramatic changes in the status of women in the West in the past fifty years, Burmese women enjoyed a degree of economic, legal, and social equality that arguably was unsurpassed either in Asia or in Europe and North America." Mi Mi Khaing (1984) concurs, devoting a good portion of her book to the subject.

But both scholars also note that Burmese gender ideologies, which are heavily informed by Buddhist precepts, not only accord far more legitimacy to males but also depict women as physically, intellectually, and morally inferior, as well as dangerous—because distracting and otherwise tempting, and polluting.[12] To elaborate, Spiro summarizes a range of Burmese Buddhist beliefs bearing on gender in relation to two ideological complexes, "the ideology of the superior male" and "the ideology of the dangerous female." The first of these complexes posits that males are superior to females "because of their sexual anatomy and *hpoun*. The Burmese regard the penis as a 'noble' organ, a 'golden flower,' and the vagina as 'ignoble' and polluting. *Hpoun*, an ineffable psychospiritual essence that is possessed only by males (and a famous female disciple of the Buddha) is usually translated as 'glory' but is perhaps more accurately glossed as 'charisma' … Since males alone are born with *hpoun*, they are innately higher than females intellectually, morally, and spiritually" (Spiro 1997:20–21). According to Burmese views, "the moral superiority of males is evinced by the alleged prevalence among females of three moral defects:" greed, lust—a "woman's sexual passion is [held to be] eight times stronger than a man's"—and assorted "evil practices" that include "habitually visiting others, making their husbands angry, [and] neglecting domestic duties" (ibid., 21–22). More generally, "[t]he spiritual superiority of males is attested to by their special place in Buddhist teaching and practice. The Buddhist initiation ceremony (*hsimbyu*) and induction into the Buddhist monastic order (*sangha*) are both restricted to males. Moreover, rebirth as a male is a sine qua non for the attainment of the three highest levels of spiritual achievement—sainthood, Buddhahood, and nirvana" (ibid., 22; see also Jordt 2005:51–60).

The second complex ("the ideology of the dangerous female"), for its part, postulates the existence of female dangers to men that are simultaneously moral, emotional, and sexual. These dangers include mercurial emotions, treachery, "love magic," "an extraordinarily powerful libido, a polluting vagina, and sexual allure" (Spiro 1997:25), any of which can threaten male authority and control along with the *hpoun* associated with it.

Spiro suggests that Burmese women, whether living in villages, urban areas, or diasporic communities in the West, tend to internalize and reproduce key features of these beliefs in much the same way and to the same general degree as Burmese men, even while they question and subvert others (cf. Belak 2002, Skidmore 2004). A more general historical point is that in pre- and early modern times, negative constructions of femininity such as these did not prevent women from assuming prestigious roles in political, economic, religious and other realms, though they may have been partly responsible for (in the sense that they could be readily invoked to rationalize) the fact that women's participation in these domains was not even more pronounced.

As for women and femininity in late twentieth-century Burma, Mi Mi Khaing dedicates much of *The World of Burmese Women* (1984) to assessments of rural women's important roles in the agricultural sector, to women's involvement as wage laborers in small- and large-scale factories (making cheroots, for example), and to the many achievements of professional and para-professional women in fields such as education and medicine. Most of these assessments, which, as we have seen, are based on research material gathered before 1980, are framed in positive terms and are quite optimistic about the future. So too are her discussions of women's participation in religious institutions. This despite the fact that—or perhaps because—she fully endorses the canonical Buddhist view that women are physically, spiritually, and morally inferior to men and thus evinces no ambivalence about restrictions on women's participation in monastic institutions or their doctrinally enshrined inability to attain *nibbana*, unless or until they are reborn as men (Mi Mi Khaing 1984:16; Spiro 1997:40–41). Also revealing are her mostly scattered and oblique comments concerning the generals who seized power in the coup of 1962, the extreme economic hardships and other difficulties their policies caused Burma's citizenry, and what impact these measures have had on women and constructions of femininity in particular. Self-censorship may be relevant here, even though she wrote most of the book while she was in residence with her well-born Shan husband, Sao Saimong Mangrai, at the University of Michigan. But this would not account for why she concludes her postscript with a salute to the women who marry soldiers and follow them to "untrammeled" border areas.

The references to these unsung heroines, like much else in the book, attest to the optimism that prevailed in many quarters during the heady days of the post-Bandung era and Burma's experiment in "Buddhist socialism." More to the point is that by most criteria, not just Mi Mi Khaing's, the first few decades after independence in 1948 not only promised many opportunities for women but also seemed likely to build on relatively positive views of femininity that, along with their less flattering counterparts, had long been part of Burmese culture.

Unfortunately, especially for women, things did not turn out as Mi Mi Khaing and millions of others had hoped. The situation went from bad to worse beginning in 1988/1989, the period that saw massive demonstrations against state policies, brutal opposition from state forces, and the emergence of SLORC (the State Law and Order Restoration Council) as the public face of the junta. This period also saw the beginnings of a shift from state socialism to state capitalism, the onset of an era of extreme geopolitical isolation, political repression, economic decline and stagnation, and attendant hardship and misery that has continued largely unabated (despite some liberalization of economic policies and cautious foreign investment in the early to mid-1990s) to this day. Annual per capita income in Burma is among the lowest in all of Asia, commonly estimated to be roughly a fourth (or less) of neighboring Thailand's and a sixth (or less) of Malaysia's, though it may be as low as US $110; and the country is plagued with high infant mortality rates, a collapsing infrastructure, etc. (Taylor 2004:183; see also Skidmore 2004). Annual inflation rates in the double—sometimes, triple—digits are the norm. And the country's banks and other financial institutions are routinely plundered by a military apparatus that has maintained itself through the creation and control of a monopolistic "narcoeconomy" based on large-scale opium cultivation, the production and trafficking of heroin, the manufacture and sale of amphetamines, and the mining (often through forced labor) and sale of precious gems and semi-precious stones (rubies, diamonds, jade, sapphires, pearls, gold, etc.) from the country's border areas, many of which remain under the control of insurgents. Tertiary educational institutions in urban areas have been closed (or forcibly dispersed) for much of the past two decades; university students and many other groups, including virtually all ethnic minorities, are suspect; propaganda machines, especially in Rangoon, are permanently cranked up; and urban neighborhoods believed to support the causes of students involved in uprisings in 1988, 1996, and 1997 have been bulldozed, their residents forcibly relocated to the outskirts of Rangoon, typically with little if any advance warning, compensation, or material assistance in their new environs. Particularly in urban areas, moreover, all movement is monitored and informers are everywhere, which is why the owners of ubiquitous sidewalk teashops endeavor to make sure that there is sufficient distance between tables to preclude eavesdropping. In light of circumstances such as these, some scholars (e.g., Skidmore 2004:59–63 et passim) have described Burma as an incipient fascist state, emphasizing that the only thing preventing Burma from joining the ranks of truly fascist states (such as Germany, Italy, and Japan during World War II and the years leading up to it) is the junta's inefficiency in successfully pressing capitalist institutions into the service of totalitarian ideological agendas, and vice versa. More generally, "the urban landscape [since 1988] has become charged with the possibility of violence and the uneasy silence of waiting," and many Burmese, numb with fear and anxiety, thus "wait for the end of the regime or the coming of the fifth and final Buddha, Arimettaya. No one seems to mind which comes first" (ibid., 11, 37).

Because of the situation outlined here, crushing poverty is endemic, as are hunger, malnutrition, and largely preventable (particularly water-borne) diseases. Short- or long-term prostitution is one of the few options available to women who endeavor to make ends meet. This is all the more true with the signing by President George W. Bush of the "Burmese Freedom and Democracy Act of 2003, which effectively closed down the Burmese garment industry, a major export earner" (ibid., 82) and one of the largest employers of women and teenage girls in urban areas and the shanty towns and satellite communities that have sprung up in their shadows.

Estimates of the numbers of Burmese women involved in commercial sex work are wildly inconsistent, from a few hundred thousand or less at the low end of the continuum to more than 1,000,000 at the high end, the latter figure being more realistic, especially if one includes women from Burma who are currently employed as sex workers in neighboring Thailand and China.[13] The prevalence of Burmese women who have been forced to turn to prostitution to make ends meet—perhaps "one-third of all women of reproductive age in the peri-urban townships" of Rangoon in the mid-to-late 1990s (ibid., 162)—does in any case have a number of profound implications, both for the bodies and lives of the women involved, and for contemporary constructions of femininity. Let us take these issues one at a time.

The prevalence of prostitution in Rangoon and other urban areas as well as small towns and remote areas along Burma's border with Thailand and China does of course raise the specter of HIV/AIDS, which is a problem of immense, rapidly escalating proportions in Burma. This is evidenced by World Health Organization (WHO) estimates that at the end of 2007 there may have been 370,000 individuals infected with the virus.[14] Males make up the majority (about 60 percent) of those confirmed to be carrying the virus, typically contracting it through the injection of illicit drugs (usually heroin) and/or heterosexual prostitution; but as in other areas of Asia and beyond, rapidly increasing numbers of monogamous women are contracting the disease from husbands or boyfriends involved in intravenous drug use, heterosexual prostitution, or both. One of the many problems here is that Burmese men are generally reluctant to purchase or wear condoms, even in the face of women's insistence that they do. Making matters worse is that for reasons having to do with masculine self-image, men who are willing to buy and use condoms consistently gravitate toward those marketed as "large" (Skidmore 2004:163). Because these are typically too big for Burmese men, they tend to fall off during sexual encounters, thus rendering them entirely ineffective in preventing contraception or the spread of STDs such as HIV/AIDS. As might be expected in a country where the state's per capita expenditure on healthcare over the last decade or so appears to have averaged less than US $10 a year, treatments and facilities for women (and men) infected with HIV/AIDS are abysmal.[15] This means, among other things, extremely high rates of female (and male) morbidity and mortality from diseases such as AIDS.

Women's extensive involvement in the sale of sexual favors also informs contemporary understandings of femininity (and masculinity). Put simply, the prevalence of female prostitutes reinforces Buddhist precepts that depict women as different from and inferior to men on account of their stronger sex drives and other "base" desires and thus having intrinsically stronger attachments to the material world—all of which impede the attainment of wisdom, spirituality, merit, rebirth on a higher plane, and of course nirvana. It does of course "take two to tango" as is sometimes said in the West, but because double standards are ubiquitous in Burma, as in the West, prostitution, which is overwhelmingly heterosexual, reflects quite poorly on femininity but has little if any negative impact on constructions of masculinity. (The fact that male-bodied prostitutes such as *acault* tend to be feminized probably contributes to these dynamics as well.) These developments help activate or bring to the fore those components of Buddhist gender ideologies that portray women in negative terms compared to men. If only in a relative sense, this dragging down of femininity by women's involvement in prostitution simultaneously contributes to the polarization of male and female and the conceptual elevation of males and masculinity as a whole.

In a climate such as this it is perhaps to be expected that the Generals' attempts to discredit the 62-year-old leader of the opposition movement, Aung San Suu Kyi, have entailed an overdetermined demonization of femininity. This demonization reverberates throughout urban and peri-urban enclaves and, to a lesser extent, throughout rural settings as well, though there is no way of measuring the extent to which it may have undercut or otherwise qualified support for Aung San Suu Kyi or her party, which clearly enjoys more popularity than the Generals but (like Aung San Suu Kyi herself) has been barred from public life. Key elements of this strategy involve the construction and dissemination of narratives focusing on the fact that Aung San Suu Kyi is a woman and that, like all women, she uses female guile and manipulation to achieve her divisive goals, in this case, leadership of the National League for Democracy (the major opposition party). Like all other women, she is also said to be driven by lust and is portrayed as otherwise unfit for an office that involves leadership of the country and stewardship of its cultural patrimony and other resources.

Aung San Suu Kyi's long-term marriage to a Briton (Michael Aris, who died in 1999), coupled with her having given birth to two "half-caste" children, adds to her sins and other deficiencies as far as the xenophobic junta is concerned, simultaneously rendering her both multiply hybrid and multiply transgressive, an overdetermined threat to nation and state sovereignty by any criteria. This is partly because her husband was non-Burmese and partly because he belonged to the "race" which colonized Burma and which, aided by or otherwise in league with the US, is waiting for signs of weakness borne of civil disobedience and disunity to wrest control of the country from its rightful stewards and thus plunder its wealth and plunge it back into colonial servitude. The impending likelihood of an invasion by Western, specifically US, forces was in fact the official reason given for the junta's abrupt relocation of all government ministries from Rangoon to a secret mountain retreat near Pyinmanaa, 200 miles to the north, on November 13, 2005, beginning precisely at 6:37 a.m., a time apparently chosen by well-placed astrologers for its auspiciousness (Mydans 2005).

Aung San Suu Kyi's sins and deficiencies include not only her base femininity and her sexual and reproductive transgressions that involve treason to "race" and nation. For on these and other grounds the Generals also depict her as "wild" and "uncivilized" like shamanic *nat kadaw*, who traffic in the occult, are married to and at times possessed by *nat*, and are well known for behavior that transcends normative expectations keyed to gender and various other domains of practice and desire. Indeed, the junta, which endeavors to position itself through dual-gendered kinship idioms as caring and benevolent ("the army is father, the army is mother") does not simply liken her to a *nat kadaw* or a *nat*; it explicitly categorizes her in these terms, in some contexts as a *nat kadaw*, in others as a *nat*—as for different reasons do some of her supporters (Houtman 2005:134 passim). In doing so the junta seeks to exploit its charges' longstanding ambivalence toward spirit mediums and the spirit world as a whole, including the mythic legacy, which is well developed in popular culture, of *nat* as threats to the sovereignty of

Buddhism and ruler(s) alike. Relevant in this connection is the regime's media-hyped involvement in the renovation and regilding of Buddhist pagodas and shrines (most notably, Shwedagon Pagoda), along with its earmarking of funds for the construction of new Buddhist monuments. These moves are aimed at garnering for itself a modicum of the orthodox religious legitimacy that it has squandered by arresting, torturing, and killing monks suspected of pro-democracy leanings. For many Burmese, however, the Generals' reputed involvement in sorcery and alchemy has the opposite effect.

The grim picture of state repression and widespread fear sketched out in the preceding pages should not obscure important comparative historical points, once of which is that "traditional" modalities of transgendering and same-sex relations are accorded more legitimacy (e.g., are less stigmatized) in Burma than in most other Southeast Asian contexts (e.g., Iban, Ngaju Dayak, Malay). At the same time, the situation of Burmese women is by any criteria far worse than that of women in other Southeast Asian venues discussed here. These patterns exist partly because of the way the junta has reversed and otherwise botched Burma's development, locking the country in downward economic spirals. Also relevant is that while the junta, in sharp contrast to its Malaysian counterpart (discussed in Chapter 5), has not seen fit to launch far-reaching campaigns against those involved in transgendering or same-sex relations (for a variety of reasons, they are less prominent on the radar as embodiments of threatening difference), it has undercut the status of women, eroded the legitimacy of all things associated with femininity, and subjected women and girls from most walks of life to all varieties of marginalization, danger, and risk. This has been done partly by effecting political and economic policies requiring women to engage in prostitution or to work and travel at night (which is taken by many to involve prostitution). Female sex workers are often raped by police; conversely, women who have been sexually assaulted by the authorities are often cast out of their homes, figuratively if not literally, and forced into prostitution. These and attendant dynamics marginalize women and render them more susceptible to abuse, disease, and early death (Belak 2002, Skidmore 2004, Talikowski and Gillieatt 2005).

It is not altogether clear how the specific policies at issue may be eroding the legitimacy of male-bodied individuals engaged in conventional modalities of transgenderism and same-sex erotics, though we have seen that there is a strong conceptual link between *acault* and prostitution, part of which exists due to widespread unemployment and across-the-board economic stagnation. It is probably not coincidental that recent years have seen efforts on the part of gay rights activists (like Aung Myo Min) to create a space for males inclined toward same-sex relations that is not feminized in any way. In the Burmese context, attempts to masculinize the same-sex relationships of male-bodied persons is part and parcel of more encompassing trends involving the polarization of masculinity and femininity, even while it may simultaneously reflect sincere efforts to create a liberatory space free from the constraints of heterogender strictures. Ironically, efforts by strongly anti-government, "this-worldly" human-rights activists like Aung Myo Min to create gay masculinities resonate with the pronounced valorization of masculinity that is promoted by draconian military policy and canonical Buddhism alike.

We also need to bear in mind that notwithstanding the climate of fear and repression that I have described here, some observers of Burma see much hope for the future. There are, put differently, a number of openings and counter-flows, just as there are relegitimization processes of the same general sort documented for Bugis, Malays, and other Southeast Asians. Grounds for optimism include not only the widespread support accorded Aung San Suu Kyi's National League for Democracy but also movements on behalf of gays, lesbians, and the transgendered, such as those headed by Aung Myo Min. Women's extensive involvement in lay Buddhist movements merits mention as well insofar as it may help counter the ideological implications of widespread female prostitution and otherwise contribute to more positive views of women (Jordt 2005). The proliferation of Burma-focused NGOs, especially in neighboring Thailand and in cyberspace, also bodes well for the future. But the fact that most NGOs cannot operate freely in Burma is obviously cause for concern. The latter situation serves as a stark reminder of the state's refusal to countenance the existence of organizations or movements that champion and embody pluralism; it is also a clear index of the junta's commitment to scaling down the pluralism that has long been a prominent feature of Burma's cultural landscapes.

Conclusion

Despite the overall thrust of the long-term historical processes outlined here and in the preceding chapter, a good deal of gender pluralism existed in many (perhaps most) areas of Southeast Asia well into the twentieth century. This generalization applies to the case studies examined in this chapter and to numerous other societies (e.g., in Bali, Java, Sumatra, Vietnam, Thailand, and the Philippines) mentioned in passing. In many of these settings, individuals engaged in transgenderism and same-sex relations were commonly involved in ritual activities associated with spirit cults and wedding festivities, and even when they were not, they continued to be accorded one or another degree of legitimacy—as did their normatively gendered partners—at least through the 1960s (or thereabouts). More broadly, even though some of the relevant anthropological accounts bearing on transgenderism and same-sex relations during the mid-to-late twentieth century suggest a certain dismissiveness, ambivalence, and, arguably, a euphemized violence of exclusion, they also document cultural scenarios and social attitudes that are in many respects relatively positive, albeit less so than in earlier times. These same generalizations apply to many culturally variable categories bearing on women and femininity.

This being the case, one could look at the proverbial glass as either half empty or half full. I shall first consider the "half-empty" perspective and briefly enumerate three broadly encompassing sets of dynamics that have eroded gender pluralism over the long term and since the 1960s in particular, a period characterized by "deep change" that was typically more profound, in terms of pace, scope, force, and overall intensity than transformations that occurred in earlier times. First, forces of political centralization, many of which have involved the expansion and consolidation of state power at the expense of local polities (among Iban, Ngaju Dayak, and Bugis, for example). Second, the development and mass appeal of nationalist and modernist discourses extolling the virtues of rationalized religion, science, technology, economic progress and secular education (which have clearly affected the Burmese and all other cases considered here). And third, processes of urbanization, bureaucratization, and industrialization, coupled with the rise of (mostly capitalist) market economies (also pervasive though wildly uneven throughout the region). These dynamics have entailed widely redounding institutional and cultural rationalization that eroded the moral underpinnings of agrarian communities and the pluralism-friendly cosmologies in which they were embedded (as is particularly evident among the Iban and Ngaju Dayak; also, albeit less overtly, among the Malays, as we shall see in the next chapter). They simultaneously contributed to increased social differentiation and stratification, along with new modalities of surveillance, discipline, and control harnessed to the production of heightened normativity in all areas of social life. Consequently, many local "priesthoods," however gendered or sex(ualiz)ed, have been shorn of their legitimacy and many rituals involving androgynous or female spirits and deities have been abandoned. In addition, throughout much of the region transgendering—like same-sex sexuality, bisexuality, and femininity—has lost many of its positive associations with the sacred. In places such as Malaysia, its long-standing centrality in royal palaces and the reproduction of local polities and cosmologies exists primarily in scattered memories, colonial monographs, and dusty archives. And, as regards its contemporary loci, it tends to be most visible in secular realms of fashion and entertainment, and the increasingly surveilled and disciplined private domain. When viewed from a long-term perspective, it is clear that myriad variants of transgendering and same-sex sexuality have been secularized and stigmatized, and that some of them have been explicitly pathologized and criminalized as well. It is also clear that many transgendered individuals, especially if involved in same-sex sexuality or bisexuality, have been recast as contaminating as distinct from sacred mediators who are perversely if not treasonously muddling and enmiring the increasingly rigid and dichotomous terms of sex/gender systems long characterized by fluidity and pluralism alike.

It is not merely the demise, reduced salience, or transformation in local schemes of cultural value of mediating (or third) categories that has contributed to or entailed the increased dichotomization of masculinity and femininity and a constriction of pluralistic sentiments and dispositions bearing on gender and sexuality, especially femininity and female sexuality. So too has commercial sex work, which is quite pervasive in some of the settings we have considered here (e.g., among urban-dwelling Iban and in Burma), though arguably less of a problem in these cases than in other Southeast Asian nations such as Thailand and the Philippines (Enloe 1990, Bishop and Robinson 1998, Peletz 2007).

Since the beginning of the colonial era, as we have seen, commercial sex work in Southeast Asia has been mostly of a heterogender if not specifically hetero-sexual variety, usually involving masculine, male-bodied clients and feminized, female-bodied prostitutes (or masculine/male clients and feminized male-bod-ied sex workers), much like its early modern predecessor, temporary marriage. Without question, contemporary prostitution provides certain outlets for males desirous of sexual contact (and in some cases certain kinds of experiences that may otherwise be unavailable to them). It is moreover constructed and appar-ently experienced by some female sex workers among the Iban and others as a liberatory ("life-style") "choice" (see, for example, Law 1997), albeit a choice exercised in an environment typically lacking meaningful educational and employment opportunities. In the majority of the contexts considered here, however, prostitution is multiply stigmatized and tends to give rise to modern, more or less secular discourses that portray women as dirty, disease-bearing, and dishonorable, just as it highlights negative features of "traditional" gender ide-ologies, typically grounded in one or another version of religious orthodoxy, that are highly unflattering to women and all things associated with femininity. On this score there is ample justification for viewing large-scale commercial sex work as detrimental to pluralism.

I hasten to add two points. First, the political-economic and attendant dynamics that give rise to large-scale prostitution—including, most notably, state policies and globalizing forces that are conducive to economic stagnation and to endemic poverty, malnutrition, hunger, and the like—commonly go hand in hand with widespread efforts on the part of political elites to repress their citizen-subjects and to inject fear if not terror into all realms of their pub-lic and private lives. And second, these latter efforts, even if only partly suc-cessful, tend to engender widespread suspicion and mistrust of variously construed Others and are thus, by definition, inimical to pluralism. Such being the case, the larger nexus of political-economic and attendant dynamics at issue here is more directly implicated in the constriction of pluralism than is prosti-tution per se. This is especially so when the predatory state policy initiatives at issue aim to—or have the effect of—creating terror throughout the land, as in the instance of Burma, in which case we are dealing squarely with state-spon-sored terrorism. Michael Walzer (2004a:51) has recently observed, "the pecu-liar evil of terrorism [is] not only the killing of innocent people but also the intrusion of fear into everyday life, the violation of private purposes, the inse-curity of public spaces, the endless coerciveness of precaution." To rephrase Walzer's observations for our purposes, we might say that the trust essential to pluralism is seriously eroded if not impossible to retrieve from the wellsprings of routine sociality when fear intrudes into everyday life, when private purposes are violated, when public spaces are insecure, and when people are endlessly coerced by the precautions necessary to avoid prolonged detention, torture, or worse at the hands of uniformed authorities, their undercover minions, or others forced reluctantly to aid their cause.

If on the other hand we view the proverbial glass as "half full," we need to ask a different question: Why is gender pluralism still relatively robust in many Southeast Asian societies, despite the cultural, political, and historical forces long arrayed against it? A partial answer to this question is that despite the inroads of normalizing forces of capitalism and governmentality that endeavor to mandate a "drive toward homogenization" (Pandey 2006:16), many Southeast Asian systems of myth, ritual, and cosmology continue to be culturally salient, and continue to encourage imaginative play conducive to the creation of implicit cultural models valorizing relativism, pluralism, and different ways of being in the world. Also germane, particularly since pluralistic sentiments and dispositions begin at home, is a nexus of domestic and social structural dynamics that includes relatively high rates of abandonment and divorce; widespread fosterage and adoption; and systems of kinship terminology involving classificatory terms of reference and address, birth-order names, and teknonymy—all of which serve to valorize the conceptual and other shifts involved in changing places and viewing things from different perspectives. Owing partly to their synergy, these dynamics engender relationality, temporal flux, and reversal, and otherwise encourage conceptual and moral relativism.

Another factor that has helped reproduce, broaden, and otherwise bolster sentiments and dispositions conducive to pluralism has to do with agency and resistance on the part of those targeted by forces hostile to pluralism. Evidence bearing on Sulawesi's past suggests that throughout (written) history, the Bugis *bissu*, aided by the nobility whose "white blood" and prerogatives they both symbolized and safeguarded, actively resisted efforts to undercut their prestige and succeeded in convincing many people of the righteousness of their cause. So too apparently did the largely "lay" *calabai* and *calalai*, many of whom benefited directly from the spaces of legitimacy that *bissu* ritualists and the dynamics that supported them helped create. *Bissu*, *calabai*, and *calalai* alike clearly derived advantage from the political openings and opportunities for cultural advocacy that emerged after the fall of Suharto in 1998, as did Muslim feminists and variably situated advocates of civil society and transnational lesbianism, some of whom forged strategic alliances with *bissu*, *calabai*, *calalai*, and/or normatively gendered women. Gendered resistance on the part of the Iban and Ngaju Dayak during the period since the 1960s is less well documented, though we saw that some Iban women turned to commercial sex work during this time rather than submit to the deteriorating conditions to which increasingly large numbers of Iban women were subject. This form of resistance might be said to have backfired insofar as it fueled the emergence of increasingly reactive heteronormative discourses depicting women in public domains as dirty, potentially disease-bearing, and dishonorable, though there are clearly different vantage points and scales of analysis that need to be distinguished here and with respect to all other forms of resistance we might want to consider.

We also saw (in Chapter 3) that untold numbers of Chinese women in late colonial-era Singapore refused to enter into heterosexual marriage or other partnerships involving men (such as concubinage and prostitution), opting instead to reside in all-female "vegetarian houses" ordered partly in accordance with Buddhist precepts and devotion to the deity Guanyin, and to pair off with like-minded women with whom they undertook vows of "sworn sisterhood" that commonly entailed same-sex relations. These relations were among the most subversive of all challenges to heteronormativity in that they were couched in symbols, idioms, and metaphors of (same-sex/gender) siblingship as distinct from (heterogender) marriage. The latter, recall, comprised the reigning trope not only for the vast majority of conventional unions, but also for most varieties of same-sex relations in Southeast Asia during the early modern era and the period since. The impact of such relations, which continue into the present, is difficult to gauge. They have not dislodged the heterogender hegemony (about which more below), but they do provide an historical legacy that Singaporean gays and lesbians are able to invoke to claim a space for themselves in the island-nation's past, present, and future.

One could easily cite other instances of colonial-era and postcolonial resistance to the normalizing forces of governmentality and state-sponsored economies, the movements spearheaded by Burmese gay rights activist Aung Myo Min and opposition leader Aung San Suu Kyi being prominent examples (see, e.g., J.C. Scott 1985, Stoler 1985, Ong 1987). My concern here is not to describe and analyze such resistance but to suggest that, taken collectively, acts of everyday resistance on the part of those who either embody or champion gender and sexual diversity or are associated with cultural-political arrangements linked to it are among the factors that have contributed to the relatively pronounced degree of pluralism we see in many quarters of present-day Southeast Asia, despite the various constrictions and other transformations that have occurred in these areas.

I turn finally to two sets of issues having to do with the proliferation of sexual and gender diversity that has occurred in the postcolonial era and the last few decades in particular owing partly to massive urbanization and the growth of new middle classes and urban subcultures engaged with globalizing discourses (the subject of the following chapter). The first involves a loosening of the hegemonic "deep structure" that long informed subjectivities as well as the directionality and the embodiment of "potential[ly] erotic enterprises," to draw upon Judith Butler's (1993:110) terminology. I use the term "loosening" here partly because we are not dealing with the shattering of a hegemony in a Gramscian (1971) sense, nor with an epistemic rupture or succession à la Foucault (1978), Morris (1994), Garcia (1996), or Altman (1996, 2001). The evidence for this "loosening," which comes from Burma, Thailand, Malaysia, Indonesia, and many other parts of Southeast Asia, includes the emergence in the past few decades of (at least) two newly delineated classes of individuals. One is composed of male-identified men who are erotically involved with other men. The main example I discussed in this connection is Burma's Aung Myo Min and the subculture focused around gay masculinity he has endeavored to create; but I also noted in passing that similarly oriented subcultures have developed in Thailand, Malaysia, Vietnam, and elsewhere in the region. What is new and distinctive about the men involved in these subcultures is that their subject positions and subjectivities are defined not only by their male gender but also by their sexual orientation as gays or men who have sex with men.

The other newly designated group consists of female-identified women who are erotically drawn to other women. What is historically novel and unique about these women is that their subject positions and subjectivities are informed not simply by their female gender but also by their sexual orientation as lesbians or women who engage in sex with women. Consider in the latter connection the referents and meanings of the terms *tom* and *dee*. These terms (and variations like *T*, *T-bird*, *tibo*, and so on) derive from the English "tomboy" and "lady," respectively, and are commonly used in Indonesia, Thailand, the Philippines, and elsewhere in Southeast Asia (including Malaysia, at least in the case of *tom*, *tomboy*, etc.) and beyond to designate female-bodied individuals who engage in same-sex relations, one or another form of transgenderism, or both. There are some important variations in the ways these terms are used (and the specific meanings they convey) from one national context to the next— and within these contexts as well—(Johnson, Jackson, and Herdt 2000) and I thus focus here on Thailand, specifically the Bangkok region as described by Megan Sinnott (2004), who has produced the most nuanced and sophisticated anthropological study of *tom* (*thom*; masculine females) and *dee* (*dii*; feminine females involved with *tom*) to date.[16]

The emergence in Bangkok in the past few decades of *dee* identities and subjectivities is in many ways highly revealing of both the scope and limits of changes occurring in Thailand and elsewhere in Southeast Asia. What separates *dee* from normative Thai women is not their gender identities or styles of dress or comportment, all of which are broadly congruent with the contours of Thai femininity, but their sexual orientation: the fact that they are attracted to, desirous of, and erotically involved with women rather than men. To reiterate a point made earlier, what is new and distinctive about these women is that their subject positions and subjectivities are defined not only by their female gender but also by their sexual orientation as women who engage in erotic activities with other women. Partly because gender identities in Southeast Asia have always subsumed and effectively defined sexual orientations, scholars like Dennis Altman (1996, 2001) see in these kinds of developments (including those involving gay men) evidence of the ways that "Asian homosexualities" are being "Americanized," "Westernized," or otherwise reconfigured by transnational, globalizing developments (see also Morris 1994 and Garcia 1996, and rejoinders by Jackson 1997 and Sinnott 2004, and Johnson 1997, respectively).

In my view, however, these shifts are not as dramatic as they may appear at first glance. I say this partly because in Thailand and elsewhere in Southeast Asia feminine-identified *dee* tend to form erotic relationships exclusively with masculine-identified *tom*, in contrast to masculine-identified *gay* men whose sexual relationships do not necessarily involve feminized *gay* men, though they sometimes—perhaps typically—do. These relationships, though (homo)sexualized, are still heterogender as far as most of the participants and others are concerned. As such, they fit comfortably within the heterogender matrix that has long been a central component of sex/gender systems throughout Southeast Asia (the Chinese Singaporeans discussed earlier constitute a partial exception). For these and other reasons I regard the emergence of new subject positions and sexual subjectivities in Southeast Asia as involving processes that while commonly appropriating global terms and identities, usually do so in ways that are heavily informed by indigenous categories and their interrelations, key features of which continue to serve as templates for the localization of things global with respect to form and content alike, much as Sahlins (1981, 2004) has observed for other processes of historical change in the Pacific and far beyond (cf. Jackson 1997, Johnson 1997, Blackwood 1999, and Boellstorff 2004a).

If on the other hand the new subject positions and subjectivities that Sinnott documents for Bangkok involved relationships that were simultaneously homosexual *and* homogender (i.e., of the same sex and similarly or identically gendered) they could pose truly serious challenges to the locally prevalent cultural hegemony. Note though that it would not be the *sexual* patterning—the homosexuality—of these relationships that would raise the specter of subversion vis-à-vis local taxonomies and hierarchies and the values and interests they serve. Rather, the real threat of subversion would come from the way they are *gendered*—the fact that they would be homogender. Note too that eroticized homogender relationships between female-bodied individuals reportedly strike the majority of Thais, Bugis, and other Southeast Asian women involved in transgender practices, same-sex relations, or both, as aesthetically and morally offensive, and otherwise beyond the pale, a view shared by their more normatively oriented sisters (see, for example, Sinnott 2004:87–88 and Davies 2007:26–28, 68). Their counterparts however—eroticized homogender relationships involving phenotypic males—do not necessarily evoke negative sentiments among male-bodied persons involved in transgender practices, same-sex relations, or both, though they apparently offend most male-bodied individuals in society at large. There are, to repeat, burgeoning subcultures growing up around these latter (male-bodied/homogender) relations in Burma, Thailand, Malaysia, and other nations in Southeast Asia. As in other contexts discussed in this chapter and elsewhere, male-bodied individuals, however gendered, continue to enjoy an appreciably broader range of experiences and opportunities than their female-bodied counterparts in terms of the directionality and embodiment of potentially erotic enterprises (and much else).

Four points follow. First, pluralism is always relative, never absolute. Second, much like sovereignty in Ong's (1999, 2006) work, pluralism is usefully conceptualized in terms of clines or gradations. Third, however pluralistic Southeast Asia is at present—or has been in the past—we are clearly dealing with regimes of graduated pluralism keyed to systems of stratified reproduction defined as encompassing networks of cultural-political relations that facilitate certain groups' nurturance and reproduction while discouraging or precluding those of others. A fourth point (which is an elaboration of the third) has to do with the two-fold nature of the clines or gradations at issue. On the one hand these clines involve different degrees of legitimacy (or prestige/stigma) accorded certain kinds of embodied activities and relationships (e.g., transgender practices and same-sex relations) as distinct from others (associated with unacceptably "close" mating [incest] and liaisons construed as adulterous, for instance). On the other hand they entail a favoring of one or more subject populations over others, for example, male-bodied persons over female-bodied persons, partners to heterogender relationships over those involved in homogender relations, and so forth.[17]

A second, related set of issues I want to comment on by way of concluding this chapter has to do with *au courant* concepts such as heteronormativity. I have deployed the latter concept throughout this book—albeit with caveats and ambivalence—but it is ultimately too ethnocentric and otherwise problematic to be of much heuristic or other use at this historical juncture or, indeed, at any point in the six hundred or so years with which this book is concerned. The prefix "hetero" in widely accepted definitions of heteronormativity refers uncritically to hetero*sexuality*, thus dubiously privileging sexual difference over gender difference. An important article that appears in the 2002 *Handbook of Lesbian and Gay Studies*, edited by Diane Richardson and Steven Seidman, for example, offers the following definition: "Heteronormativity can be defined as the view that institutionalized hetero*sexuality* constitutes the standard for legitimate and expected social and sexual relations. Heteronormativity insures that the organization of hetero*sexuality* in everything from gender to weddings to marital status is held up as both a model and as 'normal'" (Ingraham 2002:76; emphasis added). Many who use this term collapse or ignore the heterosexual/heterogender distinction altogether, assuming in the process that ostensibly bedrock sexual(ized) difference is invariably *the* defining feature of personal identity, the difference that matters most. Terms such as heteronormativity were developed to expose and undermine certain kinds of normalizing discourses. Ironically, many who deploy them often inadvertently reinscribe some of the same silences, elisions, and euphemized violence they seek to lay bare and critique.

Lawrence Cohen (1995) and Gayatri Reddy (2005) have drawn attention to conceptual and epistemological problems such as these that have vexed debates among anthropologists and South Asianists concerning the caste-like group of eunuchs and hermaphrodites known as *hijras*, India's so-called "third sex." Cohen's argument that not all difference (embodied in "thirdness") is the same is germane to our understanding of practices involving transgression and resistance, whether or not they are gendered and/or sexualized. Tze-Ian Sang (2003:92), as noted earlier, has argued that in late Imperial China, "*compulsory marriage, compulsory sexual service, compulsory reproduction,* and *compulsory chastity* are more apt than *compulsory heterosexuality* as descriptions of women's fate ... [in] traditional Chinese patriarchy" (emphasis in original); that during this time "intimacies with women" were ultimately "inconsequential;" and that "what determines a woman's gender conformity or non-conformity is ... her relations with men, *not* her relations with women. Female-female desire does not … make her a gender outcast as long as it cooperates with the imperative of cross-sex marriage. *In sum, female-female desire by itself is not taboo; marriage resistance is.*" (ibid., 93; emphasis added). In general support of these views, many of which when appropriately rephrased also pertain to male-bodied persons, I would underscore that the most deeply rooted and widely ramifying taboos throughout Southeast Asia during the 600-year period with which I have been concerned have never been engaging in transgender practices or enacting same-sex desires. Such practices and desires were perfectly legitimate as long as they occurred in certain contexts and involved bonds that were conceptualized in relation to heterogender (but not necessarily heterosexual) marriage. Heterogender marriage of one sort or another was in fact enjoined on everyone, with the notable exception of Buddhist monks and other ascetics (certain categories of *bissu*, for example) who undertook religious vows requiring celibacy. Hence the most deeply rooted and widely ramifying taboo in question involved resistance to marriage, albeit marriage involving heterogender relationships that were variably embodied and sexed.

The salience of one or another form of marriage in this formulation may seem reminiscent of the West during the past 600 years, but the apparent commonalities should not obscure the equally striking differences. The latter include both a wider berth for marriage in Southeast Asia (allowing for heterosexual unions as well as same-sex marriages in certain contexts as long as they were heterogender); and, related, the existence in Southeast Asia of marital institutions and systems of kinship and gender that were in some sense less restrictive, exclusive, and all-encompassing insofar as husbands in particular could engage in same-sex relations without necessarily calling into question their loyalties to their wives, their commitments to matrimony, or their masculinity. Although I cannot explore the issue here it merits remark that from a broadly comparative (global) perspective, the West, not Southeast Asia, is anomalous in these areas, and that the anomalies are probably best explained by the peculiar development of the Church in the West and the ways that Church policy helped shape Western institutions of kinship, marriage, gender, and sexuality over the last millennium (Duby 1983, Goody 1983, 1996, Jordan 1997). Max Weber (1922 [1963]:239) summed up some of the key contrasts in his comparative-historical observation that the teachings of Christianity, with their "demand of absolute and indissoluble monogamy went beyond all other religions in the limitations imposed upon permissible and legitimate sexuality."[18] Most relevant for our purposes is that important "East-West" contrasts of the sort at issue here are elided and obscured by uncritical usage of terms such as "heteronormative."

5 Gender, Sexuality, and Body Politics at the Turn of the Twenty-First Century

This chapter examines some of the central tensions, paradoxes, and ironies of the historical trajectories documented in previous chapters. I am especially concerned with social and cultural dynamics related to the paradoxical fact that an important range of transformations in pluralistic sensibilities and dispositions involved a *contraction of pluralism* and that roughly contemporaneous transformations in various domains of social practice and cultural valuation witnessed a *proliferation of diversity*, much of which, at least from the perspective of conventional standards of legitimacy, lies (far) beyond the cultural pale. The two sets of movements though at first glance seemingly disparate, opposed, or both are part of a single dynamic process that has also entailed the fragmentation of authority and crises of governance owing to the more or less concurrent emergence of competing loci of power and prestige that have helped birth new standards vying for legitimacy, some largely local, others derived from or informed in important ways by exogenous, globalizing sources.

In the pages that follow I explore these processes by concentrating largely on Malaysia, a nation-state that is often described in textbooks and travel brochures as "the crossroads of Asia" due to its strategic location along the waterways of Asia and its rich ethnic diversity. I begin with a consideration of mid-to-late twentieth-century discourses bearing on various "traditional" subject positions that commonly involved practices that were transgressive with respect to gender and/or sexuality. Continuing with an analysis of the narratives of "Asian values" that were articulated in the late twentieth century by political elites in Malaysia as well as Singapore, Japan, and elsewhere in the Asia Pacific region, I link the production and deployment of these discourses in Malaysia in the early 1990s to state-sponsored projects of modernity, to the proliferation of sociocultural diversity entailed in these projects (and in the state's generally enthusiastic albeit ambivalent embrace of globalizing forces generally), and to the rise of social intolerance that also saw the production of new forms of (sexualized) criminality. I proceed with a description and analysis of the Pink Triangle, a Kuala Lumpur-based NGO that was formed in 1987 to provide information and social services to people whose sexual proclivities and other bodily practices put them at risk for HIV/AIDS and other forms of potentially fatal harm. Brief profiles of the various communities served by the Pink Triangle provide an entrée to the urban/sexual underground and the struggle for sexual equality. So too does the ensuing discussion, which builds on interviews with activists in the gay, lesbian, and transsexual communities to illustrate how variably situated groups of Malaysians engage the vicissitudes of "tolerance" and open secrets, and the extremely arbitrary governmentality that scholars like Agamben (2005) consider to be a defining feature of neoliberal globalization. The concluding section of the chapter addresses some of the comparative and theoretical implications of these dynamics, focusing partly on possible scenarios for the future and why struggles for sexual equality and the discursive trajectories linked with them in Malaysia and elsewhere in Southeast Asia may diverge in significant ways from what we have seen in the West.

Transgendered Ritualists and Pondan

My contention in Chapter 4 that there was a fair degree of gender pluralism in Southeast Asia well into the twentieth century (though less so than in earlier times) is amply supported by data from the Malay Peninsula (West Malaysia; hereafter Malaysia). Malaysian data bearing on the 1960s are all the more noteworthy in light of highly repressive developments that have occurred in recent years, some of which illustrate how the culture of the state can impact local societies and cultures alike, especially in the case of the Malays, who currently number about 13,000,000 and thus comprise some 51 percent of the nation's overall population of 25,000,000 people.

In the east-coast state of Kelantan, for instance, which borders southern Thailand and has long been regarded by Malays and others as a bastion of "traditional" Malay culture and an epicenter of "Islamic conservatism," Douglas Raybeck reported that in the late 1960s Malays "regard[ed] homosexuality as peculiar, different, and even somewhat humorous, but they ... [did] *not* view it as an illness or as a serious sin" (1986:65; emphasis added). As noted earlier, Raybeck also encountered several "specialized homosexual villages" in or around the state capital, Kota Baru, one of which adjoined the palace of the Sultan who formerly enjoyed the means to maintain troupes of performing artists and all varieties of other specialists. These villages were composed exclusively of male couples engaged in same-sex erotics whose primary breadwinners made their living as transvestite performers of a Thai-origin dramatic genre known as *mak yong*. *Mak yong* performers were esteemed for their artistic skills and could outearn the heteronormative majority inhabiting neighboring settlements who comprised most of their audience. The specialized villages in which many Kelantanese *mak yong* artists resided in the 1960s were not outcast communities to which gender transgressors known to be involved in same-sex intimacies were banished. Nor is there evidence to suggest anyone harassing these enclaves or otherwise bothering their members.[1] These communities were well known to other villages, to local as well as regional and state-level religious and secular authorities at all levels, including of course the Sultan of Kelantan, who was their royal patron, and to Malay (and Malaysian) society at large. Indeed, the surrounding Malay communities and political-religious elites such as the Sultan did not simply "know about" these unique villages; they actively supported them and in the case of the Sultan clearly helped constitute them.

Data bearing on *mak yong* are reminiscent of James Peacock's (1968) findings on the symbols, idioms, and metaphors of *ludruk* and other forms of proletarian drama in Java (see also Keeler 1987) insofar as they too indicate a historical shift from palace-oriented performances to a genre geared toward an audience of "common folks," to quote Malaysia's leading expert on the subject (Mohd. Chouse Nasuruddin 1995:5). Arguably more germane are two additional historical points about the communities at issue. First, due to religious and political developments I discuss elsewhere (Peletz 2002) and will mention briefly in due course, such same-sex villages no longer exist. Second, even though these villages are a thing of the past and in the twentieth century were in any case largely confined to Kelantan (so far as we know), the pluralism suggested by their existence is broadly consistent with the situation elsewhere in the Malay Peninsula during the same general period (the 1960s through the late 1980s).

Consider, for instance, a case from the state of Kedah that I regard as deeply allegorical. It involved a male transvestite turned *alim* (Islamic religious scholar, man of learning) named Ismail bin Yaha, who was born around 1951 and "earned his livelihood by sewing clothes and serving as a 'female' dancer in local dance troupes" (Sharifah Zaleha Syed Hassan 1989:61). "In his twenties Ismail had become increasingly conscious that his dancing and his wearing of female clothing were contrary to Islam," but "he could not abandon these interests. Then, one night in the month of Ramadan, Ismail had a vision of heaven" which led him to give up his transgenderism, though not before "joining other transvestites to perform in [the state of] Perak a few nights after his ... vision" (ibid., 61–62). Shortly thereafter he "lost consciousness for about three days. When he regained his senses, he gave up dress-making, dancing, and female attire. He also conducted a *samak* (special purification rite) for his house" ostensibly because "the building materials ... had been purchased from the shop of a Chinese 'infidel.'" Most important, even though he had no religious education, he donned the white robes of an *alim* and began preaching to villagers "about the tortures they were likely to experience in hell, if they neglected their religious duties" (ibid., 61).

Based on interviews and on her study of official records relevant to this case, anthropologist Sharifah Zaleha Syed Hassan reports that Ismail immediately drew a large following and that "[lay] people began to interpret the radical transformation of his outlook, religious commitment, and life style as manifestations of divine intervention" (ibid.). Indeed, even though Ismail had been heavily involved in transgender practices for most if not all of his adolescent and adult life, he became so revered by members of the public that authorities linked to the increasingly bureaucratized and rationalized administrative bodies charged with regulating religious affairs feared he would soon be accorded the status of a prophet. After interviewing Ismail, an official committee decided that he was a *fasid* ("impious Muslim") and "declared ... [his] preaching as *kurafat* (tempting) and *bathil* (false). Since his understanding of Islamic philosophy was virtually nil, the Committee recommended that the Religious Council disallow Ismail from expounding his views on Islam ... and the ... otherworld ... for fear of confusing people and tarnishing their faith" (ibid., 62–63).

The story gets more interesting, for even after the authorities did their best to undermine Ismail's religious credentials and overall status, he went on to assume "a new and *more prestigious* role ... as a healer" (ibid., 63; emphasis added). There is no way of assessing how (if at all) Ismail's history of transgendering may have figured into the legitimacy accorded him as *alim* or healer but it seems obvious that his transgendered past was not an impediment to his assumption of either role. On the basis of my research in Malaysia since the 1970s, I would argue that it probably bolstered his legitimacy in both roles, at least as far as the lay public (comprising ordinary Muslims) was concerned. From an analytic perspective this case does in any event have deeply allegorical dimensions. It highlights not only various linkages between transgendering and ritual roles, but also both the relative permeability and interchangeability of some such roles, even at present, as well as their historic differentiation and seg-regation, a key feature of institutional rationalization in Weber's sense.

The relatively pluralistic community sentiments concerning institutional-ized transgendering that I have described for Kelantan and Kedah are consistent with my fieldwork observations in the state of Negeri Sembilan in the 1970s and 1980s. During that time, normatively oriented Malays still exhibited con-siderable tolerance and respect for individuals involved in transgendering, assuming they merited tolerance and respect on other grounds as well, though this is not to suggest a transgender let alone gay paradise. Such individuals tend to be referred to as *pondan*, which covers much the same semantic field as the terms *bapok* and *banci/waria* in Singapore and Indonesia, respectively. *Pondan* and certain corresponding terms in other parts of Southeast Asia, such as the Tagalog *bakla*, have multiple (sometimes mutually contradictory) referents. But they typically denote an adolescent or adult male who either dresses or adorns himself like a woman, walks like a woman, behaves sexually like a woman (in the sense of having sex with men), or acts like a woman in other ways. The encompassing nature of the *pondan* concept works against the cultural elabora-tion of distinctions (found in English and many other languages) among transvestism, transsexualism, intersexuality, homosexuality, and effeminate behavior. Note also that an individual's real or imagined proclivities with regard to "sexual-object choice" have never been a primary marker of the *pondan* category. *Pondan* is in any case a mediating rather than supernumerary category though this is not necessarily true of otherwise broadly analogous con-cepts in Southeast Asia, such as the Thai *kathoey* (Morris 1994, Jackson 1997).

Pondan can certainly be a term of derision (but in my experience it is usually not). And the depiction of *pondan* in literature, theater, film, and other venues of public culture suggests that the larger society views them with a fair degree of ambivalence (Khoo 2006), as is also true of *bakla* and *bantut* in the Philippines

(Manalansan 1995, Johnson 1997, Rafael 2000) and Thailand's *kathoey* (Jackson 1997, Morris 2000). But the more important point here is that in contemporary Malay culture there is an explicit conceptual link between *pondan* and transgendered individuals generally on the one hand, and certain types of ritual services and domains of cultural mediation on the other. We see this clearly in the linkage between *pondan* and *mak andam*, which is a term denoting ritual practitioners whose roles include planning weddings and attending to and beautifying brides. (Some of Malaysia's most celebrated "wedding specialists," as I call them, are *pondan*, and *pondan* are disproportionately represented among wedding specialists, especially male wedding specialists.) *Mak andam* help select propitious dates for marriage ceremonies, just as they dress and adorn the bride and mediate relationships between bride and groom and their respective kin. Aided by Quranic chants and spells, special oils, and other ritual paraphernalia, they are also centrally involved in the literal and figurative creation of beauty. At the same time, these specialists are key agents in status transformation and cultural brokerage that involve linking variously defined local worlds with Western and Islamic fashions, bodies of knowledge, and attendant sensibilities. In this they are much like the transgendered *bakla* beauticians and parloristas of the northern/Christian Philippines and their *bantut* counterparts in the Muslim south (Manalansan 1995, Johnson 1997, Cannell 1999).

Brief elaboration from the field notes I kept during my research in the village of Bogang (1978–1980, 1987–1988) will help flesh out some of these points and others relevant to them. I retain the ethnographic present tense for most of my remarks, which date from the second period of fieldwork.[2]

Villagers in Bogang often invoke the term *pondan* when discussing people like Razak (age 34) and Mustapha (age 30), both of whom belong to the wealthiest lineage in the community but, like many other young people, males especially, have long since moved out of the village. (I might add that neither of these individuals is a ritual specialist.) The term is typically used to indicate that Razak, who is married to a woman and frequently returns to the village on weekends, and Mustapha, who has never married and rarely returns home, really enjoy spending time with women, and do in fact spend far more time with women than most "normal" men. People sometimes add that Razak and Mustapha are effeminate in gesture, speech, and walk; that they are very good cooks; or simply that they are "like women" (*macam perempuan*). But there is no additional reference to or implication about their sexual orientation; in most contexts this simply does not come up. Sexual orientation, as mentioned earlier, is not a primary marker of the *pondan* category.

While many *pondan* marry and have children, villagers' occasional expressions of (mock?) surprise about *pondan* who marry suggest that, at some level, the concepts of *pondan* and marriage are mutually incompatible. It is sometimes said of *pondan*, especially after someone has commented on how effeminate or otherwise involved in transgenderism they are, "Yes, and can you believe they are married!" Similarly, villagers who heard that a woman who had been married to a village *pondan* (Razak) for 11 months and was, sadly, still a virgin (*anak dara*), were not at all surprised, since, as one woman put it, "He is, after all, a *pondan*." Razak's uncle told me that Razak and his wife had no children because Razak has a sickness or disease (*penyakit*), but this was not a biologized interpretation of why he is a *pondan*.

On the other hand, when Razak's marriage showed signs of breaking up some months later, few of the comments about the problems involved made mention of Razak being a *pondan*, focusing instead on his poor choice in selecting a wife who couldn't cook, look after a house, etc. It merits remark in any case that when Razak was teased incessantly and directly accused by his mother's sister of being a *pondan* (or *bapok*), he got extremely upset with her, offering in the process, in what was a very unMalay move, to show her that he wasn't, i.e., that he (still?) had a penis and/or testicles.

Mustapha's parents seem relatively unconcerned that he is a *pondan*, but they are clearly very disappointed that he has no apparent interest in getting married, let alone marrying properly. Both his parents were distraught when they learned that the young woman he was spending time with in Kuala Lumpur was half-Chinese and half-Indian. Making matters worse, she knows nothing of cooking or other domestic tasks, and likes to spend money on restaurants and discos. These were the primary regrets Mustapha's father mentioned to me on a number of occasions, though he was also saddened by the fact that Mustapha rarely returned home anymore. The reason for this, according to his father, was out of embarrassment for having failed in a business enterprise in Kuala Lumpur, for which he had borrowed M$5,000 from his mother, a sum he is in no position to repay.[3]

There are no specific occupational niches monopolized or favored by, or closed off to, *pondan*. As noted earlier, however, some *pondan* are wedding specialists or *mak andam* (as occurs among the Bugis, in the Philippines, and elsewhere in the world as well); and, generally speaking, there is a conceptual link between *pondan* and *mak andam*. The best known and most skillful *mak andam* in Negeri Sembilan is in fact a *pondan* from Bogang named Zainal.

I first met Zainal in 1979 or 1980, but it was not until my second period of research that I had the opportunity to talk with him at length. I had run into him at a village wedding, in December 1987, and had taken pictures of the bride he helped make up, which I later sent to him along with an invitation to come to the house for lunch. Zainal arrived sporting eyeliner and toting a large imitation-leather bag of the sort made for slide projectors and accessories, and a bag containing three photo albums of his work. The first bag contained women's jewelry—necklaces, chokers, belts, gold pins, etc.—and a ceremonial dagger (*keris*), the *kain sengkit* that grooms wear around their waists, some colored eggs (*bungga telor*), and miscellaneous items he deploys in his professional capacity as *mak andam*. The photo albums, for their part, contained pictures of various brides he had made up, photos and clippings of wedding gifts and bridal chambers that he uses to help people decide what they want to have done for their weddings, and some newspaper and magazine clippings featuring stories about his work.

Among the very first things Zainal mentioned to me as he sat down and began unpacking his things was that he was "very gifted," that he had been aware of this from an early age, and that God had given him his special talents. His father, who eventually became a high-ranking member of the Survey Department, had also been very clever at school, and had in fact been raised by an *orang putih* ("white person," Westerner) from the time he was fifteen or so until he was about seventeen.

Although both his parents are from the predominantly rural district of Rembau, Zainal grew up in various areas of the country, but never in a village, and has traveled widely. His mother (still living) resides within the confines of Bogang, he said, but she really doesn't know anything about "village ways" of making a living. In fact, she never planted rice, tapped rubber, or raised animals because "she never had to do any of these things." By way of rounding out the picture, Zainal added that each and every one of his (six or seven) siblings has high status: One is a lawyer, one has a Ph.D., another is in the army (or married to a high-ranking army officer), and so on.

When Zainal was in school he realized that he had a flair for making decorations, and for the field of fashion generally. Eventually this led him into the business of *mak andam*, which he began professionally in about 1969. At first he didn't charge the women who asked him to make themselves up, though sometimes they would give him a few *ringgit*. Later he began charging for his services, and at the time of the interview he made a fair amount (he did not specify how much) from this line of business, though his full-time job was at the Survey Department. His fee for a village wedding was usually around M$400 (though he sometimes did them for free), but he charged more for the weddings of urban Malays, particularly since his fees were structured in part around what people could afford and included the cost of materials used to adorn both the bride and the bridal chamber. One of the most expensive weddings he helped arrange was that of a child of a large housing developer in Seremban. The bridal chamber alone cost more than M$30,000, mostly for the price of an imported Italianate bed.

Zainal's work has taken him throughout the Peninsula and to other countries as well. Much of his overseas travel is in connection with his involvement in a Negeri Sembilan cultural organization, which has sponsored his trips to Singapore, Indonesia, Japan, and Turkey. He has also been to Hong Kong, though that may have been a pleasure trip, courtesy of a British friend (an estate manager), who paid his way. The impression I got was that the estate manager was gay and that he and Zainal were lovers for a while, perhaps before Zainal got married, though Zainal never came out and said this.

Zainal mentioned a few times that he was the only male *mak andam* in all of Negeri Sembilan, and that he was also the best known of all *mak andam* (women included) in the entire state. As for why other males didn't become *mak andam*, Zainal said that they might be embarrassed to do this kind of thing because it was regarded as women's work, but he had no other comments on the subject.

In response to one of my questions, Zainal explained that he recited incantations and prayers to enhance the beauty of the bride, to make her more radiant and attractive, and that he also applied special oils that had been passed down to him for this purpose. The incantations and prayers were nothing elaborate, he assured me, but they did make the bride look better. Such things were not used on *janda* (widows and divorcees) however, since they were "already old" and "aren't pretty anymore" (*tak cantik lagi*).

Zainal also mentioned (this, too, in response to one of my questions) that people occasionally asked him for advice related to sexual matters. These requests for information typically came from those who "haven't mixed much," like village girls who had never worked in factories, for they did not usually receive any advice or information about sex or physical intimacy from their mothers, or from anyone else. As a consequence, they really didn't know how to behave when they were approached for the first time by their husbands, and they were understandably scared, he said, adding "we were scared at first too, right?" But Zainal didn't usually bring up topics bearing on sex, because he did not think it was his place to do so. And he worried about his reputation: "What would people think of me if I just started talking to them about sexual matters? They would surely think that is very inappropriate."

I interviewed Zainal in a fairly structured way on various aspects of gender, thinking that he might have a unique perspective. As indicated by the synopsis of the interview (Peletz 1996:265–267), he did not. Prompted perhaps by my questions on gender and sexuality, Zainal went into considerable detail about genitalia and related topics. When I asked him about circumcision, for example, he said that this was done because it was very unbecoming to have a "long penis that just hung down there like that" (he indicated with his finger), adding that it wasn't clean or healthy either, since "all that stuff just collects there." Zainal then related a story about one of his non-Malay friends (the British estate manager), who wasn't circumcised. Zainal chastised him for being uncircumcised, and so he (the friend) ultimately agreed to undergo the surgery while he was back in England. He proceeded to send Zainal pictures of his newly circumcised penis, one *duduk* ("sitting" or "lying down"), the other one *berdiri* ("standing up"). This was related with much laughter on Zainal's part, though he was watching my reactions closely to see what I thought of his story. The friend in question was apparently the same man who had invited Zainal to Hong Kong (all expenses paid), and who later asked Zainal to come to Los Angeles and stay with him. Zainal was a bachelor at the time and considered the invitation very seriously. But when he told his mother about the possibility of his going to America, she cried and cried; so he decided not to go, especially since his father was quite ill at the time.

Zainal also told me that he has a "gay friend" (his expression), a Christian, as I recall, who lives in Melaka or Port Dickson and hosted the big New Year's Eve party that Zainal attended. Zainal emphasized that he "loved parties," and that he stayed at this one until about 2 a.m. His response to my question about whether he took his wife to the party was "no," followed by, "there are some things that you just don't talk about with your wife, right?" At about the same time in the conversation, he said that one of his friends (the gay Christian again?) had lots of pornographic magazines and some pornographic videos as well, one of which showed people at various "nude clubs." It was, I think, during this part of the conversation that Zainal asked about "free sex" (his expression) in America, but, for better or worse, I didn't provide much information on the subject. I should perhaps add that I never asked Zainal if he considered himself (or realized that others regarded him as) a *pondan*. Nor did I broach any other topics bearing on *pondan*. The main reason for not addressing any such issues is that, at the time, it seemed impolite and otherwise inappropriate to do so.

As the afternoon wore on, I grew tired. Zainal, however, continued to be very animated, though he may have eventually sensed that my energy was waning. Before leaving, he offered to dress my wife and me in formal wedding attire, promising to make us up very elaborately. He would need a bit of advance notice, however, and the evening would be best. He would dress us in our home, thus making sure that the outfits and decorations fit well with the décor and style of our house. Zainal also insisted that we come up to Seremban and spend the night, and that we would have lots of fun cooking, eating, and talking together. He added that he would be very upset if we went back to America without first saying goodbye.

A number of themes emerge from my interview with Zainal, but I will confine my comments to a few of the more basic issues. Since Zainal used the term "gay" in referring to one of his (Christian?) friends, I should first reiterate that this term was not a feature of village- or national-level discourse at the time of our interview (1988). Neither were English-origin terms such as "homosexual," "sodomist," or "sodomy"—or their Malay counterparts. In the last decade or so, however, these and related terms have come to be widely circulated in the government-controlled media, which has been pressed into service by political and religious elites to help "shore up traditional morality" threatened by the proliferation of diversity with respect to gender, sexuality, and much else. Not coincidentally, the circulation of these terms has gone hand-in-hand with the emergence of identities defined as *gay*, *lesbian*, and the like, a theme explored more fully in due course.

Among the things that struck me most forcefully during the interview with Zainal was how articulate and cosmopolitan he was, and how proud he was both of his accomplishments as a *mak andam*, and of his enviable status (both ascribed and achieved) in general. His status concerns were expressed toward the beginning of the interview, when he laid out his genealogy and cultural pedigree along with his broad travel experiences and the educational attainments and professional accomplishments of his siblings and their spouses. It is significant that Zainal's masculinity and overall status were by no means compromised by the fact that he was a *pondan* (though his simultaneous involvement in conventional marriage and parenthood may have been a factor here); indeed, he derived considerable esteem from the role of *mak andam*, which, especially in the case of male *mak andam*, is clearly linked to the status of *pondan*. This situation contrasts rather markedly with what one finds in Western societies, where transgenderism of any variety typically entails a loss of status (stigma).

Transgenderism in Western societies is commonly viewed (particularly in official discourses) in strongly negative terms, as highly "unnatural," an abominable violation of God's will. It does, moreover, elicit ambivalence, hostility, and, on occasion, violent outbursts from non-transgenderists, especially males. Such is not the case among Malays or most other Southeast Asians, who have long displayed a relatively accepting, accommodating, and "relaxed" attitude toward such phenomena. That Malays and other Southeast Asians do not seem very threatened by various kinds of gender transgression is probably related to the fact that in certain respects (e.g., in terms of language, kinship terminology, and the like) gender is not all that strongly marked in Southeast Asian societies and cultures; and that, as such, behavior which blurs the boundaries of gender categories is less problematic and threatening with respect to the basic structure of the universe (which, by some criteria, is relatively ungendered, as just noted, and, by others, is dual-gendered or androgynous). Questions of markedness aside, gender categories tend not to be arranged in a strongly asymmetric fashion (male and female are viewed in many contexts as complementary in non-hierarchical ways) and do not constitute the foundation of social hierarchy. Hence, transgenderism does not pose a serious challenge to the basic social hierarchy, which tends to be structured in terms of descent, age, birth order, and, in recent times, social class, though its co-existence, in cases like Zainal's, with more conventional gender arrangements such as heterosexual marriage may be relevant to the lack of serious threat it represents.

It remains to underscore that villagers' attitudes toward *pondan* might be decidedly less accommodating if the ranks of local *pondan* included phenotypic females. In response to my questions on the subject, I was told that no female-bodied *pondan* existed in Bogang but that one would most likely encounter them in Kuala Lumpur (the nation's den of iniquity). Other anthropologists have reported broadly analogous conversations from the 1960s, 1970s, and 1980s, some of which make no provision for even the hypothetical possibility of same-sex relations among women (see, e.g., Raybeck 1986:65). Local attitudes might also be far less accommodating if there were transgenderists living full-time in Bogang, especially if such individuals were, in addition, engaged in publicly recognized and acknowledged same-sex liaisons. The 1996–1997 case of "the woman who shook the nation," discussed below, illustrates both of these points. It also underscores that Malay-style pluralism is not nearly as robust as its Bugis counterpart, particularly when it comes to female-bodied individuals who act on desires (or engage in other practices) that transcend or transgress heteronormative ideals.

I mentioned earlier that sexual orientation is not a primary marker of the *pondan* category and thus want to clarify that some *pondan* wear their sexuality on their sleeves. Such was clearly the case with Zainal, whom I (and my wife) assumed from the outset was on some level gay and in any case was far more interested in talking about sexuality and (male) genitalia than any Malay I have ever encountered. Some of this may well have been related to his being a *pondan*. (Bogang's two other *pondan* are also decidedly "cheeky" by Malay standards.) Also relevant perhaps is that Zainal clearly viewed me as a Westerner and a Christian to boot, someone who was "free," like him, of many sexual and gender constraints, and thus appropriately positioned to discuss sexual matters.

I have not seen Zainal since 1988, but in 2000 a mutual friend from a village near Bogang who was visiting the US provided me with an update on his activities and whereabouts. The mutual friend, a 58-year-old *hajjah* with advanced degrees whom I refer to as Rokiah, mentioned that she had recently seen Zainal (now in his early to mid-sixties) as he had come to her sister's house, during which time he asked for money since "they are like family." It wasn't clear exactly how much Zainal requested, though I recall Rokiah citing the figure of M$200, this perhaps being the sum that her sister decided to give him. Zainal had claimed that the money was for his wife, that she was too embarrassed to ask for it or simply preferred not to raise the issue herself. But when Rokiah or her sister later encountered the wife and made a remark about the money, she knew nothing about it and appeared both thoroughly surprised and distressed. According to Rokiah, the money is undoubtedly intended for the overtly homosexual Indian fellow that Zainal is always seen going around with. Rokiah mentioned that Zainal is also homosexual (her term, if I recall correctly), commenting in addition that he wears heavy eye-liner. When I responded that he had long worn eyeliner (as least since my second fieldwork), she responded, "Well yes, but now it is much more pronounced," and that Zainal has become "more obvious," "more emboldened." Apparently he has retired from his job in the Survey Department, has moved out of the house he long shared with his wife and children, and now lives with his Indian lover.

Rokiah felt that for a variety of reasons Zainal's practice as a *mak andam* was no longer thriving. For one, because of a change in religious sensibilities, which has been discernible since the early 1990s or so and is especially noticeable in rural areas, the families (and particularly the mothers) of brides do not feel comfortable with male *mak andam* applying their make-up and otherwise beautifying them, since this involves touching their faces. The problem is not that many *mak andam* are *pondan*; it is that they are men. This is why one of Rokiah's sisters would not allow a (male-bodied) *mak andam* to help dress and adorn her daughter for her wedding ceremony. Rokiah also noted that Zainal is of an older generation, and that in cities, people who might seek out a male *mak andam* would "go for a younger one," someone of the "new generation." These latter comments suggest that stores of knowledge and expertise with respect to temporally inflected realms of "style" and cultural mediation continue to be important components of the symbolic capital of *mak andam*, as they have long been for Zainal, whose professional expertise as a wedding specialist involves marshaling and deftly melding together bodies of knowledge bearing on local pharmacology and ritual practice, Quranic chants and prayers, as well as Italianate furniture and other trends in fashion and consumption that prevail in overseas venues as diverse as Indonesia, Turkey, and Japan.

When Rokiah and I discussed the fallout from the Anwar affair (considered below) and other current developments, she underscored that recent years had most definitely witnessed a stigmatizing of *pondan* and a (homo-)sexualizing of the concept. Indeed, most if not all *pondan* are now assumed to be—or better put, are now *suspected of being*—homosexual. In these dynamics we see a measure of support for Dennis Altman's (1996, 2001) contention that processes of globalization are resulting in the "sexualization" of Asian gender categories and attendant identities, though we should not assume from this that Altman's other arguments, concerning the impact of Western discourses and institutions, are necessarily as simple and straightforward as he suggests (a theme addressed in Chapter 4). Rokiah also made the important point that many homosexuals would not necessarily be characterized as *pondan*, presumably because they do not identify or present themselves in public as feminized males, thus implicitly referencing the recent emergence in Malaysia of masculine-identified gays.

She mentioned too—this in response to my question about possible historical precedents for *mak andam, pondan,* and the like—that the (eunuch) guardians of the *Kaabah* in Mecca are "like *pondan*" although they do not cancel out women's ritual ablutions. These remarks are of interest for two reasons. First, in keeping with long-standing Malay conceptualizations of the embodied universe and its constituent features (bodies, persons, etc.), Rokiah posited a feature (of likeness) conceptualized in terms of gender (both subject positions are feminized, "less than masculine," or both), *not* sexuality. This despite her qualifying remark that there is also a difference between eunuchs and *pondan* (the former do not cancel out women's ritual ablutions, the latter do), which is keyed to anatomical contrast but not sexuality per se. And second, her remarks do not invoke one or another symbol of the Malay past (such as *sida-sida* or *pawang*) but rather a sacred symbol of Islam and of the Islamic heartlands in particular, thus indexing a pronounced historical shift in local Malay Muslim identities that has occurred over the past century, one that simultaneously involves a movement from an emphasis on Malayness to an emphasis on being Muslim, albeit in a larger context defined by nationalist ideologies that endeavor to elide distinctions between "Malay Muslimness" and Malaysian national identity (Peletz 1994, 1997, 2002, Willford 2006).

The connection between *pondan* and wedding specialists is of particular interest when viewed from a long-term perspective. Transgendered wedding specialists might be seen as "legacies" of one segment of the class of transgendered priests and courtiers (*sida-sida*) that existed in pre-Islamic Malay kingdoms.[4] Present evidence does not allow for documentation of all transformations in Malay transgendering as they unfolded over time. Indeed, it may well be that the available sources will never permit a fully documented genealogical reconstruction, as may also be true of Thailand (Jackson 2003), the southern Philippines and many other locales in the region (Johnson 1997), areas of Sulawesi being, again, the partial exception. It merits emphasis, however, that even in the new millennium (mostly male-bodied) *sida-sida* continue to play a role in the *yang dipertuan besar*'s royal court at Sri Menanti (Negeri Sembilan) (as discussed in Chapter 2). As in earlier times, they cross-dress and are charged both with overseeing ceremonial protocol and with safeguarding the food, drink, clothes, etc., of royalty.

Two other categories of such legacies that existed in Malaysia well into the twentieth century merit brief consideration here even though but also because they are now largely defunct. The first consists of performers of *mak yong* theater and related dramatic and musical genres, many of whom, as noted earlier, enjoyed royal patronage, were linked to palaces in other ways, and engaged in transgender and explicitly same-sex practices. The second is composed of *pawang* or shamanic specialists, who might be seen as the "most lineal" of the legacies of pre-Islamic *sida-sida*, especially in light of the strongly animist and Hindu-Buddhist tenor of their most public, community-wide rituals. *Pawang* were formally associated with indigenously defined district-level and state polities, were held to have "white blood" and extremely potent spiritual powers vested in and symbolized by their sacred regalia, and were depicted in nineteenth- and early twentieth-century British accounts (e.g., Maxwell 1907 [1982]:214–22) as belonging to hereditarily defined groups like certain of the Borneo ritual specialists discussed earlier. In the nineteenth and twentieth centuries, some male-bodied *pawang* were possessed by female spirits or deities, clothed themselves in women's attire, wore their hair long like women, and were on occasion involved in other transgender practices (miming women's gait, etc.) (Winstedt 1961:59). Similarly, in the late nineteenth century at least some female-bodied *pawang* engaged in ritual transvestism, though unfortunately we do not know much more than that (Swettenham 1895 [1984]:153–54 passim).

At present, practitioners of the latter varieties no longer exist, and *sida-sida* aside, transgendered wedding specialists thus make up the only community of transgendered ritualists in contemporary Malay society. It remains to reiterate that unlike their counterparts among the Bugis and Burmese (and in other Asian settings such as Java, the Philippines, India, China, and Japan), the vast majority of Malays who are currently involved in transgender practices and/or same-sex relations lack genealogies imaginatively linking them to the past that they might draw upon to help legitimize and frame their subject positions and subjectivities. (I have never met gay Malays—or other gay Malaysians—who evince any familiarity with the transgenderism of *sida-sida*, for example). For present-day Malays, the past is iconically associated with the rural, the backward, and the feudal (and the "ritual excesses" of the nation's disenfranchised Tamil Hindu minority [Willford 2006]), much as it has been at various junctures in the history of Bugis society and many others. It is (truly) another country, and it does not help much—indeed, it hinders the cause(s)—to go there. Dynamics of gender and sexuality are deeply imbricated in the contemporary cultural politics of race, ethnicity, religion, and class, and these are such as to require "forward-looking," cosmopolitan discourses and identities that resonate with the imperatives of globalization informed by a moderate and progressive but strongly heteronormative Islam. This is supremely ironic in that according to political and religious elites the much touted flexibility (technological, occupational, residential) promoted if not necessitated by neoliberal globalization precludes "flexibility" with respect to gender and sexuality.

The fetishization of ethnic and racial categories and attendant identities that has occurred in Malaysia since the early 1970s (a process building on colonial-era constructions, including nineteenth-century Social Darwinian notions of immutable racial and other naturalized "essences," and the kinds of binaries foregrounded by sexologists) has entailed a dichotomization, purification, and overall hardening of virtually all categories that are, or could conceivably become, relevant to identity (Peletz 1997, 2002, 2005, Willford 2006). Hence in recent years transgendered wedding specialists—along with men who have sex with men (many of whom self-identify as gay), women who engage in sex with women (tom boy, dyke, peng-kid, etc.), transsexuals (mak nyah, pak nyah), and transgendered individuals of all other varieties, races, and religions—have been very much under siege. So too have heterosexual teenage girls and young women suspected of "moral laxity" (boh sia) (Tan Beng Hui 1999, Stivens 2002). I discuss the contours of some of these communities, the climate(s) of siege, and some of the openings, counter-flows, and relegitimization processes, all of which are decidedly less robust than in the Bugis case, later in this chapter. Suffice it to note here that certain of the repressive dynamics in question, some of which also have "productive" dimensions in Foucault's (1978) sense, are due to the cultural-political crises generated by Prime Minister Mahathir Mohamad's sacking, jailing, and pillorying of Deputy Prime Minister Anwar Ibrahim in 1998 on highly dubious charges of sodomy, bribery, and corruption. (In a gross caricature of justice, Anwar was subsequently convicted of sodomy and corruption and served six years in prison.) Others are due to more encompassing processes that involve state strategies since the early 1980s to institutionalize heterosexism and homophobia—and since the 1990s, "Asian values"—as national policies. The latter in turn are integral parts of expansive state projects geared toward cleansing and tidying up both locally defined and globally inf(l)ected masculinities, femininities, sexualities, and kinship and marriage practices (e.g., adoption) alike, and "replacing" rural Malay society and culture in their entirety with a new class of urban-dwelling Malay capitalists ("new Malays," "new Muslims") whose social and cultural proclivities will enable them to compete successfully not only with local Chinese and Indians but also with other Asians and Westerners. It merits remark here that Malaysia is among the most successful of the "non-Confucian" Asian tigers, has sustained a pace of rapid development that is probably second to none in the Muslim world, and, much like Singapore, is invariably subject to "national crises" spun by political and religious elites to legitimize heightened normativity in domains of kinship/gender and sexuality and, indeed, in all areas of social life.

"Asian Values" and New Types of Criminality

Narratives of "Asian Values" and the Rise of Social Intolerance

It is perhaps most useful to examine discourses of "Asian values" by taking as our point of departure some of the more encompassing narratives and narrative products in which they are embedded.[5] In this regard we are fortunate that in 1999 Malaysian Prime Minister Mahathir published yet another highly controversial and deeply revealing book, entitled *A New Deal for Asia*, which contains a good deal of material on "Asian values." *A New Deal for Asia* follows Mahathir's earlier volumes, most notably, *The Malay Dilemma*, published in 1970, and *Meeting The Challenge*, which first appeared in 1976 in a Malay-language edition as *Menghadapi Cabaran*.[6] *A New Deal for Asia* is also profitably viewed in relation to a 1995 book that Mahathir co-authored with prominent Japanese politician (and former Governor of Tokyo) Shintaro Ishihara, which was entitled *The Voice of Asia*. The two volumes are remarkably similar in at least two ways: first, they espouse more or less identical discourses of "Asian values," a phrase that I set off in quotes throughout the discussion here; and second, they are both works of cultural production that are appropriately viewed as models of and for neoliberal economic reasoning in Asia as it headed into the new millennium (Ong 1999, Peletz 2002). A key difference is that *The Voice of Asia* appeared in 1995, at the height of the Asian economic boom, and is highly triumphant; Mahathir's *A New Deal for Asia*, in contrast, was written after the financial crisis that began in Southeast Asia in 1997 and is far more humble though still thoroughly infused with Mahathir's trademark race-chauvinism and Manichean obsessions.

One of the central arguments of both books is that Asians should "just say no" to Western models of development and democracy. (The original title of *The Voice of Asia* was *The Asia That Can Say No*.)[7] Both books cite "adaptability, flexibility, and tolerance" as quintessentially Asian values; and both explain that, in the Asian view of things, "society, state, and family are more important than the individual." Similarly, both books contend that "Asian values" are diametrically opposed to the values of "the West," which is said to have witnessed the "separation of religion from secular life and the gradual replacement of religious with hedonistic values." In the words of Mahathir, the result is that "materialism, sensual gratification, and selfishness are rife … . [There is] diminished respect for marriage, family values, [and] elders, and [a proliferation of] single-parent families, … incest, … homosexuality, … [and] unrestrained avarice. [More generally, people's] … moral foundations [are] crumbling, … and [they] are suffering all kinds of psychological and physical … decay, … stress, and … fear" (Mahathir and Ishihara 1995: 80–81).

Many of Mahathir's remarks about "Asian values" are, at base, about Asian "family values," and are curiously reminiscent of the so-called "family-values" debates in the US. I make this point for two reasons: first, to cut across the Kiplingesque divide between East and West undergirding Mahathir's comments, and second, to draw attention to the fact that exceedingly under-specified references to "family values," Asian or otherwise, necessarily involve what semioticians and linguists refer to as "floating signifiers." Such signifiers have multiple, often contradictory referents and are thus capable of being harnessed to wildly divergent political agendas. Of more immediate concern here is that like Lee Kuan Yew and his successors (e.g., Goh Chok Tong) in Singapore, Mahathir has made it clear in interviews and public speeches that, in his view, human rights, democracy, and civil society of the sort held up as Western ideals simply don't work in Asian countries like Malaysia, Singapore, and Indonesia. Indeed, Mahathir maintains that Western ideals should not be viewed as values to strive for, and that those who suggest otherwise are arrogantly ethnocentric, if not overtly racist, and bent on seeing Muslims fail in Asia and elsewhere.

Having sketched out a few features of the narrative of "Asian values," I would like to turn to a historical question: Where did this discourse on "Asian values" come from? Or, put differently, What variables promoted the discourse? In answering this question I focus on the Malaysian and Singaporean variants of the discourse, and on the dynamics most relevant in those contexts.

Among the most obvious factors that contributed to the emergence of recent discourse on "Asian values" are the phenomenal post-war economic growth of Japan, South Korea, Taiwan, and Hong Kong, as well as the more recent and, in some ways, more spectacular economic success stories, at least through July 1997, of Thailand, Malaysia, Singapore, and Indonesia. As is well known, politicians, scholars, and others on both sides of the Pacific invoked one or another set of "Asian values" to help explain these phenomena. The specific discourse of "Asian values" that has been retailed by Mahathir is also an outgrowth of his "Look East Policy," inaugurated in 1981. While the moral and material entailments of the latter policy were notoriously unclear to many government spokesmen, Mahathir apparently had in mind "The East" as represented only by Japan and South Korea.[8] Conspicuously excluded from promotions and discussions of the policy were references to Taiwan and Singapore, most likely because of their ethnic Chinese majorities and the resulting political dis-ease that this might create on the home front, particularly in light of the local cultural politics of race. The policy was in any case offered as an antidote to blind imitation of the West, and meant not so much trading only with Japan and South Korea but emulating their hard work, diligence, and much touted valorization of the group over the individual. One reason the policy was quietly discontinued after a while is that its architects never studied the extent to which Japanese and Korean patterns were in fact transferable to Malaysia. In the end, Japanese reluctance to engage in technology transfer led Mahathir to accuse them of favoring a "colonialist relationship" with Malaysia.

We might also consider Mahathir's views concerning the origins of Japan's phenomenal post-war economic success. Mahathir has long credited this success to Japan's "slavish imitation of things Western." Appearances, then, are not always what they seem, which is to say that from Mahathir's point of view, the "Look East" policy entailed looking to two particular East Asian nations that had either successfully imitated the West, or successfully reworked their emulations of things Western into locally meaningful patterns ostensibly suitable for export to other Asian nations.

The discourse on "Asian values" was also fueled by a variety of political crises, all of which were arguably related to issues of globalization and sovereignty. One such crisis developed from the 1993 Vienna Conference on Human Rights, which witnessed extensive Western critiques of Malaysia's record on issues of human rights, and a spirited counter-argument cast partly in terms of "Asian values." A somewhat similar crisis unfolded as a consequence of Singapore's arrest, detention, and subsequent caning of the all-American Michael Fay, who was found guilty of damaging 18 cars by spray-painting them with graffiti. As the latter crisis began to unfold in late 1993 and early 1994, politicians, public intellectuals, and media figures on both sides of the Pacific invoked what were heralded as "traditional values" to justify their allegiances in the war of positions that developed. Lee Kuan Yew, for example, repeatedly cited the need to defend "Asian values" against Western incursion. He also insisted that Westerners do not understand Asians, who place the interests of the group over the interests of the individual and are quite content to be ruled by what he euphemistically referred to as "strong governments" as long as they deliver economic prosperity.

As it turned out, Michael Fay survived both the flogging and the media frenzy he encountered on his return to the States. The discourse on "Asian values" enunciated by Lee Kuan Yew also survived and prospered in Singapore, elsewhere in Asia, and far beyond, thus raising two sets of issues. The first has to do with matters of heterogeneity: Not all Asian leaders agree with the Mahathirs, the Lee Kuan Yews, and the others who traffic in the discourse of "Asian values." Martin Lee, for example, former Chairman of Hong Kong's Democratic Party, has argued that we need to "put to rest the myth of 'Asian values': that democracy and human rights are Western concepts inimical both to Asia and to economic growth" (M. Lee 1998). In this view, the notion of "Asian values" is a sloppy and ideologically loaded term. Many scholars, student leaders, and others in mainland China would appear to feel the same way, and are highly critical of the ways the concept of "Asian values" has been invoked by government leaders in Beijing to rationalize the oppressive activities of the state, including the tragedy of Tiananmen. In much the same fashion, former opposition leader Kim Dae Jung, who went on to become President of South Korea, has repeatedly emphasized that "Asian values" have never precluded democracy (Rosenthal 1997).

The second issue has to do with the deeply ironic fact that Asian leaders, like Mahathir, Ishihara, and Lee Kuan Yew, espouse an essentializing Orientalism of the sort that literary critic Edward Said excoriated in his now classic (1978) study of Western literary representations of "the Orient." Said was dealing primarily with the literature on the Middle East, as opposed to East Asia, but his basic argument applies here as well. Much like the nineteenth-century construction of "the Orient" produced in the West, the notion of "Asian values" articulated by Mahathir and others is not only cast in wildly unqualified, absolute terms; it also presupposes a monolithic, eternally unchanging, homogenized "Asian" (as well as an undifferentiated, immutable, sexually anarchic, and terminally decadent "Western"), whose essential features transcend time, space, gender, class, occupation, and local cultural identity. Another of Said's arguments, that Orientalism is both a product of domination and a key resource deployed to help effect and reproduce that domination, is also relevant here. Indeed, the very same argument could be made about the new variant of Orientalism subsumed under the rubric of "Asian values" (Kessler 1999). Like its predecessor, it is, to paraphrase a point made by Sylvia Yanagisako (1995) in another context, an incomplete, selective, and in many ways deeply nostalgic and sentimentalizing narrative that renders invisible various types of experiences and meanings in the name of forging unity out of diversity. More ironic still is that this discourse not only accepts as given the very imperial-era and thoroughly Kiplingesque chasm between East and West that millions of people in "the Orient" have fought to eradicate, owing to its inherently racist and dehumanizing features, to say nothing of its ideological functions (Syed Husin Alatas 1977, Said 1993, Ong 1999); it also helps to reproduce the invidious imperial legacy (intellectual, cultural, and political) that those who articulate it are so loath to own in most public settings.

There are many other ironies and curious features of this discourse, some of which appear as silences, elisions, and conflations. Consider, for example, the cultures and nations that are conspicuously absent from the discourse. In the Southeast Asian context, the Philippines would seem to be the most glaring omission, explicable perhaps by the relatively poor showing of the Philippine economy in recent decades, though an arguably more likely explanation is that for Mahathir, the notion of a Christian Asian is at one and the same time an oxymoronic hybrid and a deep categorical treachery. Also generally absent from the discourse is any mention of Burma, Cambodia, Laos, or Vietnam. Moving beyond Southeast Asia, one is struck by the lack of references to South Asia and West Asia (the Middle East). Clearly, then, as Ong (1999) has also discussed, both the timeless and the "new Asians" touted in this discourse are either Muslims, or are people who adhere to a mélange of Confucianism and Buddhism. As suggested a moment ago, however, only certain types of Muslims (Shi'ites are definitely out) and certain types of Buddhists and Confucians are potential candidates for this discursively privileged status of "Asian," new or otherwise.

It is equally important to consider the flip side of the coin of "Asian values." Where, in other words, might one find repositories of "'traditional' Asian values?" And how do they figure into Mahathir's narratives? If we confine ourselves to Malaysia and to what Mahathir has written about Malay culture in its rural, ostensibly "more traditional" forms, the deeply ideological nature of this discourse becomes all the more evident. So, too, do the enormous "development" challenges that Mahathir and like-minded politicians have set for themselves and their countrymen since the early 1970s.

In *The Malay Dilemma*, Mahathir writes of Malays that they are "courteous," "gentle," "formal yet tolerant," self-effacing," "passive," and "withdrawn," but with "a clear sense of righteousness;" they are also "resigned," "complacent," "soft," "weak," and "indolent"—"afflicted by a seemingly permanent stupor," "uninterested in work," and, more generally, "fatalistic ... feudalists ... in the grips of unadjusted minds" that are "in need of rehabilitation." Malays also exhibit "a complete failure to relate cause and effect," and are "never committed to anything."

In these comments we see an example of self-Orientalizing that is far more extreme than anything Mahathir has disseminated in more recent speeches and publications like *A New Deal for Asia*. As alluded to earlier, we also see the enormous challenges—associated with economic "development," with the forging of a national identity, and with the creation of a viable nation—that Mahathir and others have sought to identify and overcome during the last four decades. To fully appreciate these points, we need also consider Mahathir's attitudes toward local Chinese. In *The Malay Dilemma*, Chinese are depicted in stark, racialist terms as "adventurous," "hard," "aggressive," "predatory," and "inherently good at business"—because "instinctively thrifty" and given to "secret deals, private arrangements and water-tight ... family" and guild organizations. Perhaps most revealing in light of Mahathir's subsequent emphasis on the cultural kinship said to obtain among the "New Asians" are the following remarks, which appear toward the very end (p. 175) of *The Malay Dilemma*: "In Malaysia we have three major races ... . Their physiognomy, language, culture, and religion differ;" "*there is no dialogue;*" ... . "[they] have practically *nothing in common*" (emphases added).

Particularly when viewed in light of *The Malay Dilemma*, Mahathir's contemporary ruminations on "Asian values" provide clear illustration of Yanagisako's previously noted point that Orientalist discourses are selective and sentimentalizing narratives that render invisible various types of experiences and meanings in the name of forging unity out of diversity. If such is the case, we might then ask: At whose expense is such unity forged? Put differently, which societies or sectors of society are marginalized in—or as a consequence of the deployment of—this discourse on cultural kinship?

I have already provided a partial answer to these questions in my comments about those nations and regions of Asia (including the Philippines, Vietnam, South Asia, etc.) that are conspicuously absent from the discourse on "Asian values." Of more immediate relevance are sectors of society such as women and ethnic minorities like the Iban and Penan of Sarawak who, as a consequence of globalizing forces, are subject to new forms of discrimination and new constraints on sovereignty that vary considerably from one group to the next. Aihwa Ong examines some such groups and their variegated predicaments in *Flexible Citizenship* (1999), which presents incisive analyses of *fin-de-siècle* state practices, citizenship regimes, and systems of graduated sovereignty in Malaysia and elsewhere in Asia and the Pacific. Some of the same groups are discussed in another important volume on the region that was also published in 1999, Milne and Mauzy's *Malaysian Politics Under Mahathir*.

Curiously absent from both of these texts, however, are even brief considerations of the communities of subalterns that are arguably *most* subject to discrimination and marginalization in the particular variants of modernity and "Asian values" that Malaysian officialdom have embraced. I refer to gays, lesbians, bisexuals, transvestites, and all others engaged in gender and/or sexual transgression of a home-grown and/or more cosmopolitan variety. Suffice it to note that while modern-day trends entailing the stigmatization and criminalization of transgender practices and same-sex relations might be said to date from the early 1980s, they became much more pronounced beginning around 1994, and have been especially intense since the onset of the Asian financial crisis in mid-1997. Some of the relevant developments and trends since the mid-1990s merit brief consideration here. (Others will be discussed further along.)

Two of the main objectives of the New Economic Policy (NEP) and many other state programs implemented in the last 40 years have been to eliminate poverty, especially among Malays, and to effect a restructuring of the relationship between "race" and economic function. The realization of these twin objectives has entailed (among other things) effectively encouraging Malays to abandon their rural economic traditions (rice farming, rubber tapping, and the like) so as to become increasingly involved in small-scale trade and business activities as well as the larger-scale entrepreneurial endeavors and other urban economic niches that are (also) conducive to the creation of a new middle class of urban Malays (*Melayu baru*, or "new Malays"; see Shamsul 1999, Andaya and Andaya 2001:333–336, Peletz 2002). Such programs have been successful in many respects, not least in terms of encouraging mass Malay migration from rural areas to state capitals throughout the country, but also, and more importantly, to the extremely cosmopolitan federal capital, Kuala Lumpur, which, like certain other urban centers in the region (Bangkok, Jakarta, Manila) has long had a reputation for sexual license of different kinds. For a variety of reasons, many of which are relevant to an understanding of the growth of subcultures of transgenderists and cosmopolitan gays and lesbians in urban areas in the US like San Francisco and New York City, these patterns of migration and urbanization contributed to the increased visibility of Malaysians involved in transgender practices and same-sex relations in particular, especially during the economic boom years of the 1980s and the early to mid-1990s. So too albeit in different ways did the phenomenal growth of the global sex industry in neighboring Thailand, the peaking of the AIDS crisis there during the period 1992–1993, and the resultant attention that the latter crisis came to receive from Thai officials, various governments in the region (including Malaysia's), and world health organizations and NGOs of various kinds (Bishop and Robinson 1998). Such heightened visibility could have resulted in a number of very different outcomes. The effect in Malaysia, however, was that those engaged in gender and/or sexual transgression encountered more organized opposition that included redoubled efforts not only to undercut their visibility and legitimacy, but also to eliminate them altogether, all in the name of "Asian (family) values."

As one example, in the second half of 1994, the state-run radio and television network (RTM; Radio and Television Malaysia) banned transvestites and gays from appearing on its programs.[9] According to the Information Minister, Mohamed Rahmat, the action was taken "in line with the national policy which focuses on the importance of health and family values," the bottom line being "We do not want to encourage any form of homosexuality in our society." Shortly thereafter, Prime Minister Mahathir, in a statement critical of Western countries that provide one or another degree of legal recognition to lesbian and gay couples, said: "Such a concept of the family is crazy and contrary to religious teachings. It will only produce illegitimate children who may, in turn, have incestuous marriages with their siblings."[10]

The next few years saw the appearance of numerous accounts in the government-owned and -controlled media—typically short but alarmist—of "gay clubs," such as the one that appeared in the June 22, 1995 issue of *The Sun* (a Malaysian daily), which carried the headline "Gay Clubs Not Allowed." The gist of the story was that "gay clubs" were illegal ("not allowed to be registered in the country"). The main objective of the piece, however, seems to have been to invite readers to participate in and thus enhance efforts to eliminate same-sex sexuality by providing intelligence to the authorities, for it included the line, "*If you have information on any gay club, inform Deputy Home Minister Ong Ka Ting*" (emphasis added). Similar headlines—"Gay Clubs Are Not Allowed to be Registered in Malaysia," "69 Held in Raid at Club for Gays"— have become commonplace. According to one of the stories appearing beneath such a headline, "Police detained 69 men, including 12 foreigners, at an exclusive club believed to be for gays in Jalan Raja Laut [Kuala Lumpur] here yesterday … . The club, which is operating without a license, is a shophouse which was converted into an exclusive club equipped with a gymnasium, sauna, and rooms specially for gays. All the detainees were taken to the headquarters for urine tests." Like many others of this ilk, the account excerpted here draws attention to or at least raises the specter of multiple illegalities— operating a business establishment without a license; using illicit drugs (to be detected by urine tests); and engaging in same-sex erotics in gymnasiums, saunas, and "rooms specially for gays." Of comparable if not greater significance, it also draws explicit ties between same-sex sexuality, drug use, and foreigners.

In light of this kind of negative publicity, it is not surprising that subsequent years saw the Kuala Lumpur Town Council and the Malaysian Youth Council beseeching the government to take strict measures to abolish any form of homosexual activity in the city. One such appeal occurred in connection with a Gay Pride Event that had been scheduled for June 28, 1998. Invitations to the event had been distributed and promoted via the club's website, which, as the appeal emphasized, was used for "international exposure."[11] As might be expected, the event was cancelled.

In recent years, moreover, the police have raided *mak nyah* beauty contests in Kuala Lumpur and elsewhere. In a number of celebrated cases, the police have arrested the Malay (Muslim) contestants, but not the non-Muslim *mak nyah* in the pageants. Such partisan behavior was also evident during a more conventional all-female beauty contest held in Selangor in June of 1997. In that case (the Miss Malaysia Petite Pageant), the Malay winner and two other Malay contestants were arrested at the end of the show. Middle-class Malays and other Malaysians I spoke with in 1998 felt that it was highly ironic, to say the least, that the police sat through and presumably enjoyed the entire show before arresting any of the participants. They also argued that it was unfair that the Malay contestants were singled out in these cases, some of them adding that the authorities "surely have better things to do." Similar arguments were advanced by members of Malaysia's leading Muslim feminist organization, Sisters in Islam, whom I also interviewed in 1998. Moreover, as noted by Mohammad Hashim Kamali (2000:280), a highly respected Professor of Islamic Law and Jurisprudence at the International Islamic University Malaysia, "within two weeks of arrest, the three young women were charged, found guilty and each fined … [M$]400, … a display of efficiency that the Syariah Courts are hardly known for."

A decidedly different perspective emerged in the course of an interview I conducted in 1998 with the Chief Judge who presides over the Islamic court system of the Federal Territory of Kuala Lumpur. The gist of his comments on the subject—"Nowadays, with people moving into the city and with modern change and such, there are all sorts of things going on …. People think they can do anything"—imply that the massive flow of villagers and rural culture into the city is disorderly and unsettling; and that "we have to draw a line somewhere." These comments resonate deeply with the perspectives of Mary Douglas (1970), Gayle Rubin (1984), Kath Weston (1998), and others, who contend that sexualities are particularly politicized and contested during times of rapid and unsettling sociocultural change. They also suggest that non-normative ("deviant") sexualities are an easy target for politicians and others who seek to exert control over the circumstances of such change and to maintain or broaden their constituencies in the process.

New Types of Criminality: Azizah, Anwar, and Beyond

At present, homosexual practices are heavily criminalized throughout Malaysia insofar as oral and anal sex between same-sex (and "opposite"-sex) partners, which are covered by Sections 377A and 377B of the national Penal Code, are categorized under the rubric of "carnal intercourse against the order of nature and gross indecency." Such acts are liable to punishment by imprisonment for up to twenty years as well as whipping, even if they are consensual. Moreover, any act defined as "gross indecency" between two men or two women, whether public or private, is a criminal offense that can lead to two years' imprisonment. This includes attempts to establish contacts between same-sex partners (i.e., "cruising"). Partly because such cases are prosecuted by the police and thus usually require the filing of reports from someone directly involved, there have been few "successful" prosecutions of gay men, and even fewer of lesbian women. It is essential to bear in mind in any event that these are secular laws *not* religious laws. Contrary to the assumptions of many Westerners, we are not dealing with yet another example of a "medieval Islamic rigidity" with respect to gender and sexuality. Indeed, the precedents for these particular laws and many of the specifics of their language were introduced by the British during colonial times, initially in the Indian Penal Code of 1860, which was subsequently incorporated with slight amendments into the penal codes of the Straits Settlements (1872), the Federated Malay States (in stages, beginning in 1874), the Unfederated Malay States, the Federation of Malaya and so on.[12]

One prosecution leading to the conviction of transgendered woman involved in same-sex relations that merits consideration in this context was widely covered in the Malaysian press on a more or less daily basis from December 1996 to March 1997. This case, which is the subject of insightful work by Tan Beng Hui (1999) to which I am much indebted, involved two young women (Azizah Abdul Rahman, aged 21, and Rohana Mat Isa, aged 20) residing in the state of Kelantan. Azizah, described in many accounts as a "tomboy"—and, more significantly, as the "woman who shook the nation,"—habitually dressed in male attire and according to press accounts "otherwise looked and behaved like a man" (Tan Beng Hui 1999:289). Partly because Azizah had also taken a man's name and possessed a male identity card, she succeeded in convincing the local religious authorities (among others) that she was a male and could thus marry her partner. Azizah is also said to have fooled her bride and the witnesses at her wedding, and, more seriously, to have "disgraced Islam."

Although or perhaps because this case was the "first … of its kind in Malaysian history" (ibid., 289), Azizah was charged on two relatively pedestrian criminal counts: "impersonating a man," and "using another person's identity card." These offenses fall within the jurisdiction of the secular courts and were the most clear-cut and least complicated transgressions to prosecute since the question of proof is less vexing and exacting than would be the case if charges of a specifically sexual nature were heard in the religious courts. These charges carried the additional advantage that their prosecution could be overseen by the federal government, something which would not occur if the charges had been of a religious nature and had thus been tried in the Islamic courts, especially since the latter are under state (rather than federal) jurisdiction.

Upon learning Azizah's true (female) identity, Rohana's father sought to have the marriage annulled—an issue that, significantly, was never pursued by Rohana herself, even though Rohana claimed that throughout the course of their relationship she had been deceived as to Azizah's real (female) identity and was not herself a lesbian. But there were complications with respect to an annulment because it was not altogether clear that a valid marriage had been contracted in the first place. Similarly, while Azizah and Rohana did engage in sexual contact (involving, among other things, mutual caressing and Azizah applying her hands to Rohana's vagina) that was construed as illicit (as *zina*, hence actionable), their possession and use of "sexual aids" in the form of a dildo, though apparently outrageous to public sensibilities, was more problematic as a specifically religious offense since in the eyes of many Islamic jurists penetration by a dildo does not constitute "real sexual intercourse." Issues such as these prompted state authorities in Kelantan and elsewhere to tighten their Islamic Family Enactment(s) so as to prevent—or at least more clearly criminalize and penalize—unions of this sort (as discussed below).[13] They also resulted in the local *kadi* threatening to bring charges of a religious nature against Azizah; though he never did so, he eventually annulled the marriage, apparently having decided that it had been a valid union in a narrow legal sense.

In the state of Kelantan, where the two lived, there were no laws currently in force specifically prohibiting sexual relations among women, though such had been proposed by the PAS-controlled state government a few years earlier in its attempt to institute some of the more severe Islamic criminal laws and punishments specified in the Quran (i.e., "*hudud* laws"). The actual implementation of such laws, which was stalled and ultimately scuttled by the federal government, could have resulted in Azizah (and Rohana?) being found guilty of offenses subsumed under the rubric of *musahaqah*, this being defined as "a *ta'zir* offense consisting of an act of sexual gratification between females by rubbing the vagina of one against that of the other … [the punishment … for which] shall be at the discretion of the Court" (Rose Ismail 1995:116–117). The penalty proposed for this crime is not altogether clear, although the punishment for its "male counterpart," that is *liwat*, which is construed as an offense "consisting of carnal intercourse between a male and another male or between a male and a female other than his wife, performed against the order of nature, that is through the anus," might be the same as that for *zina* (adultery/illicit fornication); to wit: one hundred lashes and a year's imprisonment, or stoning to death with stones of medium size.[14]

Investigation of Azizah's background revealed that she was a Malay Muslim whose citizenship status was that of a Thai national permanently resident in Malaysia. Apparently born in Malaysia, she was raised by an aunt, and at age 13 had gotten pregnant by a (young Malay?) man with whom she eloped to Thailand. He turned out to be a poor husband, and rather than suffer abuse at his hands, Azizah proceeded to divorce.[15] Even though she had a child to raise, she subsequently decided that she did not want to be supported by or dependent on any man, and that she would have relationships with women instead. Information released in the course of the trial revealed in addition that she had married Rohana "for love," but also partly because Rohana, facing family pressure, had threatened to break off their eight-year relationship if they didn't get married.

The sentence that Azizah received from the judge who heard the case resulted in her serving 24 months in prison. According to media accounts, "the demonic son-in-law" was eventually "rehabilitated." She later appeared in Islamic headgear (a *tudung*), proclaiming that "she regretted her erroneous ways" and that her future plans and desires included "conventional marriage."

Significantly, though not surprisingly, press accounts of the case repeatedly emphasized a number of related themes bearing on Azizah's biography; most notably: (1) her lower-class background; (2) the fact she had been adopted and raised by an aunt and was perforce deprived of her "real" mother's ("natural") love, affection, and guidance; and (3) that she was of foreign (Thai) origins in the sense that she had lived in Thailand for a number of years since eloping there at age 13. The more general message driven home by media accounts and official pronouncements about the case was that Azizah's misguided and mis-spent youth and waywardness had resulted not merely in a failed, "broken" (het-erosexual) marriage, a subsequent turn toward homosexuality, massive deception, and criminal illegality that shocked the entire nation. It also landed her in prison, effectively orphaned her son, and disgraced both her family and Islam alike.

At the height of the dramatic, sensationalist, and in many respects salacious media coverage of this incident (more specifically, just a month after Azizah's conviction and some two weeks before the *kadi* annulled the marriage), a some-what similar incident came to light in the neighboring state of Terengganu. A key difference, however, is that this case involved a male couple, who, it should be noted, received but a fraction of the media coverage accorded Azizah and Rohana (a mere five days, as opposed to three solid months). The headlines concerning this case underscored that "a *transvestite* ... tried to marry a man [by] posing as a woman" (emphasis added). The accompanying articles explained that "the marriage was called off after the bridegroom discovered the true gender of his prospective wife."[16]

It is not merely that the media coverage of this incident paled in comparison to the media attention lavished on Azizah and Rohana. The sentence meted out to the offending cross-dresser in this instance—an illiterate 15-year-old shop assistant by the name of Fauzi Yaacob, who was wearing a shirt, jeans, women's shoes, and two earrings in his left ear when arrested and was apparently so attractive and so convincingly "female" that he had already received five marriage offers—was also much lighter (a jail term of roughly seven as opposed to 24 months). This despite the fact that on at least two previous occasions Fauzi had been arrested by the police on similar if not identical grounds ("posing as a woman").

The differences in the media coverage and sentencing in these incidents are pronounced, making clear that when cross-dressing or other transgender behavior of this sort involves men it is far less offensive to legal and socio-cul-tural sensibilities than such behavior on the part of women. But we should also note the similarities in these cases and the way they were handled by the media. One obvious implication of the media coverage in both instances is that those involved in same-sex relations resort to transvestitism to marry and deceive, and, conversely, that transvestitism is merely a "cover" for same-sex sexuality.

Another is that "gender woes" of all varieties have come to plague Malaysia; that insufficient vigilance on the part of parents and others is partly to blame; and that parents, teachers, schools, and religious and political leaders and their associations need to be pressed into service to prevent the further spread of such sinful, unnatural, and profoundly corrosive and threatening behavior. It is thus not surprising that during the media circus surrounding these incidents a minister in the prime minister's department, Datuk Dr. Abdul Hamid Othman, offered a detailed public commentary on the Fauzi case, in which he "link[ed] gender woes to upbringing:" [17]

> *Boys brought up as girls has been the main reason they become transvestites ... . Some parents who have sons and yearn for a daughter end up dressing one of their sons as a girl, buying him bangles and allowing him to develop female character-istics.* They fail to realise the danger because the child, confused about his gender, grows up thinking he is a woman trapped in a man's body.
>
> Parents need to be told the importance of bringing up their children according to the child's *natural gender.* A daughter should realize she will eventually become a wife and a son should know he will be a husband someday, not the other way around ... . Parents [need] to take up parenting skills and adopt the *zero tolerance* concept in family life, religion, and law. Zero tolerance means parents will not endure or allow room for wayward-ness in the family. They will not adopt the *tak apalah* [it doesn't matter] atti-tude.
>
> UMNO want[s] to *wipe out the problems of transvestites* in its war against social ills. The religious and social welfare bureaus of UMNO ... [will] meet ... to discuss the matter ... . *UMNO branches, religious departments, schools, parent-teacher associations, and the media ... [will all] be utilized to spread the message on proper parenting skills.* [emphases added]

I shall return to some of Datuk Hamid's comments shortly. In the meantime it merits emphasis that partly because of the notoriety and backlash generated by such cases—some felt that they were "a sign that the world is coming to an end"—but also because of the (almost always tense) political climate and the resultant tendency to find groups on whom to place blame for society's ills, various jurisdictions in Malaysia sought to increase the penalties for same-sex rela-tions and to outlaw sexual contact between women that involves "rubbing the vagina of one against that of the other." The more general point is that those whose sexual orientations constitute a significant departure from stereotypical gender roles are increasingly subject to discrimination and harassment in the form of verbal and physical abuse, detention and arrest, and curtailment or loss of educational, employment, and other economic opportunities.

In May 1998, for instance, the state of Johor, following the example set by the Federal Territory of Kuala Lumpur, passed legislation, which was subsequently approved by the Sultan and became official law in 1999, that introduced whip-ping as an additional penalty to punish Muslims convicted of sexual offenses such as "sodomy," "lesbianism," and "extra-marital sex." State Executive Councillor and Islamic Affairs Committee Chairman Datuk Abdul Kadir Annuar explained that the move was to check growing social problems and moral decadence in the state, and that whipping and increased fines would henceforth be provided for, under amendments to the *Syariah* Criminal Procedure Code Enactment 1997 and the *Syariah* Criminal Offenses Enactment. Specifically, the new enactments, which also apply to "those spreading deviationist teaching, pimps and purveyors of promiscuous relations," provide for a mix of six strokes of the rotan, fines up to M$5,000 and imprisonment of up to three years upon conviction.[18] Similar enactments have been introduced in other states.

As for some of the broader trends, transgender practices have become heavily stigmatized, criminalized, and medicalized, and have also come to be defined increasingly in terms of sexuality and sexual pathology in particular, whereas even in the 1980s this was not the case. The criminalization of *pondan*, *mak nyah*, same-sex sexuality, and other variants of gender and/or sexual transgression is not only a strategy geared toward the cleansing of locally defined masculinities, femininities, and sexualities; moves along these lines and attendant strategies are also central components of more encompassing schemes of governmentality that have three analytically distinct though related objectives. First, the creation and policing of modern middle-class families and subjectivities that will hopefully help bring about a transnational Asian renaissance. Second, the reinscription of various types of authenticity and identity that are held to be conducive to this renaissance. And third, the promotion of an array of nationalist and transnational narratives bearing on "Asian values" that emphasize a timeless, tradition-bound, patriarchal, strongly heterosexual, and otherwise essentialized "Orient" (which is cast in sharp relief to an equally timeless and essentialized "West" represented as bereft of traditions other than those entailing sexual anarchy and terminal decadence). Efforts to stigmatize and criminalize transgender practices in Malaysia, Singapore and elsewhere in Southeast Asia in the name of "Asian values" are also key features of strategies aimed at legitimizing and easing the profoundly dislocating socio-cultural transformations effected by state projects of modernity in conjunction with the boom-bust cycles of global capitalism to which the state projects in question are ambivalently wed. To help illustrate these arguments we shall proceed to the case of Anwar.

Nationalist and transnational discourses on "Asian values" were frequently invoked by Malaysian politicians and others in connection with the case of Anwar Ibrahim. This case dominated Malaysian politics and mediascapes from September 1998 through mid-2000 and is widely viewed as one of the most severe political crises in the nation's history since the devastating post-election "race riots" of May 13, 1969 that resulted in the deaths of hundreds of people and the destruction of the homes and property of about 6,000 residents of Kuala Lumpur. Setting aside for the moment the structural tensions, political disputes, and personal differences between Anwar and Mahathir (and their respective supporters) that helped foment the crisis,[19] we might say that it began on September 2, 1998, which is when Anwar, Mahathir's extremely popular heir-apparent, was stripped of his official titles and duties, which included deputy prime minister and minister of finance. Shortly thereafter, Anwar, who is also the former head of both the International Islamic University and the Malaysian Islamic Youth Organization (ABIM), was detained under the Internal Security Act. He was subsequently charged with five counts of sodomy (under Section 377 of the national Penal Code), and other sexual impropriety (adultery), and various counts of bribery and corruption, all keyed, ultimately, to the accusations of sodomy. During the initial months of his incarceration, he suffered life-threatening injuries at the hands of his jailers, much as he and many others predicted would happen when he was first arrested.

There are three quick points to register before getting into the specifics of this case and the fallout to which it (and the developments leading up to it) gave rise. First, the majority if not all of the charges against Anwar seemed politically motivated if not altogether bogus—at least three of the five men who supposedly acknowledged having been sodomized by Anwar, for example, later emphasized that their "confessions" were coerced. Second, generally peaceful marches and rallies protesting Anwar's treatment were met with truncheons, tear gas, plastic bullets, water cannons, police brutality, a large number of arrests, and pronouncements from Mahathir and his supporters that the repressive measures at issue were clearly necessary and altogether in keeping with "Asian values." And third, the mockery of a trial that resulted in Anwar's conviction was characterized by gross discrepancies in the accounts of government prosecutors and "witnesses," and by all varieties of other "irregularities."

The first phase of Anwar's trial, focusing on charges of bribery and corruption, began on November 2, 1998, and eventually resulted in conviction on four different charges of "corruption" in the form of "abuse of power," specifically, that Anwar illegally used his powers of office to thwart the police investigation of the sodomy charges against him. This phase of the trial formally ended on April 14, 1999, at which time Anwar was sentenced to six years in jail. The hearings lasted a full 78 days, thus making this phase of the proceedings alone the longest criminal trial in Malaysian history.

The second phase of the Anwar trial began on June 7, 1999 and was concluded on August 8, 2000, at which point Anwar was sentenced to an additional nine years in prison. This phase focused on allegations of sexual crimes; the alleged offenses include an adulterous liaison (Anwar is married) with one of his private secretary's female in-laws, which falls under the category of *zina* (illicit fornication/adultery). Far more widely publicized, indeed, the most frequently referenced charges, were the accusations that he engaged in same-sex relations (as the "active" partner or "inserter") with five different men and was thus guilty of multiple counts of sodomy or *liwat*.[20]

At first glance the charges against Anwar might seem quite disparate and variegated. But there is a common logic underlying and linking them, for just as each of them entailed an allegation that Anwar transgressed one or another cultural code of fidelity or moderation, so too does each transgression constitute treason (*derhaka*). To elaborate on the issue of fidelity: Anwar stood accused (and was, recall, convicted) of engaging in corruption and bribery, and thus of being unfaithful to his office, to his political patron (the prime minister, who was central to his attainment of office), and to idealized political traditions (that brook neither corruption nor bribery) as well as to the ruling political party (UMNO), the electorate, the Malay "race," the Muslim community, and the nation. Similarly, we have seen that Anwar was charged with various counts of (heterosexual) adultery and numerous counts of (homosexual) sodomy, and thus obviously stood accused of being unfaithful not only to his wife, but also both to his family as a whole (whose trust he is said to have betrayed), and to the nation generally, especially since the nation is held to be built up, and to depend for its very survival, on strong families formed around stable, enduring conjugal bonds that are ideally monogamous and otherwise exclusive.

As for the theme of moderation, the issues here are perhaps more straightforward: to be charged with and convicted of corruption and bribery is obviously to be held up as someone who wields illegal and otherwise excessive power, a crime of immoderation and excess that is all the more serious in the case of an elected official who is vested with more power and authority than anyone else in the entire country save the prime minister. The charges of (heterosexual) adultery might be said to speak for themselves insofar as they too clearly suggest immoderation and excess, in the sense of someone who is not capable of satisfying their ("excessive") sexual urges within the context of marriage, and thus must turn to other women and to illegality for their satisfaction. It is no small matter here that the extremely widespread counter-hegemonic discourse suggesting that, the official line notwithstanding, men have more (not less) "passion" (*nafsu*) than women and are for this reason ultimately less (not more) responsible than women, is fueled by precisely this type of immoderate behavior on the part of men. Such behavior (men "playing around," needing more than one mate, etc.) is specifically cited by many women (and some men) as the grounds upon which they base their view that, compared to women, men are ultimately more *gatal* ("scratchy," "itchy," or "horny") and ultimately less responsible (Peletz 1995, 1996). To the extent that this discourse impacts all men negatively, it also entails "letting down the (male) side," hence a form of betrayal and infidelity.

The charges of homosexuality also raise the specter of immoderation and excess, particularly since same-sex sexuality, not being seen by Malays as reproductive, is viewed as a form of self-indulgent and gratuitous sex, and, at least in the official discourse disseminated in the present-day context, as behavior that is sinful as well as pathological in both the social and medical senses of the term in that it is pursued only for perverse pleasure. Noteworthy in this connection is that one of the widely publicized (though undoubtedly coerced if not altogether manufactured) statements attributed to one of the men (Azizan Abu Bakar) said to have been sodomized by Anwar proclaimed, "His [Anwar's] insatiable lust shows that he is someone who could be classified as chronic"; ... this [chronic insatiable lust] exerted intense pressure on my spirit and mind;" and it was this "intense pressure" that was responsible for the fact that he [Azizan] unwittingly and ultimately unwillingly (given his compromised willpower) became Anwar's "homosexual slave" (*hamba homoseksual*).[21] The image of Anwar as extremely immoderate (excessive) is further reinforced by the foregoing reference to slavery, which in the Malay context necessarily brings to mind images of royalty, who kept slaves in former times, and continue to enjoin their subjects to refer to themselves, when addressing royalty, by a term whose principal meaning is that of slave (*hamba*), though it also means something like "your humble servant." The clear implication is that Azizan was a slave to the royal Anwar, royal in any case being associated in the current political climate with all varieties of increasingly contested excesses and immunities, including those associated with criminalized sexuality.

In official Malay culture all such immoderate behavior is highly inappropriate and extremely transgressive, particularly in light of the proper and moderate conduct that is expected of a national leader who is vested with the title of minister of finance and whose mandates obviously include proper ("rational") stewardship of national resources in the broadest sense of the term. To greatly oversimplify, and to mix metaphors, Anwar's transgressions amount to his having indulged and inflamed his passions (*nafsu*) to the point of a Dionysian frenzy that is altogether unacceptable in light of the Apollonian moderation expected of political leaders, and of men generally.

The charges of homosexual offenses become all the more serious and overdetermined when one looks more closely at some of the particulars of the men Anwar is said to have sodomized, especially those of the two men whose statements and overall circumstances received the most extensive and unrelenting press coverage (partly because, they were, according to press accounts, the first to be charged after government probes into the allegations made in a book that was widely circulated by Anwar's detractors in June and July 1998). The two men are: Sukma Darmawan Sasmitaat Madja, an Indonesian by birth who, in addition to being Anwar's adopted brother, was an interior designer and businessman, and a permanent resident in Malaysia, thanks in no small measure to Anwar's having facilitated his application for Malaysian citizenship; and Munawar Ahmad Anees, from Pakistan, a friend and former speechwriter and lecturer. The fact that the first of these men was Anwar's adopted brother and was thus related to Anwar through ties of kinship, necessarily raised the specter of incest (*sumbang*). Incest is (among other things) an offense against keeping separate that which should be separate, of failing to maintain proper boundaries, and in former times it could eventuate in capital punishment. The alleged incest was all the more serious in this instance since it confounded, in addition, the most basic of all boundaries—male and female. The fact that both of these men were foreigners raises additional, deeply unsettling questions about inappropriate mixing, about breaches of national security, and about "letting down the side" (Malays), especially since one of them enlisted Anwar's help in obtaining much coveted Malaysian citizenship.

Whether or not Anwar was guilty of any of these crimes (and most Malaysians, along with most foreign observers, had very strong doubts about the veracity of the charges and the integrity of the process by which they were adjudicated), it is clear from many indications that Anwar was also being charged, albeit unofficially, with treason (*derhaka*), and that the case for treason was in many ways difficult to refute. To clarify, I need to explain that while the Malay term *derhaka* has meanings which include certain Western understandings of the term "treason" (violation of allegiance to one's nation or sovereign, especially the betrayal of one's nation by waging war against it or by consciously or purposely acting to aid its enemies), it also evokes images of the most unheard-of breaches and inversions of the divinely ordained and simultaneously naturalized social order, such as incest (*sumbang*) and cannibalism, both of which (also) involve an unacceptable partaking of "one's own." Incest, cannibalism, and treason are explicitly linked in Malay culture, through myths and aphorisms, including the expression, "like a chicken eating its own flesh" (*macam ayam makan daging sendiri*), which is sometimes invoked when people talk of incestuous unions. Such unions are seen as involving a preying on and consuming of one's own, much like domesticated chickens consuming the flesh of their consociates when they eat the scraps of cooked chicken that have been tossed out to them through the windows or the floorboards after a meal (Peletz 1988:53–58); and, at least in former times, they were regarded as treasonous violations of *adat*.

We may summarize the main points here as follows: (1) in Malay culture, publicly criticizing a patron or a father-like figure, and/or rising at his expense, thus "eating off" him, is a form of disloyalty and treason that can also entail symbolic cannibalism; (2) Anwar publicly differed with and criticized his former patron and father-figure Mahathir on a variety of issues relating to economic and other policy matters, including International Monetary Fund (IMF) guidelines issued to Malaysian ministries in the wake of the Asian financial crisis, and if only in this restricted sense was thus susceptible to charges of disloyalty, treason, and symbolic cannibalism; (3) offenses of treason and cannibalism are conjoined in Malay political culture with acts of incest, the latter being but one category of "bad sex;" and (4) those believed to be guilty of treason and/or cannibalism are thus likely to be—or might as well be—guilty of one or another form of bad sex such as same-sex sexuality, especially if they are allied with or conceptually linked to the West, which, in official Malaysian discourses and in popular culture generally, is *the* main source of the perversion and moral turpitude that exists both in Malaysia and in the world as a whole.

Rather than elaborating on the cultural-political dimensions of the charges against Anwar and the overall portrait of him that the government tried to paint, I shall proceed to two other sets of dynamics. One has to do with the international and domestic fallout from Mahathir's handling of the issues associated with the trial and the verdict. The other concerns the society-wide effects of the government's construction of Anwar's alleged criminality.

Mahathir's handling of the affair met with sanctions in the form of censure not only from the US and other Western nations but also from various Asian countries, including friendly neighbors such as Muslim-majority Indonesia and the Philippines, an overwhelmingly Catholic country with a small but politically significant Muslim population. It is notable that much of the censure from these very different nations was embedded in a shared discourse keyed to increasingly international standards of due process and human rights.

Far more detrimental to Mahathir's legitimacy as the Muslim leader of a predominantly Muslim nation is that his handling of the affair also met with sharp condemnation from the heads of Muslim groups, both domestic and international. Some of the Muslim protest from local and international quarters stemmed from the belief that the proceedings against Anwar should have been held in the Islamic courts. One of the more strongly worded of these international condemnations came from Shaikh Taha Jabir Al-Alwani, whose impeccable credentials include: having obtained an advanced degree in Islamic law and jurisprudence (*fiqh*) from Al-Azhar University in Cairo; having taught for many years at Imam Muhammad ibn Sa'ud University in Riyadh, Saudi Arabia; and being a Founding Member of the Muslim World League, Mecca, and a member of the International *Fiqh* Council of Jeddah. Shaikh Taha Jabir's condemnation of the sodomy trial is contained in a document that was circulated on the Internet shortly after the sodomy verdict against Anwar was announced on August 8, 2000. When I visited Malaysia in January 2001, it was also widely available in pamphlet form from sidewalk vendors and bookstores in Kuala Lumpur and elsewhere.[22]

The Shaikh states that based on Islamic law, "one can write volumes on the violations of the rights of the 'accused;'" he then goes on to enumerate a series of violations that render both the verdict and the trial as a whole illegal. The latter enumeration invokes numerous passages from the Quran and various *hadith* by way of substantiation, and also includes the following: that "the alleged offense, sodomy, is a crime of honor and character, like *zina* [adultery, illicit fornication] [that] requires four credible eyewitnesses who have witnessed the act first hand, with no barrier or obstruction;" that "if there is the slightest discrepancy in their testimony, the whole case is to be dismissed and the witnesses or accusers are guilty of slander or libel;" that Anwar was denied the opportunity to "call and cross examine a key witness in the person of the Prime Minister," who had privileged access to a good deal of material evidence and was also a critically important character witness; and that the government was guilty of numerous counts of witness tampering and attorney intimidation.

The Shaikh's overall assessment of the trial and the verdict is summed up in his remarks that it was "an embarrassing conviction to the Malaysian Judiciary System. It has disgraced the great name of Malaysia. The judge should have upheld the values of Justice and *Shari'a* and the ethics of his profession by dismissing the case outright. It is judges like him who are the subject of the Hadith of the Prophet ... 'two out of every three judges end up in Hell fire.'" The Shaikh continues by emphasizing that the trial was a "violation of justice, the *Shari'a* law in form and substance" and "a gross violation of the defendant's Human Rights." Lest anyone miss the bottom line of his professional, *syariah*-based judgment, he concludes his statement by underscoring that "Anwar Ibrahim should be declared innocent ... [and] released immediately," and that "his accusers should be tried for slander and libel."

Mahathir's treatment of Anwar forever changed the Malaysian political landscape. This is partly because the Anwar affair, especially the blatant perversion of the judiciary for narrowly political purposes, not only created and "mobiliz[ed] domestic groups that then influence[d] authority structures" within the state, as Stephen Krasner (1999:32–33) has put it with respect to analogous dynamics elsewhere in the world; it also "alter[ed] domestic conceptions of legitimate behavior, [and] subject[ed] domestic institutions and personnel to external influence." Having already mentioned some of the external pressure brought to bear on domestic institutions and personnel in the wake of Anwar's arrest, I would underscore that the Anwar affair also gave rise to all varieties of other phenomena. These include: new national-level political parties (most notably, *Parti Keadilan Nasional* [The National Justice Party], generally known as *Keadilan*, which is headed by Anwar's wife, Dr. Wan Azizah); new national-level political coalitions (the Alternative Alliance [*Barisan Alternatif*], composed of *Keadilan* and PAS, among others); a multitude of local NGOs with transnational connections; and a plethora of new books, articles, periodicals, Web sites, chat rooms, and other media products—each insisting in its own way that business as usual (corruption, croneyism, nepotism, and "money politics") was no longer acceptable, and that new standards of transparency, accountability, and efficiency were vital to the nation's institutional (particularly economic) health and wellbeing, as well as its political standing and prestige in the international community.

More generally, the Anwar affair seriously alienated large segments of the Malaysian population, polarized the Malay community, and politicized Malay women and youth in particular, one immediate result of which was that many Malays, including (apparently) disproportionately large numbers of women, voiced their opposition to Mahathir and UMNO in the general elections held in November 1999 by casting their votes either for *Keadilan* or for the major Islamic opposition party, PAS. One consequence of the shift away from UMNO, which also occurred in subsequent by-elections, is that PAS gained control of the state government in Terengganu, which borders the state of Kelantan, the other major PAS stronghold. These dynamics in turn encouraged Mahathir to take women's concerns more seriously, or at least to create a Ministry of Women's Affairs (later to become the Ministry of Women, Family, and Community Development). While this may have been a Pyrrhic victory for women, it is indicative of the shifting political landscape that official announcements concerning the creation of this ministry in January 2001 were immediately followed by widely publicized press releases from leaders of the *mak nyah* (male-bodied transsexual) community, who expressed the hope that state-sponsored efforts to promote greater public awareness of issues of gender would lead to their formal recognition and acceptance as a "third sex."

The electorate's swing toward PAS (which was reversed after September 11 [Peletz 2005]) is usefully viewed in the context of changes that occurred in the PAS-controlled state of Kelantan earlier in the 1990s. Beginning in the early years of that decade, the state government introduced a variety of legal, administrative, and policy proposals aimed at making the judicial and other institutions of their states "more Islamic," the more encompassing objective being to encourage their Muslim residents and ultimately Malaysia's entire Muslim population—and some would say all non-Muslims as well—to adopt a "more Islamic" way of life. In some cases, the changes that have been implemented or proposed seem heavily laden with symbolism but relatively inconsequential in "real-life" terms, such as separate supermarket check-out lines for males and females, and the abolition of "unisex" hair salons. In other instances, the measures at issue have far broader social and cultural consequences or potential implications. I would include in the latter category the Kelantan government's 1990 banning of shadow-puppet theater and related genres of popular dramatic art that were long central to local Malay cultural identities;[23] and the legislative and other measures pursued by Kelantan authorities in the early 1990s in an effort to implement *hudud* laws.[24] The formal implementation of the latter (*hudud*) laws was stalled and ultimately scuttled by the national government, but many Malays and non-Malays fear that it is only a question of time before such laws are introduced in Kelantan and elsewhere in the Peninsula. Not surprisingly, recent years have also witnessed enhanced legitimacy and prestige accorded to Islamic scholars and men of learning (*ulama*), especially in Terengganu and Kelantan, but elsewhere as well, along with greatly stepped-up activity on the part of the increasingly high-profile Islamic Center (*Pusat Islam*), which is based in Kuala Lumpur and has as one of its key mandates the reduction of vice among Muslims and the upgrading of Muslim morality generally. These developments have gone hand in hand with the apparent upsurge in support among Malays, particularly youth, for Islamization programs of various kinds. Some Malaysians feel that trends such as these are responsible for the increase in censorship and self-censorship that characterizes many variants of contemporary political and social discourse, and for the overall constriction of pluralistic sensibilities and dispositions as well as discursive spaces commonly associated with civil society.

For mostly obvious reasons, developments of the latter sort exacerbated the conundrums of legitimacy and sovereignty facing Mahathir (especially since UMNO is seen as relatively secular compared to PAS), just as they exacerbate the quandaries facing his successors (e.g., Abdullah Badawi, r. 2003–present), however Islamist, accommodationist, or secular they may be. The same is true of other dynamics that have contributed to divisions and polarization among Malays. More generally, political and other disunity among Malays is seen by many Malays and other Malaysians as a grave threat to Malaysia's sovereignty, as are the processes of economic and political globalization over which a more sovereign Malaysia might be able to exercise a modicum of control. In this connection it merits emphasis that many Malaysians view economic and political globalization as more or less synonymous with neo-colonial domination by Western powers that differs from its colonial-era counterparts primarily by being more invidious, pervasive, and hegemonic (cf. Ong 2006:1 passim). Indeed, in the views of some, the experience of globalization is likened to being (date) raped, as discussed below.

Mahathir's handling of the Anwar affair, including, especially, his government's construction of Anwar's alleged criminality, changed the political landscape in other ways as well. Perhaps most obvious has been the highlighting of same-sex sexuality, and its stigmatization, criminalization, and medicalization, in the myriad contexts comprising public culture. It is not simply the case that local papers were filled with what were, in the Malaysian setting, shockingly detailed and lurid accounts of the charges against Anwar and the evidence introduced by the government to prosecute him: stained mattresses, samples of blood, pubic hair, and semen, and scientific reports detailing the findings of anal probes, all of which were front-page news. Equally shocking to the sensibilities of many Malaysians was the constant bandying about—in government speeches, newspapers, and radio and television broadcasts—of terms such as *liwat*, the latter being the (Arabic-origin) Malay term for sodomy that prior to Anwar's arrest was generally unknown even to highly educated Malays.[25]

Similarly, much media attention was lavished on Mahathir's repeated reminders that homosexuality is a disease of Western origin that is criminalized in Malaysia. Extensive media play was also accorded Mahathir's pronouncements that "in Malaysia we reject such extreme acts," and that "We accept men as men and women as women," the factually erroneous implication of which is that Malaysians have never tolerated or accepted men or women who deviate from normative definitions of masculinity or femininity, respectively. Needless to say, the state-controlled media also made much of Mahathir's very public, bottom-line position(s), articulated as: Malaysians need to "distance themselves from misguided Western ideas, such as accepting homosexuality as a human right," and "I cannot accept a man who is a sodomist as leader of the country."[26]

It remains to consider the consequences of the media frenzy surrounding the Anwar case and some of the dynamics it engendered. Most relevant here are the deployment of discourses and the whipping up of public sentiment against same-sex sexuality and gender transgression of all varieties. Manifestations of these discourses and sentiments include the increased frequency of police raids on certain parks, malls, restaurants, bars, parking lots, and other locales seen as friendly to gays, lesbians, and the transgendered. Such raids on the part of the overwhelmingly Malay police force typically result in the widely publicized arrest, detention, and drug testing of their patrons, especially the foreigners among them, who, as is typically emphasized in press accounts, are usually *Western* men. They also commonly involve the publication in the newspapers of photos of those arrested, resulting in serious repercussions of various kinds.

Such raids are also partly responsible for the waves of fear and panic periodically experienced by members of Malaysia's gay, lesbian, and transgendered communities, who, especially if they are members of one or another ethnic minority (Chinese, for example), rightfully fear discrimination and harassment in the form of verbal and physical abuse, detention and arrest, and the curtailment or loss of educational, employment, and other economic opportunities.

Another consequence of these developments is in some ways much more ominous. I refer to the formation of community-based vigilante groups, made up largely of Malays, who have taken to monitoring activities in their neighborhoods that they deem to be "immoral" or "un-Islamic." Such groups, which apparently began forming around 1994, assisted in the arrests of some 7,000 people from 1994 to 1995 alone, and have been encouraged by government officials to "fight homosexuals" and wipe out same-sex sexuality in its entirety. As one high-ranking government official put it, "We certainly do not want to see our country turning into another replica of Western countries."[27]

One of the groups that was explicitly anti-homosexual was launched on October 21, 1998—not coincidentally, a mere seven or eight weeks after the first broadly public airing of sodomy charges against Anwar. From the outset, this group, known as the People's Anti-Homosexual Volunteer Movement (PASRAH), disclaimed any political motivation, even though most of its members appeared to belong to the inner circle of the ruling UMNO party, and even though its founding chairman, Ibrahim Ali, was both a member of the UMNO Supreme Council and a staunch supporter of Prime Minister Mahathir. One of the group's self-described goals was to bring about the closing of all bars, recreational centers, and other establishments frequented by gays, lesbians, and bisexuals (PASRAH cited some 13 such spots in Kuala Lumpur), who were estimated by PASRAH to number approximately 24,000 in Kuala Lumpur alone.[28]

The more general goal of PASRAH, which claimed the existence of some 50 like-minded organizations, was to press for legislation and other measures that would eliminate homosexuality in its entirety, on the grounds that it is a defiling Western import that is profoundly threatening with respect to race and nation because it jeopardizes the reproduction and strengthening of Islamic and Malaysian values specifically, and "Asian values" in general. In this connection we might recall that some of the more "puritanical" and "conservative" Malay Muslims in Malaysia, many but not all of whom are associated with PAS, seek the passage of legislation that would result in same-sex erotics being penalized with the punishment sometimes meted out in Islamic countries for heterosexual adultery/fornication (*zina*), which can include caning or whipping (involving as many as 100 lashes), and, in some cases, capital punishment.

The formation of PASRAH in October 1998, coupled with the emergence of numerous ("50," if PASRAH estimates are to be believed) like-minded organizations, is but one manifestation of a type of cultural cleansing that has been going on in Malaysia during the past few decades. Such cultural cleansing is geared toward purging Malaysia of what are perceived to be contaminating and otherwise unacceptable cultural influences, in this instance of foreign, especially Western, origin. These disturbing developments were condemned by local human rights organizations, such as SUARAM (*Suara Rakyat Malaysia; The Voice of the Malaysian People*), which insisted that attempts by PASRAH members to incite discrimination and condemnation of a minority group was a "misguided form of support for the Prime Minister."[29] The establishment of organizations such as PASRAH was also decried by certain prominent individuals, such as Marina Mahathir, a highly respected journalist, author, and businesswoman, as well as the daughter of then Prime Minister Mahathir and a longtime President of the Malaysian AIDS Council. Marina publicly articulated the well-founded fears that such "hate campaigns" might promote intolerance, "inflame public prejudice against gays and lesbians," and "make anti-social acts such as harassment of certain groups acceptable."[30] The daughter of the prime minister is one of the very few individuals in the country who can safely criticize developments of this sort, and she may be partly responsible for the fact that PASRAH's formal, "above-ground" existence appears to have been short lived.

In this context it is relevant that some of those I interviewed in January 2001 insisted that PASRAH continued to operate, but not in an official or "above-ground" capacity. Others I interviewed, including Marina, told me that PASRAH no longer existed in any form, not even as a shadow organization, and that its founding members had likewise ceased to hold important political positions of any variety. Many who were of the latter opinion, along with some who felt that PASRAH was indeed alive and well (though underground), hastened to emphasize the following themes. Whatever its current status and scope of operations, PASRAH is but one example of an increasingly common type of "morally corrective" organization and cultural-political sensibility. And in some ways more germane, each and every urban and rural community in the country has as part of its system of local governance at least one committee or council charged with upholding public morality and bringing morally suspect or "wayward" individuals to the attention of local government authorities or their superiors.

There is, I believe, a more important point in all of this: those threatened by dynamics involving the formation of the many PASRAH-like vigilante groups that continue to operate are not simply individuals involved or believed to be involved in same-sex relations. Also very much threatened are men and women involved in transgender practices who do not engage in same-sex activities, as well as *all men perceived to be effeminate* and *all women perceived to be masculine*, especially since being effeminate in the case of a male and masculine in the case of a female is increasingly construed as a major sign or symbol of being "a homosexual" (*seorang homoseksual*).

Developments and dynamics of the latter sort and are increasingly evident in various spheres and regimes of governmentality—including national and state legislatures, the secular and religious courts, as well as other sub-systems of law and administration—and in other public institutions and agencies that have come to exercise ever greater control over the most intimate of private domains, such as the bedroom. Here we might recall the speech made by Minister Datuk Abdul Hamid Othman in February 1997, at the height of the public controversies surrounding the cases of Azizah and Fauzi. Reassuring his audience of the government's redoubled efforts to combat transvestitism, other "gender woes," and "social ills" more generally, he announced new plans to draw upon and actively recruit the personnel and other resources of political parties (UMNO branches), religious departments, schools, parent-teacher associations, and the media, to "spread the message on proper parenting skills," including the message that parents need to *learn* "proper" parenting skills. In this context, as we have seen, "proper" parenting means adopting a *"zero tolerance concept"* in "family life, religion, and law," which is to say that parents should neither endure nor allow room for "waywardness in the family," nor "adopt the *tak apalah* ['it doesn't matter'] attitude" when it comes to the gender(ed) and potential sexual(ized) proclivities of their children.

Thus targeted by these new campaigns is not only the social tolerance long exhibited by Malay parents toward certain types of gender(ed) conduct (such as male experimentation with female dress, adornment, and comportment), but also children's "polymorphous" behavior with respect to sex (what Freud referred to as their "polymorphous perversity") and gender alike. But much more is at issue. Indeed, what is involved here are at least four broadly encompassing and critically important developments: (1) the targeting and, more significantly, the problematizing of childhood and adolescent sexualities; (2) the harnessing of pedagogical institutions to better supervise and regulate "the problem" of childhood and adolescent sex, what Foucault (1978:104) spoke of as the "pedagogization of children's sex"; (3) the tacit and unmarked admission, which is highly subversive with respect to much of the official discourse on the subject, that at least in the case of those given to cross-dressing, local "gender woes" are *not* entirely or even primarily of Western origin and may in fact be the direct result of parenting traditions long enshrined in *local* culture; and (4) the equally tacit and unmarked though ultimately far more subversive admission that gender identities and sexual orientations are not the direct, unmediated by-product of one's genital constitution or otherwise ascribed at birth (in a sociological sense), but are achieved (also in the sociological sense) and thus capable of being malleable, hybrid, and protean, much like religious, ethnic, and other identities.

Attendant developments have entailed the emergence of entirely new discourses that are simultaneously cause and effect of the production of "a whole machinery for speechifying, analyzing, and investigating" (Foucault 1978:32) a related series of themes. These include but are not limited to the following: "sodomy" and "homosexuality;" "sodomy and homosexuality as perversion," and "sodomy and homosexuality as perversion of Western origin"—all of which are related through complementary opposition and are otherwise deeply constitutive of the discourses on "Asian values" that have proliferated in Malaysia, Singapore, and elsewhere in Asia since the early 1990s. The highly politicized "incitement to discourse" that has given rise in mediascapes and elsewhere to the "veritable discursive explosion" (Foucault 1978:17) bearing on sodomy, homosexuality, and perversion bears a loose family resemblance to some of the historical trajectories that Foucault has described for France and other parts of Europe in the eighteenth and nineteenth centuries. So too does the transposition of certain categories that has occurred in the course of the "discovery of sexuality" and the "invention of homosexuality" in particular. To paraphrase Foucault's (1978:43) observation that in France, whereas "the sodomite had been a temporary aberration, the homosexual was now a species," we might say that in Malaysia, whereas the transgendered *pondan* had long been seen (and in many respects still is regarded as) a temporary aberration, "the homosexual," like "the sodomist" (the two terms tend to be used interchangeably in Malaysia), is clearly a species, "a personage, a past, a case history, and a childhood, in addition to being a type of life, a life form, and a morphology, with an indiscreet anatomy and possibly a mysterious physiology" (Foucault 1978:43), though some of this occurs with certain types of *pondan* as well. A key difference from France is that the *pondan* was never sexualized in the way that the French sodomist was, which is to say that in the Malaysian context we see a move from an aberration that was gendered though neither sexualized, stigmatized, nor criminalized; to a species, which, in addition to being (homo)sexualized is also stigmatized and criminalized.

One other comparison with France worth noting has to do with Foucault's observation that in sixteenth- and seventeenth-century France, moral categories of "excess" and "debauchery" were both culturally elaborated and of broad socio-political concern. This is because they were envisioned as simultaneously cause and effect of "heredity," and thus always implicated in potentially anxious discourses on "the health of the race" and "racial—and/or national—degeneration." Of additional interest here is Foucault's (1978:118) point that in eighteenth- and nineteenth-century France, the moral category of "perversion" eclipsed that of "excess/debauchery," such that the series "excess/debauchery, heredity, degeneration" was superseded by the series "perversion, heredity, degeneration." Obvious differences in time frame aside, here too we see a loose family resemblance to the Malaysian case, though the latter might be said to be in the midst of an epistemic or discursive transition, one highlighted most visibly by the combination of charges against Anwar, which, as we have seen, include (if only implicitly) accusations of excess, debauchery, *and* perversion. That charges of perversion were meant to be the most damning of all accusations is, I think, additional evidence of the trajectory to which we have alluded, especially since allegations that officials have engaged in adultery, corruption, and the like have become so commonplace in the Malaysian political setting that something "truly scurrilous"—because truly perverse—had to be concocted in order to have the desired result of destroying Anwar's spiritual and religious credentials and overall moral character, hence his political legitimacy.

As discussed briefly in Chapter 3, Foucault (1978:101) has shown that the appearance in nineteenth-century France of an extensive series of psychiatric,

jurisprudential, and other "discourses on the species and subspecies of homosexuality, inversion, pederasty, and 'psychic hermaphrodism' [not only] made possible a strong advance of social controls into this area of 'perversity;' ... it also
made possible the formation of a 'reverse' discourse: homosexuality began to
speak in its own behalf, to demand that its legitimacy or 'naturality' be acknowledged, often in the same vocabulary, using the same categories by which it was
medically disqualified." We might thus ask if something along these lines has
also occurred in Malaysia; or, put differently, if there is any Malaysian evidence
bearing on such matters that might support Foucault's (1978:95) frequently
cited observation, which I paraphrase, "where there is knowledge/power, there
is resistance." Before answering such questions it is well to add a bit more complexity to Foucault's position by emphasizing that "reverse" discourses emerge
not as phenomena contained within discourse alone, but also as a result of more
"sociological variables" such as the creation of new landscapes of human agency
like the city, the Internet, business enterprises that are not dependent on state
patrons, etc.[31] Some of these landscapes invite heightened control and repression at the hands of different categories of elites, but others allow for the quotidian practices of anonymity, autonomy, and self-determination (in choosing a
place to live, a career, or a mate, for example) that ultimately lead some people
to articulate and enact alternative definitions of their selves and their futures.
This argument resonates with my earlier elucidation of the fact that modernity
has both bright sides and dark ones. It is not contrary to the Foucauldian emphasis on discourse, but it adds another more complex layer than Foucault offers,
one that is consistent with Malaysia's historical and contemporary experience of
institutional differentiation, spatialization, and movement.

Malaysian evidence of these dynamics and discourses does in fact exist, as
Tan Beng Hui (1999) has noted with respect to the discourse on "Asian values"
and the particular ways it has singled out same-sex sexuality, cross-dressing, and
transgender practices of all varieties as being "un-Asian."

> The discourse on Asian values has also "benefited" the homosexual
> (female and male) community in Malaysian society. The constant cautions
> against homosexuality and other forms of social "evil" have given these
> various phenomena—as well as the actors behind them—a prominence
> never before seen in Malaysia. The Asian values discourse has inadver-
> tently ended up publicly acknowledging and naming the presence of
> homosexuality in Malaysia. Furthermore, the very idea of needing to con-
> tain homosexuality and to "get rid" of it is premised on a recognition that
> homosexuality not only exists but that it can also be promoted. This is
> extremely significant since it implies that sexual identities are not natural,
> fixed, and immutable as they are commonly made out to be.
>
> (Tan Beng Hui 1999:287)

In the essay cited here Tan does not go as far as saying that either home-
grown or more cosmopolitan gender transgressors or sexual outlaws have also

begun speaking publicly on their own behalf, to demand that their legitimacy or "naturality" (to use Foucault's term) be acknowledged. But the very existence of her work is a clear indication of burgeoning developments along these lines. Additional evidence of such trends appears in the related article published by Malaysian scholars and activists in 1996 under the pseudonyms of "Rais Nur and A.R.," which provides an overview of the lesbian movement in Malaysia and the ways that lesbians and gays are persecuted by the state; and in essays posted on the Internet in 1998 and 1999 by Alina Rastam and Nadiah Bamadhaj, which discuss the Anwar case in the context of the need for Malaysians to lobby for the legal and cultural recognition of sexual rights—especially the sexual rights of gays, lesbians, and transsexuals—as human rights. More generally, the Internet has facilitated a veritable explosion of discourses concerning not only sexual orientation and sexual rights in the Malaysian setting, but also the experiences of gay and lesbian Malaysians living abroad, increasing numbers of whom have sought and been granted political asylum in the US and Canada on the grounds of their membership in social groups or communities that are subject to persecution in Malaysia. Anwar's conviction on sodomy charges, coupled with his August 8, 2000 sentencing to an additional nine years in prison, may well have helped insure that, at least in the short run, some of these discourses remain relatively underground in Malaysia—or largely confined to cyberspace. But there is every reason to believe that these discourses will multiply exponentially in the years ahead, and that those involved in their production and dissemination will eventually seek a multiplicity of more public venues to assert their legitimacy and naturality.

Since the production and world-wide circulation of all such discourses, like those of Muslim feminists, local and Western NGOs and specifically human-rights organizations that we consider later in this chapter, are very much part and parcel of processes of globalization, I would like to conclude this discussion of "Asian values" and new types of criminality with a few remarks on globalization and nation-state sovereignty. Saskia Sassen (1996, 1998) has written insightfully on the subject, but as Ong (1999) correctly points out, Sassen sometimes gives the impression that she conceives of the dynamics in essentially zero-sum terms, that "more" globalization leads inexorably to "less" nation-state sovereignty. Ong suggests that we transcend zero-sum problematics, and that we look instead at the ways that globalizing phenomena pose new challenges to nation-states, and thus help elicit new strategies of governmentality, new regimes of citizenship, and new systems of graduated sovereignty—all of which can be pressed into service to negotiate globalizing forces in a variety of different ways. This is a vital corrective that I heartily endorse. But I would also register a friendly caveat and underscore that it is a theoretical or analytic perspective based on "the outsider's" point of view, what anthropologists, drawing on the distinction that linguists make between phonetics and phonemics, used to call an "etic" perspective. "Etic" perspectives need to be distinguished from their "emic" counterparts, the views and sensibilities articulated by the people whose social lives and cultural products we aim to describe and interpret.

It seems crucial to maintain the distinction in the present context. I say this because Mahathir and other Southeast Asian leaders, and good numbers of their countrymen, seem to experience, understand, and represent forces of globalization—including the financial meltdown and the plethora of economic, political, and moral crises to which it gave rise—as a devastating assault on their multiple sovereignties, including the integrity of their imagined communities, body politics, and invariably sexed and gendered bodies.

According to Mahathir's widely retailed worldview (*A New Deal for Asia*), forces of globalization have unleashed on Southeast Asia the unbridled greed and other base passions of unruly herds of foreign currency traders and speculators like George Soros. Mahathir has been explicit in insisting that such groups, along with the IMF and related organizations, have totally undercut the rights of Asian leaders to defend their countries and control their destinies, and have in these and other ways completely disregarded principles of national sovereignty. Mahathir's nationalist discourses since mid-1997 are in fact strikingly reminiscent of the narratives of women who have been subject to (date) rape. They are in any case redolent with symbols, idioms, and overt imagery of victimization through theft, assault, and humiliation; of the laws of the jungle; of fault lines that can be widened and prised open; of shattered certainties and stolen futures; and perhaps most revealingly, of the violent penetration that necessarily results from having been unwittingly open and receptive to id-driven, wanton foreigners hell-bent on the creation and subsequent domination of a borderless world. In this connection we need also bear in mind that Anwar was widely depicted in the press and elsewhere as a supporter of the IMF and an ally of the West in general. Given this overall discursive context, the allegations that Anwar illegally penetrated and otherwise violated a variety of Malaysian and other men, at least one of whom was related to him through bonds of kinship, are deeply allegorical. Indeed, it is hard to think of a political narrative that is more conducive to exploiting local fears and anxieties about being insufficiently vigilant in safeguarding the integrity and sovereignty of bodies, families, and body politics from the real or imagined onslaught of globalization.

The Pink Triangle, the Urban/Sexual Underground, and the Struggle for Sexual Equality

In January 2001 I was talking to a young Indian man in a dilapidated building in the Chow Kit section of Kuala Lumpur who told me quite matter of factly—and in almost impeccable English—that he had once been a drug addict. He added that he had been clean for some time, and that he was now working to help people who were still caught in the grip of addiction. Our conversation had unfolded rapidly and was somewhat disjointed, so when he proceeded to ask me if I had seen all of the "fixing" going on in the streets and sidewalks outside the building, I wasn't entirely sure what he meant. Partly because I used to do construction work in the summers, I assumed that he was referring to the noisy and seemingly incessant jackhammering, road repair, and other construction activities that are more or less permanent features of most every part of Kuala Lumpur, including Chow Kit. I was wrong, of course, as I quickly realized when I was invited to look out the nearest window of the third-floor office that served as the venue of our conversation. There on the sidewalk across the street, in broad daylight and in plain view, amid piles of garbage and newspapers swirling around in the hot morning wind, were a couple of young men shooting up. One had his shirt pulled up so that he could inject himself in the abdomen; the other had dropped his pants to his ankles in order to more easily inject his drug of choice (most likely heroin) into his groin.

These were some of the most jarring and disturbing images I had ever seen in Malaysia—or anywhere else; and to this day they remain seared in my mind. Thinking back to that day, I should have expected to encounter these kinds of scenes. I was, after all, in one of the more run-down parts of the infamous Chow Kit, a largely working-class and predominantly Chinese neighborhood that is also home to large numbers of Indonesians and other (Asian and African) immigrants and is well known throughout the country as a teeming red-light district if not *the* epicenter of Malaysian vice and crime. As one published source puts it, "several of its streets are lined with seedy brothels" and "according to one estimate, there are about 8,000 IDUs [intravenous drug users], sex workers, and transsexuals living and working in the area" (UNAIDS 1999:38). Chow Kit is also the city's main containment zone for vice and crime. Police, political and religious elites, and other state-appointed guardians of morality often turn a blind eye to what goes on openly there (as they also do, albeit to a lesser degree, in the more upscale Bukit Bintang area) in the hope that such strategies, along with greater vigilance elsewhere, will help "keep it in the neighborhood."

The Chow Kit neighborhood is home to the main office of an NGO known as the Pink Triangle (also commonly referred to since 2003 or 2004 as the PT Foundation [Yayasan PT]).[32] The official *raison d'être* of the Pink Triangle is to provide information and services to communities that are at risk for HIV/AIDS and/or subject to discrimination on account of involvement in sexual practices that fall outside the range of local heteronormative ideals. The Pink Triangle is one of a multitude of cosmopolitan, progressive NGOs that have sprung up in Malaysia in the past few decades, many of which are vital to the development of sensibilities conducive to the strengthening of civil society and democratic pluralism. In relation to the vast majority of other Malaysian NGOs, however, the Pink Triangle is highly unique. Its uniqueness lies in its implicit promotion of sexual rights as human rights. Most other NGOs in Malaysia, including those with explicitly feminist agendas, steer clear of any positions along these lines, and are, in almost all cases, overtly hostile to them. Hostility of the latter sort is also characteristic of all political parties in Malaysia, even though the majority of them do espouse one or another variant of equality or justice with respect to gender.

This section of the chapter has four objectives. The first is to present an overview of the services provided by Pink Triangle along with heretofore inaccessible data bearing on the basic contours of the largely underground communities they aim to assist—all of which, to borrow a phrase from Gayle Rubin (1984), find themselves well "beyond the charmed circle(s)" of society insofar as they engage in sexual and other bodily practices that are overtly stigmatized if not criminalized. My second objective is to discuss selected features of the discourses articulated by Pink Triangle staff both in their literature and public pronouncements, and in the interviews I conducted with them in 2001, 2002, and 2008. My third goal is to examine some of the latter discourses in relation to those articulated by political and religious elites (herein glossed as "official discourses"). The fourth and final objective of the discussion is to provide data conducive to comparative and theoretical perspectives on the current status and future of struggles for sexual equality in Malaysia and other regions of Southeast Asia on the one hand and the West on the other. Before turning to these matters and to the ways in which the Pink Triangle and variably located social actors engage "tolerance," open secrets, and governmentality, additional background information is in order.

Background and Context

I noted earlier that travel brochures and academic texts commonly describe the Muslim-majority nation of Malaysia as "the crossroads of Asia" owing to the country's strategic location along the waterways of Asia as well as its rich ethnic and religious diversity. The ethnic mosaic is usually discussed in terms of four major categories. "Malays," all of whom are Muslims, make up about 51 percent of the total population. "Chinese," who are usually described as practicing a syncretistic blend of Buddhism, Confucianism, and Taoism, compose about 26 percent. "Indians," most of whom are Hindus, though some are Sikh, Christian, or Muslim, account for about 7 percent. And "Others," including hill-dwelling aborigines, Eurasians, etc., make up the remaining 16 percent (Government of Malaysia 2000).

The Malaysian case is of much greater significance than the country's demographic girth—some 25 million people—might suggest at first glance. One set of reasons for this is that Malaysia is among the most successful of the "non-Confucian" Asian tigers and has also sustained a pace of rapid development that is probably second to none in the Muslim world. Another is that Malaysian Prime Minister Mahathir (r. 1981–2003), far more than any of his predecessors, successfully projected both the Malaysian case and his particular ideas on political-economic modernization as an emulable model for other regions of the world. Mahathir has frequently claimed, for example, that the Malaysian model of growth-led development that is simultaneously informed by transcendent Islamic values and "smart partnerships" linking the civil service, the private sector, and political leaders is a preferred alternative to Western-style development in other Muslim-majority nations and in much of the southern hemisphere as a whole. In his "role as 'emissary' for the South," Mahathir has also offered "a post-Bandung discourse of Malaysian-style 'economic nationalism' for peripheral states to follow [that is] fashioned around themes of political solidarity with poor and developing countries" (Hilley 2001:99). Mahathir's messages were well received in many quarters, both at home and abroad. This is partly because in the course of a mere generation or so Malaysia catapulted itself into the slender ranks of Muslim countries with appreciable middle classes and burgeoning if still precarious civil societies (Abdul Rahman Embong 2002). Circumstances such as these help explain why Malaysia has become a locus of nationalist, transnational, and academic discourses concerning "Muslim modernities," "Asian modernities," and "alternative modernities" generally (Ong 1999, 2006, Peletz 2002; see also Appadurai 1996, Eickelman and Piscatori 1996, Rofel 1999, Hefner 2000, Knauft 2002).

Ethnic distinctions and antagonisms in Malaysia are infused with far-reaching religious, political, and economic significance, and have been exacerbated by development strategies of the postcolonial government. This is most evident with the NEP (1971–1990), which sought to eradicate poverty among all Malaysians and to "restructure society" by undermining the material and symbolic connections between ethnic categories on the one hand and economic standing and function on the other. By pursuing policies to help the predominantly rural and agricultural Malays "catch up" economically with Chinese and Indians, the government has placed tremendous emphasis on "race" (on being a Malay or a non-Malay) as a criterion in allocating government loans and subsidies and other scarce resources (university scholarships, start-up funds for businesses, etc.). These policies heightened the awareness of distinctions between Malays and non-Malays and made them all the more politically and economically salient.

The NEP also exacerbated class antagonisms within the Malay community. Although its programs helped create a Malay middle class and enriched some Malays quite substantially, they left other Malays no better (and, in some cases, relatively worse) off than before in terms of material standing and access to social justice. Reactions to the NEP have taken many forms, including active and passive resistance to the Green Revolution implemented as a key feature of the NEP in many areas (J.C. Scott 1985), and disaffection from the central clique of the ruling political party and from the party in its entirety.

Dissatisfaction with the government's commitment to modernity and the NEP in particular has also fueled Malaysia's Islamic resurgence. The resurgence is sometimes referred to as the *dakwah* movement. The term *dakwah* means to invite or call one to the Islamic cause, or to respond to the invitation or call, hence missionary work, including making Muslims better Muslims. The resurgence is usually said to date from the early 1970s, even though it is most appropriately viewed as an outgrowth of earlier developments in Islamic nationalism and reform, such as those associated with the *Kaum Muda* ("Young Group") movement of the 1920s and 1930s (Roff 1967). The *dakwah* movement is thoroughly home-grown but has also been inspired by Islamist groups and Islamic revivalism in Indonesia, Pakistan, Egypt, Libya, and other parts of the Muslim world.

Most scholars approach the resurgence as a response if not a form of resistance to one or more of the following analytically related and culturally interlocked sets of developments. The first development concerns the postcolonial state's Western-oriented modernization policies (noted above), which entail a heavily interventionist role for the state with respect to economic planning, distribution, and capitalist processes as a whole. These policies are widely seen as contributing to Malaysia's over-dependence on Western capital; to the economic success of Chinese and Indians relative to Malays; and to upper-class corruption and decadence (sexual and otherwise) as well as deracination and moral and spiritual bankruptcy throughout the Malay community. The second development involves the simultaneous shifting and hardening of class interests and animosities, especially between the newly emerged middle class and an entrenched (aristocratic) ruling class. The third development is the tightening of ethnic boundaries, particularly those separating Malays and Chinese. These boundaries have become increasingly pronounced and freighted in recent decades owing largely to NEP-era practices highlighting race in the allocation of scarce government resources. The NEP is thus commonly regarded as having encouraged cultural assertiveness—some would say chauvinism—among Malays (Chandra Muzaffar 1987, Zainah Anwar 1987, Willford 2006). This cultural assertiveness is especially evident as regards Islam, the practice of which, along with speaking the Malay language and observing Malay "custom" (*adat*), is a defining feature, and increasingly *the* key symbol, of Malayness. More broadly, scholars generally view the *dakwah* movement as a powerful vehicle for the articulation of moral opposition to government development policies, traditional as well as emergent class structures, other ethnic groups, or some combination of these or related phenomena (Shamsul A.B. 1983, Nagata 1984, Chandra Muzaffar 1987, Zainah Anwar 1987, Muhammad Abu Bakar 1987, Husin Mutalib 1993, Peletz 1997, 2002).

Dakwah organizations are highly diverse and their objectives are in certain respects mutually incompatible. However, they all share an overriding concern to revitalize or reactualize (local) Islam and the (local) Muslim community by encouraging stronger commitment to the teachings of the Quran and the *hadith*, in order to effect a more Islamic way of life (*din*). So, too, does the major opposition party, PAS (Parti Islam Se-Malaysia; the Pan-Malaysian Islamic Party), the successor to the Hizbul Muslimin (Islamic Party) formally inaugurated in 1948, which has a decidedly populist orientation and has been a key player in Malaysian politics since shortly after its formation in 1951. Strictly speaking, PAS is not part of the *dakwah* movement, though many of its objectives are espoused by some segments of the movement. The most basic of these objectives is the creation of an Islamic state with the Quran and the Sunnah as its constitution.

The relationships between the various segments of the movement and the state merit careful consideration, for they have fueled many political and religious dynamics in contemporary Malaysia. PAS, for example, has frequently charged the ruling party (UMNO, the United Malays National Organization) with failing to safeguard the interests and well-being of the Malay community, especially with regard to Islam. PAS has also claimed that the ruling party has sold out to local Chinese and Indians as well as foreign capitalists, all of whom are seen as having contributed both to Malaysia's underdevelopment and dependence on foreign markets and to its moral decadence and spiritual bankruptcy.

In such a religious and political climate the ruling party has to work overtime to validate its Islamic credentials—relegitimize the party and the state—and thus coopt, or at least undercut, both the Islamic resurgents and the opposition party. This means going forward with its own far-reaching, but ultimately rather moderate Islamization program, which is simultaneously a consequence of the *dakwah* phenomenon and a key factor in its promotion along state- and regime-friendly lines. This program to "out-Islamicize" the opposition, which does at times have those qualities of an arms race that Gregory Bateson (1936), in a very different context, referred to as "schismogenesis," has included: the creation of an international Islamic university, an Islamic stock market, and a nation-wide system of Islamic banking and insurance (all geared ultimately toward meeting the material and other needs of the urban middle classes and assuring them that one can be both authentic Muslims and members of a modern middle class); the building and refurbishing of prayer houses and mosques; the passage of countless legislative measures bearing on Islam and Islamic law specifically; the cooptation of charismatic Muslim intellectuals, partly by offering them influential posts in the administration; and the "Islamization" of Kuala Lumpur's monumental architecture and skyline. Broadly speaking, state strategies overseen by Mahathir succeeded in undercutting PAS and other Islamist groups (e.g., ABIM), and in retaining the support of urban middle-class Malays who are most responsive to *dakwah* appeals. So too to some degree have the strategies of his hand-picked successor, Abdullah Badawi, who assumed office in October 2003 and achieved success during the first few years of his tenure as prime minister through a combination of neoliberal economic reasoning, authoritarian governance, and the promotion of a moderate and relatively inclusive and progressive (though strongly heteronormative) Islam.[33]

A more general, comparative point to emphasize is that cultural-political dynamics in contemporary Malaysia have a good deal in common with dynamics reported for other Muslim-majority nations such as Indonesia and Egypt. National elites in all three of these countries (like their counterparts in many other Muslim-majority settings) tend to be committed to variously defined projects of modernity that seek both the development of educated hence economically competitive urban middle classes and the revitalization or reactualization of the "essence" of real or imagined Islamic traditions. In Malaysia as elsewhere in the Muslim world, widely ramifying debates revolve around whether the "essence" in question entails core Islamic values such as justice, equity, and humility, which is more or less the position of Malaysia's ruling party (UMNO), or, as others, including the country's main opposition party (PAS), would have it, programs of Islamic law that encompass the specific subset of crimes and punishments known as *hudud* that involve harsh physical punishments for certain criminal offenses—amputation for theft, flogging for fornication, stoning to death for adultery, and so on.

The broader context in Malaysia as elsewhere involves a nexus of developments that is currently transforming much of the "modernizing southern hemisphere:" massive out-migration from rural to urban areas coupled with a rapid growth of urban middle classes; a more or less simultaneous expansion of secondary and tertiary educational institutions as well as factories and worker housing complexes, all of which afford opportunities for new types of interactions between males and females and all varieties of sexual experimentation and play; and the monetization of social relationships coupled with the commercialization of almost all aspects of life, including the most intimate. More generally, global circulations of diverse forms of capital and technology—and of workers, tourists, and other consumers from the West, the Middle East, East Asia, and other locales—have spawned disparate discourses that have contributed to a mind-boggling proliferation of standards and choices bearing on social relationships, presentation of the self, care of the body, and the most basic and intimate modalities of pleasure and desire. In this context, families and households along with the bodies and minds of individuals (and many other locally relevant units) emerge as target and terrain for the competing and at times mutually contradictory projects of different groups of political and religious elites. These dynamics in turn give rise to the often mind-jarring juxtapositions encountered by consumers of media- and cityscapes that Walter Benjamin (1936 [1968]) famously noted as one of the consequences of print capitalism and newspapers specifically (cf. B. Anderson 1991, Appadurai 1996, de Certeau 1984). Descriptions and analyses of such juxtapositions are standard fare in culturally oriented treatises on globalization and anthropological accounts of the "Other," though no less thought-provoking for having become somewhat *de rigeur.*

The August 11, 2002 issue of *The Star* (*Sunday Star*), an English-language newspaper that enjoys wide circulation in Malaysia, especially in Kuala Lumpur and other urban areas, provides graphic illustration of the kinds of cultural juxtapositions, standards, and choices that currently barrage Malaysians on a daily basis. Page 6, for example, leads off with a story written by a Malay (Mustafa Kamal Basri), entitled "Terengganu Plans Syariah Jails," which focuses on plans by officials in the then PAS-controlled state of Terengganu to build prison facilities for people convicted or suspected of violating *syariah* laws, including the *hudud* laws that Terengganu officials were seeking (unsuccessfully, as it turns out) to have implemented throughout the state. Vying for the reader's attention, indeed, right below the article on "*syariah* jails," is a large color photograph of Austin Powers, "the swinging London spy" (played by Mike Myers), who directly engages the reader with his "twinkling" eyes and infectious signature "grin" (a crooked, toothy smile that lights up his face but seems as much snarl and grimace as anything else) while sitting in the driver's seat of a 1960s-style car identified in the caption as his "time-travelling 'Pimpmobile.'" The headline of the article adjacent to the photograph, "Yeah Baby! Austin Powers Is Coming Soon," advertises the upcoming nation-wide release of "Austin Powers in Goldmember," which, as the text of the article (written by Chinese journalist Renee Choong) makes clear, "squash[ed] recent rumours that the movie," described as "hugely popular," had been banned.

Most of the remainder of page 6 is devoted to an advertisement headlined, "Menopause: Does Nutrition Play a Role?" Targeting Chinese women in particular, this ad underscores the importance to "women after 40" of including in their daily diet herbal extracts and nutritional supplements so as to ameliorate the "troublesome symptoms" of menopause and "enhance quality of life during menopause and the decades afterward." Filling up the remaining space is a short article that appears under the headline, "Govt to Go After Those Responsible for Attack." This article (which carries no byline) reassures readers that the authorities will track down and apprehend the group of "about 20 Thais," described as "rice smugglers," who attacked Malaysian police in Rantau Panjang, near Kelantan's border with Thailand; that "border patrols would be increased" as would cooperation between Malaysian and Thai officials; and that the overall situation was "deplorable" owing to the "possible riot" caused by "up to 100" locals who "swamped the area during …[the] commotion."

We see in this montage a nexus of intertwined themes. The most obvious include: (1) the need to better control serious crime through harsher Islamic punishments, the building of new prison facilities, and the hiring and training of volunteer wardens; (2) the existence of political contests and stalemates between different groups of elites (here state- and federal-level authorities, associated with PAS and UMNO, respectively) concerning the implementation of Islamic law and, more generally, the definition and place of Islam and Islamic morality in modern-day Malaysia; (3) the local availability and huge popularity of Western media products and attendant discourses emphasizing sexuality and all varieties of individualism, materialism, and hedonistic self-indulgence, which most Malays and many others in Malaysia (groups of youth being the major exception) view as altogether corrosive of public morality if not inherently crimeogenic; (4) the importance both of properly maintaining bodies (especially aging female bodies) and basic qualities of life, and of protecting them from processes threatening their decline (here the forces of "nature"); and (5) the need for additional vigilance (and resources) to police national boundaries so as to lessen their permeability and thus reduce criminality and deplorable developments conducive to "possible riots" and the breakdown of social order across the board.

Viewed from a different angle, one might see a much simpler, more straightforward message here, a message that simultaneously enjoins fear, insecurity, and consumption. Whichever of these or other messages the reader draws, page 6 of the August 11, 2002 edition of *The Star* provides us with a valuable optic through which to view a significant range of contemporary dynamics that shape both the milieu in which the Pink Triangle operates and the more encompassing contours of the struggle for sexual equality.

The Pink Triangle and the Urban/Sexual Communities it Serves

The ethnic and other diversity, and the mind-jarring juxtapositions I have outlined in the preceding pages are readily apparent in the offices and operations of the Pink Triangle, an activist-oriented outreach organization founded in 1987, which currently boasts around 50 paid staff, the vast majority of whom hail from the communities they serve. The business cards and much of the other literature that the Pink Triangle distributes tend to be printed in Malay and English, though some of their material is available in Chinese. This literature makes clear that the Pink Triangle is primarily concerned with five (formerly six) distinct though at times overlapping communities. The ethically neutral, medicalized, "social work"-style terminology deployed to refer to these communities is noteworthy for being more or less identical to the terminology employed by similarly oriented NGOs in Sydney, San Francisco, Johannesburg, and Rio de Janeiro. This is to say that it is part and parcel of an increasingly global discourse bearing on sexualities, bodily practices, and desires in the age of AIDS. The utilization of such discourse is one index of the Pink Triangle's cosmopolitan orientation. I suspect that it simultaneously heightens the organization's vulnerability in the fields of Malaysian cultural politics as a "Western outpost," hence a source of moral turpitude that is implicated in erosions of sovereignty and national decline.

In referring to the communities targeted by the Pink Triangle for educational outreach and other services, I will use the terminology and abbreviations utilized by Pink Triangle staff and their publication in the first few years of the new millennium, much of which remained unchanged through my 2008 visits to their offices. In the official language of the Pink Triangle, these communities are as follows: (1) Men Who Have Sex with Men (also known by the abbreviation MSM); (2) Commercial Sex Workers; (3) Intravenous Drug Users (collectively referred to as IDUs); (4) Transsexuals; and (5) People Living with AIDS (who, as a group, are often designated as PLWA). Another community that is targeted by their services according to some but not all of their official literature is (6) Women Who Have Sex with Women, sometimes referred to by the abbreviation WOW, which stands for Women on Women. As suggested by its name, the WOW branch of Pink Triangle does not assume that women who have sex with women necessarily self-identify as *homosexual* or *lesbian*, or in terms of other locally relevant categories. In this they are like the MSM branch, which eschews the assumption that men who have sex with men invariably self-identify as *homosexual*, *gay*, or *pondan*. The fact that WOW is listed on some of the Pink Triangle's publications but not others—and by the time of my 2008 trip to Malaysia had been formally discontinued, apparently because the women involved in the program did not feel that it was sufficiently attentive to their needs and interests—points to the marginalization of lesbians within the organization as a whole. More importantly, it signals the marginalization, even within the sexual underworld—and the world of NGOs ostensibly geared toward serving those who find themselves situated beyond the charmed circle—of the community composed of women who have sex with women.

To appreciate the challenges faced by the Pink Triangle as well as their heroic efforts to create a more just, equitable, and caring society, we need to know something of the services they provide. Briefly stated, these include: educational outreach geared toward condom use, safe sex, and other forms of harm reduction, as well as counseling and referral for a broad range of occupational/economic, medical, and legal issues. In addition, the Pink Triangle sponsors social events and fundraisers; staffs telephone hot-lines, shower facilities, and "safe havens" for anyone in need; and provides bleach kits to help disinfect syringes and needles. To round out the picture we need to have some sense of the demographic and sociological contours of the communities Pink Triangle staff seek to educate and otherwise assist and serve. The rough sizes and ethnic and class compositions and structural locations of such communities, for example, are important to try to estimate, even if the estimates are highly tentative.

The size of the MSM population in the city and the country as a whole is understandably difficult to gauge in light of the repressive political climate in recent years coupled with the existence of both secular and Islamic laws that criminalize same-sex relations; for obvious reasons, men who have sex with men don't rush forward to be counted. Some Pink Triangle staff and other knowledgable professionals and activists have told me that the MSM population amounts to at least 5,000 in Kuala Lumpur, whose overall population is about 1.6 million, and at least 20,000 in Malaysia as a whole. I should add, though, that these are very conservative estimates; others suggest figures that are five to ten times higher. Chinese, who constitute the largest ethnic group in Kuala Lumpur, also comprise the majority of those who attend Pink Triangle functions oriented toward the MSM community. But Pink Triangle staff assured me that they do not therefore assume that the majority of MSM in the city or the more encompassing Klang Valley area (whose population exceeds seven million) are in fact Chinese. For a variety of reasons, Chinese MSM in the Kuala Lumpur region, most of whom are of the working class, may simply be more inclined to take advantage of Pink Triangle's programs than their Malay or Indian counterparts.

Such may also be true of the community of women who have sex with women, which may be roughly similar in size to the MSM population and does in any event appear to be predominantly Chinese, though this may reflect the preponderance of Chinese in the Kuala Lumpur area, the greater involvement of Chinese in activities and organizations geared toward women who love women (and in the world of NGOs generally), or both. The various communities formerly subsumed under the Pink Triangle's WOW rubric are characterized by a great deal of heterogeneity with respect to class and ethnicity (even though, as noted, Chinese appear to predominate, if only in numbers), and with respect to self-identification in terms of sexual/gender identities and erotic orientations. Some members of these communities self-identify as *lesbian* or *dyke*, others as *tomboy*, *peng-kid* (sometimes rendered as *pengkid* or *pengkit*; from the English "punk kid"), *butch*, or *femme*, or in terms of two or more of these labels. There are also women who have sex with women who do not draw upon any of these labels in thinking about or referring to themselves or like-minded souls (broadly defined), partly because they have little if any knowledge either of like-minded others or of the terminologies that they utilize to designate themselves and the communities with which they identify.

The Malaysian Chinese social activist, community organizer, and scholar who profiled these communities in an important 1996 article (co-authored with "A.R") under the pseudonym Rais Nur, describes herself both as "an androgynous Malaysian lesbian feminist" and a "fairly out lesbian" (Reinfelder 1996:xi). Rais emphasizes that "butch/femme roles" in particular are "taken very seriously" by Malaysian lesbians, in sharp contrast to the West, where one sometimes encounters frequent switching of sartorial styles and other gendered codes either "as a fashionable thing to do" or as "a way of subverting essentialist notions of sex and gender" or "parodying notions of identity/sexuality as stable and immutable rather than fluid and constantly changing" (Rais Nur and A.R. 1996:73). This kind of code switching tends not to occur in Malaysia, where "the emphasis on roles [within the lesbian community, broadly defined] is very restrictive, and those who resist defining themselves in such a way often find that they are treated with distrust and hostility by their peers, as are lesbians who change identifications" (ibid., 74).

The number of commercial sex workers in the Kuala Lumpur area and in Malaysia generally is also difficult to estimate. This is partly because secular law criminalizes solicitation, just as Islamic law criminalizes all varieties of pre- and extra-marital sex in addition to "illicit proximity" (*khalwat*), and, in some states (such as Kelantan), specifically singles out prostitution as a criminal offense as well. As with MSM, commercial sex workers don't rush forward to be counted. That said, sources suggest the existence (in the mid-1990s) of at least 16–22,000 sex workers in Kuala Lumpur, and perhaps as many as 142,000 in the country as a whole (Lim 1998:7). The vast majority are locally born women (mostly Chinese, though Malays constitute about a third of the locally born group). Of the foreign-born sex workers, Thais top the list in terms of sheer numbers, with Indonesians a close second and Filipinos a somewhat distant third.

Intravenous drug users (IDUs) make up another of the marginalized and at risk communities that the Pink Triangle aims to assist through educational outreach and other services. For mostly obvious reasons, including fear and experience of being shunned and incarcerated, their numbers are also hard to gauge with precision. The figures for this group that I have encountered exceed 180,000 for the nation as a whole, but these could well be unrealistically low (since they pertain only to *detected* IDUs). Most IDUs are young men, and the majority, by far, are Malay. This is the group that is at greatest risk for HIV/AIDS in the sense that most of the confirmed cases of HIV/AIDS in Malaysia were contracted from sharing contaminated syringes and needles.

Transsexuals, who are generally referred to as *mak nyah* (even though strictly speaking this term designates only male-bodied transsexuals)[34] are also targeted by the Pink Triangle for various kinds of services. Numbering between 5 to 7,000 in Kuala Lumpur and perhaps 20 to 30,000 in the country as a whole, most members of this community are Malays who were born in male bodies but feel they are female. Male-bodied transsexuals (*mak nyah*), who I focus on here because of the paucity of data on their female-bodied counterparts (*pak nyah*),[35] tend to dress as women and to seek sexual partners who self-identify as straight (or bisexual) men, never fellow *mak nyah* or those who identify as *gay*. Many *mak nyah* take female hormones as well as vitamin supplements that will lighten and beautify their skin; a small percentage have also had sexual reassignment surgery, but since such surgery is forbidden among Muslims in Malaysia, except for those born intersexed (hermaphroditic [*khunsa*]), these procedures are not viable options for most *mak nyah*. Some 65 to 70 percent of the city's *mak nyah* are involved in commercial sex work and are thus subject to multiple forms of stigma, risk, and harm. Extensive research by Teh Yik Koon (1998, 2002) suggests that most transsexuals in Malaysia are at best marginally employed, and that the majority have been beaten and/or rejected by their families, and arrested and jailed at least once, all of which is consistent with information I obtained from interviews with *mak nyah* in 2001, 2002, and 2008.

The interviews I have conducted with *mak nyah* indicate that some consider themselves women or "like women." All apparently use female pronouns in referring to themselves and other *mak nyah*, want to be addressed and treated like women, and assume the female/receptive role in sexual relations. They also eschew labels such as transvestite, cross-dresser, and *pondan*, feeling that each of these terms is derogatory or otherwise offensive because it diminishes or trivializes their subject-positions and subjectivities—by implying, for example, that *mak nyah* simply enjoy dressing as women on occasion and are in other relatively superficial ways given to female gestures, comportment, and the like, practices which they could cast off as easily as changing their clothes. These dismissive views reflect painful ignorance of their lived realities.

We come, finally, to the last of the six communities served by Pink Triangle, which is designated as people living with AIDS (PLWA). Malaysian Ministry of Health estimates indicate that this community consists of around 80,000 individuals (as of mid-2008), but the actual figures could be three to four times higher. The vast majority of confirmed cases of HIV/AIDS, some 73 percent of them, occur among intravenous drug users. (There may be some bias in these data, however, since those who utilize drugs and are incarcerated face mandatory testing for HIV/AIDS, whereas other sectors of the population do not and thus seek HIV/AIDS testing voluntarily or not at all, possibly skewing the data.) In 1995, men accounted for over 96 percent of the total infections reported, women making up the remaining 4 percent. By 2006, however, one of every seven new infections involved a female. Almost all of the latter cases have occurred among married women who contracted the virus from husbands involved in intravenous drug use.

The figures on HIV/AIDS, prostitution, and the like that I have cited for Malaysia may strike some readers as relatively low, especially when compared to the distressing figures from neighboring Thailand (or Burma), not to mention the terribly grim statistics reported for India, China, and Sub-Saharan African countries like South Africa and Zimbabwe. In Thailand, where there may be as many as 2,000,000 women involved in commercial sex work, the number of cases of HIV/AIDS hovers around 600,000.[36] Such figures obviously dwarf those I have cited for Malaysia, but these comparisons are in some respects altogether irrelevant—at least or especially as far as Malaysians are concerned. Malaysia is after all a much less populous country (just over a third the size of Thailand), with a very different history and course of development. And its economy is far less dependent than Thailand's on tourism, which figures prominently in the demand side of the sex industry that has fueled Thailand's AIDS epidemic. On the other hand, the scope of Thailand's problems are quite relevant to Malaysians inasmuch as they serve as a grim warning of what the Malaysian future could conceivably hold. Because Malaysia and Thailand share an extremely porous border, Thailand necessarily looms large in Malaysian imaginaries and in the Malaysian state's strategies to police its citizens and national borders. This is especially so in the aftermath of September 11 and in the wake of the US "war on terror" which has seen renewed attention focused on the growing militance and escalating violence in Thailand's southern/ Muslim provinces (McCargo 2008). Particularly relevant here are brothels in Bangkok that cater specifically to Malaysians (Bishop and Robinson 1998:102) and the steady trickle of Malay and other Malaysian men, mostly married, who travel from northern Malaysian states like Kelantan to Thai border towns such as Sungei Golok for short-term assignations and typically resume relations with Malaysian women on their return.

Official Discourses on Communities in the Urban/Sexual Underground

In light of the information I have provided concerning the sizes and rough contours of the communities the Pink Triangle serves, it should be obvious that the staff of this small, under-budgeted NGO have their work cut out for them. It remains to make clear that the Pink Triangle receives a degree of support and official public recognition from the state for some—but not all—of its programs. At the risk of oversimplification, the state accords support and public recognition to the programs aimed at intravenous drug users, people living with AIDS, and, to a lesser extent, commercial sex workers, but *not* to the programs aimed at transsexuals, men who have sex with men, or women who have sex with women. One reason for this has to do with the nature of the discourses articulated by the country's political and religious elites. I gloss these as "official discourses," though not because they constitute an ostensibly "monolithic system ... [or] a finite set of texts" but rather because the term allows us to speak of "a series of ... [elite-generated] discourses, each adapted to a specific historical situation yet having in common certain elements with others" (Spurr

1993:1–2, cited in Proschan 2002a:438). Official discourses concerning the first two of these groups (IDUs and PLWA) are heavily biologized and medicalized in the sense that the reigning narratives bearing on their stigmatized bodily practices and the threats they pose to the well-being of society, race, and nation tend to be cast in biological and medical discourses keyed to the master symbols of physiological and/or psychological addiction and its consequences in terms of often fatal contagion. (Most cases of HIV/AIDS, recall, are contracted through the sharing of contaminated syringes and needles.) Narratives bearing on commercial sex workers are not biologized or medicalized in the same way; they do not focus on addiction, for example. But commercial sex workers are also seen as needing medical treatment and therapy, including moral and specifically religious (i.e., Islamic) reeducation. In short, because the discourses bearing on these three communities are medicalized, their members are accorded a degree of acceptance and legitimacy that they would otherwise be denied.

What then of the official discourses bearing on the other three groups, namely transsexuals, men who have sex with men, and women who have sex with women? Are they biologized or medicalized as well, with some of the same implications for a measure of social acceptance? The short answer is: it depends which of these groups one is talking about. Transsexuals tend to be portrayed in state-controlled media and other public venues as suffering from an unfortunate physiological and/or psychological condition that is "not their fault;" hence they are seen as needing medical treatment, psychological counseling, moral and religious guidance, and, no small matter here, understanding and acceptance from the Muslim community and society at large. However, this is not to say that in the official view of things they should be allowed to cross-dress or that the secular and Islamic laws bearing on cross-dressing and impersonating a member of the "opposite sex" should be rescinded. The point is simply that because they are seen as suffering from a biological/medical condition that is "beyond their control," they should be accorded understanding and respect, and treated insofar as possible like anyone else, or at least like others situated at the outer reaches of the charmed circle.

Two other dynamics merit brief remark here insofar as they help motivate public views of male-bodied transsexuals that are far more positive than public views of same-sex relations involving phenotypic males who are not transsexuals. The first has to do with the folkloric and touristic appeal of certain communities of transsexuals and their public ritual celebrations. A case in point involves the 500-strong group of Hindu transsexuals who gathered at Sri Karumarlamman temple in Klang in mid-2001 to celebrate the traditional full-moon festival (Paurnami Madha Villa) and to give thanks to Jai Mataji, the Mother God and protector of transsexuals.[37] This celebration, which drew transsexual Hindu devotees from all over Malaysia—and from Singapore and as far away as London—involved lavish and colorful dress, along with song, dance, prayer, and offerings and refreshments of various kinds. As might be expected in a country that is in many respects committed to multiculturalism, the festival was reported more or less respectfully and rather matter of factly in the state-controlled press, which saw fit to include flattering photos. And it appears to have proceeded without any hitches or negative repercussions for the participants. Many of the same generalizations pertain to secular beauty contests involving transsexuals, particularly if the official rationale for holding them is to raise money for one or another socially acceptable and compelling cause such as helping PLWA. It should be recalled, though, that these secular pageants are occasionally raided by the police, as are more conventional beauty contests. What is most interesting about these raids is that the authorities typically arrest the Muslim contestants but not the non-Muslims who participate in the pageants. This suggests that the patrolling of religious and racial boundaries and more encompassing hierarchies is of highest priority, and clearly more compelling than the surveilling of national morality per se—or, put differently, that the safeguarding of national morality is construed by political and religious elites as more or less isomorphic with the policing of religious and racial boundaries bearing on Malay Muslims and the (Malay-Muslim dominated) hierarchies to which they are keyed.

The second dynamic that is relevant to official views of transsexuals being more positive than official views of men defined as homosexual or gay has to do with the gendering both of mak nyah and of their erotic relationships with others. Male-bodied transsexuals are not entirely assimilated to the category "male" (lelaki); more generally, they consider themselves and are seen by others as both "less male" and "more female" than any other culturally salient community of phenotypic males. Because mak nyah are viewed as different from "normal" males (and from females) and are sometimes held to comprise a "third sex" or "third gender" ("females trapped inside male bodies"), their sexual relations with normatively gendered males, while homosexual from a culturally muted anatomical perspective, tend to be construed as heterogender. As such, they are easily accommodated within the implicit heterogender matrix that for many centuries now has allowed for and in some (especially ritual) contexts encouraged sexual relations and marriage between individuals with similar anatomies assuming they were held to be differently gendered. The more general point is two-fold: first, a range of practices and desires that fit comfortably within a heterogender matrix has long been accorded legitimacy, at least if they involve(d) male-bodied individuals or transgendered ritual specialists (be they phenotypically male or female); and second, gender difference has long subsumed and encompassed sexual difference—associated with anatomy, physiology, sexual activity, and the like—rather than vice versa.

It remains to emphasize that the medical and therapeutic discourses that dominate many official narratives bearing on transsexuals as well as IDUs and PLWA are not invoked or otherwise implicated when it comes to men who have sex with men or women who have sex with women (assuming that transsexualism is not involved). One reason for this is that participation in same-sex sexual relations that are viewed by society at large as homogender (due, for example, to the fact that one or both partners to the relationship cultivates an androgynous persona that undercuts heterogender distinctions) tends to be seen in terms akin to a "life-style choice," the emphasis being on the issue of "choice." Partly for this reason, and partly because same-sex sexual relations of a homogender sort tend to be regarded as an altogether unacceptable entailment of modernity and the transnational flows of goods, services, discourses, and technologies that is a hallmark of globalizing dynamics driven by Western forces and interests, men who have sex with men and women who have sex with women receive far less moral and other support from society at large than do transsexuals. For the same general reasons, state agents are disinclined to grant public recognition and legitimacy to Pink Triangle programs dealing with these communities.

The Struggle for Sexual Equality

I mentioned earlier that the Pink Triangle is involved in the struggle for sexual equality in ways that the vast majority of other progressive and cosmopolitan NGOs in Malaysia are not. This generalization raises a number of questions, one of which concerns what the Pink Triangle actually does either to help bring about cultural-political conditions conducive to sexual equality, or, put differently, to ameliorate the climate of inequality long tolerated and in many respects promoted by state laws and policies coupled with extra-legal initiatives undertaken by national political and religious elites. In answering this question we might begin with the most general and in some ways most obvious point: the mere existence of the Pink Triangle as a "self-consciously non-governmental" organization cannot help but challenge the legitimacy of the state's (usually implicit) claim that "the state alone is properly responsible for all political and social action" (Lev 1990:151). This is no small matter in a context such as Malaysia, where the social contract that the state "offers" its citizens in return for unwavering loyalty entailing political silence is said to include all varieties of protection and pastoral care. This questioning of the state's claims to a "patrimonially conceived monopoly of political legitimacy" (ibid.), one that defines the state as the sole legitimate actor with respect to social and political action, becomes all the more subversive of state legitimacy when we factor into the mix that the communities the Pink Triangle serves are composed of people whose sexual and other bodily practices present serious, life-threatening risks (both to themselves and to their families and to the Malaysian "race" and nation alike) that are not being dealt with adequately by other institutions, including, most obviously, those of the state. Moreover, if such communities are among the most marginalized in society, and if one measure of the validity of a state's claims to legitimacy involves assessing what actions the state takes on behalf of its most marginalized populations—those occupying the bottom rungs of the ladder(s) of graduated sovereignty—then *ipso facto* the very existence of the Pink Triangle raises serious questions not only about the state's most general claims to legitimacy, but also about the legitimacy of the specific discourses bearing on the culturally interlocked domains of gender and sexuality that it seeks to instantiate. To put some of this differently, the Pink Triangle's promotion of sexual rights as human rights "symbolically identifies governmental irresponsibility and untrustworthiness and links reformers to an international network of political and ideological support" (ibid.)

The Pink Triangle's involvement in the struggle for sexual equality also proceeds along more concrete, largely community-based lines, even though it tends not to organize or participate in public demonstrations or marches let alone ACT-UP-style confrontations with authorities or members of the public. Some of these activities involve formal and informal networking in efforts to raise the consciousness of family members and others who deal directly with the ravages of AIDS. Other activities focus on raising money both from the private sector and from international sources. Members of the Pink Triangle also work with doctors, lawyers, social workers, and individuals and organizations in the fashion, entertainment, and hotel industries, in efforts to build grass-roots support for the communities they serve. And of course the Pink Triangle works closely with organizations such as the Malaysian AIDS Council, which endeavors to carry their message throughout the country.

The Pink Triangle also provides medical and other care, and, in some instances, housing, for the sick and dying who have been abandoned by family members, medical personnel, and others; helps them attend to their prayers and other religious obligations (especially important for Muslims); recites the *Yasin* (the thirty-sixth *sura* or "chapter" of the Quran, according to the traditional arrangement of *sura*) for Muslims who are terminally ill; takes care of the burial and other funeral expenses of members of the communities they seek to assist; and helps see to it that the final wishes of those near death are honored. These activities, along with others mentioned earlier (providing counseling and referral for medical, legal, and economic issues, shower facilities, and telephone hotlines, education aimed both at these communities and the general public) help convey the message that the members of the communities they serve are fully human and merit the same humane treatment as other members of society. In this, their activities pose a direct challenge to the discourses of the state, which contribute directly to many Malaysians falling through the cracks.

To flesh out the claim that the Pink Triangle is involved in the struggle for sexual equality in ways that the vast majority of other progressive and cosmopolitan NGOs in Malaysia are not requires noting in addition that many progressive NGOs that might ally themselves publicly with the Pink Triangle have avoided doing so, and have likewise refrained from taking up the issue of sexual rights as human rights. In this regard, Malaysian dynamics of pluralism and civil society are markedly less robust than their counterparts in Sulawesi, Java, and other regions of Indonesia, though so too are the outbursts of decidedly uncivil violence (some sectarian and/or communal, others more squarely criminal) that periodically plague parts of Indonesia. The extremely influential group of Muslim feminists known as Sisters in Islam, for example, has lobbied effectively for the legal and other rights of Malay and other Muslim women, and the rights of women generally. But due partly to its Faustian pact with state authorities, it has focused most of its efforts on the rights of women in the context of marriage, attempting to reform laws on polygyny, for example, and to reduce the delays and other obstacles and inequities wives face in Islamic courts (Zainah Anwar 2001, Peletz 2002, 2005, Ong 2006: Chap. 1). It has, more generally, agreed to the state-mandated stipulation that it can continue to exist as long as it limits its membership (there are currently only two dozen or so formal members of Sisters in Islam) and refrains from activities that might galvanize any kind of mass movement.

Many of these same generalizations apply to the All Women's Action Society (known by the acronym AWAM) and to other nationally well-known organizations such as *Aliran*, *Suaram*, and *Keadilan*. AWAM, for instance, has published a critically important analysis and policy statement concerning the serious problem of rape in Malaysia (Alina Rastam 2002), and has worked to safeguard and expand women's rights in a variety of domains. I want to make clear that I am not questioning the valuable accomplishments of these NGOs. They are, indeed, of vital significance. I do want to emphasize, however, that in the public positions they articulate, such organizations operate with notions of sexuality that are shackled to a narrowly defined calculus of biological repro- duction that makes no provision for sexual desire, pleasure, or play outside the context of heterosexual marriage. Due partly, perhaps, to their involvement in coalitionist politics and strategic alliances with the ruling party long dominated by Mahathir, who is known to have a strong personal dislike of same-sex sexu- ality, these and related NGOs tend to be silent and/or hostile when it comes to a woman's—or a man's—participation in consensual sexual relations with another adult of the same sex.[38]

Needless to say, such silences are not characteristic of the Pink Triangle. With a few notable exceptions, the latter organization is essentially "out there all alone" in advocating the fair treatment of all members of society, regardless of sexual/gender identity or erotic orientation. The fact that the vast majority of progressive NGOs in Malaysia—and all of the country's political parties— are opposed to defining sexual rights as human rights even when they espouse one or another form of gender equality, points to one of the ways Malaysian- style visions and instantiations of modernity differ from their Western counter- parts: Gender equality *is* acceptable and desirable as far as large and increasing numbers of Malaysians are concerned, sexual equality is *not*.

The overall dynamics are more complicated and arguably more hopeful than suggested thus far, for I have yet to say anything of substance about Marina Mahathir, an extremely energetic and accomplished media specialist and activist as well as the daughter of the man who recently completed over two decades of service as Malaysia's prime minister. Marina served as the president of the Malaysian AIDS Council from 1994 to 2004 and is without question one of the most influential women in the entire nation. It is extremely fortunate for the staff of the Pink Triangle and all of the communities they seek to represent that she is one of their most vociferous and articulate defenders. Educated partly in Europe, widely viewed as a "patron saint," and explicitly likened to Lady

Diana on account of her tireless efforts on behalf of the country's marginalized communities, Marina regularly weighs in against discrimination and intolerance of all varieties. (This partly through a weekly column in the widely read daily, *The Star*.) Her primary objectives, however, are to promote personal and collective empowerment of the sort advocated by media moguls in the West like Oprah Winfrey. As Marina repeatedly made clear in the course of our interviews (conducted in 2001 and 2002), Oprah is one of the world's public figures she most respects and admires.

Significantly, in October 1998 Marina used the considerable symbolic and other resources at her disposal to publicly denounce the explicitly anti-homosexual organization known as PASRAH, which, as noted earlier, was founded by some of her father's supporters shortly after he engineered the arrest of his deputy prime minister (Anwar), on largely bogus charges of sodomy and corruption. Marina's discursive strategies in such contexts are of broad comparative and theoretical interest insofar as she invokes the sentiments, dispositions, and values conducive to racial tolerance and ethnic pluralism and attempts to scale them up by transposing them to an ever broader social canvas.

This scaling up is one of the key processes involved in the expansion of pluralism and civil society, as scholars have emphasized with reference to analogous dynamics in other regions of the world as diverse as Italy, Indonesia, and the US (see, for example, Putnam 1993, 1995, Evans 1996, and Hefner 2000, 2005). More generally, taking stock of forums and dynamics conducive to these processes is (at least potentially) of far greater significance than a body count of NGOs arrayed in opposition to the state (Hefner 1998, 2000). This is doubly true in cultural political contexts such as Malaysia. For as Marina and a veteran Pink Triangle staffer who is a leading spokesperson for the nation's *mak nyah* community made clear to me, most Malaysians view public demonstrations and confrontational politics of the sort that are commonplace in the West as both offensive and inappropriate—and likely to be altogether counterproductive. This means that foreign scholars, journalists, human rights workers, and activists looking for evidence of Malaysian patterns of resistance to heteronormativity or other institutional arrangements that are intrinsic (or keyed) to structures of domination need to look beyond the usual quarters (e.g., public protest, collective or otherwise) and consider "backstage" and "underground" arenas involving "hidden transcripts," much as James Scott (1985, 1990) has suggested. It also means that we need to pay particularly close attention to practices involving discursive transpositions of the sort for which Marina has become justly renowned and revered. Contra Scott and many of his interlocutors, such practices may be exceedingly public and straightforward, in the sense that they do not involve "topsy-turvy" fantasies or millennial reversals, but are no less subversive of established inequities.

At least equally telling in all of this is that Marina holds no formal position in the machinery of governance and has seen her own media productions censored by the Ministry of Information and the highly secretive Censorship Board (e.g., when one of her scheduled television broadcasts included a portion of an interview with a young woman who spoke in positive terms of her sexual relationship with another woman). These circumstances point to the highly tenuous, partly because thoroughly uninstitutionalized, nature of the support that exists for individuals and communities who transgress heteronormative ideals. This support is all the more precarious in a milieu such as Malaysia, which has been dominated in recent decades by political and religious elites who have endeavored via legal and political initiatives and various kinds of cultural struggles to institutionalize heteronormativity, heterosexism, and homophobia as national policies. A more general, theoretical point that bears on the development of pluralism and civil society in Malaysia and far beyond is that in present-day Malaysia there are few channels or mechanisms through which pluralistic sentiments originating among citizens, including those with "strings" (or "cables" [*kabel*] in local parlance), can effectively inject them into the institutionalized workings of the state. Put differently, while this injection, feedback, or synergy is necessary for the expansion of pluralism and civil society, it exists in relatively short supply in contemporary Malaysia, not to mention certain other places we discussed earlier such as Burma.

Engaging "Tolerance," Open Secrets, and Governmentality

Thus far in this chapter we have considered the ways in which various groups of political and religious elites along with certain NGOs and nationally prominent figures have endeavored to negotiate selected features of difference, identity, and legitimacy in Malaysia at the turn of the twenty-first century. In the remainder of the chapter I provide additional—"ground-level," actor-oriented—perspectives on these negotiations, though I should make clear at the outset that the perspectives in question derive from highly cosmopolitan urban-dwelling activists, each with at least a few years of Western education, and that their experiences and perceptions cannot necessarily be generalized to all Malaysians—gay, lesbian, or otherwise. My goal in the pages that follow is to illustrate the ways in which individuals occupying specific subject positions engage (experience, understand, help transform) Malaysia's much touted "tolerance," the flip side of the repression that I have focused on in this chapter. We shall see that they do so partly by participating in the construction of collective social fictions ("open secrets") that facilitate their creation of meaningful identities in the context of a cultural-political climate characterized by extremely arbitrary governmentality, which scholars such as Giorgio Agamben (2005) see as a disturbing if not defining characteristic both of late modernity and of the global spread of neoliberalism in particular (cf. Ong 2006).

Before turning to the interview material that comprises much of the remainder of this chapter, I want to underscore that it is easy to misconstrue Malaysia's cultural-political climate from afar, especially if one relies overly much on the perspectives of scholars and foreign journalists given to eliding distinctions between legal and political initiatives on the one hand, and their actual implementation (if any) on the other. Cultural-political dynamics in the east coast states of Terengganu and Kelantan provide a case in point. We have seen that the PAS-controlled governments in each of these states have endeavored to expand the jurisdiction of *syariah* in recent years, with Kelantan drafting legislation in 1993 that, if successfully implemented, would have introduced harsh *hudud* codes that specify amputation of limbs for theft, flogging for fornication, stoning to death for adultery, and so on. The proposed legislation would also make it a criminal offense for women to engage in sexual relations with one another. Terengganu's state government followed suit around 1999, claiming that Islamic law and the moral codes entailed therein offer a much preferred alternative to the secular law regimes promoted by the ruling party that had long proved to be patent failures, judging especially from the prevalence of society-wide moral slides, widespread corruption, and crimes against women in particular. Kelantan is also well known, at least among some Malaysians and many Malaysia watchers, as a place of extreme gender segregation, as evidenced by the presence in some supermarkets of gender-segregated checkout lines, as well as gender-segregated hair salons, and the like.

When one looks more closely at on-the-ground realities, one sees a somewhat different picture. During a week-long visit to Kelantan in 2002, for example, I observed one supermarket in Kota Baru (the state capital) with gender-segregated checkout lines (eight in all) but did not see any such lines or analogous patterns elsewhere, with the unremarkable exception of public toilets. Each checkout line was identified by overhead signs of distinctively male or female headgear (a head adorned by a *songkok* signifying the "male line," a head framed by a mini-*telekung* denoting the "female line"). But even a few moments' observation made clear that neither shoppers nor store employees paid them all that much heed. Some middle-aged men followed women who appeared to be their wives into the "female only" line, for example, doing so without any discernible hesitation and without provoking any apparent consternation or sense of impropriety. I suspect that adolescent or adult females who mistakenly or otherwise found themselves in the "wrong (male) line" would not have occasioned much alarm either, as is true of youngsters I have observed in Negeri Sembilan sitting with the "wrong group" of children who form gender-segregated lines in front of the *imam* at the local mosque when he offers them after-school instruction in Quranic recitation (*mengaji*).

Arguably far more relevant is that the *hudud* law codes that state governments in Kelantan and Terengganu have sought to introduce have *never* been implemented in these states or anywhere else in Malaysia, despite the impression one sometimes receives from formal presentations at conferences and from research proposals and conversations involving Malaysia-watchers and others. *Hudud* legal codes have never attained the status of law in Malaysia due largely to opposition from the federal government, which is adamantly opposed to their introduction both on the East Coast and throughout the country as a whole. The fact that state political and religious leaders sought to have these laws introduced is definitely meaningful, and was certainly alarming to many non-Malays who feared they would be subject to Islamic law in family matters and much else. It did, moreover, provoke outrage among Muslim feminists and others on the grounds that the legal initiatives, if actually implemented, would prove highly detrimental to women owing to problems in meeting high evidentiary standards (the necessity of four credible witnesses in a case of rape, for example) that could result in their being found culpable of crimes they did not commit, such as *zina* (fornication/adultery), and thus subject to unwarranted punishment. At least equally significant though is that the legal initiatives in question never became the law of the land (and may never do so).

Further tempering if not shattering the stereotypes is that Kelantan's capital continues to be renowned for certain beaches that attract local Malay males (among others) seeking sexual liaisons with other males—despite the PAS-inflected moralities that prevail in certain quarters. Similarly, the islands off the shores of Terengganu continue to enjoy a reputation as places where young tourists from Malaysia and beyond come for snorkeling, scuba diving, turtle-watching, and partying. Some of the partying involves Westerners, especially Australians, whose sun-bathing attire or lack thereof sometimes offends the predominantly Malay locals who take offense at public displays of various kinds, including public nudity, public sex, public drunkenness, and public urination. More germane is the "open secret" that some of the rather wild partying that occurs in beach bungalows and similar digs involves groups of same-sex Malaysians, particularly males.

The first interview I want to discuss here involved one of the directors of the Pink Triangle, who I shall refer to as Kadir. In a 2002 interview (conducted mostly in English), forty-something Kadir recounted that he had been part of a group of "about twenty *gays*" who had recently taken a trip to one of the islands off Terengganu. They spent much of their time playing snooker, drinking beer, and dancing together, "many without their shirts on," he added. At one point he turned to one of his friends and asked rhetorically—and incredulously—"And do you realize we're in Terengganu, under *hudud* law?". The question thus posed elides the distinction noted earlier, between legal initiatives and on-the-ground realities; for as we have seen, *hudud* law has never been in effect in Terengganu or elsewhere in Malaysia. But given the thrust of Kadir's remarks (concerning the large group of Malaysian *gays* who partied for a few days without inviting unwanted attention), they are more revealing for highlighting both the dangers of generalizing from sensational headlines and other accounts erroneously suggesting the existence in Malaysia of *hudud* laws and the morality supposedly associated with them, and some of the remarkable silences, elisions, and contradictions in the fields of Malaysian public culture.

In the course of our conversation Kadir also mentioned having organized a separate three-to-four-day trip, with "some 30 to 40 *gays*," the term "*gays*" being used broadly here to encompass *mak nyah* and perhaps other gender transgressors and sexual outlaws who do not in fact self-identify as gay, much like the inclusive if not homogenizing designation *pondan*. Shortly after they arrived at their hotel, he realized that a group of *ulama* (Islamic religious scholars; sing. *alim*) who were attending a conference were also booked at the hotel, and that their stays overlapped by a day or so. Kadir related how one of the *alim* became interested in a *mak nyah* in his (Kadir's) party and even proposed to her that they go up to his room; this, according to Kadir, gave her the "fright of her life" and she ran away from him. In a similar (iconoclastic, subversive, and ironic) vein, Kadir related how transsexuals in Kuala Lumpur's Chow Kit neighborhood have told him that they "love it when the UMNO General Assembly convenes in town," because "it's great for business," adding a bit later in the conversation, "most Malays are bisexual," a comment that, given the context of our conversation, I took to refer to Malay males but not females.

I did not press Kadir on the possibility of hyperbole in the latter statement, taking it instead as a commentary both on the fluidity that he perceived and apparently experienced in Malay male sexuality, including his own, and on the relative tolerance he feels Malays exhibit toward sexual and gender variability, as compared with Chinese and Indians. The fact that Kadir is of mixed ethnic background (part Malay and part Chinese) is arguably relevant here. Because he is not fully Malay and is phenotypically (somewhat) Chinese, I suspect that Kadir is not fully accepted in all of the Malay circles in which he moves. Hence like others who sometimes find themselves on the "outside," he is not only more critical of the Malay-controlled power structure (including UMNO leaders, Islamic religious scholars, etc.) than Malays normally are, unless they strongly identify with one or another opposition party, but also more inclined to focus on what he takes to be hypocrisy on the part of political and religious elites. Interesting in this connection is Kadir's view that much if not most of the sodomy (his term) involving youth that occurs in Malaysia takes place in or around Islamic boarding schools (*pondok, pesantren*) and is initiated by religious teachers who sodomize their charges (typically young Malay boys). Noteworthy as well is that when I asked Kadir about the possibility of *sida-sida* existing in earlier times or at present in royal palaces in his native Johor, he claimed to know nothing of such roles or of any others from former times that might help legitimate the existence of contemporary Malaysians involved in sexual and gender diversity, as occurs in parts of Indonesia, Native North America, and elsewhere—only that in his experience all *mak andam* (wedding specialists) are *mak nyah*, as are those who perform "belly dances" (his term) at weddings. That said, he also commented with a smile that Tungku M., one of the grandsons of the first Agung (King), is "as *gay* as you can get; very, very *gay*." Kadir added that "he used to introduce his boyfriends as his 'bodyguards'" and that he never married. The extent to which one might reasonably generalize from these observations is subject to debate, as are some of Kadir's other remarks about the daughter of a sultan in a northern Malaysian state who is an out lesbian, having flaunted her erotic orientation to lesbian groups and having otherwise made little effort to conceal her sexual proclivities. Such remarks do in any case resonate with the sexual and gender diversity long associated with ruling families, royal palaces, and those in their employ.

Partly because I posed a series of question geared toward ascertaining how if at all the Anwar crisis had affected communities of gays, lesbians and the transgendered, we spoke a fair amount about changes in the cultural-political climate over the past few years and how he and others negotiate their identities and live their lives without drawing unwanted attention. Like numerous others I queried on these topics, Kadir was reluctant to generalize on many issues, such as whether most gays/lesbians/transgendered (hereafter "GLT," following his usage) people experienced discrimination or persecution in their own lives, preferring instead to look on the bright side, a useful survival strategy to be sure. In answer to one of my questions on the subject he maintained that he had never experienced any persecution on account of being gay, though he also made clear that he is not out to his family, his co-workers, or most others.

He said that much is "tolerated" and proceeded to mention five openly gay saunas and two openly gay discos that are frequently advertized in published sources bearing on the urban/sexual underground (*Blue Boy*, *Liquid*), in addition to well known cruising spots. He added that a tremendous amount of information is available on websites that can be accessed by initiating searches using the keywords "gay" and "Malaysia," and that the *mak nyah* community hosts beauty pageants a few times a year. Advertised mostly by word of mouth or on the Internet, these pageants are held in some of Kuala Lumpur's big hotels (such as the Federal). They are formally defined as "private" parties, but the hotel management, the authorities, and everyone else knows what and who these galas involve, especially since they attract and are sometimes publicly supported by the city's rich and famous and are frequently the occasion for upscale fundraisers to benefit worthy social causes, such as people living with HIV/AIDS.

Unlike neighboring Thailand, however, Malaysia has no gay newspapers, magazines, or other periodicals. And Kuala Lumpur's gay saunas, discos, and massage parlors are periodically raided by the police (as occurs elsewhere in the country as well)—every year or so, he estimated, in response to my question on the relative frequency of these occurrences. But so too he hastened to add are karaoke bars that cater to straight crowds, the larger issue being that the periodic shows of force are less crackdowns on gays per se than components of more broadly cast anti-vice campaigns carried out by the police and Islamic religious authorities in an attempt to "flush out" and apprehend "criminal elements" involved in drug use, solicitation, and the like. These blitzes often last a week or so, with authorities converging at one establishment one night, raiding another the following night, and so on. Due to the ubiquity of cellphones, those most Asian of accoutrements, the onset of a police raid at one locale is immediately broadcast both to the owners and likely patrons of similarly oriented venues that might be targeted, and to lawyers, members of the Bar Council, and others with strings or "cables." Consequently, the blitzes are not nearly as effective as they might be.

To illustrate the general point about "cables," Kadir related that when Anwar was sacked by Mahathir and charged with sodomy, he immediately telephoned Marina to ascertain if a campaign of persecution focusing on gays was under way. He also called Marina around the time (a little over a month later) that PASRAH announced its existence in a press conference, information about which was leaked to him by a friend in the media before it was reported in the newspapers. In both cases, Marina was ready with a counter-offensive, assuring him, "No, but don't make any official/public statements, don't do anything, stay low." Marina's public statement was extremely savvy, in that she focused on the issues of tolerance and discrimination, implying if not stating directly, "We cannot have intolerance and discrimination in a (multiethnic) society such as ours." She did not actually come out and say that Malaysians need to make space for and defend gay rights, though she did invoke the brutal gay-bashing and murder in the US around that time of Matthew Shepard, warning that Malaysia could conceivably degenerate to the level of the US. She focused instead on the compelling "slippery slope" argument: "Who might be next?" More generally, Kadir remarked on how humble and down to earth Marina is, typically driving herself around in her own small car, summing up his sentiments at one point by exclaiming enthusiastically, "She is marvelous, she's our Lady Diana!"

Kadir's previously noted comment that "most Malays are bisexual" appeared to be in response to one of my questions about whether tolerance had decreased or increased in the previous year or so. The implication of the remark was that because of their personal predilections for sexual diversity, Malays are inclined toward tolerance of sexual and gender variability in others, as long as it is not flaunted. "But we don't come out publicly and take the issues to the streets and advocate gay rights," implying that this would be quite counter-productive in Malaysia, especially since it would be anti-government or perceived as such. This theme came up at various points in our conversation: in many respects you can live your life as you wish and are quite alright—as long as you don't go against the government.

Kadir did not think much if anything had changed for the gay community since September 11, which proved to be a watershed for the Mahathir regime and for Malaysia generally, as discussed elsewhere (Peletz 2005). In this connection he mentioned an incident that could have given rise to a major scandal but did not, as did a number of others I interviewed in 2002. The incident began with a tabloid story reporting that the head of Puteri UMNO (the UMNO organization established on behalf of young women), was a lesbian, that she had a female lover, and that she had used UMNO funds to buy her lover a car. Kadir maintained, as did others I interviewed, that she is indeed a lesbian, that she does not hide it, that she drives to hotels in her fancy, well-known car, checks in and has trysts with her lover(s), and that no one really cares. When the story spilled over into the mainstream media, Keadilan, the opposition party headed by Dr. Wan Azizah (Anwar's wife), came out with a statement the gist of which was that she should take legal action against the tabloid (sue its owners) if the story is false and resign if it is true. The deputy prime minister (Abdullah Badawi), in contrast, apparently advised her to pursue a simpler course of action: just sue the tabloid. Interestingly, Prime Minister Mahathir is said to have counseled her to ignore the whole thing, telling her that it was simply a political ploy to pull her down. Not surprisingly, Mahathir did not heed his own advice; shortly thereafter his people revoked the tabloid's license to publish.

Arguably most significant about this case, especially when viewed alongside the Anwar affair, is that it illustrates both the arbitrary deployment of power by the executive branch and the key conditions that enable it, foremost among them being the excessive (unchecked and unbalanced) concentration of power and authority in that branch. "If Mahathir wants to make an issue of real or imagined 'deviant' sexual orientation, he will," and an Anwar-like debacle may follow, with all that was involved in perverting and undermining the judiciary and provoking a national political crisis. Alternatively, "if he chooses *not* to take action against the individual in question," because (unlike Anwar) he or she is a staunch ally, "he will simply ignore the whole thing" (the critical exception being the offending tabloid, which had its license revoked). A more general point about the architecture of Malaysian politics that Kadir underscored is that if Mahathir wanted all the gay venues—saunas, discos, bars, cruising spots, and so on—closed down, "they would be gone in an instant." "There are no laws on the books to preclude this kind of scenario," as Kadir pointed out, and even if there were, they could be ignored with impunity. I should add that the same is true under Mahathir's hand-picked successor (Abdullah Badawi), though this is not something Kadir and I discussed since the new prime minister had not yet taken over the reins of governance. A more or less identical situation obtains in neighboring Singapore, as well as in Burma, as we have seen, though my conversation with Kadir did not engage these latter subjects in any detail.

Scenarios of the sort described by Kadir bring to mind the dynamics that Weber had in view when he wrote of the arbitrariness and ultimate irrationality of "traditional" rule in Muslim societies, a patrimonial form of governance he glossed as "sultanism." Like "*kadi*-justice," which was characterized for Weber by ostensibly arbitrary, ad hoc, and irrational decision-making on the part of Islamic judges (*kadi*), Weber saw sultanism as an impediment to the development of rational capitalism, partly because it precluded safety of person, property, and profit, and thus hindered the growth of a relatively free-wheeling and autonomous middle class committed to rational capitalism. Weber thus felt that sultanism (and its absence) constituted a powerful explanation of difference between the developmental trajectories of East (largely failed) and West (mostly successful, except for their negative implications for the spirit of "brotherliness" and the psyche and soul). One of the many ironies of the Malaysian situation is that the Islamic courts overseen by *kadi* are far less arbitrary and corrupt than their secular counterparts (especially those dealing with high-stakes civil, as distinct from criminal, matters) which were bequeathed to Malaysians by British colonial authorities and continue to operate, at least in theory, on the basis of British (or British-derived) law and attendant "judicial customs" including the official use of English in the courtroom and (until relatively recently) judges' donning of black robes and powdered wigs. The same might be said of sultans (most of whom inherit their titles and prerogatives, and are largely ceremonial figure-heads) in relation to elected officials, who are ostensibly more like their Western counterparts.

Arguably more relevant than the substance and irony of these latter contrasts are the variegated ways in which arbitrary governmentality figures into the conceptual and analytic schemes of prominent social theorists such as Weber and Agamben. For Weber, arbitrary governmentality was the exception that explained failure to attain the (to him desired) norm, Western-style modernity driven by rational capitalism. For Agamben (2005), by contrast, writing nearly a century after Weber, arbitrary governmentality *is* the norm, particularly but not only in (late) modern Western states committed to or unwittingly swept up in projects of neoliberalism. For driven as they are by unrelenting concerns with transnational and other corporate profit, market "discipline," pro-business political cultures, and a "downsizing of democracy" (Duggan 2003), these invariably entail perennial states of exception where "necessity creates its own law"—and "all law is 'situational law'" (Agamben 1998:16, 2005:24), much as Weber erroneously claimed in his characterization of the workings of Islamic courts (Peletz 2002). In his recent (2005) work, Agamben focuses largely on the US and the implications of post-September 11 developments such as the Patriot Act for the institutions and culture of democratic governance. That many of his observations and insights are deeply relevant to Southeast Asian contexts is suggested by Kadir's (Agambenesque) remarks, by the Anwar affair, by the wholesale destruction, with little if any advance notice, of non-Muslim (especially Tamil Hindu) sites of worship and entire non-Muslim (especially Tamil Hindu) communities to make way for Kuala Lumpur's "development" (Willford 2006, Baxstrom 2008), and by everyday occurrences in Burma and Singapore (see also Ong 2006).

In response to my question about the feasibility of being out to one's family, Kadir remarked that only about 10 to 15 percent of gays in Malaysia are out to family members. Kadir, for example, is not out to his parents, at least he has never come out and told them explicitly. But he has lived with his lover for 16 years; they not only share a house, they sleep in the same room. His parents "must know," but they've never discussed it with him (and vice versa) and even if he were ready to tell them, he must ask "whether they are ready to hear the news." He mentioned a few times that the issue of coming out is very complicated, that people need to think not just of whether or not they are ready to come out, but "whether their parents and others are really ready to hear the news. It's selfish not to think of that." Referring to Malaysia but clearly commenting on the scene in the West as well, he said that he hears many gays speaking about "coming out as 'empowerment.'" But he feels that this is "often quite selfish: empowerment, blah, blah, blah .... Are the parents necessarily ready to hear all of this? So selfish."

Lots of gays and lesbians in Kuala Lumpur do in any case live with their lovers, though some reside with their parents. In Malay society, especially in urban areas away from one's hometown, it is actually much easier to live with someone of the same sex than with someone of the "opposite" sex. There's no issue of *khalwat* ("illicit proximity;" a criminal offense for Muslims in Malaysia) if a male stays with another male in the same hotel room, for example.

I discussed my dilemmas with respect to being an "expert witness" for asylum cases involving gay, lesbian, and transgendered Malaysians (addressed further in the Epilogue); for example, that the issue of persecution is not as straightforward as it seemed to be a few years earlier (e.g., 1998–2000), though one can look at developments in recent decades and over the long term and see clear trends entailing the declining legitimacy of once revered transgendered ritual specialists, as well as their stigmatization, criminalization and medicalization. During the Anwar episode, members of the gay community felt very much under siege and were petrified, partly because they did not know what was going to happen, and they are still anxious because of the laws, but at present they are not in a constant state of fear. If you let it (the political situation, the laws, etc.) bother you, it will. Otherwise you can ignore lots of it. That said, the low numbers of people who are out make clear that there is still much to be afraid of as far as most are concerned. Kadir, recall, is not out to his family or his colleagues at work, owing largely to the fact that he is a senior manager at a large, state-run enterprise and does not want to risk his job and career.

As to whether he is fearful of *hudud* and such: "there are so many other issues they [the government] has to address—drug use, illegal immigrant workers—realistically, this cannot be one of their priorities." He acknowledged, however, that if a crisis developed, it would pose serious problems, for "the GLT community is complacent. They don't think as a community. Nobody comes to the legal aid clinics we organize, and people don't take to the streets," the more general observation being that there are "many fence-sitters in Malaysian politics." If PAS came to power nationally, "they would have so many other things to do. I'm not worried about what they might do about homosexuality. In Kelantan and Terengganu, for example, they have never targeted or focused on homosexuality or transsexuals, even though there are well-known cruising spots right in Kota Baru. Recently, there was a big conference/seminar in Melaka on *mak nyah* that was organized by faculty at UKM [Universiti Kebangsaan Malaysia], partly because there are so many transsexuals on the UKM campus" whose existence raised questions in scholarly and other circles. "And people like Kartini and Sulastri [the country's most outspoken *mak nyah*] can go in and out of the country without any problems. It's being anti-government that poses the biggest threat."

Kadir also mentioned Singapore in this connection, suggesting that things are much better on the Malaysian side of the causeway than in that tightly controlled city-state. This is due partly to laws on slander and libel, many from the colonial era, which the Singaporean government famously invokes against political opponents (a strategy used to good effect in Malaysia as well). The other part of the problem is Singapore's deployment of undercover agents, outfitted in "short shorts" and the like, to entice and entrap gay men, who, if apprehended, are subject to fines up to S$20,000 and incarceration for as long as 20 years. (The logic and wording of the colonial-era statutes in question are basically the same as Malaysia's, as is also true of their counterparts in Burma, India, and Pakistan, falling under Section 377 of the National Penal Code, or its equivalent, in each of these former British colonies.) As far as most people are concerned, this kind of entrapment does not occur in Malaysia.

I want to conclude my remarks on this interview with a series of loosely related comments on networks. During our three-hour conversation, Kadir received a number of calls and text messages on his cellphone, thus reinforcing my sense that he was thoroughly enmeshed in a variety of different networks. As he gleefully reported to me at one point, one of the messages confirmed that the government had agreed to an enormous increase in its appropriations for the Pink Triangle: some M$4 million per year over the next ten years, compared with funding during the previous year that was on the order of M$120,000, if I understood correctly. Whether the Pink Triangle would receive all of the money allocated was of course a different story, as Kadir made clear; but the news was definitely cause for celebration, as was the success of the extensive networking and lobbying that helped bring it about.

Some caution is in order here, lest we mistakenly assume that these kinds of networks and the burgeoning subcultures with which they are associated are spread evenly across the capital or other large cities let alone the nation as a whole. Put differently, the fact that Kadir and the people with whom he is in regular contact are extensively involved in networking and other kinds of associational activities does not mean that the majority of people Kadir might want to mobilize either participate in such networks or associational opportunities, or are even dimly aware of their existence. As is also clear from the accounts of Malaysians living in the diaspora, many Malaysians with non-normative gender identities and sexual orientations are completely unaware that there are others "like them" and, for fear of ridicule and other stigma, must endure various kinds of associational constraints, despite the presence in Kuala Lumpur and certain other large Malaysian cities of organizations, movements, and virtual spaces aimed at educating and otherwise helping them or simply celebrating—or easing some of the moral and other burdens of—their existentially solitary existence. The principle exception to this generalization involves those who think of themselves as gay or lesbian (or as a tom boy, dyke, peng-kid, etc.); for those who identify with these subject positions do so based partly on their recognition of the existence of others "like themselves," or "people like us" (abbreviated as PLU), an increasingly common codeword on the Internet.

Speaking of broader issues, Kadir opined that Malays are much more tolerant of gender and sexual transgression than the nation's other main "races" (Chinese and Indians); and that racial tolerance leads to other kinds of tolerance, including tolerance toward gays, mak nyah, and the like. "The [main] problem here," however, is not that Chinese and Indians are not as tolerant as they might be. It is, rather, "the [Malay] ayatollahs," an Iranian-inflected shorthand referring to "people with PAS mentality." One might assume from our interview and from the other material presented in this chapter that "the ayatollahs" are no match for the Internet or for the globalizing discourses of a broadly liberal sort that often circulate there. While generally speaking this seems true, it is important to underscore that in Malaysia as elsewhere, religious groups of all stripes (including PAS) utilize the Internet to good effect. So too do various kinds of illiberal organizations and factions situated squarely within the overwhelmingly secular state apparatus and the attendant system of electoral politics. These points are clear from the controversy surrounding Mahathir's ill-fated (October 2001) declaration that Malaysia is an "Islamic state," a declaration that was condemned (online and elsewhere) by Muslim feminists among others, some of whom were then attacked on the Internet and in all varieties of other media for ostensibly lacking the religious credentials to weigh in on such matters (Peletz 2005). They are also readily apparent from the government's more recent (2007–2008) threats to deploy the dreaded Internal Security Act, the Sedition Act, or both, against various Internet bloggers and online writers. At greatest risk here are those identified via state cyber-surveillance either as having criticized the police, the ruling party, or certain officials and ministries for corruption, or for having written about other "sensitive issues" including but not limited to the prerogatives of race, religion, or royalty. Like almost everything else associated with (late) modernity, the kinds of networks and resource mobilizations that the Internet facilitates have new liberatory potential but can also be pressed into service in a variety of absolutist and otherwise deeply repressive ways.

I turn now to interviews from my 2001 and 2002 fieldwork involving a self-described "androgynous, lesbian-feminist activist," community organizer, and scholar who is probably in her early 40s and has published important articles on women and sexual rights in Malaysia. These interviews (also conducted in English) provided confirmation of many points emphasized by Kadir as well as contrasting perspectives on certain key issues. Rais, as I shall call her, in keeping with the pseudonym she utilized in her 1996 article on the lesbian movement in Malaysia, is of Chinese ancestry, resides in Kuala Lumpur, and at the time of our interviews was working for an internationally oriented women's organization geared toward monitoring women's rights in the Asia Pacific region and helping to insure various nations' compliance with recent human rights protocols. She spent a number of years in the West, where she obtained both a B.A. and an M.A., and is thoroughly conversant with Western academic discourses on women, gender, and sexuality, including some of the latest cutting-edge scholarship in the field of queer theory.

Like many of the activists, judges, lawyers, academics, and others I spoke with in the early years of the new millennium, Rais lamented what she saw as the rise of ethnic and racial intolerance in recent years, insisting that "things are much worse now in term of racial segregation and polarization." She spoke of the Kampung Medan incident (February 2001), which saw at least six people killed in an impoverished, shanty-town section of Kuala Lumpur when fighting broke out between Malay and Indian men, some of whom had been attending a wedding, others a funeral. The government-controlled press provided superficial coverage of the incident for a short time, but as Rais made clear, even if an official investigation was launched, nobody heard the full story, especially since government officials "advised" people via the media that they should not talk about it and should "move on." This is just one of the examples that Rais cited. She felt that the schoolbooks are also partly to blame for the tense climate—a climate that one Kuala Lumpur-based lawyer of South Asian ancestry repeatedly described to me as a "powder-keg"—perpetuating racial stereotypes as they do. So too in Rais' view is the school system in its entirety, to say nothing of the rampant chauvinism, especially on the part of Malays.

I asked Rais whether in her view gays and lesbians have a "well-founded subjective fear of persecution" (a key issue when Malaysians and others seek political asylum in the US), to which she responded, "Yes, very definitely, and if you are partly out, you have to be very careful who you tell." Rais acknowledged that many of the lesbian women and gay men she knows have not directly experienced police harassment or other forms of persecution because of the degree to which they are forced to live their lives closeted and underground. The culture of secrecy, concealment, and accommodation is such that people are generally extremely discreet, engaging in various practices of self-censorship, and otherwise remaining in the closet—all the more so if they are Chinese. (In this respect she is relatively unusual; she characterizes herself as a "fairly out lesbian," as we have seen, describing "the extent of her outness ... [as] subject to family constraints, actually just her mother!" [Reinfelder 1996:xi].) Because they are usually successful in masking their sexual orientations, problems don't usually arise. *Dykes* (her term) typically gather in one another's homes, under other auspices, and thus tend to go about their business without attracting much attention. But, as she pointed out, "there are lots around, you see them in the malls, just as you see transsexuals in their locations," at the cosmetic counters of upscale department stores, for example.

The overall climate of repression and uncertainty impacts identities, interactions, and patterns of sociality in other ways as well, partly because it makes for a lack of trust in relationships of all varieties. It is precisely this lack of trust that leads female-bodied Malaysians given to same-sex erotics to think long and hard before adopting or improvising on one or another of the locally available subject positions (*lesbian, dyke, tomboy, peng-kid, butch, femme*, etc.), let alone casting off one such subject position for another. As Rais put it in one of her published essays that I cited earlier, "butch/femme roles" especially are taken quite seriously by lesbians in Malaysia, in marked contrast to the West, where "postmodern notions of parody, irony, and 'genderfuck'" may entail frequent switching of gendered performative styles "as a fashionable thing to do" or a way of parodying or "subverting essentialist notions of sex and gender ... as stable and immutable rather than" hybrid, fluid, and protean (Rais Nur and A.R. 1996:73). Even though the extent to which female-bodied individuals identify as masculine, feminine, androgynous, or "men trapped inside women's bodies" (the classic statement of what it is to be a *pak nyah* both in Malaysian medical and social-work discourse and in the Western sexology that helped generate that discourse) is perhaps best described in terms of a variety of cross-cutting continua, the kind of code switching at issue here tends not to occur in Malaysia. In Malaysia, "the emphasis on roles [within the lesbian community, broadly defined] is very restrictive," and those who endeavor to buck the system often meet with "distrust and hostility" from their peers (ibid., 74). For these and other reasons, Western emphases on what Rais glossed as "postmodern notions of parody, irony, and 'genderfuck'" strike lesbians and others in Malaysia and many other regions of the Global South as culturally inappropriate, somewhere between curiously misplaced and grossly ethnocentric, much like Western exhortations that everyone should come out of the closet.

Adolescent and adult experiences and understandings of the vicissitudes of trust and distrust obviously build on earlier templates laid down in familial and household contexts. It is thus revealing that some people with whom I discussed issues of same-sex sexuality among Malaysian women explained what they took to be the disproportionate numbers of Chinese in Malaysia's lesbian community with reference to Chinese females' disaffection from the patriarchal dimensions of Chinese kinship and marriage, which are of course unpalatable to some (apparently small numbers of) Chinese males as well. As a Kuala Lumpur-based journalist of Chinese background who beyond family circles is a partly out lesbian with some experience of male lovers and a gay brother (who has likewise kept his sexual orientation from their parents) once quipped to me, ostensibly referring to her fondness for Jack Daniels whiskey: "The only man you can really trust is Jack; he always treats you the same." Perspectives such as these resonate with Rais' views concerning the capricious, personalistic nature of Malaysian politics: "Things could change in a day if Mahathir decided that they should." They are, moreover, thoroughly in keeping with Kadir's previously noted (Agambenesque) comment that if Mahathir wanted all of Kuala Lumpur's gay venues (saunas, discos, bars, cruising spots, etc.) closed down, "they would be gone in an instant."

The fear and uncertainty experienced by Chinese and other non-Malays living in Malaysia is exacerbated by dissension and strife that exists within the ruling political party (UMNO) and in relations between UMNO and the Islamist opposition party, PAS. More generally, it is no accident that Kadir (a Malay, and a male) is far more optimistic and upbeat than Rais (who is Chinese, and female) on the present and future of ethnic and race relations, gender pluralism, and related matters such as PAS's initiatives to expand the jurisdiction of Islamic law—even though as a Muslim, Kadir would be more directly impacted by the laws, which, in theory at least, would not pertain to non-Muslims such as Rais. Unlike Kadir, Rais sees in PAS an ominous threat, and "PAS people" (as she and many others put it) definitely frighten her. When I raised Kadir's arguably encouraging point about PAS not having targeted gays, lesbians, *pondan*, and the like either in Kelantan or in Terengganu, she countered by reminding me that Kelantan's initiatives to implement *hudud* laws make clear provision for the criminalization of homosexuality, including lesbianism; the penalties for these offenses would indeed be quite severe.

Of related but more immediate concern to Rais and other feminist activists is that the period since the mid-1990s or so has seen greatly expanded efforts on the part of state officials and Islamic religious authorities to regulate all aspects of female sexuality. Such efforts stem partly from cases such as that of Azizah (and Rohana) and partly from media exposés concerning *boh sia*, i.e., Malay and other teenage girls and young women in certain areas of Kuala Lumpur who were reported to be drinking beer and other liquor and engaging in "one night stands" and other forms of casual sex with older men (Rais Nur and A.R. 1996, Stivens 1998, 2002). The moral panics that ensued in various quarters spawned legislative and other measures aimed at eliminating these practices, partly by broadening legally salient definitions of the types of behavior that constitute "offenses against public decency."

Judging from the work to which she devotes herself and from comments made in the course of our interviews and in print, it is clear that Rais regards progressive NGOs and community ("grass roots") activism as providing much hope for the future. It is also evident that Rais sees no way around the hard work required to organize communities, build networks and coalitions, raise funds, and otherwise create the kinds of social capital that will facilitate progressive change. This is especially true in the Malaysian context, where a few well-placed phone calls or email messages—to Marina Mahathir, for example—could yield funds or other assistance for one or another short- or long-term project. In settings such as Malaysia, it is tempting for progressive NGOs to try to avail themselves of the material and other assistance that can be got through personal requests for help or networks built up through chains of patron-client relations. In the long run, however, Rais feels that this kind of "quick fix" is counter-productive, for it creates no ongoing community networks or coalitions, and none of the expansive social capital required to sustain progressive change.

There are in any case two additional challenges confronting Rais and similarly oriented lesbian activists. One of these challenges, mentioned in our discussion of the Pink Triangle, is that like most other progressive NGOs, prominent women's groups like Sisters in Islam have been reluctant to join Rais and other activists from the lesbian, gay, and transsexual communities in calling for the recognition of sexual rights as human rights (Ng, Maznah, and Tan 2006). Rais is well aware that groups such as Sisters in Islam are constrained both by "the Islamic position" (her expression) on same-sex sexuality and by their extensive, deeply embedded involvement in coalitionist politics with the likes of UMNO, whose fortunes soared in the aftermath of September 11, due partly to Mahathir's deft tarring of PAS as a "terrorist organization" (Peletz 2005). And while the post-September 11 period also saw great increases in the credibility and overall legitimacy of groups like Sisters in Islam, there was apparently no "spillover effect" or scaling-up of pluralistic sensibilities or dispositions that directly benefited the gay, lesbian, or transgendered communities. The fact remains that Malaysian citizen-subjects and their formal associations cannot usually take a proactive stance; for the most part they can only react to a particular case when it comes up in the press, and then primarily by discouraging discrimination. It helps that a number of other women's rights groups have formed in Malaysia in recent years, many of them, like the one Rais works for, with an international focus, though such a focus can of course divert attention and valuable resources from local realities.

The other dilemma Rais mentioned is that the Pink Triangle appeared to be in shambles, on the verge of disintegrating—a situation that persisted through 2006 or thereabouts (at which point the Ministries of Health and of Women, Family, and Community Development earmarked significant funds for their operations): "What do you expect when you have a bunch of gay men running it?" she asked rhetorically; "they are too interested in their social lives." The bottom line for Rais is that organizational and development efforts are ad hoc and haphazard—she made passing reference to prominent members of the Pink Triangle attempting to collect money from passers-by in a mall. Rais' latter comments may help explain the unfortunate shuttering in 2002 of the Ikhlas Drop-In Center, located in the Chow Kit section of Kuala Lumpur, which was one of only two Pink Triangle facilities that existed in the capital and in Malaysia as a whole at the time. (The other was the Pink Triangle headquarters, also located, as we have seen, in Chow Kit.) The Ikhlas outreach programs thus terminated had served intravenous drug users as well as the transsexual community, especially mak nyah, to whom we now turn.[39]

The life experiences of mak nyah illustrate a range of engagements with "tolerance," open secrets, and governmentality that is quite different from— and in some ways much more dramatic, brutal, and repressive than—what we have seen from interviews discussed thus far. This is partly because most mak nyah cross-dress on a more or less permanent basis and thus engage in transgender practices that are criminalized under secular law and Islamic legal codes alike. (For the Muslims among them, cross-dressing thus entails involvement in at least two separate and distinct forms of criminality and renders them liable to criminal prosecution in two separate venues.) The mak nyah community's relatively extensive engagement in commercial sex work (recall that, according to informed estimates, some 60 to 70 percent of Kuala Lumpur's mak nyah are involved in prostitution) also contributes to them finding themselves routinely confronting the forces of governmentality in ways that gays and lesbians typically do not. Mak nyah also push the envelope as far as their parents are concerned, whereas gays and lesbians typically do their best to make sure that their parents remain in the dark as to their sex/gender identities, with mak nyah typically experimenting in cross-dressing from an early age, performing women's work around the house, participating in stereotypically female pastimes and occupational pursuits, and otherwise insisting to their parents and others that despite outward appearances they are really (emotionally, psychologically, spiritually) female. As noted earlier, many perhaps most mak nyah have been beaten by their parents, literally thrown out the door(s) or window(s) of their natal homes, arrested, beaten, and in some cases sexually assaulted by the police, and subject to other forms of humiliation, torture, and abuse. Gays and lesbians are less likely to have these kinds of experiences for the simple reason that they invest much time and energy in the kinds of impression management that will enable them to pass muster as normatively gendered and sexed. Such is much less likely to occur in the case of *mak nyah*, whose main concerns with respect to impression management focus on "passing" for (or as) women. Because Islamic officials in Malaysia issued a *fatwa* (authoritative ruling) in 1983 that prohibited sex-change operations for Muslims on religious grounds, Muslim *mak nyah* tend not to have the operation (though they could do so in Singapore or Bangkok) and therefore have a harder time passing as women than non-Muslim *mak nyah* or the Muslims who had the operation before it was declared religiously unacceptable. The situation in Malaysia is thus very different from Muslim nations such as Iran, where some leaders encourage sexual reassignment surgery as a way to "cure" and ultimately eliminate homosexuality.

Mak nyah identities and the subject positions and subjectivities associated with them are of very recent origin. They first emerged in the early 1980s in the context of efforts by a dozen or so predominantly Malay male-to-female (MTF) transsexuals who had undergone sexual reassignment surgery (in the days when it was still legal for Muslims in Malaysia to do so) to form an informal self-help organization, what would nowadays be referred to as an NGO. Assisted by Dr. Khairuddin Yusof, a Malay gynecologist at the University of Malaya Hospital who served as their spokesman and advocate, and by other medical personnel specializing in sex-change operations, they established an informal organization called The *Mak Nyah* Society, combining the term *mak*, a contraction of the term *emak* or "mother," which is also used by mothers and other women as a first-person pronoun, with *nyah*, which is short for *nyonya*, a term referring to women from Melaka of mixed Chinese-Malay ancestry that connotes elaborate make-up and hair styles hence an exaggerated femininity. To be a *mak nyah* is thus to be a "very feminine or womanly mother," or an "I (person or self) who is feminine/woman," unambiguously if not redundantly female in any case—ironic, perhaps, given the ambiguity and lack of redundancy in their femininity.

The immediate goals of The *Mak Nyah* Society were apparently three-fold: first, to persuade the state's Registration Department that their earlier, male names should be struck from their Identity Cards (all Malaysians are required to carry one of these) and replaced with their new, female ones; second, to convince the state's Welfare Department that it should provide them with funds to establish small businesses; and third, to obtain official state recognition for their organization (Teh 2002:123). They achieved short-term success with respect to the first two goals, but not the third. I should clarify that for reasons related to dynamics of surveillance, discipline, and control, the Malaysian state requires that all political parties and other organizations—or "societies" as they are sometimes called—be formally registered and licensed, thereby ideally insuring that their official *raison d'être* and routine activities be clarified, approved, and subject to monitoring and governance. The state's refusal to grant *mak nyah* a license (official recognition) should not be read as a lack of state concern with their existence. It is rather a refusal to grant them legitimacy.

It is not clear how the individuals who came together in the early 1980s conceptualized their identities prior to the invention of the designation *mak nyah*, though it is possible that at least some of them thought of and referred to themselves as *wadam*, this being a contraction of the Malay terms *wanita* and *adam*, the former denoting a woman, the latter Adam, thus indicating either a feminized male or a masculinized female (Teh 2002:123). What is clear is that the impetus for carving out a new identity was motivated by deeply felt existential dissatisfaction with extant gender categories such as *lelaki* (male), *perempuan* (female), and *pondan*, which, as we have seen, typically refers to a male-bodied individual who walks like a woman, talks like a woman, spends too much time with women, or behaves like a woman in other ways such as by having or preferring sex with men. Neither of the first two terms ("male," "female") spoke to their embodied experiences or to other aspects of their lived realities. Nor did the third term (*pondan*)—or regional variations on the theme—offer them an intellectually or emotionally meaningful identity, suggesting to them as it did misleading and otherwise offensive similarities between what they took to be superficially "feminine males" on the one hand and their own experiences and self-understandings as "women trapped in men's bodies" on the other. As one *mak nyah* put it, apparently referring in part to the larger society's ambivalence toward *pondan* (reflected, for example, in the ways they are sometimes dismissively and demeaningly depicted in venues of public culture), "Who wants to be labeled a *pondan* ... if they can help it" (Teh 2002:52).

It is worthwhile to devote a bit more attention to how the *mak nyah* community first constituted itself. For the ways it did so reveal a great deal about the incentives and constraints bearing on the creation of new sexual and gender identities in contexts such as Malaysia, just as they shed new light on important debates concerning the formation of sexual and gender identities in non-Western settings that have ranged across a number of different academic disciplines. We have already noted part of the answer to the question concerning the initial constitution of the *mak nyah* community, for we mentioned that all of the original members of the *mak nyah* society were post-operative MTF transsexuals. The question then becomes, How or on what grounds did they obtain the surgery? The short answer is that, as typically occurs in the West, they were required to undergo a long series of extensive interviews and examinations—with medical doctors, psychiatrists, psychologists, and others—to prove that they did indeed display clear evidence of a long-term if not permanent condition conforming to the reigning biomedical profile of "transsexualism" as established by cosmopolitan medical standards of Western origin. The colonial-era and subsequent circulation throughout Asia and much of the rest of the world of discourses of sexology and Western biomedicine as a whole is directly relevant here. For in Malaysia, as elsewhere, these discourses provided the specific range of techniques, examinations, and standards of proof and authenticity central to the construction of normativity and abnormality alike.

Much has been made in the literature spanning a number of different academic disciplines of the ways that Western medical and scientific discourses imposed various types of binaries and dichotomies ("heterosexual vs. homosexual," "male vs. female," "normal vs. abnormal," etc.) on non-Western landscapes of gender and sexuality that were characterized both by a fair degree of fluidity and permeability and by the relative absence (or de-emphasis) of strictly binary or dichotomous constructions. And rightly so. But we also need to recognize that just as Western science contributed to the "abnormalization" of a good deal of non-Western gender and sexual diversity, it also provided terms, conditions, and categories that have been creatively appropriated (and in some cases radically transformed) by postcolonial subjects who seek to fashion meaningful identities for themselves and otherwise negotiate fields of governmentality and the terms in which they lead their daily lives. In contexts where "traditional" gender terminologies and the more encompassing discursive/cosmological matrices in which they are embedded do not adequately provide for these individuals' subject positions and subjectivities, their appropriations from the West, even if quite literal, may be experienced as extremely liberating and, in some cases, veritable life savers, particularly when, as among Malay and other Muslim *mak nyah*, serious clinical depression is a widespread problem and culturally informed biomedical interventions aimed at alleviating it have seen some measure of success (Teh 2002). In this view, which builds on Foucault's (1978) insights but is more empirically grounded and nuanced than many of Foucault's arguments and many posthumous transpositions of Foucauldian perspectives to non-Western settings, modern Western biomedicine both delineated and in this sense helped create the "problem," and, much like Lévi-Strauss's (1967) famous Cuna shaman, offered terms, conditions, and categories to help render it intellectually and emotionally meaningful and thus to some degree (clinically or pragmatically) manageable.

Dynamics such as these are important to bear in mind since many of the debates about the modern sex/gender identities that obtain outside the West focus heavily on the symbols, meanings, and negotiations of terms and identities—*gay*, *lesbian*, *tomboy*, and the like—that are of clear Western provenance, however much they may have been reworked and transformed in non-Western settings. Incisive analyses have sometimes compared and contrasted the semantic domains of these terms with the semantic domains of lexical items that are of much greater antiquity, such as the Thai *kathoey* (e.g., Morris 1994, Jackson 1997) and the Filipino *bakla* and *bantut* (e.g., Johnson 1997, Cannell 1999, Manalansan 2003). But they sometimes do so without devoting sufficient analytic attention to the broader landscapes of gender and sexuality. These landscapes include the shifting and contested contours of normative masculinity and femininity (as we saw in Burma) as well as the existence of native-language categories bearing on transgression which derive from or to one or another degree map onto Western terms other than "gay"—such as *mak nyah*—and which have been coined in recent years to distinguish certain subject positions and subjectivities from those associated not only with indigenous categories (such as *pondan*) but also with those linked to more recent terms of Western-origin like "gay."

I should perhaps be more explicit here and emphasize that *mak nyah* seek to differentiate themselves both from male-bodied *pondan*, who are invariably feminized, and from those who consider themselves or are seen by others as *gay*, regardless of how the latter are gendered. This despite the fact that some *mak nyah* have experimented with *gayness* in the sense that they donned a *gay* identity for a while, only to reject it since (*inter alia*) it is typically seen as requiring male attire. In seeking to create for themselves a largely feminine identity, *mak nyah* might be seen as working at cross-purposes to those Malaysians who endeavor to carve out a space for *gay* masculinity, *lesbian* femininity, and other relations that do not readily conform to a heterogender matrix. Put differently, *mak nyah*'s commitments to feminized identities coupled with their strong desires to form erotic relationships exclusively with masculine males is thoroughly consistent with the (heterogender) deep structure of the Malay universe of gender and sexuality, particularly the contrastive directionality of embodied desire. Dynamics such as these go a long way toward explaining why by some criteria *mak nyah* occupy one of the more privileged spaces accorded those who live their lives beyond the charmed circle, and, related to this point, why they pose far less of a challenge to conventional categories and hierarchies than certain groups of gays and lesbians, if not gays and lesbians in their entirety.

It is revealing in any case that their experiences of one or another type of medicalized "gender dysphoria" motivated *mak nyah* to launch an NGO so as to obtain formal recognition and legitimacy from the medical establishment and from political and religious elites and society at large. In earlier centuries, the forging of ties between certain categories of transgenderists and elites in a position to help endow them with society-wide legitimacy was also commonplace. But of course it would not have involved the formation of an NGO, and might have first entailed journeying into the forest, consulting with or appealing to the spirits or to those who specialize in trafficking with them, or engaging some other domain of the occult, as still commonly occurs in places like Burma (and to some degree among the Bugis). The largely but not exclusively secular and public-health oriented tack pursued in the Malaysian context by *mak nyah* (some Muslim *mak nyah* have also sought formal recognition from *ulama*, *mufti*, and other religious leaders who they have approached with questions concerning appropriate ritual procedure related to prayer, burial, and the like) speaks clearly to the prevalence of medicalization in the Malaysian setting (evidence for which is also clear among the Bugis), and to the emergence of new loci and standards of authenticity and legitimacy, which is symptomatic of the fragmentation of authority discussed earlier on. It also illustrates the partial decentering of the sacred, and of religion generally, in modern Malaysian identities and public spaces of all varieties, despite the florescence and reactualization of religion—especially Islam—in myriad contexts imbricated in the fraught and highly unpredictable dynamics of identity politics.

Forming an NGO is of course no guarantee of just or equitable treatment, for at the drop of a hat any such organization may be forcefully disbanded and its public representatives and other members persecuted either by one or another group of political or religious elites or by ostensibly "volunteer" (vigilante) organizations such as the short-lived PASRAH, variations on the theme being widespread throughout Malaysia. But it does at least bestow a modicum of respectability on its members. It does, moreover, provide an important object lesson to all those who are watching patiently from the ubiquitous sidelines or "sitting on the fence(s)" (*duduk pagar* in local parlance), eager to see how they and others of "their (variously defined) kind" ("people like us") might fare in the fields of identity politics and minority representation. Perhaps more critically, though, it indexes a willingness to negotiate processes of medical and political domestication, just as it confirms some measure of Gramscian "consent" to play by the modern rules of political and civic engagement in a system characterized by extremely arbitrary governmentality and gradations of sovereignty and pluralism alike.

Conclusion

Among the more intriguing cultural-political developments in Malaysia, Singapore, and elsewhere in the Asia Pacific region during the 1990s was the emergence of discourses concerning "Asian values." These narratives stigmatize and endeavor to silence and disclaim all non-heteronormative genders and sexualities as decidedly "un-Asian," despite the abundant historical and ethnographic evidence indicating that transgendered practices and identities and various types of non-heteronormative sexuality—like conditions of gender pluralism generally—have a long and venerable history in Southeast Asia and the Asia Pacific world as a whole. It should thus be obvious, as scholars have noted for other reasons (Ong 1999), that narratives of "Asian values," constituted as they are by "monolithic categories and mythic binaries" (Grewal and Kaplan 1994:28), are characterized by a great deal of selectivity and cultural aphasia. They are also highly politicized in an overdetermined sense, though this should not surprise us since they are frequently pressed into service by national elites to promote new, acceptably "modern" ways of being in the world and to delegitimize and criminalize others as "backward" or "unacceptably modern." Nor is it coincidental that these discourses emerged during the 1990s, a decade that saw "economic miracles" in many parts of Southeast Asia (e.g., Malaysia, Singapore, Thailand, but, significantly, not Burma) as well as severe financial crises beginning in 1997. As albeit to a lesser degree with the 1980s, the 1990s witnessed projects of modernity which helped underwrite the economic transformations in question but which nonetheless presupposed social engineering and cultural cleansing that were extremely dislocating and otherwise deeply painful for many Southeast Asians. It is thus highly ironic, though perhaps not surprising as a strategic counter-move and an effort to create cultural ballast for an increasingly globalized and uncertain future, that political and religious elites in Malaysia, Singapore, and various other regions took such pains to formulate a discourse on "Asian values" that celebrates a timeless, eternally unchanging, and strongly tradition-bound, heteronormative and otherwise essentialized "Oriental," whose basic subjectivities and "family values" transcend time and space and are ostensibly poised to surmount all challenges they might confront.

Discourses of "Asian values" have been strategically deployed by political and religious elites motivated by (at least) two related sets of concerns. First, to provide timely reassurance to Malaysians, Singaporeans, and others targeted by the discourses that the core values they cherish are indeed safeguarded and promoted by elites, the state apparatus, and home-grown projects of modernity alike. And second, to underscore in no uncertain terms that the diverse subject positions and subjectivities (*gay*, *tom boy*, etc.) that have proliferated in recent years, due at least in part, ironically, to projects of modernity that embrace many features of globalization and neoliberalism, are decidedly "un-Asian" and will not be countenanced. In the latter regard it is essential to recall a definitional point made toward the very beginning of this book: in order for pluralism to exist, diversity must be accorded legitimacy. Just as diversity without legitimacy is not pluralism (it "falls short"), increased diversity need not entail an augmentation of pluralism. Indeed, because greater diversity is often perceived to be a threat to established values and arrangements and the various interests they serve, it may contribute both directly and indirectly to a constriction of pluralism, as is clearly the case in Malaysia, other regions of Southeast Asia, and many other parts of the world (Altman 2001, Knauft 2003).

The contemporary Malaysian state's wide-ranging efforts to institutionalize policies of heterosexism and homophobia and the cultural sensibilities associated with them has had the effect of disciplining all individuals involved in transgendering and same-sex relations, including those (such as *pondan*) who do not necessarily engage in "deviant sexual practices" but are nonetheless tarred as *gay* or *lesbian*. These state strategies, which we also see in Singapore and elsewhere in Southeast Asia as well, highlight a relationship between transgenderism and non-normative sexual practices on the one hand and political elites on the other that is obviously a far cry from the pattern of the early modern era, when political elites embraced transgendered individuals and the sexual variability associated with them for the vital role they played in the sanctification and reproduction of local polities. To express this in more general and abstract language: the long-term cultural-political developments outlined here are contributing to a further secularization, stigmatization, and criminalization of all forms of transgendering. They are also serving to redefine transgendered individuals as contaminating—as distinct from sacred—mediators who are perversely muddling and enmiring the increasingly polar and monochromatic terms of a sex/gender system long characterized by hybridity, fluidity, and pluralism. This is especially evident in the enactment in Malaysia in recent years of specifically Islamic laws proscribing cross-dressing, sodomy, and sexual relations between women, and the rise of attendant discourses and "volunteer" (vigilante) organizations that serve to increase the purview, consciousness, surveillance, and disciplining modes of both Islamic and secular courts with respect to allegedly Western-origin "perversions," "gender waywardness," and many other domains of practice and desire (Peletz 2002).

The stigmatizing and criminalizing processes we see in Malaysia and Singapore in the 1990s are not occurring in the same manner or to the same degree in every region of Southeast Asia, partly because projects of modernity vary considerably, in terms of their conceptualization, scope, force, etc., from one area of Southeast Asia to the next and are in some cases geared toward keeping the rest of the world at bay. The situation in Burma (outlined in Chapter 4) makes this clear. So too in different ways does work on Java and other parts of Indonesia by Dede Oetomo (1996) and Tom Boellstorff (1999, 2004a, 2005), which highlights the Indonesian state's relative lack of concern with non-normative sexualities. As such, both the Burmese data (bearing on *nat kadaw* and the like) and the Indonesian material cited here help counterbalance the account presented in this chapter, which focuses on one of the darker sides of modernity. So too to some extent do reports from Jakarta indicating that same-sex relations among women, many of whom have husbands, children, and outwardly "normal" (heteronormative) lives, are extremely widespread though typically hidden from family members and others because they are denied legitimacy and are seriously stigmatized (Murray 1999, Wieringa 1999; see also Blackwood 1999, 2005). That said, it is well to keep issues of legitimacy—and axes of prestige/stigma generally—in the forefront of our analyses, especially if one of our main concerns is the constriction and overall transformation of pluralist sensibilities, which, by definition, are sensibilities that accord legitimacy to various types of difference.

According to most Indonesianists, on the eve of the new millennium there were no laws in Java or elsewhere in the archipelago that criminalized sexual activity involving consenting adults of the same sex. More broadly, political and religious elites in Java often act as if sexual and gender deviance does not exist, even while they tacitly endorse censorship of such deviance and its repression by the military. Additional research will be necessary to document and explain the sharp contrast in these areas between Malaysia (and Singapore) on the one hand, and Java and Indonesia generally on the other. Suffice it to say that although there is a good deal more gender pluralism in Java and other regions of Indonesia (e.g., among the Bugis) than in Malaysia, this could change due to countervailing currents in Indonesia that are working against pluralist sensibilities bearing on gender, politics, and religion. I refer to distressing reports from post-New Order Java suggesting that members of extremist Islamist paramilitary organizations like Laskar Jihad (Jihad Militia Force; which at its peak a few years ago was some 10,000 strong) and Laskar Pembela Islam (Defenders of Islam Force) have instigated attacks on gay organizations, such as those that have occurred in Java, Sulawesi, and elsewhere in the past few years (Boellstorff 2004b, Davies 2007:76). These actions do not necessarily bear the imprint of the state, such as it is in present-day Indonesia. Nor do the offensive forays against cafés, bars, discotheques, and casinos that are believed to be the work of Laskar Pembela Islam and Jemaah Islamiyah (Islamic Community). But given the well-documented links between extremist religious organizations (of which there are dozens, all throughout Indonesia) and powerful members of military and paramilitary groups loyal to former Indonesian President Suharto and his supporters (Hefner 2000, 2002, Noorhaidi Hasan 2006), occurrences along these lines are no less troublesome. Indeed, they are perhaps even more disturbing than "plain old state-sponsored terrorism" inasmuch as they resonate with Taliban-style sensibilities and high-profile developments in other regions of the Muslim world such as Saudi Arabia and Egypt.

The direction of future developments in Indonesia and other regions of Muslim Southeast Asia remains unclear. The signs are not necessarily encouraging, especially when one considers that the extremely puritanical Salafi-Wahhabi tradition of Islam promoted by the Saudi leadership has informed both Taliban-style Islam and the Muslim paramilitary groups that have sprung up throughout Indonesia. What does seem a strong likelihood is the heightened militarization of Indonesia and insular Southeast Asia generally—at least in the short run—owing to some of the regional dynamics alluded to here in conjunction with US policy initiatives linked to "the war on terror." These developments bode ill for transgendering and perhaps for pluralist sensibilities of all kinds. This perspective is supported by the experience of the southern Philippines during the 1970s and 1980s. The increased violence spawned then as a consequence of the imposition of martial law by President Marcos and the subsequent rise of the Moro National Liberation Front placed a premium on male virtues associated with bodily strength, physical combat, military prowess, and successful warfare, thus creating conditions conducive to declines in the prestige of certain aspects of femininity and a further stigmatization of transgendered practices and identities (Johnson 1997). One can perhaps be more optimistic about the long term, hopeful that Indonesian political and religious elites work with ordinary Muslims and others to negotiate their present crises and variously defined projects of modernity in ways that build on and enhance rather than constrict the pluralistic traditions that long characterized the region.

Relevant in this connection is that in recent decades, forces of transnational capitalism and globalization, including the notoriously ungovernable Internet, have contributed to the circulation throughout Southeast Asia of Western-origin discourses bearing on genders, bodies, and sexualities. In some places (I mentioned Sulawesi and other parts of Indonesia as well as Malaysia and Burma, but the list is actually much longer, including Thailand, Singapore, and the Philippines, for example), feminist-inflected narratives bearing on women, gender, and sexual rights as human rights have helped animate largely home-grown movements aimed at contesting certain gendered and sexual arrangements entailed in conventional kinship and marriage. Also contributing to dramatic change but often working at cross-purposes to the movements noted here—and to repressive regimes of governmentality—are media concerns and other agents of corporate capitalisms. In mostly Chinese (Buddhist/Confucian/Taoist) Singapore, as in the more conspicuous cases of Thailand,

Taiwan, Japan, and the US, for instance, we see new groups of entrepreneurs who seek to capture gay markets (pink dollars) and to exploit other commercial opportunities either by creating forms of entertainment dramatizing sexual or gender ambiguity, or by focusing media attention on whatever sells, be it vociferous advocacy of feminism or of sexual rights, their denigration, or both. In this regard, Singapore has recently turned a corner and is diverging rather sharply from the trajectory it once appeared to share with Malaysia. For since 2002 or thereabouts the "economic-profit trump card of capitalist logic has ... been deployed ... [in the city-state] to argue for a more open atmosphere toward the gay community, particularly foreigners, both in pursuit of the 'pink dollar' of gay tourists and in an effort (albeit with some equivocation ...) to tap into the economically profitable creative energy of gay artists, entrepreneurs, and others" (E. Thompson 2006:332; see also K.K. Tan 2006). That Malaysia is unlikely to follow suit in the near future is perhaps best indicated by the incredible fact that in late June 2008, as this book was headed toward publication, former Deputy Prime Minister Anwar who was freed from jail in 2004 and currently heads the opposition movement, was *again* charged with sodomy—and was subsequently arrested—largely because authorities still feel that allegations along these lines are more likely to undercut Anwar's (and other critics') moral, religious, and political credentials than almost any others that might be concocted.

How long those at the helm of Singapore's ship of state will countenance this new spirit of openness toward the increasingly public activities of gays and lesbians—not to mention their ever more vociferous claims for unfettered inclusion in the official narratives of the city-state's past, present, and future—is a good question. But if Singapore's business and political elite follow the leads of East Asian economic success stories like Taiwan and Japan, we may soon see the florescence there of all varieties of enterprises and industries geared toward the aggressive marketing of things erotic and sexual, and the creation of new needs and desires in potential consumers from almost every age group and walk of life (Peletz 2007).

Such a scenario is consistent with Singapore's redoubled commitment since the Asian financial crisis of 1997–1998 to position itself as a world leader if not *the* global future of social engineering and "technopreneurial networking" (Ong 2006:181). This future places a premium *not* on the "Asian values" that were widely touted in Singapore (and beyond) in the 1990s, but on a "knowledge-driven economy" informed by "ethics that stress independent thinking and risk taking" (flexibility) and an educational system designed to "instill initiative, creativity, critical thinking ability, and entrepreneurialism" albeit in a larger cultural political climate made more hospitable, friendly, and familiar by "Asian values" (ibid., 190). Hence Ong's provocative assertion, in an essay published in 2006 but probably written a few years earlier, that at least in Singapore, "the 'Asian values' discourse is dead" (ibid., 194). The new focus on the individual as producer and consumer on the one hand, and "worthy citizen ... [who needs] to excel at self-management and to be globally competitive and politically compliant" on the other (ibid., 194), makes clear allowance for a measure of "do-your-own-thing" kind of "flexibility" in lifestyles, domestic arrangements, and erotic attachments—as long as the "greater good," Singapore's short- and long-term political stability and economic prosperity, is kept squarely in view. We need to bear in mind, however, that the kinds of "flexibility" at issue here carry a different and more negatively inflected range of meanings and connotations among the members of Singapore's Muslim-majority neighbor-nations (e.g., Indonesia and especially Malaysia); and that official equivocation vis-à-vis the gay community is more pronounced in Indonesia and in Malaysia in particular. This despite the fact that many key players in the latter two nations would be happy to assume Singapore's enviable position as one of the world's fastest growing knowledge-driven economies, perhaps even if attaining that goal required further state complicity in the construction of "open secrets" and the domestication through co-optation or repression of potential opposition that might arise on ostensibly religious or other grounds among variously situated groups of citizen-subjects.

We have seen that Burmese, Malaysians, and other Southeast Asians are putting their bodies on the line in social activism on behalf of progressive causes, doing so in ways that promise great hope for the future. An important question that arises concerns the future of struggles for gender and sexual equality in Southeast Asia and their relationship to similarly oriented movements in the West. In the US, to take one Western example, the civil rights movement helped set the stage for variously defined women's movements, all such collective struggles helping to pave the way for the battles currently being waged over gay marriage and other forms of sexual equality. Progressions of this sort, like those involving the succession of juridical discourses bearing on sexuality that Foucault (1978) documents for eighteenth- and nineteenth-century France, are by no means inevitable in Southeast Asia, even though there are some fascinating parallels. To paraphrase Margaret Jolly and Lenore Manderson (1997:22), we need to be wary of discursive genealogies and "theories of development which conceive a teleological trajectory" whereby the West "becomes a dress rehearsal for the rest of the world." There are numerous reasons why historical trajectories in Southeast Asia may not be analogous to those in the West. One reason is that in Southeast Asia, as in many other parts of the world, cultural-political responses to the onslaught of globalization and neo-imperialism emanating from the West entail powerful (re)assertions of moralities that are simultaneously represented and experienced as "indigenous," "traditional," and vehemently "anti-Western." Discourses of "Asian values" articulated in the 1990s by Mahathir Mohamad, Lee Kuan Yew, Shintaro Ishihara, and other Asian leaders and their charges provide examples of this. Another relevant dynamic is the heightened normativity in most domains of social life that is seen by the majority of Southeast Asia's political elites (including many but not all in Singapore) as necessary to sustain the new Asian capitalisms, to negotiate the rise of various forms of religious or ethno-nationalistic "fundamentalism," and to contend with the aftermath of September 11 and the vicissitudes of the

US "war on terror." The history of the region makes clear that these developments will inform a good many dynamics bearing on genders, sexualities, and body politics, though precisely how they will do so remains to be seen.

An upbeat example we might cite by way of concluding these remarks comes to us in the form of a handwritten message composed in French that Norodom Sihanouk, the then 81-year-old king of Cambodia, posted on one of his websites on February 20, 2004.[40] The king conceived the missive after having watched television coverage of the nearly 3,000 gay and lesbian couples that, with the formal blessing of San Francisco Mayor Gavin Newsom, had been granted marriage licenses in San Francisco in the week or so since February 12. The king's short but in many ways amazing message, written from his residence-in-exile in Beijing, emphasized that since Cambodian leaders had decided in 1993 to join the ranks of "liberal democracies," men should be allowed to marry one another, as should women as well as *khtoey*, who he matter of factly characterized as "neither men nor women." (Under current Cambodian law, such marriages are not possible.) The king added that *khtoey* should be accepted and treated well in Cambodia's national community, that he respects "homosexuals" and "lesbians," and that "it's not their fault because it is the Good Lord [*le Bon Dieu*] who loves [and creates] diversity in tastes and colors, ... [in] ... humans, animals, vegetables, etc."

The king's pluralistic endorsement of justice and equality for gays, lesbians, and the transgendered invites extended discussion. So too does his blanket support of diversity in "tastes and colors" and in "humans, animals, [and] vegetables," particularly in light of his deeply checkered history of dealing with political opponents during the period in which he effectively ruled Cambodian politics (from 1953 through 1970). More relevant here is that Sihanouk is a constitutional monarch who has long been highly respected and continues to be a powerful—and generally positive—symbol of and for Cambodia's past, present, and future, even though he cannot lay claim to any executive powers and is considered by many outside observers to be a tragic figure (Chandler 1991, Osborne 1994). It is no coincidence that the king and his family enjoy semi-divine status; or that as long-time patrons of the arts, particularly theater and dance, they have helped maintain the Royal Cambodian Ballet and thus insure that dances bearing witness to the glories of Angkor which "until the early twentieth century ... [were commonly performed] for the king alone, usually as an accompaniment to rituals" (M. Freeman 2004:189), continue to be performed throughout much of the twentieth century, even or especially by Cambodian gays in diasporic contexts such as California (Quintiliani 1995:74–78). Nor is it a coincidence that these Tantric-inflected dances have long included androgynous motifs (M. Freeman 2004:186–190)—or that Sihanouk's son, Norodom Sihamoni (b. 1953), who succeeded to the throne in 2004 and is widely assumed to be gay, is a highly accomplished dancer specializing in classical Cambodian ballet. Sihanouk's support of San Francisco's gay marriages and his feeling that in Cambodia state policies and the public should respect gays, lesbians, and the transgendered and accord them equal standing before the law is undoubtedly informed in part by the solidarity he feels with his son and thus falls squarely within almost any calculus of "family values" ("Asian" or otherwise). Sihanouk's position on these matters is in any case deeply allegorical insofar as it resonates both with the pluralistic stances of pre- and early modern Southern Asian elites' toward certain categories of ritual specialists and others involved in transgender practices and same-sex relations, and with the general ethos and worldview enshrined in their cosmologies. It is also in keeping with more modern-day pluralistic sensibilities of the sort that might be—but are apparently not usually—displayed by Euro-Americans in their dealings with Cambodian Americans (straight and gay alike), as discussed in the Epilogue.

It is not clear how Sihanouk's message along with short- and long-term reactions to it are playing out in the diaspora or in Cambodia, although as noted earlier Sihanouk continues to enjoy considerable popular support, as does his official website, which is reputed to receive upwards of a thousand hits a day.[41] The situation is especially uncertain in the wake of high-profile setbacks in the struggles for sexual equality that have occurred in San Francisco and elsewhere in the US. In August 2004, for example, an appellate court in California nullified the 4,000 marriage licenses issued in San Francisco earlier in the year, though in June 2008 California's Supreme Court ruled that the state could in fact authorize marriage involving same-sex partners, thus setting the stage for renewed legislative and other battles in the months and years to come. Since 2004, moreover, many states in the US have witnessed the passage by significant margins of state amendments to ban gay marriage (even though a few states such as Massachusetts and New York have moved in more progressive directions). What is beyond dispute is that the near instantaneous, mass-mediated global dissemination throughout the world of discourses extolling the virtues of sexual equality can entail new discursive and liberatory opportunities. Recall that Sihanouk's message in favor of sexual equality was sparked by events in the US that he observed on television in Beijing ("half a world away") as they were unfolding, and that his thoughts on these developments were posted on the globally accessible Internet more or less immediately. Coverage of the king's comments by Western print media, both straight and gay (e.g., *The New York Times*, *The Advocate*), was also more or less instantaneous. More generally, the circulation back to and beyond the US of the king's support for gay and lesbian marriage in San Francisco and elsewhere in America provides further encouragement and legitimacy to the struggle for sexual equality in the US and beyond, just as the struggle in the US (particularly its successes) encourages and inspires Cambodians and others throughout the world.

Epilogue
Asylum, Diaspora, Pluralism

I began this book with a consideration of certain aspects of Southeast Asia's pre-modern period. I took as my point of departure some of the ways in which people in Southeast Asian societies during that time and subsequently interwove religious and other influences "from beyond" with autochthonous material and thus helped constitute the region in ways that many scholars have come to regard as culturally and politically distinctive. I conclude the discussion by considering some of the ways that contemporary Southeast Asians move beyond the region itself. I do so for three reasons: (1) to emphasize the movement, hybridity, and porousness that have always been hallmarks of Southeast Asia both as a "culture (or world) area" and a geopolitical region; (2) to outline some of the vicissitudes of pluralism in an important diasporic context (the US), and thus to lay bare and undo binaries involving Southeast Asia "versus" the US as an exemplar of the West; and (3) to open up possibilities for future research involving translocal and global comparisons. In tracking these movements and circuits, I highlight relations between political power and claims to legitimacy as I have done throughout the book. In these final remarks, however, I do not focus on legitimacy conferred or contested by political elites situated at the apex of polities inflected by one or another set of Austronesian, Hindu-Buddhist, or Islamic themes. Nor do I focus on their colonial-era or postcolonial successors. Rather, the majority of the political elites I am concerned with are ensconced squarely within the corridors of United States power, deriving their warrants from the United States Constitution and a series of related documents bearing on immigration, naturalization, and citizenship.

The material I consider in the initial section of this epilogue is drawn from cases involving Malaysians residing in the US who have petitioned US authorities for political asylum on the grounds that they are openly gay, lesbian, or transgendered, and that if they return to their native country, they will be persecuted due to their publicly recognizable sexual orientation (specifically, that being openly "homosexual" or "transgendered" necessarily entails "a well-founded subjective fear of persecution"). I have been involved as an "expert witness" in more than a dozen such cases, and I find the narratives of asylum seekers and the process of petitioning for asylum highly instructive. Asylum seekers' narratives and the documents submitted on their behalf provide important perspectives on life in the homeland, on processes of subject-making in a diasporic context, and on the kinds of associational freedoms and other liberatory experiences gay, lesbian, and transgendered Southeast Asians expect to have in the US.

That asylum seekers have heavily idealized understandings of what life for them will be like in the US is suggested by the experiences of gay Cambodians living in this country, the majority of whom came as refugees in the wake of America's war in Indochina or the resulting horrors for Cambodia of the Pol Pot regime (1975–1979)—or were born to refugee parents already living here. In contrast to gay Malaysians pursuing asylum, gay Cambodians living in this country tend to speak of paradise lost rather than gained, summing up their views of the dissimilarities between homeland and diaspora with comments along the lines of "what we did sexually" in Cambodia "is not bad like it is here," and that while we "were teased by Cambodians," we are "hated by Americans" (Quintiliani 1995:65–66). The perspectives of gay (and straight) Cambodians on life in the US thus trouble the linear, progressivist narratives we tell ourselves about our (pluralistic) selves, just as they raise deeply unsettling questions about the constraints of normativity and similitude—and the future of difference and its proliferation—in an increasingly borderless world.

Events that occurred in Cuba in 1980 provide an appropriate entrée to understanding sexual asylum cases involving Southeast Asians and others. At that time, Fidel Toboso Alfonso, an openly gay Cuban man, was summoned to a police station and told by authorities that he faced four years in prison on account of his sexual orientation, though he had apparently broken no Cuban laws; alternatively, he was informed, he could leave Cuba on what came to be known as the "Mariel boat lift." He opted for the latter "choice" and sailed for the US, where he and other "Marielitos" were granted parole by US authorities. By 1985, however, after an arrest and conviction on drug charges, he faced mandatory deportation to his native Cuba. In the deportation hearing, he petitioned for political asylum and withholding of deportation[1] on the grounds that his return to Cuba would necessarily result in his being subject to persecution because of his "status as a homosexual." The immigration judge ruled in his favor (withholding deportation), but the Immigration and Naturalization Service (INS) appealed the ruling, arguing that homosexuals were not members of a "social group" subject to persecution as defined by the Refugee Act of 1980, the reigning document that had thus far been interpreted to apply mainly to members of ethnic or racial groups or political or religious organizations subject to state (or other political) persecution. The case was ultimately adjudicated in favor of Alfonso, partly because those "fleeing communist and communist-dominated lands were singled out for special attention" (Ong 2003:309 n18).

More important for our purposes are developments that took place in 1994. At that time, Attorney General Janet Reno, who as head of the Justice Department was in charge of the INS, ordered that the Alfonso decision should thenceforth be a legally binding precedent for INS officials dealing with cases involving applications for political asylum or withholding of deportation based on sexual orientation or identity. In Reno's (1994) words: "The case holds that an individual who has been identified as homosexual and persecuted by his or her government for that reason alone may be eligible for relief under the refugee laws on the basis of persecution because of membership in a [particular] social group."

Since 1994, gays, lesbians and transgendered individuals from dozens of countries in Asia, Africa, Eastern Europe, and Latin America have sought asylum in the US (and in Canada and Western Europe). The list of countries from which sexual asylum seekers (sexual asylees) have originated includes Brazil, Columbia, Peru, Nicaragua, Venezuela, Romania, Iran, Jordan, Turkey, China, India, Pakistan, Bangladesh, Malaysia, Singapore, and Indonesia, to name but a few. The process of seeking sexual or other political asylum in the US is generally similar regardless of one's national origins, though the outcome of the process is highly variable, depending not only on "country conditions" as understood by asylum officers and immigration judges, but also on these latter officials' professional background and gender. "Fortuitous circumstances," most notably "the personalities of the particular judges before whom cases happen [through random assignment] to come for disposition" are the most salient determinants of the outcome of cases, according to an exhaustive study (of some 400,000 asylum decisions) appropriately titled "Refugee Roulette: Disparities in Asylum Adjudication." The study concludes that the single most important action affecting the disposition of an asylee's case is the court clerk's more or less random assignment of the case to a particular judge, as illustrated by the fact that one judge approved only 5 percent of the Colombian asylum cases he was randomly assigned, while another judge in the same building provided favorable rulings in more than 88 percent of the Colombian asylum cases that were randomly assigned to her (Ramji-Nogales et al. 2007:296). These latter generalizations apply to all varieties of political asylum, not simply the subset of those cases that involve what I call "sexual asylum." My experience with Malaysians seeking sexual asylum, which is based on a far smaller number of cases (an n of 14), is presumably more comforting to those who believe that the US legal system should be characterized by regularity, consistency, and predictability, insofar as all of the cases were adjudicated in favor of asylees. Such consistency should come as no surprise since most of the cases in which I was involved occurred during the midst of or shortly after the Anwar affair. The extensive coverage afforded by the *New York Times* and other Western media was a godsend for anyone seeking to develop an argument that Malaysians who are openly gay, lesbian, or transgendered have a well-founded subjective fear of persecution by police and others.

The chambers and more encompassing spatial contexts in which asylum cases are heard, like many of the encounters between asylees and those involved in their hearings, are usefully regarded as "contact zones," following the usage of Mary Louise Pratt (1992:6–7 passim) and James Clifford (1997:Chap. 7). Pratt defines "contact zone" as "the space of colonial encounters, the space in which peoples geographically and historically separated come into contact with each other and establish ongoing relations, usually involving conditions of coercion, radical inequality, and intractable conflict." The term differs from that of "frontier" and

> is an attempt to invoke the spatial and temporal copresence of subjects previously separated by geographical and historical disjunctures, and whose trajectories now intersect. By using the term "contact," I aim to foreground the interactive, improvisational dimensions of colonial encounters so easily ignored or suppressed by diffusionist accounts of conquest and domination. A "contact" perspective emphasizes how subjects are constituted in and by their relations to each other. [It emphasizes] copresence, interaction, interlocking understandings and practices, often within radically asymmetrical relations of power.
>
> (Pratt 1992:7)

Clifford (1997:192–193) expands the notion of contact zones to include encounters that do not entail colonialism, such as ethnographic museums (Karp and Lavine 1991), for they too are "places of hybrid possibility and political negotiation, sites of exclusion and struggle" (Clifford 1997:212–213). So too of course are the sites of immigration hearings.

For Robert Chung (a pseudonym), the 33-year-old Chinese Malaysian seeking political asylum in the US whose case I focus on in these remarks, the larger spatial context of the contact zone included the Federal Building in lower Manhattan, the venue for his (Spring 1999) hearing. On the day of the hearing, as in previous months, the Federal Building was subject to intense security measures owing to the fact that the trial of the men charged with the 1993 bombing of the World Trade Center was still in progress, as were proceedings in the high-profile racketeering trial of mobster John Gotti. Large police vans blocked the sidewalk in some areas, apparently in an effort to prevent suicide car-bombers like the ones that devastated the US Marines barracks in Beirut in 1983.

Because my direct encounters with Robert were quite limited, I do not know what impressions these sights or the palpable tension in the air made on him, or how he traveled to the Federal Building that morning. Did he take a bus or cab driven by one of New York City's many immigrants? If so, did he feel any kinship or cultural affinity with them? The driver of the car who drove me from the airport to the offices of Robert's lawyers was a burly Egyptian who after hearing from me that I was in town in connection with an immigration case, complained bitterly of his wife's woes with the immigration office, one problem being that their paperwork had been languishing for a few years now. Whether he would have shared his story with Robert (or vice versa) is unclear.

As we rode the elevators up to the tenth floor of the building, one of Robert's lawyers recounted apocryphal tales about immigrants who ended up being deported due to mechanical problems with the elevators that resulted in their being stuck between floors or otherwise unable to reach the courtrooms situated toward the top of the building in time for their hearings. The waiting room to which we were relegated was like a mini-UN, packed with Indian women in saris, turbaned Sikh men, West Africans in flowing garb, large numbers of Chinese, and African American and other lawyers doing uptake interviews on the run. Many in the room appeared to have little if any command of the English language or of American law, a point driven home by exasperated lawyers engaged in hasty interviews, one of whom admonished his client for being unprepared for his hearing and warned that he did not want to squander precious capital with the judge by proceeding with cases that lacked proper documentation. It all seemed extremely chaotic, a crap shoot at best; yet clearly the fates of many families, and much more, hung in the balance.

Robert was extremely fortunate that his case was assigned to a sympathetic judge. Of Euro-American background and probably in his early 60s, the judge evinced a great deal of interest in Robert's experiences in Malaysia and in my account of country conditions bearing on gender and sexuality, especially same-sex sexuality. He asked incisive, penetrating questions of all of us, even though it was slow going for him at times, especially since his (and everyone else's) questions to Robert, along with Robert's responses, had to be translated by an interpreter conversant in English and Mandarin.

The only time I saw the judge lose patience was when the government (INS) attorney in the case, an African American woman who appeared to be in her 40s—whose main job was to impugn the testimony that Robert (and I) provided—suggested that granting Robert asylum would "open the floodgates" to gays and lesbians from all over the world. The clear implication was that an affirmative ruling on the judge's part would result in deluging the US with wave after wave of undesirable because perverted aliens. The judge was angered by this comment, responding that since this was only the first (or second) case of this sort that he had ever encountered, he did not see any open floodgates on the horizon. Apparently more upsetting to him, however, was the fact that Robert's case had reached his courtroom in the first place. He felt that the asylum officer who had previously denied Robert's petition for asylum had made an egregious mistake in doing so, and that Robert had experienced undue delays, uncertainties, and suffering as a result.

The documentation provided the judge by Robert's two lawyers included statements from social workers, a psychiatrist (or psychologist), the anthropologist, as well as city officials (local councilmen), and others who corroborated various aspects of the narrative presented in Robert's affidavit. The social workers and psychiatrist verified that Robert had been undergoing treatment for the unresolved emotional traumas he had experienced in Malaysia, just as the anthropologist confirmed that country conditions were such that Robert did indeed have a well-founded subjective fear of persecution should he return to his homeland and live an openly gay life there. The city councilmen for their part wrote that Robert was a productive member of the New York City community who held a job, paid taxes, and did volunteer work in a clinic for people living with HIV/AIDS.

Clearly, Robert had to be constructed in a certain, easily recognizable way in order to be "legible" to the judge. Just as this necessitated extensive documentation from lawyers, mental health experts, elected officials, and their proxies and allies, so too did it presuppose that Robert categorically identify himself as "a homosexual," more specifically, a "feminized homosexual"—and an "open" one at that. The establishment of these facts required that Robert painstakingly and repeatedly divulge the most intimate and traumatic details of his life experiences to a host of strangers, some of whom, like the government attorney representing the INS, were clearly hostile to him and sought to elicit inconsistent statements from him so as to undermine his credibility and have him deported. In light of these circumstances and the fact that some of the experts whose help Robert and his defense team solicited staked their professional reputations on the fact that Robert's presentation of self was consistent with that of an American-style (or at least recognizably) "open homosexual," it is no surprise that one of the very first assertions in Robert's affidavit is the statement: "I am a homosexual." Whether this narrativized sexualized identity should be taken as evidence of the formation of a new kind of Asian (American) *homo sexualis* that downplays gender identity in favor of sexual orientation is unclear, though we see analogous developments among other groups of Southeast Asians both in this nation and the homeland.

The affidavit Robert submitted for his hearing has much in common with other asylum narratives that I have examined, especially in its stark portrayal of his traumatic persecution and other disconcerting experiences in Malaysia—understandable, perhaps, in light of the purpose of the documents. (The skeptic might reason that some of these experiences are embellished if not manufactured *ex nihilo* to bolster the case for asylum, but their strong resonance with accounts of gay, lesbian, and transgendered Malaysians who have remained in their native country argue against this skepticism, as do consistencies in the multiple recounting of life experiences to therapists, legal scribes, judges, and others.) Robert's negative experiences included an early, discomfiting awareness of, in his words, being "different" from "other boys" at school, an awareness that went hand in hand with his discernible lack of interest in "boys' games" (such as soccer, marbles, and playing Samurai) and his preference for "girls' activities" (jump rope, playing with dolls, etc.). Robert's early awareness of his (feminized) and to him immutable difference and its implications was reinforced by the teasing and hazing he experienced at the hands of male classmates, coupled with a recognition around age 12 or 13 of erotic or sexual feelings toward other boys. The teasing and hazing by male age-mates quickly escalated to the point where Robert was beaten and threatened with recriminations if he told his parents, school authorities, or anyone else. So at age 14 he quit school and took up the first of a series of low-paying jobs that included assisting his father, who made a living as a carpenter, helping his mother who hawked food from a roadside stall, selling t-shirts to tourists, and working as a welder in a metal shop. Co-workers in the metal shop, the majority if not all of whom were male, quickly targeted his overt femininity, which they took as a clear sign of his being homosexual, and subjected him to various kinds of humiliation, sexual abuse, and exploitation. So too did the Malaysian police, who encountered Robert in the vicinity of Merdeka [Independence] Square—a well-known cruising spot for males seeking sexual encounters with other males—and threatened to sodomize him with a nightstick and throw him in jail if they ever saw him there again.

Experiences such as these caused Robert to fear for his safety and led to depression and suicidal impulses. There was no one in Kuala Lumpur to whom Robert felt he could turn, despite the presence there, obviously unbeknownst to him, of a burgeoning subculture of people who identified as gay or lesbian. So in 1988, by which time Robert dreamt of being a fashion designer, he left Malaysia for Singapore, hoping to find in that predominantly Chinese island-nation a more hospitable environment. Part of the appeal of taking up temporary residence in Singapore (he apparently never intended to live there permanently, an issue of some importance in his petition for asylum) had to do with the existence there of a beauty school that he had heard about from a cousin's sister. Robert enrolled in the school and spent a total of six years in Singapore (1988–1994), making brief trips back to Malaysia to visit family when the school closed for holidays. But he did not find the climate in Singapore particularly hospitable, partly because this was a time when discourses of "Asian values" and heteronormativity were ascendant. On the other hand, it was in Singapore that he came across a Chinese-language newspaper article about life for gays in the US. As Robert put it in his asylum narrative: "I decided to visit the United States in May 1994 when I read in a Chinese newspaper that homosexuals have more freedom and safety in the United States. I saw a photo of a gay pride march in New York City where people were smiling and happy. They looked comfortable with who they were. I decided to apply for a [B-2] tourist visa to visit the United States."

Robert's narrative continues as follows:

> When I arrived in New York City I saw an active gay community in places like West Village and Chelsea. I saw for myself that gay people have a freedom to associate with other gay people. I soon started feeling more self assured and comfortable in this city. I did not have to look behind my shoulder in fear of police or authorities. It was here that I made friends and met my life partner [SP] in January 1996. It took me many long sessions with my companion [SP] and my best friend [TM] to bring out my feelings and these stories. It is not in the Chinese tradition to talk about sexuality. I am expected by my parents to marry and have children. I am still not able to tell my parents I am homosexual. I still have difficulty talking about my feelings. They are very painful and not easy to relate. I repressed a lot of these feelings because I grew up in a very religious Buddaist [sic] family. It is my hope that after so much abuse and mistreatment as a homosexual including sexual abuse by co-workers and threats from police, and the fear of more abuse and mistreatment as an open homosexual if deported to Malaysia that the Immigration Court will consider granting me political asylum.

One of the interesting features of Robert's asylum narrative is the dichotomous portrayal of Malaysia (homeland) and the US (diaspora). Malaysia is rendered almost entirely in negative terms: a site of humiliation, physical and psychological abuse, persecution, sexual trauma, self-denial, forced concealment of one's core identity—a living hell. The US on the other hand is portrayed as a site of openness and tolerance, a place where one can be self-assured, comfortable, and free, a land of smiles and happiness, where one's self—any self—can flourish through association and the formation of emotionally meaningful relationships with others, including de facto marriage with a same-sex partner—in short, a "do-your-own-thing" kind of paradise. These kinds of dichotomous renderings are fairly common in accounts from the diaspora (Clifford 1997: Chap. 10), though in many cases the signs are reversed, emphasizing paradise lost rather than gained. Much obviously depends on the political and other circumstances leading up to decisions to leave one's homeland and the kinds of experiences one has in the new country.

That Robert's feelings toward his homeland include both positive and negative sentiments, and are thus more mixed than his narrative suggests, is indicated both by his desire to take his life-partner (SP) to Malaysia at some point in the future ("to show him what it is like"), and by his maintaining more or less weekly telephone contact with his mother and other family members. When I asked SP (at Robert's hearing) about the likelihood of such a trip, he expressed disdain at the thought. He was strongly disinclined to undertake any such journey, especially in light of Robert's coming-of-age experiences there and what he (SP) had learned about the country from international media coverage of the Anwar affair and the research he had undertaken to help search out and organize documents for Robert's case. Relevant as well is the sardonically titled film *Return to Paradise*, which is set in Malaysia and had been released the previous year (1998); SP (like me) had recently seen this disturbing film, the first portion of which deals with "three [American] buddies living the life in Malaysia, a life of drugs, sex, and freedom."[2] The "good life" they share does not last long, however, for they soon split up. One of them ("Lewis"), an idealistic conservationist, stays behind, intending to go to Borneo to save orangutans, while the others head back to the US to pursue their careers. Shortly after their departure, Lewis is imprisoned for possessing a sizable amount of hashish that the three of them had bought while they were still together. He is then sentenced to death, a punishment that will be commuted to jail time, he is promised, if his two friends return to take responsibility and serve three years each for their share in the crime. The two eventually agree to return to Malaysia to spare their friend the death penalty. But because of negative American press about the trial and the Malaysian judiciary on the eve of the sentencing, Lewis is dragged screaming to the gallows and hung, by which time one of his buddies had begun serving his sentence and the other had fled the country.

The film thus conveys a clear cautionary tale about the dark side of paradise "Malaysian style:" Malaysian authorities cannot be trusted; the judiciary in particular is arbitrary, irrational, and spiteful; and anyone who angers authorities or transgresses local laws and customs flirts with disaster (imprisonment, torture, bodily decay, misery) if not certain death. These themes resonate deeply with international media coverage of the Anwar affair—and with centuries of Western depictions of Islamic justice. All things considered, it is not surprising that SP had no interest in traveling with Robert to Malaysia.

Robert's asylum narrative is also broadly allegorical in ways that were culturally meaningful to the judge, which may help explain why the judge ruled in his favor. Particularly pronounced are the themes of victimization, persecution, suffering, self-denial, and stoic endurance leading to flight or quest in search of salvation, personal redemption, and self-realization. Also much in evidence are themes of hard work, a certain industriousness and restlessness of spirit, a highly developed sense of autonomy, and a clear capacity for self-reliance and self-management. Perhaps most striking, however, is Robert's remarkable personal courage. Nearly two centuries ago Alexis de Tocqueville (1835–1840 [2004]: 215, 732) observed that in the hierarchy of American values, courage is "the paramount virtue and the greatest of moral necessities for man," particularly since "Americans are taught from birth that they must overcome life's woes and impediments *on their own*" (emphasis added).

These are the kinds of themes emphasized by America's largely Protestant founders, who fled religious and political persecution in England and elsewhere in Europe and went to great lengths to insure that the new republic they established made allowance for the untrammeled expression of certain kinds of difference (e.g., of religious belief and political opinion). Not surprisingly, these are also the themes that struck Tocqueville, whose two-volume opus, *Democracy in America* (1835–1840 [2004]), remains one of the most incisive accounts of American society and politics ever written. A French lawyer of aristocratic background, Tocqueville traveled throughout America for nine months in 1831, during which time he interviewed some two hundred people from diverse walks of life (in New York, Maine, Michigan, Missouri, Georgia, Mississippi, etc.), and made systematic observations concerning all that he saw and heard. The rich civic (associational) life of Americans contrasted sharply with what Tocqueville knew to be characteristic of France and England and also helped temper the omnipotence and "tyranny of the majority," an ever-present danger in democracies that Tocqueville discussed at some length. Emphasizing the systems of checks and balances that allow for the florescence of formal and informal democracy—and pluralism—in America, Tocqueville thus underscores that laws and formal institutions (e.g., of church and state) are dialectically related to less formally codified "mores and customs," and that the latter can and must nourish—and serve as a check on—the former, and vice versa. But laws and formal institutions alone will not necessarily enable people to "escape the dominion of custom and the tyranny of opinion," especially if the "the well of public virtue has run dry" (ibid., 105, 701). The cultivation and dissemination of ethical virtues is thus key, which is why Tocqueville, like Weber and Foucault later on, is so concerned with the ethics of self-management and how these and attendant ethics are inculcated and reproduced in the citizenry.

In sum, the virtues highlighted in Robert's asylum narrative share deep resonance with many of the values foregrounded by America's founders, and, to mix
metaphors, would have been identified by Tocqueville as "the right stuff" for
America. That the judge in Robert's case ruled as he did indicates that they also
resonate with the (neoliberal) themes of our day. Congruences such as these
lead Ong (2003) to ask rhetorically whether Asian immigrants, many of whom
embody virtues highlighted in Robert's narrative, might be considered the "new
Westerners."

What difference might it have made if instead of (or in addition to) learning
about diversity in the US via Chinese-language newspaper depictions of
"happy (gay) natives" in New York City, Robert had encountered international
media coverage of other, less upbeat events, involving "gay bashing" for
example, that occurred in the US when he was coming of age in the 1980s and
1990s? One immediately thinks of the murder of Matthew Shepard in October
1998, although this occurred after Robert had immigrated to the US. Shepard
was the 21-year-old gay student at the University of Wyoming who was robbed,
pistol whipped and otherwise savagely beaten (his skull was crushed), tied to a
fence, and left to die in an isolated, rural area of Laramie by two ostensibly heterosexual men he had met in a bar and asked for a ride home earlier that
evening. The two men charged in the murder initially invoked the "gay panic"
defense, claiming that Shepard had made sexual overtures toward them and
that these overtures induced a panic so intense and uncontrollable that it
entailed temporary insanity. They later switched tactics, insisting that they had
only intended to rob him not to kill him, but were nonetheless convicted of
murder.

Shepard's tragic killing was memorialized by well-known public figures, especially in the music and entertainment industry, and eventually led to the passage of legislation concerning hate crimes. But his funeral was also picketed by
many members of the Christian right, some of whom, like their compatriots
who protested from afar, bore signs reading "Matthew Shepard Rots in Hell,"
"God Hates Fags," and "AIDS kills fags dead." International media covered
Shepard's murder and the subsequent funeral and trial at some length, and
clearly presented a very different picture of diversity (and its discontents) than
the images of the gay pride march in New York City, where "people were smiling and happy … and looked comfortable with who they were," that Robert
encountered in the Chinese-language press in Singapore.

One can only speculate as to whether Robert had heard of the cases like that
of Matthew Shepard and, assuming he had not, how familiarity with such cases
might have troubled if not radically transformed his view of the US as a "safe
space" for "people like himself." One wonders too whether Robert knew about
Vincent Chin, the 27-year-old Chinese American who was beaten to death in
recession-plagued Detroit in June 1982 as he was celebrating his final days of
bachelorhood. Chin died at the hands of two white autoworkers—Ronald
Ebons, a foreman at Chrysler Motors and his recently laid off stepson Michael
Nitz—who he had encountered in a neighborhood bar. An inebriated Ebons

mistook Chin for Japanese, calling him a "Jap," adding, "It's because of you little mother-fuckers that we're out of work." A brawl ensued and those involved were evicted from the bar. Ebons and Nitz then availed themselves of a baseball bat from their parked car and chased Chin for a full 20 minutes, finally catching him. Nitz restrained Chin while Ebons repeatedly beat him on the head with the bat, cracking open his skull and splattering his brains on the pavement. Four days later, Chin died of head injuries.

Though originally charged with second-degree murder, Ebons and Nitz brokered a deal in which they pled guilty to a lesser charge (manslaughter). The white judge, who evidently felt that their crime did not merit any jail time, sentenced each of them to three years' probation and a $3,000 fine. The senseless murder and the slap-on-the-hand sentence outraged Chinese Americans and the larger Asian American community who organized rallies and mobilized community resources across the country to pressure the federal government to pursue separate charges against the two men (for violating Chin's civil rights). The resulting jury trial exonerated the two men who murdered Chin because they assumed he was Japanese, owing to the jury's belief that the crime was not racially motivated.

My intention in citing these two hate crimes is not to suggest that the extremely uncivil views and dispositions of their perpetrators somehow typify American sentiments concerning diversity, for clearly they do not. I cite these cases, rather, to draw attention to four sets of issues. First, there are large numbers of people in the US who while not driven to premeditated murder or other violence are deeply ambivalent about if not sharply opposed to the presence in their midst of people like Matthew Shepard and Vincent Chin, to say nothing of Brandon Teena, the 21-year-old female-to-male transsexual depicted in the film *Boys Don't Cry*, who—in real life, as in the film—was also brutally murdered.[3] Second, incidents such as these, like the cultural-political dynamics that spawn them, trouble the linear, progressivist narratives we tell one another about our (pluralistic) selves and, by implication, our constructions of the differences between "us" (Westerners) and "them" (non-Westerners)—as, in different ways, do the high suicide rates among gay and lesbian teenagers in this nation and the experiences of gay Cambodians living here (to which we turn shortly). Third, hate crimes of all varieties make for good media copy that circulates widely, informing the views of many hundreds of millions of people throughout the world as to the values that Americans hold dear, in much the same way as revelations of conditions at American-run prisons at Abu Ghraib and Guantanamo Bay.[4] A fourth, related point is that had Robert's initial or lasting impression of American pluralism and its discontents been shaped by media coverage of these kinds of crimes and abuses, as opposed to gay pride marches in New York City, he might not have sought asylum here.

The kind of community that Robert and other gay asylum seekers envision in New York City and elsewhere in the US may not exist, though we should exercise caution in assuming that Robert and others who petition for sexual asylum do in fact hunger for "community"—as distinct from freedom to "be themselves" and to associate openly with whomever they choose—in the first place. Robert's narrative, recall, expresses a desire for "freedom," "safety," "happiness," being "comfortable," and experiencing "self-assurance" and "acceptance," not community per se, although one might counter that the existence of these kinds of experiences presupposes the existence of community. Kath Weston (1991: 128–129) has argued with reference to San Francisco, for example, that the notion of a gay (or lesbian) community is something of a chimera, if one means by "community" an internally undifferentiated social space characterized by unity, harmony, and equality, a place where everyone feels like they fit in, belong, and are accepted (cf. Gopinath 1996, Manalansan 2003). Part of the reason for this is that owing to the cultural-political climate, gays (broadly defined to include lesbians) in San Francisco and elsewhere must situate themselves in relation to a number of potentially divisive issues: the significance of coming out to parents and others; "popular critique[s] of the look-alike styles of 'Castro clones'; a resurgence of butch/femme relations among lesbians that [flies] in the face of feminist prescriptions for androgyny; and ... heated debate[s] about sadomasochism, ... and other marginalized sexualities" (Weston 1991:128).

Gays in San Francisco and much of the rest of the world are further divided by affiliations of class, race, ethnicity, religion, and national origins. This is readily apparent to gay Muslim residents of the US in the wake of the September 11 terrorist attacks on the World Trade Center and the Pentagon, and the Bush administration's ensuing "war on terror" (Worth 2002). Anti-Muslim sentiment directed at gay Muslims by gays who are not Muslim has been particularly painful, especially since gay Muslims cannot share their experiences with straight Muslims for fear of being rejected and disowned by parents and other relatives, barred from attending mosque services, and otherwise ostracized by the Muslim community, many members of which feel that same-sex sexuality is a Western invention that so debases religion and race alike that it merits capital punishment.

Gay Muslims living in diasporic contexts such as the US did of course experience acute alienation long before September 11. Factors such as these led to the establishment of gay Muslim organizations such as the Al-Fatiha Foundation, which takes its name from the Arabic term for "the opening." Launched in New York City in 1999 by Pakistan-born Faisal Alam (who was also instrumental in organizing a chapter in Washington D.C. in 1997), the foundation aims to help mitigate the "incredible amount of loneliness and suffering" experienced by gay Muslims in the New York City area and "to help individuals reconcile their homosexuality with their religion, in whatever way they want to do it" (Sachs 1999). One of the reasons the creation of such a network (which now boasts chapters throughout the US, Canada, and beyond) was deemed necessary was that "when he revealed his homosexuality at college in Boston, Faisal ... was asked to leave several Muslim youth groups" and was outed at the family mosque, his distressed mother insisting, "you can't call yourself a Muslim anymore" (ibid.).

People like Faisal, along with their Muslim counterparts from Malaysia, Indonesia, and other parts of the Muslim world, must contend not only with the daily fear of rejection from members of their native communities but also from the straight, predominantly Euro-American community that dominates in the new homeland. The perspectives of Cambodian immigrants who self-identify as *gay* are revealing in this regard (even though they are mostly Buddhists not Muslims), especially since they also suggest one of several possible futures awaiting successful asylees such as Robert.

Unlike the Malaysians discussed here, the circumstances of Cambodians' journeys to the US were heavily conditioned by the American war in Vietnam, Laos, and Cambodia, and the resulting horrors of the Pol Pot regime (1975–1979), which brought about the deaths, through starvation, physical exhaustion, disease, torture, or execution, of some 1.7 million Cambodians, nearly 20 percent of the country's entire population. The majority of Cambodians living in this country at present, including those who self-identify as *gay*, entered the US as refugees, in many cases after having spent time in refugee camps in Thailand, or were born to refugee parents already residing in the US. In contrast to their Malaysian counterparts, in other words, *gay* Cambodians living in this nation did not enter the US seeking (or once here petition for) political asylum on grounds of sexual orientation.

The experiences of *gay* Cambodians in the US (documented by Quintiliani 1995, who deals primarily with educated, middle-class people) are usefully considered in the context of other work on Cambodians in the diaspora (Ledgerwood 1994, Smith-Hefner 1999, Ong 2003). In southern California, the site of Quintiliani's research during the period 1992–1994, Cambodians who self identify as *gay* "describe themselves as feminine males who have the 'heart' of a woman and behave or desire to behave like a woman," their usage of the term "also signif[lying] their desire for same-sex partners" (Quintiliani 1995:17). The English-language term "gay" is thus taken to be "the closest English translation for the Khmer word *khteey*" [*khtoey*] (ibid., 17), a polysemic term like the Thai-language *kathoey* to which it gave rise. Since in Cambodia the term *khtoey* encompasses hermaphrodites, cross-dressers, effeminate males, and masculine females without specifying sexual orientation per se, its translation in the US context as "gay" indexes both a localization and a diversification of the concept of gayness.

In sharp contrast to Malaysian asylum seekers, whose narratives emphasize a hellish past in the homeland and paradise gained in the diaspora, *gay* Cambodians living in southern California portray gender sensibilities in Cambodia in relatively positive terms, particularly when compared with the negative dynamics they encounter in the US. Thus emphasized are themes of the "tolerance," "acceptance," and "respect" they were accorded, along with mainstream Cambodians' "relative nonchalance" toward gender and sexual transgression (though they also acknowledged "being teased"). Some idealizing of conditions in Cambodia is evident in these depictions—a deep irony in light of the Pol Pot regime's murderous intolerance of various kinds of difference

(Chandler 1991, Kiernan 1996). The many groups targeted for elimination by the Khmer Rouge included those working for or otherwise linked with the French colonizers or the US-backed government of Lon Nol (1970–1975), hence bureaucrats, intellectuals, urban dwellers, and anyone who spoke French or wore eyeglasses (each a sign of Western technology and decadence). In their quest to purge the Khmer "race" of ethnic and other cultural impurities, the Khmer Rouge also endeavored to eliminate Vietnamese, Chams, and other non-Khmer, as well as Khmer seen as exhibiting one or another aspect of "Vietnamese mentality." Pol Pot's disdain of religion (as "the opiate of the masses") also led Khmer Rouge forces to murder Buddhist monks and members of other religious orders, and to sack and destroy many Buddhist monuments (Boua 1991). The fate of healers (*krou*) and other ritual specialists is less clear. Some of them were most likely spared, even held up as exemplars of "the glories of Angkor," which Pol Pot sought to resurrect from the ashes of history. Others may have been seen as remnants of feudal times and would have been dealt with accordingly (hunted down, murdered), as occurred in broadly analogous circumstances with the Bugis *bissu* during the South Sulawesi Rebellion (1950–1965).

The widespread destruction of families and households that occurred during Pol Pot's reign of terror sometimes obscures the strong pro-natalist policies the Khmer Rouge sought to enforce. (Many adults who lost or were separated from their spouses were forced to marry and start new families.) These policies placed a premium on sexual activities with reproductive potential and may well have discouraged same-sex intimacy on the part of ritual specialists and others. More broadly, the emphasis on male physical prowess and bravery contributed to a climate in which effeminate males were widely disparaged if not actively targeted for elimination, though in some cases they were spared and kept for the sexual services they could provide soldiers. The more general point is that *gay* Cambodians' narratives of life in Cambodia (as conveyed to and by Quintiliani) make little if any explicit reference to the kinds of dynamics outlined here. Instead, and in a searing indictment of US "tolerance" of and "compassion" toward non-white refugee Others, they emphasize "how much better they were treated in Cambodia" as compared with America, and that, as noted earlier, "at least people [in Cambodia] didn't hate us like they do here" (Quintiliani 1995:49).

In light of their positive depictions of sentiments toward gender transgression in Cambodia and their negative experiences with racism, heterosexism, and homophobia in the US, it is not surprising that *gay* Cambodians in this country who are in their 30s and 40s (or older) evince a strong interest in "being Cambodian (or Khmer)." "Being Cambodian" entails speaking or at least being competent in the Khmer language, and displaying knowledge of Cambodian dance, food, card games, and floral arrangements. The Flower Blessing Dance, like performances of the *apsaras*, the "celestial maidens" or "heavenly dancing girls" depicted in hundreds of carvings at Angkor who "were believed to have been created from the Churning of the Sea of Milk" (Coe 2003:121), are deeply resonant symbols of Cambodian identity. This is particularly so for *gay* Cambodians, many of whom strongly identify with and go to some lengths to master these and other dances that were performed by women and presumably *khtoey* at royal palaces in the capital, Phnom Penh, and elsewhere in times past. In thus identifying with dramatic genres that are linked to the spirits and the sacred and that have long been sponsored by Cambodian royalty, *gay* Cambodians assert a cultural kinship with previous generations of Khmer (and many other groups of Southeast Asians involved in gender transgression). This identification has profound regenerative and cosmological significance insofar as heavenly unions with *apsaras* are believed to have given rise to the Khmer royal line, the Khmer people, and very name of the homeland. In one origin myth, for example, "a hermit named Kambu ... was given an *apsaras* or celestial nymph named Mera by the great god Shiva (the major patron of Khmer rulers). From this marriage sprang the Khmer royal line as well as the people themselves. The Khmer thus came to call their land Kambudesa or 'Country of Kambu', later abridged to Kambuja; it is from this latter that the modern name 'Cambodia' is derived" (Coe 2003:33).[5] The *apsaras* and those who identify with them thus share with the Bugis *bissu* and certain others in Southeast Asia that they were present at, even before, the creation.

At least as significant as how they position themselves in relation to fellow Cambodians and traditions of the past is the ways they negotiate encounters with non-Cambodians in the present and what this might bode for their future and that of other Southeast Asians living in the US. In the US, *khtoey* subject positions and subjectivities have undergone various transformations due to Cambodians' engagements with Euro-American gay culture and their associations with Hispanics and other men of color. "With the exception of the traditional interpretation of the *khteey* roles [,] ... gay-identified Cambodian men" no longer "want to go all the way and portray themselves as women publicly. The gay world [of southern California and the US generally] makes alternate, less extreme choices available to these men" (Quintiliani 1995:82–83). For both the *gay*-identified and those who are not out, "the gay world offers the social and emotional support to resist getting married without portraying themselves as a *khteey*" (ibid., 83). More generally, "Cambodian men who have sex with men and who do not want to get married" are increasingly able to look and behave "like men" and to pursue occupations other than those seen by Cambodian society as involving "women's work" (ibid., 83). Analogous openings are evident in the realm of sexual positioning in that *gay* Cambodians no longer confine themselves to the insertee role. In short, we see more flexibility and switching than formerly and a loosening of the heterogender hegemony insofar as Cambodians can more easily (e.g., with less opprobrium) engage in relations that are simultaneously homosexual and homogender.

These changes are part and parcel of more encompassing transformations that have witnessed a rise in heterosexism and homophobia within America's Cambodian community (ibid., 83). *Gay* Cambodians' growing estrangement and alienation from fellow Cambodians is experienced as the larger community pulling away from them, withdrawing its support, and viewing them as deeply disappointing—as stigmatized sources of physical contagion and social, spiritual, and moral pollution. As their nieces and nephews mingle with Anglos, Hispanics, and others at schools and playgrounds, they adopt and disseminate among family members and friends new terminologies of insult and derogation, including terms such as "fag" and "faggot," which as one *gay* Cambodian man's nephew explained, means "someone you hate or looks weird" (ibid., 50, 51). While the young boy did not understand the meaning of the term, the uncle "fears that his nephew will learn the definition and begin to despise him" just like other Americans (ibid., 51).

The partial defeminization of Cambodian *gayness* is part of a larger dynamic involving polarization and other forms of realignment and change that has occurred in the culture and political economy of the sex/gender systems of Cambodian refugees. *Inter alia*, these changes entail the emergence on the one hand of increasingly strict, dichotomous codes of gender and sexuality for the heteronormative majority, especially the female-bodied among them; and on the other, a diffuse suspicion if not denigration of femininity on the part of males, coupled with a rise in domestic violence against women. The theme of the "virtuous woman" is particularly pronounced among Cambodians living in the homeland and the diaspora even or especially in contexts where parents find it increasingly difficult to inculcate the relevant virtues (modesty, chastity, filial piety, compassion) in their daughters (Ledgerwood 1994, Smith-Hefner 1999). In the Khmer scheme of things, the attainment of female virtue requires that daughters be sequestered at home, under the vigilant tutelage of elders. But this is increasingly unrealistic for most Cambodians in a highly mobile society such as the US where unchaperoned travel to schools and jobs is often necessary and where the mass mediated temptations of shopping malls, consumerism, and sex beckon constantly. One result is that men's suspicions about female family members (reinforced by Buddhist doctrines that depict women as men's inferiors) not uncommonly "boil over," resulting in domestic violence (Ong 2003:33–35, 142–167).

The denigration of femininity and the rise of domestic violence against girlfriends, wives, and daughters that we see in many quarters of the Cambodian community in this country speak to the crises of masculinity experienced by Cambodian males living in the diaspora who find that the language and occupational skills they honed in the homeland render them ill-suited both for meaningful employment in the US, and for the role of head of household that is defined in economic, moral, and spiritual terms. Alcohol and drugs provide short-term escape from the experience of disjunction between ideals of masculine prowess and autonomy on the one hand and lived realities on the other. So too, at least for teenage boys and young adult men, does membership in gangs that valorize displays of hypermasculinity emphasizing a radical autonomy vis-à-vis women and all others. One is reminded of the broadly analogous cultural politics and ironies surrounding Burmese (and US) rappers' performances of angry and discursively violent masculinities (Chapter 4), and of the appeal in China and its diaspora of the Chinese martial arts scene (Louie 2002).

The larger issue is that like others in the US (and elsewhere), Cambodians must negotiate and otherwise contend with dimensions of their social location that are keyed to dynamics of race and class, many aspects of which are imbricated in or embedded within their gender identities and sexual orientations. The majority of Cambodians residing in the US find themselves at or below the poverty line, working—when jobs are available to them—in the low-paid service sector (e.g., in the garment industry, or as janitors or waitresses), which does not afford them the opportunity to make a living wage. As a consequence, they tend to live in cramped, sub-standard housing in low-income neighborhoods (in East Oakland and San Francisco's Tenderloin District, for example) that are rife with drugs and crime. They do not fit—indeed, in many respects they invert—the "model minority" stereotype and are thus subject to harsh regimes of discipline, surveillance, and control that are overseen by refugee organizations, medical bureaucracies, the police, and the general public, even though they are also the beneficiaries of a feminist-inflected "refugee love" that is evident in the interventions of social workers and others who seek to ameliorate the effects of poverty and structural violence, especially domestic abuse (Ong 2003: Chap. 6; cf. Rafael 2000).

Circumstances such as these help explain why *gay* Cambodians feel that they are hated by the American majority. Some—arguably much—of the ill-will *gay* Cambodians experience is due to their social location within the heavily hierarchical US racial system. This system is fundamentally binary and tends to assimilate all ethnic and "racial" groups to one or the other of the two dominant categories, "black" or "white," which are sometimes conceptualized along a continuum (Williams 1989). Cambodians, as Ong (2003) has shown, are implicitly classified as "black" or at least relegated toward the black end of the continuum, and are thus "blackened," like Jews, Irish, and the members of certain other religious and ethnic groups in former times inasmuch as they are subject to many of the same stereotypes and structural and other prejudices that have long confronted the African American community (e.g., the idea that they are lazy, lack a proper work ethic, have deficient standards of personal hygiene, and are sexually aberrant and otherwise dangerous). Insofar as they are blackened (like Arabs, Muslims, Sikhs, and South Asians generally), the experiences of Cambodian Americans differ significantly from Chinese and Japanese Americans who as exemplars of model minorities are subject to "whitening" processes that accord them honorary white status, even though as "strangers from a different shore" (Takaki 1998) they are never fully accepted as white. The contrasting gradations in respect and legitimacy accorded different groups of Southeast Asian immigrants exemplify the historically contingent and contested system of graduated pluralism that prevails in the US.

Because Southeast Asian immigrants are of divergent ethnic and class backgrounds and national origins, they have very different experiences in the US. As a consequence, we should not expect that the experiences of *gay*

Cambodians will necessarily typify those of all other gay, lesbian, or transgendered Southeast Asians who take up residence in the US. It is conceivable, for example, that the optimism expressed in Robert's asylum narrative might not be tempered in any significant way by his lived experiences in New York City, though in the absence of hard data on the subject we can only speculate on these matters. Robert, recall, identifies as ethnic Chinese (not as Malaysian), though he frames his case for asylum in terms of his being a Malaysian subject/citizen (raised as a Chinese Buddhist). As a member of the Chinese diaspora, Robert enjoys the benefits of whitening that are not accorded to Cambodians or to Malays or other Malaysians residing in the US (who are also blackened, unless they present themselves or are perceived as Chinese).

Clearly germane in this connection is that Robert's life partner (who owns a small shop and appears comfortably middle-class) is white, as are the partners of the vast majority of Cambodian *gays* in the US. The same pattern obtains among Cambodian women involved in heteronormative relationships in this country (Ong 2003:210–213). Patterns involving women "marrying up" status hierarchies ("hypergamy") are common both cross-culturally and historically though they do not necessarily involve hierarchies of race. And while the term "hypergamy" is usually confined to relationships involving heteronormative couples, we see that patterns of "raced hypergamy" also exist among feminized Southeast Asian gays in the US and that their participation in these relationships is one of the ways they negotiate the system of graduated pluralism (cf. Manalansan 2003).

The kinds of experiences that Robert and other gay Southeast Asians have in the US will depend partly on their relative successes in negotiating the historically contingent and contested system of graduated pluralism that obtains in this nation, and partly on the vicissitudes of neoliberal globalization, the "war on terror," and attendant public debates over how best to cope with immigration and the proliferation of difference, inequality, injustice, xenophobia, and violence in an increasingly borderless world. Much will also depend on the actions of political and religious elites in this country and elsewhere, particularly the manner in which they endeavor to marshal the symbolic and other capital at their disposal for the purpose of infusing pluralistic—or monistic—sentiments and dispositions into systems of governance and the thinking of the electorate.

Relevant here are policy initiatives of the Bush administration's "war on terror" along with decades-long dynamics entailing the expansion of White House powers. The events of September 11, 2001 provided Bush and his inner circle with the official rationale for the passage in October 2001 of the US Patriot Act and for a subsequent series of measures that have restricted Americans' privacy and freedoms (from "warrantless" and otherwise unwarranted surveillance, search, and seizure, for example) and effectively defined certain categories of people ("suspected terrorists," "enemy combatants," "detainees") as lacking any of the basic rights that international bodies (such as the UN) and treaties to which the US has been signatory (e.g., the Geneva Convention) have long held to be vested in all human beings. While many of these measures were signed into law in recent years without the consent or knowledge of the citizenry or Congressional leaders, it is also clear that tendencies toward an imperial presidency have been evident for some decades now, and that one of the key mechanisms for advancing this process involves declaration of a state of emergency ("state of exception") that effectively abrogates selected provisions of the Constitution. As Agamben has noted, the state of exception has roots in antiquity and was famously deployed by Presidents Lincoln and Roosevelt. More relevant though is that it "has continued to function *almost without interruption* from World War One, through fascism and National Socialism, and up to our own time [cf. Benjamin 1950 (1968)]. Indeed, *the state of exception has today reached its maximum worldwide deployment.* The normative aspect of law can thus be obliterated and contradicted with impunity by a governmental violence that—while ignoring international law externally and producing a permanent state of exception internally—nevertheless still claims to be applying the law" (Agamben 2005:86–87; emphasis added).

Some readers may concur with Agamben that these dynamics are deeply implicated in "the working of the machine that is leading the West toward global civil war" (ibid., 87); others may not. Two points are nonetheless strikingly obvious to growing numbers of people. First, recent decades have seen heightened concentrations of power in the US executive branch, reflected (*inter alia*) in the executive branch's increased unwillingness either to be subject to the checks and balances vested in the legislature and the judiciary or to abide by founding documents such as the Declaration of Independence, the Bill of Rights, and the Constitution. And second, these dynamics bode ill for pluralism both in this nation and far beyond. Nearly two hundred years ago Tocqueville expressed deep concern about these and attendant tendencies, conducive as they are to the tyranny of the majority (or the tyranny of those who claim to speak on the majority's behalf): "What I find most repugnant in America is … the virtual absence of any guarantee against tyranny … . Once it [the majority, or its elected representatives or self-designated spokespersons] has made up its mind about a question, there is nothing that can stop it or even slow it long enough to hear the cries of those whom it crushes in passing" (Tocqueville 1835–1840 [2004]:285, 290). Tocqueville thus emphasized the importance in America of associational freedoms (freedom of movement and assembly, freedom of the press, free speech, etc.), for he recognized that just as the myriad associations to which they gave rise were "in a position to struggle against tyranny without destroying order," so too did they help mitigate the effects of "the various forms of religious madness" that he saw as "quite common in the United States" of the 1830s (ibid., 623, 799).

Nearly two centuries after Tocqueville contrasted democratic systems of governance in America with their monarchical counterparts in France and England, Agamben echoed some of Tocqueville's findings in his assertion, "the clean opposition of democracy and dictatorship is misleading for any analysis of the governmental paradigms dominant today" (Agamben 2005:48). The cultural logics and institutionalized practices of governmentality in Burma, Malaysia, and the US, for instance, clearly differ from one another in dramatic ways but also share key features in common. Consider first some of the obvious dissimilarities. Burma is ruled by a military dictatorship supposedly attuned to Buddhist precepts (usually honored in the breach). Most of Malaysia's leaders, by contrast, are Muslims who rose to office through a system of electoral politics held to be compatible with progressive Muslim values; and while some of them are given to authoritarian practices, they tend to be far more responsive to democratic sentiment than their Burmese counterparts. The US, for its part, boasts a strongly democratic system commonly described as based on Christian (or Judeo-Christian) values, albeit one in which authoritarian tendencies in the executive branch have been increasingly prevalent in recent decades. Sharp differences aside, these systems share a disturbing commonality insofar as leaders in all three of them routinely invoke one or another "state of exception" to justify radical departures from constitutional and statutory provisions to which they are beholden in the eyes of the citizenry and foundational charters alike. In the first and third of these systems (Malaysia and the US), this is partly because political and other elites embrace various aspects of neoliberal globalization that place a premium on transnational and other corporate profit, market discipline, a pro-business political culture, a downsizing of democracy, and a self-managing, adaptive, flexible, and politically acquiescent citizenry—a commonality often overlooked by those who focus only on Kiplingesque divides between East and West and thus offer tautological predictions of an impending "clash of civilizations." Political elites in the second case (Burma) find themselves more ambivalently enmeshed in the neoliberal world order and do in fact endeavor to keep much of the outside world at bay. In negotiating their sovereignty in the face of foreign powers and domestic critics, they nonetheless embrace and seek to promulgate many of the same basic values as their counterparts in Malaysia and the US, particularly those conducive to corporate profit (managed by the state), discipline via (state-controlled) markets, a pro-regime business culture, a constriction of democratic spaces, and a self-managing, adaptive, flexible, and politically complacent citizenry. One unfortunate entailment of these policies in all three settings is widespread (though variable) vulnerability, insecurity, and fear.

Vulnerability, insecurity, and fear bred of social injustice or other dynamics are deeply corrosive of the trust essential to pluralism, providing fertile ground for the florescence of monistic and absolutist tendencies—and Manichean thinking—in family life, politics, religion, and, indeed, in all of social life. It follows from this that developing a critical understanding of the political, economic, and other dynamics conducive to landscapes of vulnerability, insecurity, and fear in domestic arenas (pluralism clearly begins at home) and beyond is a useful first step toward expanding the scope of pluralistic sentiments and dispositions, and scaling them up or otherwise transposing them to an ever broader social canvas. Identifying religious beliefs and practices that bear on pluralism either directly or indirectly is obviously relevant here insofar as moral truths and imperatives for ethical action are commonly grounded in religious cosmologies. Most such cosmologies are variably friendly to one or another range of human diversity even when (as is the case for many Christians and Muslims) they instill both pride and purpose as well as insecurity and fear (e.g., of damnation) in the believer and define non-believers and certain varieties of believing (but "morally lapsed") Others as paragons of evil bent on destroying the citadels of the righteously faithful and subjecting them to all varieties of unspeakable horror. Meaningful debates bearing on the institutional and other bearers of pluralism and the variables that serve to inhibit or constrain them do in any event presuppose the associational freedoms as well as the systems of checks and balances that Tocqueville championed nearly two centuries ago. Both vigilance and proactive stances are necessary to safeguard and expand these freedoms, and to help create more global space for the regimes of social justice and equality with which they are ideally associated.

Notes

1 Introduction

1 To speak of difference in the singular is of course to oversimplify, for most forms of difference or contrast are on closer inspection multiple rather than singular.

2 At least in Anglo-American intellectual traditions; it is decidedly less so in the case of many French scholars (e.g., Lévi-Strauss, Derrida, Lacan) and their interlocutors (see, e.g., Derrida 1977).

3 The phrase is Clifford Geertz's (2000:Chap 11).

4 Although I cite Weber as a source of inspiration here, the idea that assessments bearing on legitimacy are typically contested and subject to historical flux owes more to Gramsci (1971) than to Weber. As will become clear later on, my theoretical understanding of legitimacy draws heavily on both theorists and their interlocutors.

5 Clinical evidence supports this view as well; see, for instance, Jost and Major (2001).

6 Consider, for example, the otherwise incisive contributions of Sen and Stivens (1998) and Steedly (1999b). Stoler's compelling reading of Foucault's *History of Sexuality* (Volume I) in light of dynamics of race, class, gender, and sexuality during Southeast Asia's colonial era proceeds in an analogous fashion inasmuch as the analysis of "sexuality" is confined almost entirely to heterosexuality, a serious limitation that is not acknowledged until two-thirds of the way through the book and then only in a footnote (Stoler 1995:129 n93 [*sic*; 97]), as discussed in Chapter 3.

7 "Paraphrasing slightly, it is people who make legitimacy, but they make it out of resources not of their own choosing" (Zelditch 2001:51).

8 For many of the same reasons, legal scholars and others with interests in what is referred to as "legal pluralism" will want to bear in mind that the "pluralism" in my use of the term "gender pluralism" and in this book as a whole shares little in common with the "pluralism" in "legal pluralism." What is characterized as legal pluralism in many studies focusing on the ways that systems of law and law-like phenomena ("custom," "customary law") of disparate origin articulate with one another and are differentially embedded within all-encompassing hegemonic systems is often reminiscent of the apartheid-like institutional arrangements and attendant sensibilities and dispositions depicted in Orwell's *Burmese Days*, and is thus far from pluralistic in terms of the criteria that I and like-minded scholars employ.

9 Dictionary definitions of androgyny commonly note that the root term "androgyne" derives (via Latin) from Greek nouns meaning "male" and "female," and that in common parlance the term "androgynous" indicates "partly male and partly female in appearance," "of indeterminate sex," and/or "having the physical characteristics of both sexes" as in a hermaphrodite (see, e.g., *The New Oxford American Dictionary*, ed. Jewell and Abate 2001). My usage of the term generally refers not to physical embodiment but to gender, designating an explicit and emphatic combination of

culturally salient male and female characteristics (commonly entailing processes of "dual-gendering") but not their confusion, underrepresentation, or absence. For an important discussion of these and attendant issues (with a different twist) that focuses on Melanesia and the Kodi district of Sumba (Eastern Indonesia), see Strathern (1988) and Hoskins (1998:187–190 passim), respectively.

10 In keeping with these definitions I considered restricting the terms "female" and "male" to contexts where I referred to the "physical embodiment of a person" (Blackwood 2005:849 n1) and thus to utilize them as synonyms for a "female-bodied person" and a "male-bodied person," respectively, regardless of how the body is gendered (e.g., as feminine/womanly, masculine/manly, androgynous, or "other"). The contrasting set of terms "woman" and "man" could thus be reserved for instances where I sought to designate a person's gender, like the glosses "feminine" and "masculine" (as in Blackwood 2005). For my purposes, however, terminological conventions such as these, though potentially useful, create at least as many problems as they are meant to resolve. There are at least three reasons for this: (1) the vast majority of Southeast Asian languages, like the vast majority of people who read, write, and speak English, do not make any such rigorous semantic distinctions; (2) the objective and semantic overlap for those who speak English (and other languages) of terms such as "female" and "woman" (and "male" and "man") and their equivalents or analogies often renders it unfeasible and unproductive to maintain these (or attendant) contrasts; and (3) the distinctions at issue presume a knowledge of both (physical) embodiment and gender subjectivities and identities that is not always evident, and for these and other reasons risk being arbitrary, artificial, and (wildly) inaccurate. Suffice it to add that in certain contexts I do find it useful to utilize terms such as "female-bodied" and "male-bodied" (as well as "phenotypically female" and "phenotypically male") to emphasize that I am referring to a person's embodiment, and that terms like "feminine"/"womanly" and "masculine"/"manly" are used primarily to designate a person's gender rather than the kind of body one has.

11 I generally use the term "heteronormative" to convey the idea that some societies regard both exclusive heterosexuality and a system of two sharply differentiated genders ("male" and "female") as the moral norm, though I do so for convenience and with some misgivings because: (1) as it is commonly understood, the term implicitly (if not explicitly) privileges sexuality over gender (see, for example, Ingraham 2002:76); and (2) many who utilize the term elide or ignore the sex/gender distinction, problematically lumping together relationships that for certain analytic purposes ought to be separated, e.g., those that are heterosexual (involving persons of different physical embodiment) and those I gloss "heterogender" (which involve persons who are differently gendered but may have the same kinds of ["male" or "female"]) bodies. In early modern Southeast Asia, same-sex ("homosexual") relations that were heterogender were commonly accorded a degree of legitimacy, but this was rarely if ever the case (so far as we know) with same-sex relations construed as homogender. For these and other reasons, elisions in common understandings of the term "heteronormative" give rise to all sorts of conceptual and analytic problems (as discussed at the end of Chapter 4).

12 Concerning this last dynamic, compare, for instance, the Trobriand case described by Weiner (1976) with strongly patriarchal systems in which, at least in their ideal typical forms, men and all things male are accorded more prestige "across the board."

13 While it may strike many readers as obvious that there is no intrinsic connection between one or another variant of transgendering (e.g., cross-dressing) on the one hand and specific forms or practices of sexuality on the other, certain scholars adopt a different perspective on some of the relationships at issue. Bornstein (1995:134–135), for example, contends that at least in the West all gays and lesbians—not simply "butch" or masculine lesbians, or "queens" or feminine men—merit inclusion in the category "transgendered" (along with transsexuals, bisexuals, etc.).

This perspective derives partly from the assumption that in the West "gay men and lesbians are more consciously excluded by the culture for violations of *gender* codes (which are visible in the daily life of the culture) than for actual sexual practices (which usually happen behind closed doors …);" and that, as a consequence, "lesbians and gay men actually share the same stigma with 'transgendered' people: the stigma of crimes against gender" (1995:134–135; emphasis in original). Bornstein goes on to observe that "while 'transgendered' people may not in fact practice gay or lesbian sex, and so may not themselves be lesbian or gay, gays and lesbians are invariably perceived as 'transgendered.'" Suffice it to add that while Bornstein's position is somewhat problematic, it helps sensitize us to the fact that many of the normative regimes and transgressions discussed in the following pages are more about "about" gender than sex (cf. Elliston 1999, Johnson et al. 2000).

14 The phrasing here owes much to Stallybrass and White (1986:110).

2 Gender Pluralism and Transgender Practices in Early Modern Times

1 The term "Austronesian" designates (a) a group or "family" of some 1,200 languages of common origin that are spoken primarily in insular Southeast Asia, the Pacific (especially Polynesia and Micronesia), and parts of Madagascar, and (b) the historically related cultures associated with those languages. People speaking proto-Austronesian languages originated in southern China. Beginning around 4,000 BCE, they began a series of southerly migrations that eventually resulted in the spread of Austronesian languages and cultures to Taiwan, the Philippines, Borneo, and other parts of insular Southeast Asia, as well as coastal (southeastern) Vietnam, many parts of the Pacific (Samoa, Tahiti, Hawaii, etc.), and certain areas of the Indian Ocean such as Madagascar (Reid 1988:3–5, Bellwood 1997:97–154 passim). In light of subsequent discussion, I should emphasize that the languages commonly referred to as Indonesian, Malay, Javanese, Balinese, Acehnese, Iban, Ngaju Dayak, and Bugis are all members of the Austronesian language family, as are Tagalog and most of the other languages spoken in the Philippines; and that, especially during early modern times, the societies and cultures of the native speakers of these languages had a good deal in common though each was of course unique in its own way.

2 As noted in the Introduction, historians, anthropologists, and others writing about the region commonly refer to the era extending roughly from the fifteenth to the eighteenth centuries as Southeast Asia's "early modern period." The deployment of the term in the Southeast Asian context, like its use in scholarship on China, Japan and other areas outside Europe, has of course led to spirited debate in some quarters (see, for example, Rafael 1993). The growing consensus, however, is that Southeast Asia's involvement in commercial, political, and attendant developments of global scope beginning in the fifteenth century, along with "the quickening of commerce, the monetization of transactions, the growth of cities, the accumulation of capital, and the specialization of function" that occurred throughout much of the region during the sixteenth and early seventeenth centuries (Reid 1993a:2), was a watershed in relation to the earlier, "classical" period; and that it was likewise (albeit in different ways) fairly distinctive when viewed against developments of the "late modern period," which saw a stunting and reversal of some of these processes owing largely to the growth and florescence of European mercantilism and capitalism as well as full-blown colonialism. For further discussion of these matters, see Reid (1988, 1993a, 1993b), Lieberman (2003), and B. Andaya (2006:Chap. 2 passim).

3 Many of the (prehistoric) dates cited here and in the ensuing few pages are tentative; some of them, moreover, are contested. The dates and chronology of developments outlined in the next few pages derive mainly from Higham (1989, 2001) and Bellwood (1997) and the research they summarize.

4 Mandala derives from "a term for an administrative unit or country in ancient India" (White 2003:124).

5 This, in any case, is the strong version of the argument; the weak version is that these cultural forms valorized both ambiguity and relativity (see Beatty 2002; cf. Trawick 1990).

6 O'Flaherty (1980) provides a good discussion of this theme; see also Roscoe (1996).

7 My discussion of *hijras* is adapted from Peletz (2007).

8 As Ann Gold has noted, "at a higher level to understand her [the female goddess] as simultaneously wielding weapons and full of grace is an important theological and devotional truth." A more general point is that in Hinduism, "the grace-giving element of female deities is fused with the fearsome" to a greater degree than suggested by many conventional depictions of female capacities to devour and destroy (personal communication, August 13, 2006 and October 31, 2006; see also Gold 2007).

9 Anthony Reid's (1988, 1993b) path-breaking work on the history of Southeast Asia is far more sophisticated than Murphey's, especially when dealing with matters of women and gender. But like Murphey, Reid devotes minimal attention to transgender practices (though he refers to cross-dressed ritual specialists in a few contexts) and even less to non-heteronormative sexualities. One of the few occasions where Reid addresses such matters is in connection with Burmese myths that purport to explain why Burmese women "wrapped their cloth only once [as opposed to twice] around the body, so that it opened when walking to show the leg up to the thigh." Reid notes, "Numerous early European observers made much of the indecency of this practice, and ascribed it to an early queen anxious to divert Burmese men away from homosexual proclivities," to which he adds, "Like many such tales, this tells us more about European attitudes than Burmese" (Reid 1988:88). The clear impression one receives from passages such as these is that European and other foreign references to Southeast Asian practices that were transgressive with respect to heteronormative sexuality were entirely fanciful projections or rationalizations that bore no connection to Southeast Asian realities. Barbara Andaya's more recent (1994, 1998, 2000a, 2006) work addresses these matters in a less dismissive way and provides exemplary descriptions and analysis of both the lived realities of heteronormative women in early modern Southeast Asia history and the issues (at once methodological, historiographic, and cross-cultural) that confront scholars involved in reconstructing such realities. For the most part, however, Andaya does not deal substantively with issues bearing on transgenderism or same-sex practices although she does provide incisive commentary on "sexual [and gender] ambiguities" associated with anatomical intersexuality (hermaphroditism) and cross-dressing.

10 There is a voluminous literature on the *bissu* in Dutch, French, English, Bugis, Indonesian, and other languages; English-language sources include Van der Kroef (1956), Errington (1989), Pelras (1996), L. Andaya (2000), and Davies (2007).

11 Indeed, "ancient Indian and Indonesian cults are intertwined to such a degree that it is often impossible to decide whether certain elements of religion in … Southeast Asia are Austronesian under an Indian name or Indian influenced by Austronesian tradition" (De Casparis and Mabbett 1992:311).

12 It is not feasible here (because it would require an additional volume) to discuss the relevance of the terms "third sex" and "third gender" for these cases or others in Southeast Asia that have been described in similar terms (see Morris 1994, L. Andaya 2000).

13 I have chosen these six cases partly because the historical and/or ethnographic literature allows for descriptions and analyses of gender and sexuality that are relevant to the main concerns of this book. Insofar as four of the six cases are drawn from insular (Austronesian) Southeast Asia, the discussion as a whole is somewhat skewed toward Southeast Asia's insular regions. The inclusion of Burmese and Siamese/Thai

cases offsets this skewing (and otherwise expands the purview of the discussion), and thus makes clear that despite significant differences between insular and mainland Southeast Asia (and within each of these regions as well), there are important commonalities throughout this world area. The Philippines and to a lesser extent Java are not addressed as fully as they might be, partly because more detailed discussions of this material would further unbalance my coverage of Southeast Asia. Another relevant factor is that these cases are described in some detail elsewhere (see, for example, Garcia 1996, Johnson 1997, Cannell 1999, Manalansan 2003, and Brewer 2004 on the Philippines; and Keeler 1990, Brenner 1995, 1998, Sears 1996, Blackwood 1999, 2005, Boellstorff 1999, 2004a, 2005, Murray 1999, and Wieringa 1999 on Java and Indonesia generally).

14 The Bohemian Grove, owned and operated by the Bohemian Club of San Francisco, is a private, wooded compound of several thousand acres located on the Russian River in Sonoma County that for over a century has served as a retreat for men from California and elsewhere who belong to the upper echelons of the nation's political elite. Domhoff (1974) has produced the definitive study of the Grove, whose members have included thousands of nationally prominent corporate leaders and captains of industry, and many US presidents (e.g., Hoover, Eisenhower, Nixon, Ford, Reagan, and George H.W. Bush). Research conducted by James Vaughn in the mid-to-late 1990s makes clear that cross-dressing by men (including false breasts, wigs, heavy make-up, and skirts and dresses) still occurs in plays, skits, and other contexts (many of which involve bacchanalian rituals); that certain men make themselves up to look like drag-queens, while others seek to appear indistinguishable from "sexy" women; and that some of the men who participate in these retreats also engage in heterosexual prostitution in nearby towns (Vaughn 2006). As Domhoff (1974:27) observes and as Vaughn's research indicates, many of the Grove's myths, rituals, and symbols focus on sex; indeed, "the [latter] topic is outranked as a subject for light conversation only by remarks about drinking enormous qualities of alcohol and urinating on redwoods." Much of the humor at these kinds of retreats is misogynist and homophobic, a critically important reminder that not all gender- (or sexually-) transgressive behavior is indicative of pluralistic sentiments or dispositions. The ways in which "othering" practices such as those that occur in the Bohemian Grove and in other exclusively or predominantly male institutions (fraternities, the armed forces) contribute to male bonding and social cohesiveness of other kinds has been variously addressed by Domhoff and Vaughn as well as Gregor (1985) and Sanday (1990).

15 The term "Iban" designates a congeries of culturally and linguistically related peoples living mostly in the second and third Divisions (administrative districts) of Sarawak, many of whom were referred to in Western accounts of the mid-nineteenth century as "Sea Dayaks," often abbreviated as "Dayaks." Owing partly to factors discussed by Pringle (1970:Chap. 1), the term "Iban" was not widely used as a marker of ethnic or cultural identification prior to World War II.

16 By the late 1800s, "The *manang bali* as an institution" was apparently "confined … to the remote tribes of the Sea Dyaks [Iban] … [and was] not in vogue among [those living in] vicinity to the Malays, who invariably ridicule the practice, and endeavour to throw it into disrepute" (H.B. Low n.d. I:271; cf. P. Graham 1987:94).

17 The term "Ngaju" has been widely used in the ethnographic literature on Borneo for well over a century. It typically designates the various linguistically and culturally related groups of Dayak residing "along the southward-flowing rivers of [that portion of] the island" currently known as Central Kalimantan but should not be taken to imply either a "distinct cultural entity or … corporate identity" (Miles 1966:1; cf. Schiller 1997a:14–16 passim).

18 Notwithstanding their social and cosmic importance, the *basir*'s femininity could also be a source of derision—or at least had come to be so by the mid-nineteenth

century. Thus Hardeland (1859) reported expressions such as "*mambesei kilau basir*, to paddle like a *basir*, i.e., idle, sluggish; *kilau basir keton, jawn hunyin keton malawan*, you are like a *basir* (i.e., cowardly, womanly), you have no courage in the face of obstacles." More generally, by the mid-nineteenth century the varied meanings of terms like *babasir* and *basibasir* included not only the idea that one was "like a woman (in clothes and bearing)" but also, as such, "weak, idle, slack" (Scharer 1946 [1963]:57).

19 In Scharer's time, *balian* were sometimes viewed as "slaves in the possession of their owners, but they no longer worked in fields" or actively participated in household tasks. "The profit ... they brought to their masters lay in the fact that they were hired out as prostitutes, singers, and dancers, and also as priestesses, at feasts and on other occasions" (Scharer 1946 [1963]:53). Both in the distant past and at the time of Scharer's research, "daughters of freemen occasionally became *balian*," usually because "they were seduced into it, or a disappointment in love. ... Hardeland [1859] states ... that it is felt to be a shameful thing if a relative ... [of a freeman] becomes a *balian*," that a brother might even murder his sister for doing so (ibid., 54). The (probably rare) imposition of such an extreme sanction by the brother of a "free" woman who became a *balian* speaks to the severity and broadly polluting and stigmatizing potential of an "ungrammatical," descent-based status transgression since the woman was likened to a "slave" or "debtor" in the possession of her "owner" (thus implicating the origins of her siblings and other relatives), rather than someone enjoying the "free" status to which she and her siblings and various other kin were entitled at birth.

20 Both *basir* and *balian* were involved in "sacred prostitution" in ritual contexts, according to Scharer (1946 [1963]:58, 135–136, 139). Most of the details remain unclear, though Scharer (135–137) reports that "the organiser of ... [various] ceremon[ies] and the representatives of the total community have sexual intercourse with the *balian* and the *basir* before and during the sacred service, and this is related to the entry of the *sangiang*, viz. the total godhead, into the pit of the stomach of the officiants... . The sacred service is a divine ceremony for, through, and with men [humankind]," is followed by a ritual battle, and is thus strongly reminiscent of Tantric themes discussed earlier in the chapter.

21 To suggest that the obligations of a "slave" or debtor were mostly of a ritual nature is not to imply that they were of little consequence; in some cases, the ritual obligations in question required that one be offered (or "offer" oneself) in ceremonies entailing human sacrifice (Scharer 1946 [1963]:46–47).

22 In discussing Bugis history, I draw on the ethnohistorical research conducted by Pelras (1996) and on ethnographic and historical studies published by L. Andaya (2000), Gibson (2005), Davies (2007) and others. Some of Pelras' historical assertions have been challenged on archeological grounds by Caldwell (1995), Bulbeck (1996), and Bulbeck and Prasetyo (2000) but the debates are beyond the scope of the present discussion.

23 I am indebted to the Malay Concordance Project (a digital corpus of Malay texts) for this information, and to Ian Proudfoot, the director of the project, for clarification of various bibliographic and other issues (personal communication, October 29, 2005, August 29, 2008). See Proudfoot n.d.

24 The complexity of these circuits derives partly from the fact the Islamic law prohibits castration.

25 Shamsul A.B., personal communication, August 17, 2002, May 23, 2008.

26 Douglas Raybeck, personal communication, August 4, 2000.

27 Not all scholars accept Anderson's depiction of "traditional Javanese sexual culture." Ricklefs' (1998) analysis of Javanese manuscripts and other indigenous sources suggests that same-sex relations were more problematic in Javanese court culture

than Anderson implies, particularly from the point of view of Islamic teaching. It may be relevant that a manuscript produced during the early 1600s serves as Anderson's point of departure, whereas Ricklefs focuses on a later period, 1726–1749. (See also Keeler 1990:148–150, Day 2002:128 passim.)

28 Anthropologists and other scholars have spilled much ink on the meanings of these practices and whether they were undertaken for women's pleasure, so that men could demonstrate their virility and/or ability to withstand pain, or for some combination of these or other reasons (e.g., "to curb sodomy"). A common but contested interpretation that receives mythic support from Burma (as noted in the text) and from many other Southeast Asian sources is that practices such as these are broadly indexical (and a sharp reminder) of the extent to which men took women's concerns—with pleasure, for example—seriously. In this view, men's willingness to undergo painful genital surgery attests to the high status of Southeast Asian women and is thus a clear marker of the region as a distinctive "cultural area" (see, for example, Reid 1988:148–149, Brown, Edwards, and Moore 1988). Some aspects of this view have merit; but variations of these practices have been reported for aboriginal Australia, India, and elsewhere far beyond Southeast Asia, including, not least, in the "West's postmodern phallocentrism that impresses some observers as ultrapunk" (Boon 1991:729), contexts where women do not necessarily enjoy the prerogatives long accorded their sisters in Southeast Asia. Factors such as these lead scholars like James Boon (1990:8–12, 54–60, 1991:729–730) to reject the idea that the balls, bells, pins, and spurs surgically inserted into men's penises at different points in Southeast Asian history were necessarily—always and everywhere—"women pleasers demanded by relatively autonomous females" (1991:730), and to call for additional research on the context-specific meanings of these practices and their symbolic and other resonance with key cultural features of the societies in question (cf. D. Brown 1991, B. Andaya 2006:64).

29 For a classic statement on the marginalization of gender in the discipline of history, see Joan W. Scott (1999). Concerning the marginalization of gender in the history of Asia and Southeast Asia in particular, see Barbara Andaya (1998, 2006).

30 Bowring's estimate of the numbers of Chinese living in Siam in the mid-nineteenth century appears quite high. David Wyatt (2003:203) suggests that the figure is more on the order of 300,000, though he notes that it increased to around 792,000 by 1910.

31 These transgendered ritualists assume various mediating roles, like their early modern predecessors. But they also differ from them in critical ways. Most relevant is that they are distanced from contemporary centers of power and prestige and formally disavowed and disdained by political and religious elites, some of whom nonetheless eagerly if ambivalently avail themselves of their services.

32 Not all anthropologists concur as to the antiquity in the Thai context of the conceptual linkages between *kathoey* and mediumship—or that of transgendered ritualism generally (see, for example, Jackson 2003), even though such antiquity is well established as far as numerous Thai specialists (e.g., Morris 2000) are concerned and is moreover well documented for neighboring (culturally similar, historically intertwined) Burma and indeed for much of Southeast Asia since the beginning of the early modern era. Although considerable work in these areas remains to be done, it is relevant in my view that none of the most extensive and incisive studies of early modern Southeast Asian history (e.g., Reid 1988, 1993b, Lieberman 2003, B. Andaya 2006) makes a case for Thai exceptionalism with regard to these matters.

33 As in Burma, Buddhist law codes in Siam/Thailand have long prohibited "true *kathoey*" (hermaphrodites) from serving as witnesses and from claiming shares of inheritance (Sangermano 1818 [1893]:235, 237, Crawfurd 1830 II:129, Bowring 1856 [1969] I:177, Jackson 1998).

3   Temporary Marriage, Connubial Commerce, and Colonial Body Politics

1 In Theravada Buddhist contexts such as Ceylon/Sri Lanka, Burma, and Siam/
Thailand, this engagement ultimately gave rise to what some scholars have referred to
as "Protestant Buddhism" (see, e.g., Gombrich and Obeyesekere 1988). The latter
term draws attention to the development of currently widespread forms of Buddhism
that both "originated as a protest against the British [and Europeans] in general and
against Protestant Christian missionaries in particular" but simultaneously "assumed
salient characteristics of that Protestantism" (ibid., 7). According to scholars of
Buddhism like Oliver Freiberger, the term "Protestant Buddhism" highlights "the
'Protestant' character of Buddhist revival movements" such as one sees in colonial-era
and postcolonial Sri Lanka and mainland Southeast Asia, which emphasize "the
agency of laypeople (e.g., founding meditation centers independent from the
monastery); overcoming the 'superstition' of folk rituals and beliefs; and searching for
the 'original' Buddhism by studying foundational [Pali] texts"—many of which were
translated into English by Western (mostly Protestant) scholars with a strongly
Protestant sense of the "true" (textual) locus of Buddhism—all "without the monks'
mediation" (personal communication, April 30, 2008). Most relevant for our purposes is that proponents of these variants of reformed Buddhism typically adopted the
strongly binary notions of gender and sexuality characteristic of Western Protestants,
just as they came to embrace "the general repression of overt sexuality" and the "adoption of Victorian sexual mores" on the whole (Gombrich and Obeyesekere 1988:255
passim; Bechert 1984; Schopen 1991, Loos 2006). Protestant Buddhism is a variant of
Buddhist modernism in much the same way that the "Muslim Puritanism" described
by Peacock (1978) constitutes a variation on the theme of Islamic modernism (see, for
example, Hefner 2000, Peletz 2002). In the pages that follow I do not employ terms
such as "Protestant Buddhism" or "Muslim Puritanism" to distinguish certain "modern" forms of these religions from their more "traditional" forebears. But it should be
clear that we are dealing with dynamic (not static or "fixed") religious traditions
whose entailments with respect to gender and sexuality are highly variable both historically and cross-culturally, and, more specifically, that the "same" traditions that
embrace gender pluralism in some historical and ethnographic settings may provide
the basis for its constriction in others.

2 Rates of female literacy appear to have been relatively high during the first half of
Southeast Asia's early modern period, especially when considered alongside those
prevailing in Europe and other world areas at the time (Reid 1988:215–225,
B. Andaya 2006:53–55). Girls and young women were typically instructed in the arts
of reading and writing by their mothers, elder siblings, and other kin who helped their
charges compose courting songs and "love letters" that were inscribed on palm leaves,
joints of bamboo, or comparable material and subsequently shared with their love
interests or potential mates, though in some contexts their skills were also deployed to
help keep track of debts and commercial transactions. This tradition declined in subsequent centuries due largely to the effects of religious and other changes described in
this chapter and the next (see also Reid 1993b: Chap. 3). Suffice it to mention here
that Islam, Buddhism, Christianity, and other World Religions privilege males as
guardians and interpreters of religious texts and other sacred objects, and, accordingly,
as specialists charged with explicating canonical doctrines and most issues bearing on
genealogy, ceremonial precedence, liturgical orders, and ritual as a whole. Monastic
traditions in Buddhism and Christianity, moreover, like Islamic practices involving
the recitation of the Quran and other sacred texts, have long contributed to the spread
of male literacy in Southeast Asia (as elsewhere); and while their custodians and proponents have not usually actively discouraged female literacy, they have been known
to espouse the view that it is dangerous in light of its potential to facilitate the pursuit
of inappropriate romance on the part of girls and young women (Reid 1988:220).

3   In many cases there are few if any concrete differences between concubinage and prostitution. "Concubine" typically designates someone who "is kept" or to some degree maintained in a material sense in exchange for the provision of sexual and other services, and thus overlaps with "mistress." The term "prostitute" (or "commercial sex worker") on the other hand is usually taken to mean someone who provides sex for money, gifts in kind, or one or another type or range of service(s). One of the problems with terms such as these in Southeast Asian contexts (and many other areas) is that both short- and long-term relationships that focus around or otherwise involve sex also commonly entail many other kinds of transactions ("gifts," "favors," and the like), and are not necessarily conceptualized either as concubinage or prostitution, or in other broadly comparable terms.

4   Also contributing to the acceptance of concubinage were the encumbrances on marriage between members of the Dutch East India Company and non-Christians, legal precedents for which date from as early as 1617. Part of the rationale for these and other restrictions on the return to Europe of anyone "married to a native or mixed-blood woman" had to do with "a fear of '[inter-racial] multiplication' in the Netherlands" (Ming 1983:69; cf. Gouda 1995:112).

5   *Nyai* is "a Javanese word ... denot[ing] both a respectable woman of middle age, and [more relevant here] the mistress or concubine of a European" (Ming 1983:71).

6   Of further relevance are the kinship idioms informing these bonds and the ways they differed from idioms cloaking most variants of same-sex relations in colonial Southeast Asia. Relationships of "sworn sisterhood" obviously involve symbols and idioms of female siblingship, though it is also likely that idioms of male siblingship were sometimes invoked by these women, as is the case with Buddhist nuns in Singapore who insist "that it is as males that all are reborn in the Pure Land and in anticipation of this call each other brothers" (Topley 1956:82). The relevance of siblingship in these relationships is noteworthy since symbols and idioms drawn from heterosexual marriage (rather than one or another modality of siblingship) structured most variants of same-sex relations in Southeast Asia both in colonial times and long before. How might we explain the contrast? A partial explanation might lie in the fact that especially in Chinese-speaking settings, sibling ties imply a much greater degree of equality than bonds of marriage. The inequalities of (Chinese) marriage, after all—and of (Chinese) heterosexual relations generally—were what many of these women sought to avoid. It thus stands to reason that they would refrain from constructing their same-sex bonds in symbols and idioms they took to be exploitative and otherwise highly problematic. Probably relevant as well is that the members of vegetarian houses adopted lifestyles that were to one or another degree modeled on the lives of Buddhist ascetics; celibacy, for instance, albeit celibacy that was apparently defined primarily in heterosexual terms, was in fact a prerequisite for attainment of leadership positions in these houses and in the larger, umbrella organizations subsuming them. For this reason too same-sex unions modeled on or otherwise cloaked in the terms of heterosexual marriage would entail a jarring dissonance. One might conceivably suggest, finally, that "the exception that proves the rule" at issue here is best understood as a Chinese pattern that does not (and should not be expected to) conform to long-standing albeit historical variable configurations associated with Southeast Asia as a cultural area (or a series of overlapping cultural areas).

7   The emergence in the nineteenth century of the scientific field of sexual science or "sexology" (about which more below) provides clear evidence of these trends, as does the fact that a disproportionate number of those working in this and allied fields were inclined toward same-sex erotics.

8   The latter two volumes were not available to Stoler at the time she submitted her (1995) book for publication, but the vast majority of the published sources cited in their bibliographies, which, taken together, run some 59 pages, clearly were.

9   For further discussion of these important points, see Thomas (1994).

4 Transgender Practices, Same-Sex Relations, and Gender Pluralism Since the 1960s

1 The term "gay" is widely used throughout Southeast Asia but its meanings vary according to locale and socio-linguistic context and its connotations are not necessarily the same as those associated with its usage in English-language settings (though there is considerable overlap). In some circumstances, the term refers primarily to certain categories of phenotypic males (e.g., male-bodied transsexuals and their effeminate male counterparts) who have sex with other males; in many perhaps most others, it has broader meanings, denoting any male (or female-bodied) individual erotically oriented toward same-sex relations who may or may not engage in heterosexual relations including conventional marriage. I italicize terms such as "*gay*" (and "*lesbian*") when I seek to emphasize one or another Southeast Asian identity or Southeast Asian-language usage. I use regular font when deploying the terms to convey their now conventional English-language meanings (e.g., a person inclined toward erotic relations with others of the same sex). When quoting published material, I retain the author's conventions.

2 Indeed, the term "*balian* ... is no longer used to apply to female [ritual] specialists" (Schiller 1997a:154 n3).

3 Population estimates for the Bugis are not as precise as they might be, but this seems a relatively realistic figure (Gibson 2005:7).

4 Since most citizens of Burma ("Burmese") are lowland-dwelling ethnic Burmans and since many of the sources consulted for this book do not specify whether or not the "Burmese" to whom they refer are ethnic Burmans (as distinct from Shan, Karen, Rakhine, Kachin, or "Other"), I use the term "Burmese" to gloss both ethnic Burmans and other citizens of Burma, unless noted otherwise. References to "Shan," "Karen," etc., on the other hand, designate ethnic minority groups whose members reside both in the highlands of Burma and beyond its borders (e.g., in neighboring Thailand)

5 "It is not unusual for young men or married men to have sex with an acault" (Coleman et al. 1992:317).

6 Jane Ferguson, personal communication, February 23, 2008 and June 28, 2008.

7 I follow Burmese gay-rights activist Aung Myo Min in using the term "lesbian" here, even though some Burmese women involved in same-sex relations may eschew the term, as occurs in Thailand and some other parts of the region (see Than Win Htut 2005, discussed below).

8 All quotes in the ensuing section are from the brief online article cited in the text, obtained from the website located at <http://www.mizzima.com/archives/news-in-2005/news-in-feb/20-February%2005-25.htm>, accessed on December 13, 2005.

9 But Burmese law criminalizes same-sex sexual activities under the rubrics of "sodomy" and "unnatural behavior" (under Section 377 of the National Penal Code).

10 See Chapter 3, note 1.

11 "For women to uncover their legs, or even to bare their arms fully, remains in Burma a highly charged, and highly compromising, move. Even on stage, few women appear willing to generate the unflattering associations that displaying much of their body in public would inevitably give rise to" (Keeler 2005:225).

12 Burmese gender ideologies have much in common with those of Theravada Buddhists in Thailand and Cambodia (Kirsch 1982, 1985, Keyes 1984, Van Esterik 2000, Ledgerwood 1994, Smith-Hefner 1999) and are in some respects strikingly similar to those of Malay Muslims (Peletz 1995, 1996, 2002) though they are cast in different symbols and idioms and pressed into service in somewhat different ways.

13 Accurate figures bearing on the number of Burmese women involved in commercial sex are difficult to come by. Sources such as Asia Watch and The Women's Rights Project (1993), Belak (2002), and Skidmore (2004) provide mostly qualitative information, though they concur that there is an epidemic of sexual trafficking

involving ever younger women and girls and, more generally, that increasing numbers of women and girls find themselves pressed into trading sex for one or another kind of material compensation (see also Talikowski and Gillieatt 2005). Skidmore's (2004:162 et passim) assessments suggest that the relevant figures for Rangoon may be in the hundreds of thousands and, for the nation as a whole, well over a million.

14 WHO estimates bearing on HIV/AIDS in Burma were obtained from the "UNAIDS/WHO Epidemiological Fact Sheet on HIV and AIDS, 2008 Update" for Myanmar, located at <http://www.who.int/globalatlas/default.asp>, accessed September 26, 2008.

15 This point is well documented in written accounts (e.g., Skidmore 2004). It was also clear from a brief visit to Burma that I made in January 2005, during which time I toured a few clinics and talked with doctors, nurses, and others about the nation's healthcare.

16 For a variety of reasons I suspect that some of Sinnott's findings bearing on subject positions and subjectivities in the Bangkok region may be broadly applicable to Rangoon and other urban areas of Burma; but in the absence of substantive data on these matters, my views on this point must remain speculative.

17 While the notion of "graduated pluralism" bears a loose family resemblance to concepts that Ong has developed, it is also quite distinct from them and is asked to do very different kinds of work. "Graduated pluralism," as I have explained, is intended to help us understand certain dynamics bearing on gender, sexuality, and body politics in Southeast Asia over the past 600 or so years. The concept of "graduated sovereignty," in contrast, though also developed primarily in relation to Southeast Asian material, refers to processes in which "the state makes different kinds of biopolitical investments [both] in different subject populations" ("privileging one gender over the other," for example) "and in certain kinds of human skills, talents, and ethnicities," along with its willingness in some cases, even as it "maintains control over its territory, … to let corporate entities set the terms for constituting and regulating some domains" (Ong 1999:217). Ong deploys the concept of graduated sovereignty primarily to designate post-Fordist dynamics that have arisen with neoliberal globalization, commonly associated with the post-1970s era, suggesting that hyper-rational states and transnational corporations driven by wills to power and profit and other largely utilitarian agendas are invariably the key players in driving these dynamics. My explication of the notion of graduated pluralism accords more significance to the cosmological underpinnings of state apparatuses and the conceptual schema informing the ethos, worldview, and practice of agents of governmentality and their proxies and charges, and the ways some of these cosmologies and conceptual schema are dialectically related to myth and ritual as well as domestic and social structural arrangements.

18 Bryan Turner's brief elaboration of Weber's insight with reference to Puritanism merits note here, particularly since it also pertains to the doctrines of many other Christian denominations: "By making marriage a vocation equivalent to traditional religious vocations, Puritanism" construed divorce as unacceptable, just as it rendered "alternatives to divorce—adultery, homosexuality, prostitution—equally unthinkable" (B. Turner 1996:140).

5 Gender, Sexuality, and Body Politics at the Turn of the Twenty-First Century

1 Douglas Raybeck, personal communication, August 4, 2000.

2 Many of the names employed in this chapter and the Epilogue are pseudonyms that I utilize to protect the anonymity of my informants.

3 During my 1987–1988 fieldwork one Malaysian *ringgit* (M$1) was worth approximately US $0.39. Subsequent years witnessed extreme fluctuations in the value of the *ringgit*, which is currently (August 2008) valued at about US $0.31.

4   My use of the term "legacy" builds on Grewal and Kaplan (2001).
5   Some of the material in this chapter is adapted from previous publications (Peletz 1996, 2002, 2005).
6   Due to limitations of space I focus my comparative remarks on the first of these books.
7   The precedent for this volume was Ishihara's (1990) *The Japan That Can Say No*.
8   For a comprehensive discussion of these and related matters, see Milne and Mauzy (1999).
9   "Malaysia Bans Gays, Transvestites from Television," Reuters News Service, August 17, 1994.
10   "Malaysia Bans Gays From Television and Radio," *The Washington Blade*, August 24, 1994.
11   "Malaysian Gay Pride Event Suffers," *Sunday Metro*, June 28, 1998
12   I am indebted to M.B. Hooker for this information (personal communication, December 13, 2000).
13   *The Star*, January 22, 1997.
14   For clarification of the variation in punishment, see Rose Ismail (1995:114).
15   Tan Beng Hui (1999:295).
16   "Transvestite Who Tried to Wed Held," *The Star*, February 19, 1997.
17   "Minister Links Gender Woes to Upbringing," *The Star*, February 19, 1997.
18   Prior to these amendments, the maximum penalty for the sexual offenses at issue involved a fine of M$1,000 and six months' imprisonment.
19   See Funston (1999), Milne and Mauzy (1999).
20   The distinction between "active" and "passive" roles in same-sex encounters involving male-bodied individuals is the subject of less cultural elaboration in Malaysia (particularly in Malay circles) than in other settings such as Latin America (see, for example, Kulick 1998), though it is nonetheless meaningful in certain contexts. The fact that Anwar was assumed to be the "active" partner vis-à-vis the men with whom he was alleged to have sexual relations may help explain why the sodomy charges leveled against him did not feminize him or raise substantive or enduring questions about his masculinity.
21   See "Translation of Azizan Abu Bakar's Sworn Statement" and "Translation of Handwritten Retraction Letter by Azizan Abu Bakar," *The Star*, December 22, 1998.
22   The Malaysian version (complete with Arabic and English translation) that I purchased in Kuala Lumpur in January 2001 bears the title *Pendirian Syari'at Terhadap Hukuman Bersalah Ke Atas Dato' Seri Anwar Ibrahim* [*Syariah Review of the Guilty Verdict Passed on Dato' Seri Anwar Ibrahim*].
23   The ban does not extend to "folkloric" presentations organized by state officials.
24   As far as many Muslim scholars are concerned, the *hudud* laws enforced in much of the Muslim world are based on questionable interpretations of Quranic injunctions (see, for example, Rose Ismail 1995, Mohammad Hashim Kamali 2000).
25   As Shamsul (2000:229) has noted, "terms like 'sodomy,' 'homosexuality,' 'anal sex,' 'pubic hair,' 'semen,' 'bodily liquids,' 'masturbation,' 'sexual intercourse,' and 'DNA'" came to be defined and discussed "in graphic legal and scientific detail in the court, almost non-stop for weeks on end."
26   "Malaysia PM Says Gay 'Big Sin,'" *News Planet*, September 25, 1998.
27   Cited in "Malaysian Squads Target Gays," *Sydney Star Observer*, February 23, 1995.
28   "Combating the 'Gay' Threat," *The Straits Times*, October 22, 1998.
29   *New Straits Times*, October 23, 1998.
30   Ibid.
31   Thanks to Robert Hefner for encouraging me to emphasize these points.
32   In 2003 or 2004 the Pink Triangle formally changed its name to the PT Foundation [Yayasan PT]. I retain the earlier designation in keeping with the time frame of my

discussion, much of which focuses on the period 2001–2002 and the years immediately preceding it.

33 Abdullah's political fortunes have since declined, however, and by mid-May 2008 many people, including his former patron Mahathir, were calling for his resignation.

34 I address the meanings of this term later in the chapter.

35 There is virtually no published data I know of that focuses on *pak nyah*, aside from Rais Nur and A. R.'s (1996:73) remarks that "peng-kids often feel that they are men trapped in women's bodies," that "they bind their breasts as well as use men's underwear and aftershave," and that they "are renowned as very loyal and extremely attentive and generous to their girlfriends." I might add that my questions to *mak nyah* about *pak nyah* met with quizzical looks, blank stares, or both, and that the seasoned Pink Triangle staffers with whom I discussed such matters claimed to know nothing about them. Future research on gender and sexual diversity in Southeast Asia needs to give priority to Malaysia's *pak nyah*—and lesbian—communities along with their counterparts in Burma, Cambodia, Laos, and Vietnam, even if this means reallocating some scholarly resources from the extremely well-studied contexts of Thailand and Indonesia.

36 See Peletz (2007:71–72, 92–93 n2 and n3, and Works Cited) for brief discussion of these figures and some of the relevant sources.

37 See Loong Meng Yee and Elan Perumal (2001).

38 Various activists I interviewed in 2008 noted, for example, that in recent years Chandra Muzaffar, long-time head of the progressive reform movement known as *Aliran*, has come out strongly against Western-style gay marriage, identifying it—along with globalization—as one of the most serious threats currently facing Malaysian society.

39 These outreach programs have since been reinstated and expanded, thanks to federal funds allocated to the Pink Triangle in 2006 or 2007.

40 The message bore the title "Mon 2eme Texte Pour le 20 Fevrier 2004, Droleries, par Norodom Sihanouk" ["My Second Text for 20 February 2004, Curiosities, by Norodom Sihanouk"] and was accessed from Sihanouk's official website, located at <http://www.norodomsihanouk.info/>, on February 25, 2004.

41 This in any case is the figure provided by Wikipedia under its entry for Sihanouk, <http://en.wikipedia.org/wiki/King_Sihanouk>.

Epilogue: Asylum, Diaspora, Pluralism

1 There are important differences between granting asylum and withholding deportation but they are not germane to the present discussion.

2 From the notes on the back cover of the DVD version of *Return to Paradise*, released by Universal Studies in 2002.

3 See Harding (2000) for a cogent description and analysis of the culture of one such Christian community.

4 Recall that Marina Mahathir cited the Matthew Shepard case in her public denunciation of the People's Anti-Homosexual Volunteer Movement (PASRAH) that formed shortly after her father, the prime minister, engineered the downfall of his protégé Anwar. I might add that Matthew Shepard's legacy is also mentioned in a number of asylum narratives I have reviewed.

5 "It is popular to claim that the dance style of Angkor's *apsaras* of the twelfth century is perfectly preserved in the Royal Cambodian Ballet dance style. Unfortunately, this is romantic nonsense. A world of difference separates the elaborately costumed, chaste, and refined Cambodian dancers of today from the bare-breasted, hip-swinging beauties of Angkor" (Brandon 1967:59).

Bibliography

A. Samad Ahmad, ed. 1979. *Sulalatus Salatin* (*Sejarah Melayu*) [Malay Annals]. Kuala Lumpur: Dewan Bahasa dan Pustaka. Malay Concordance Project, <http://mcp.anu.edu.au>.

——. 1987. *Hikayat Amir Hamzah* [The Saga of Commander Hamzah]. Kuala Lumpur: Dewan Bahasa dan Pustaka. Malay Concordance Project, <http://mcp.anu.edu.au>.

Abdul Rahman Embong, ed. 2002. *State-Led Modernization and the New Middle Class in Malaysia*. London: Palgrave Macmillan.

Agamben, Giorgio. 1998. *Homo Sacer: Sovereign Power and Bare Life*. Stanford: Stanford University Press.

——. 2005. *State of Exception*. Chicago: University of Chicago Press.

Agrawal, Anuja. 1997. "Gendered Bodies: The Case of the 'Third Gender' in India". *Contributions to Indian Sociology* 31(2):273–297.

Aldrich, Robert. 2003. *Colonialism and Homosexuality*. New York: Routledge.

Alina Rastam. 1998. "Out of the Closet and Into the Courtroom? Some Reflections on Sexuality Rights in Malaysia". *Saksi* 2, <http://www.saksi.com/novdec98/alina.htm>.

——, ed. 2002. *The Rape Report: An Overview of Rape in Malaysia*. Kuala Lumpur: Vinlin Press Sdn. Bhd.

Altman, Dennis. 1996. "Rupture or Continuity? The Internationalization of Gay Identities". *Social Text* 48:77–94.

——. 2001. *Global Sex*. Chicago: University of Chicago Press.

Andaya, Barbara W. 1994. "The Changing Religious Role of Women in Pre-Modern Southeast Asia." *South East Asia Research* 2(2):99–116.

——. 1998. "From Temporary Wife to Prostitute: Sexuality and Economic Change in Early Modern Southeast Asia." *Journal of Women's History* 9(4):11–34.

——. 2000a. "Delineating Female Space: Seclusion and the State in Early Modern Southeast Asia." In *Other Pasts: Women, Gender, and History in Early Modern Southeast Asia*, ed. Barbara W. Andaya, 231–253. Honolulu: Center for Southeast Asian Studies, University of Hawaii Press.

——, ed. 2000b. *Other Pasts: Women, Gender, and History in Early Modern Southeast Asia*. Honolulu: Center for Southeast Asian Studies, University of Hawaii Press.

——. 2006. *The Flaming Womb: Repositioning Women in Early Modern Southeast Asia*. Honolulu: University of Hawaii Press.

Andaya, Barbara W. and Leonard Andaya. 2001. *A History of Malaysia*, 2nd ed. Honolulu: University of Hawaii Press.

Andaya, Leonard. 1981. *The Heritage of Arung Palakka: A History of South Sulawesi (Celebes) in the Seventeenth Century*. The Hague: Martinus Nijhoff.

——. 1993. *The World of Maluku: Eastern Indonesia in the Early Modern Period*. Honolulu: University of Hawaii Press.

——. 2000. "The Bissu: Study of a Third Gender in Indonesia." In *Other Pasts*, ed. Barbara Andaya, 27–46. Honolulu: Center for Southeast Asian Studies, University of Hawaii Press.

——. 2001. "Aceh's Contributions to Standards of Malayness." *Archipel* 61: 29–68.

Anderson, Benedict O'G. 1990. "Professional Dreams: Reflections on Two Javanese Classics." In *Language and Power: Exploring Political Cultures in Indonesia*, 271–298. Ithaca: Cornell University Press.

——. 1991. *Imagined Communities: Reflections on the Origin and Spread of Nationalism*, rev. ed. London: Verso.

Anderson, Warwick. 1997. "The Trespass Speaks: White Masculinity and Colonial Breakdown." *American Historical Review* 102(5):1343–1370.

An-Na'im, Abdullahi. 2008. *Islam and the Secular State: Negotiating the Future of Shari'a*. Cambridge: Harvard University Press.

Appadurai, Arjun. 1981. "The Past as a Scarce Resource." *Man* 16:201–219.

——. 1986. "Theory in Anthropology: Center and Periphery." *Comparative Studies in Society and History* 28(2):356–361.

——. 1996. *Modernity at Large: Cultural Dimensions of Globalization*. Minneapolis: University of Minnesota Press.

Aragon, Lorraine, 2001. "Communal Violence in Poso, Central Sulawesi: Where People Eat Fish and Fish Eat People." *Indonesia* 72:45–79.

Aronson, Jacob. 1999. "Homosex in Hanoi? Sex, the Public Sphere, and Public Sex." In *Public Sex/Gay Space*, ed. William L. Leap, 203–221. New York: Columbia University Press.

Asia Watch and The Women's Rights Project. 1993. *A Modern Form of Slavery: Trafficking of Burmese Women and Girls into Brothels in Thailand*. New York: Human Rights Watch.

Atkinson, Jane. 1989. *The Art and Politics of Wana Shamanship*. Berkeley: University of California Press.

Aung-Thwin, Michael. 1985. *Pagan: The Origins of Modern Burma*. Honolulu: University of Hawaii Press.

Ballhatchet, Kenneth. 1980. *Race, Sex and Class Under the Raj: Imperial Attitudes and Policies and their Critics, 1793–1905*. New York: St. Martin's Press.

Bateson, Gregory. 1936. *Naven: A Survey of the Problems Suggested by a Composite Picture of a New Guinea Tribe Drawn from Three Points of View*. Stanford: Stanford University Press.

Baxstrom, Richard. 2008. *Houses in Motion: The Experience of Place and the Problem of Belief in Urban Malaysia*. Stanford: Stanford University Press.

Beatty, Andrew. 1999. *Varieties of Javanese Religion*. Cambridge: Cambridge University Press.

——. 2002. "Changing Places: Relatives and Relativism in Java." *Journal of the Royal Anthropological Institute* 8:469–491.

Bechert, Heinz. 1984. "Buddhist Revival in East and West". In *The World of Buddhism: Buddhist Nuns and Monks in Society and Culture*, ed. Heinz Bechert and Richard Gombrich, 273–285. London: Thames and Hudson.

Belak, Brenda. 2002. *Gathering Strength: Women from Burma on Their Rights*. Chiangmai: Images Asia.

Bellwood, Peter. 1997. *Prehistory of the Indo-Malaysian Archipelago*, rev. ed. Honolulu: University of Hawaii Press.

Belo, Jane. 1935 [1970]. *Traditional Balinese Culture*. New York: Columbia University Press.

Benjamin, Walter. 1936 [1968]. "The Work of Art in the Age of Mechanical Reproduction." In *Illuminations: Essays and Reflections*, ed. Hannah Arendt, 217–251. New York: Schocken Books.

——. 1950 [1968]. "Theses on the Philosophy of History." In *Illuminations: Essays and Reflections*, ed. Hannah Arendt, 253–264. New York: Schocken Books.

Bishop, Ryan and Lillian Robinson. 1998. *Night Market: Sexual Cultures and the Thai Economic Miracle*. New York: Routledge.

Blackwood, Evelyn. 1999. "Tombois in West Sumatra." In *Female Desires: Same-Sex Relations and Transgender Practices Across Cultures*, ed. Evelyn Blackwood and Saskia Wieringa, 181–205. New York: Columbia University Press.

——. 2005. "Gender Transgression in Colonial and Post-Colonial Indonesia." *Journal of Asian Studies* 64:849–880.

Blackwood, Evelyn and Saskia Wieringa, eds. 1999. *Female Desires: Same-Sex Relations and Transgender Practices Across Cultures*. New York: Columbia University Press.

Bleys, Rudi. 1995. *The Geography of Perversion: Male-to-Male Sexual Behavior Outside the West and the Ethnographic Imagination, 1750–1918*. New York: New York University Press.

Bloch, Maurice. 1989. *Ritual, History, and Power: Selected Papers in Anthropology*. London: Athlone Press.

Boellstorff, Tom. 1999. "The Perfect Path: Gay Men, Marriage, Indonesia." *QLQ: A Journal of Lesbian and Gay Studies* 5(4):475–510.

——. 2004a. "Playing Back the Nation: *Waria*, Indonesian Transvestites." *Cultural Anthropology* 19:159–195.

——. 2004b. "The Emergence of Political Homophobia in Indonesia: Masculinity and National Belonging." *Ethnos* 69(4):465–486.

——. 2005. *The Gay Archipelago: Sexuality and Nation in Indonesia*. Princeton: Princeton University Press.

Boon, James A. 1977. *The Anthropological Romance of Bali, 1597–1972: Dynamic Perspectives in Marriage and Caste, Politics and Religion*. Cambridge: Cambridge University Press.

——. 1979. "Balinese Temple Politics and the Religious Revitalization of Caste Ideals." In *The Imagination of Reality: Essays in Southeast Asia Coherence Systems*, ed. A.L. Becker and Aram A. Yengoyan, 271–291. Palo Alto: Ablex.

——. 1990. *Affinities and Extremes: Crisscrossing the Bittersweet Ethnology of East Indies History, Hindu-Balinese Culture, and Indo-European Allure*. Chicago: University of Chicago Press.

——. 1991. Review of *The Penis Inserts of Southeast Asia: An Annotated Bibliography with an Overview and Comparative Perspectives*, by Donald E. Brown, James W. Edwards, and Ruth P. Moore. *Journal of Asian Studies* 50(3):729–730.

Bornstein, Kate. 1995. *Gender Outlaw: On Men, Women, and the Rest of Us*. New York: Vintage.

Boua, Chanthou. 1991. "Genocide of a Religious Group: Pol Pot and Cambodia's Buddhist Monks." In *State-Organized Terror: The Case of Violent Internal Repression*, ed. V. Schlapentokh et al., 277–240. Boulder: Westview.

Bourdieu, Pierre. 1977. *Outline of a Theory of Practice*. Cambridge: Cambridge University Press.

Bowen, John. 1993. *Muslims Through Discourse: Religion and Ritual in Gayo Society*. Princeton: Princeton University Press.

———. 2003. *Islam, Law, and Equality in Indonesia: An Anthropology of Public Reasoning*. Cambridge: Cambridge University Press.

Bowrey, Thomas. 1680 [1905]. *A Geographical Account of Countries Round the Bay of Bengal*, ed. R.C. Temple. Rpt. Cambridge: Hakluyt Society.

Bowring, Thomas. 1856 [1969]. *The Kingdom and People of Siam*, 2 vols. Rpt. Singapore: Oxford University Press.

Brac de la Perrière, Bénédicte. 1989. *Les Rituels de Possession en Birmanie: Du Culte d'État aux Cérémonies Privées*. Paris: Éditions Recherche sur Civilisations, ADPF.

———. 1996. "The Burmese Nats: Between Sovereignty and Autochthony." In *The Link with Nature and Divine Mediations in Asia*, ed. Bernard Formoso, 45–60. Providence: Berghahn.

———. 1998. "'Être épousée par un naq': Les implications du mariage avec l'esprit dans le culte de possession birman (Myanmar)." *Anthropologies et Sociétés* 22(2):169–182.

———. 2005. "The Taungbyon Festival: Locality and Nation-Confronting in the Cult of the 37 Lords." In *Burma at the Turn of the Twenty-First Century*, ed. Monique Skidmore, 65–89. Honolulu: University of Hawaii Press.

Brandon, James R. 1967. *Theatre in Southeast Asia*. Cambridge: Harvard University Press.

Brenner, Suzanne. 1995. "Why Women Rule the Roost: Rethinking Javanese Ideologies of Gender and Self Control." In *Bewitching Women, Pious Men: Gender and Body Politics in Southeast Asia*, ed. Aihwa Ong and Michael G. Peletz, 19–50. Berkeley: University of California Press.

———. 1998. *The Domestication of Desire: Women, Wealth, and Modernity in Java*. Princeton: Princeton University Press.

Brewer, Carolyn. 1999. "Baylan, Asog, Transvestism, and Sodomy: Gender, Sexuality, and the Sacred in Early Colonial Philippines." *Intersections: Gender, History, and Culture in the Asian Context* 2, <http://www.sshe.murdoch.edu.au/intersections/issue2/carolyn2.html>.

———. 2000. "From Animist Priestess to Catholic Priest: The Re/Gendering of Religious Roles in the Philippines, 1521–1685." In *Other Pasts*, ed. Barbara Andaya, 69–86. Honolulu: University of Hawaii Press.

———. 2004. *Shamanism, Catholicism, and Gender Relations in Colonial Philippines, 1521–1685*. Burlington, VT: Ashgate.

Brooke, Charles. 1866 [1990]. *Ten Years in Sarawak*, 2 vols. Rpt. Singapore: Oxford University Press.

Brooke, James. 1848. *Narrative of Events in Borneo and Celebes, Down to the Occupation of Labuan: From the Journals of James Brooke, Esq*. London: John Murray.

Brown, Donald E. 1991. "The Penis Pin: An Unsolved Problem in the Relations Between the Sexes in Borneo." In *Female and Male in Borneo*, ed. Vinson Sutlive, 435–454. Williamsburg, VA: The Borneo Research Council.

Brown, Donald E., James W. Edwards and Ruth P. Moore. 1988. *The Penis Inserts of Southeast Asia: An Annotated Bibliography with an Overview and Comparative Perspectives*. Occasional Paper No. 15, Occasional Paper Series, Center for South and Southeast Asian Studies, University of California at Berkeley.

310   Bibliography

Brown, R. Grant. 1915. "The Taungbyon Festival, Burma." *Journal of the Royal Anthropological Institute of Great Britain and Ireland* 45:355–363.

Bulbeck, F. David. 1996. "The Politics of Marriage and the Marriage of Polities in Gowa, South Sulawesi, During the 16th and 17th Centuries." In *Origins, Ancestry, and Alliance: Explorations in Austronesian Ethnography*, ed. James Fox and Clifford Sather, 280–315. Canberra: Department of Anthropology, Australian National University.

Bulbeck, F. David and Bagyo Prasetyo. 2000. "Two Millennia of Socio-Cultural Development in Luwu, South Sulawesi, Indonesia." *World Archaeology* 32(1):121–137.

Burton, Sir Richard. 1886 [1973]. *The Sotadic Zone*. Boston: Milford House.

Butler, Judith. 1990. *Gender Trouble: Feminism and the Subversion of Identity*. New York: Routledge.

——. 1993. *Bodies That Matter: On the Discursive Limits of "Sex"*. New York: Routledge.

Caldwell, Ian. 1995. "Power, State, and Society Among the Pre-Islamic Bugis." *Bijdragen tot de Taal-, Land- en Volkenkunde* 151(3):394–421.

Cannell, Fenella. 1999. *Power and Intimacy in the Christian Philippines*. Cambridge: Cambridge University Press.

Carsten, Janet and Stephen Hugh-Jones, eds. 1995. *About the House: Lévi-Strauss and Beyond*. Cambridge: Cambridge University Press.

Certeau, Michel de. 1984. *The Practice of Everyday Life*. Berkeley: University of California Press.

Chandler, David P. 1974. "Royally Sponsored Human Sacrifices in Nineteenth Century Cambodia: The Cult of Nak Ta Me Sa (Mahisasuramardini) at Ba Phnom." *Journal of the Siam Society* 62(2):207–222.

——. 1991. *The Tragedy of Cambodian History: Politics, War, and Revolution Since 1945*. New Haven: Yale University Press.

Chandra Muzaffar. 1987. *Islamic Resurgence in Malaysia*. Kuala Lumpur: Fajar Bakti.

Chou Ta-Kuan. 1297 [1993]. *The Customs of Cambodia*. Trans. Paul Pelliot [and J. Gilman d'Arcy Paul], 3rd ed. Bangkok: The Siam Society.

Clements, Alan. 1992. *Burma: The Next Killing Fields?* Berkeley: Odonian Press.

Clifford, James. 1997. *Routes: Travel and Translation in the Late Twentieth Century*. Cambridge: Harvard University Press.

Coe, Michael D. 2003. *Angkor and the Khmer Civilization*. New York: Thames and Hudson.

Coedès, George. 1966. *The Making of Southeast Asia*. Berkeley: University of California Press.

Cohen, Lawrence. 1995. "The Pleasures of Castration: The Postoperative Status of Hijras, Jankhas, and Academics." In *Sexual Nature/Sexual Culture: Theorizing Sexuality from the Perspective of Pleasure*, ed. Paul Abramson and Steven Pinkerton, 276–304. Chicago: University of Chicago Press.

Cohen, Shelee. 1995. "'Like a Mother to Them': Stratified Reproduction and West Indian Childcare Workers and Employers in New York." In *Conceiving the New World Order: The Global Politics of Reproduction*, ed. Faye Ginsburg and Rayna Rapp, 78–102. Berkeley: University of California Press.

Coleman, E., P. Colgan, and L. Gooren. 1992. "Male Cross-Gender Behavior in Myanmar (Burma): A Description of the Acault." *Archives of Sexual Behavior* 21:313–321.

Connolly, William E. 2005. *Pluralism*. Durham: Duke University Press.

Covarrubias, Miguel. 1937 [1972]. *Island of Bali*. Rpt. Singapore: Oxford University Press.

Cox, Hiram. 1821 [1971]. *Journal of a Residence in the Burmhan Empire*. Rpt. London: Gregg International Publishers.

Crawfurd, John. 1820. *History of the Indian Archipelago, Containing an Account of the Manners, Arts, Languages, Religions, Institutions, and Commerce of Its Inhabitants*, 3 vols. Edinburgh: Archibald Constable and Co.

——. 1830. *Journal of an Embassy From the Governor-General of India to the Courts of Siam and Cochin China; Exhibiting a View of the Actual States of Those Kingdoms*, 2nd ed. 2 vols. London: Henry Colburn and Richard Bentley.

——. 1834. *Journal of an Embassy from the Governor General of India to the Court of Ava*. 2 vols. London: Bentley, Bell, and Bradfute.

Cummings, William. 2002. *Making Blood White: Historical Transformations in Early Modern Makassar*. Honolulu: University of Hawaii Press.

Dampier, William. 1697 [1717/1906]. *A New Voyage Round the World*, 2 vols., ed. John Masefield. London: E. Grant Richards.

Davies, Sharyn Graham. 2007. *Challenging Gender Norms: Five Genders Among the Bugis in Indonesia*. Belmont, CA.: Wadsworth.

Day, Tony. 2002. *Fluid Iron: State Formation in Southeast Asia*. Honolulu: University of Hawaii Press.

De Casparis, J.G. and Ian W. Mabbett. 1992. "Religion and Popular Beliefs of Southeast Asia Before c. 1500." In *The Cambridge History of Southeast Asia, Vol 1. From Early Times to circa 1800*, ed. Nicholas Tarling, 276–339. Cambridge: Cambridge University Press.

Derrida, Jacques. 1977. *Writing and Difference*. London: Routledge and Kegan Paul.

Despres, Leo A. 1968. "Anthropological Theory, Cultural Pluralism, and the Study of Complex Societies." *Current Anthropology* 9(1):3–26.

Deveaux, Monique. 2000. *Cultural Pluralism and Dilemmas of Justice*. Ithaca: Cornell University Press.

Domhoff, G. William. 1974. *The Bohemian Grove and Other Retreats: A Study in Ruling-Class Cohesiveness*. New York: Harper and Row.

Douglas, Mary. 1970. *Natural Symbols: Explorations in Cosmology*. New York: Pantheon.

Drewes, G.W.J. 1976. "Further Data Concerning 'Abd Al-Samad Al-Palimbani." *Bijdragen Tot de Taal-, Land- en Volkenkunde* 132(2/3):267–292.

Duby, Georges. 1983. *The Knight, the Lady, and the Priest: The Making of Modern Marriage in Medieval France*. New York: Pantheon Books.

Duff-Cooper, Andrew. 1985. "Notes About Some Balinese Ideas and Practices Connected with Sex from Western Lombok." *Anthropos* 80:403–419.

Duggan, Lisa. 2003. *The Twilight of Equality? Neoliberalism, Cultural Politics, and the Attack on Democracy*. Boston: Beacon Press.

Eck, Diana. 2001. *A New Religious America: How a "Christian Country" Has Become the World's Most Religiously Diverse Nation*. New York: HarperCollins.

Eickelman, Dale and James Piscatori. 1996. *Muslim Politics*. Princeton: Princeton University Press.

Eisenbruch, Maurice. 1992. "The Ritual Space of Patients and Traditional Healers in Cambodia." *Bulletin de L'Ecole Française d'Extrême-Orient* 79(2):283–316.

Eliade, Mircea. 1951 [1972]. *Shamanism: Archaic Techniques of Ecstasy*. Princeton: Princeton University Press.

Elliston, Deborah. 1999. "Negotiating Transnational Sexual Economies: Female Mahu and Same-Sex Sexuality in 'Tahiti and Her Islands'." In *Female Desires*, ed. Evelyn Blackwood and Saskia Wieringa, 230–252. New York: Columbia University Press.

El-Rouayheb, Khaled. 2005. *Before Homosexuality in the Arab-Islamic World, 1500–1800*. Chicago: University of Chicago Press.

Engels, Frederick. 1884 [1972]. *The Origin of the Family, Private Property and the State*. New York: International Publishers.

Enloe, Cynthia. 1990. *Bananas, Beaches, and Bases: Making Feminist Sense of International Politics*. Berkeley: University of California Press.

Errington, Shelly. 1989. *Meaning and Power in a Southeast Asian Realm*. Princeton: Princeton University Press.

Evans, Peter. 1996. "Government Action, Social Capital and Development: Reviewing the Evidence on Synergy." *World Development* 24(6):1119–1132.

Fabian, Johannes. 1983. *Time and the Other: How Anthropology Makes Its Object*. New York: Columbia University Press.

Fardon, Richard. 1990. "Localizing Strategies: The Regionalization of Ethnographic Accounts." In *Localizing Strategies: Regional Traditions of Ethnographic Writing*, ed. Richard Fardon, 1–35. Edinburgh: Scottish Academic Press.

Feinberg, Leslie. 1996. *Transgender Warriors: Making History From Joan of Arc to Dennis Rodman*. Boston: Beacon.

Finlayson, George. 1826 [1988]. *The Mission to Siam and Hue, 1821–1822*. Singapore: Oxford University Press.

Firth, Raymond. 1940. *The Work of the Gods in Tikopia*. London School of Economics and Political Science, Monographs on Social Anthropology, 1 and 2.

Fitch, Ralph. c. 1592 [1811]. *The Voyage of Mr. Ralph Fitch, Merchant of London, to Ormus, and so to Goa in the East India [1583–1591]*. In *A General Collection of the Best and Most Interesting Voyages in All Parts of the World*, Vol. 8, ed. J. Pinkerton, 406–425. London: Longman, Hurst, and Rees.

Fjelstad, Karen, and Nguyen Thi Hien, eds. 2006. *Possessed by the Spirits: Mediumship in Contemporary Vietnamese Communities*. Ithaca: Southeast Asia Program, Cornell University.

Foucault, Michel. 1978. *The History of Sexuality, Volume I: An Introduction*. New York: Vintage.

Freeman, Derek, 1983. *Margaret Mead and Samoa: The Making and Unmaking of an Anthropological Myth*. Cambridge: Harvard University Press.

Freeman, Michael. 2004. *Cambodia*. London: Reaktion Books.

Fukuyama, Francis. 1992. *The End of History and the Last Man*. New York: Free Press.

Funston, John. 1999. "Malaysia: A Fateful September." *Southeast Asian Affairs* 1999, 165–184.

Furnivall, J.S. 1939. *Netherlands India: A Study of Plural Economy*. New York: Macmillan.

——. 1948. *Colonial Policy and Practice: A Comparative Study of Burma and Netherlands India*. Cambridge: Cambridge University Press.

Gailey, Christine. 1987. *Kinship to Kingship: Gender Hierarchy and State Formation in the Tongan Islands*. Austin: University of Texas Press.

Galvao, Antonio. c. 1544 [1971]. *Treatise on the Moluccas, Probably the Preliminary Version of Antonio Galvao's Lost Historia Das Molucas*, ed. and trans. H. Jacobs. Rome: Jesuit Historical Institute.

Garcia, J. Neil C. 1996. *Philippine Gay Culture: The Last Thirty Years*. Quezon City: University of the Philippines Press.

Geertz, Clifford. 1960. *Religion of Java*. Glencoe, IL: Free Press.

——. 1973. *The Interpretation of Cultures*. New York: Basic Books.

——. 1980. *Negara: The Theatre State in Nineteenth-Century Bali*. Princeton: Princeton University Press.

——. 2000. *Available Light: Anthropological Reflections on Philosophical Topics*. Princeton: Princeton University Press.

Geertz, Hildred. 1961. *The Javanese Family*. Glencoe, IL: Free Press.

George, Kenneth M. 1996. *Showing Signs of Violence: The Cultural Politics of a Twentieth-Century Headhunting Ritual*. Berkeley: University of California Press.

Gibson, Thomas P. 2005. *And the Sun Pursued the Moon: Symbolic Knowledge and Traditional Authority Among the Makassar*. Honolulu: University of Hawaii Press.

——. 2007. *Islamic Narrative and Authority in Southeast Asia: From the 16th to the 21st Century*. New York: Palgrave Macmillan.

Gold, Ann. 2007. "Gender." In *Studying Hinduism: Key Concepts and Methods*, ed. Sushil Mittral and Gene Thursby, 178–193. London: Routledge.

Gombrich, Richard and Gananath Obeyesekere. 1988. *Buddhism Transformed: Religious Change in Sri Lanka*. Princeton: Princeton University Press.

Gomes, Edwin H. 1911. *Seventeen Years Among the Sea Dayaks of Borneo: A Record of Intimate Association with the Natives of the Bornean Jungles*. Philadelphia: J.B. Lippincott Co.

Goody, Jack. 1983. *The Development of the Family and Marriage in Europe*. Cambridge: Cambridge University Press.

——. 1996. *The East in the West*. Cambridge: Cambridge University Press.

Gopinath, Gayatri. 1996. "Funny Boys and Girls: Notes on a Queer South Asian Planet." In *Asian American Sexualities: Dimensions of the Gay and Lesbian Experience*, ed. Russell Leong, 119–127. New York: Routledge.

Goriaeva, Lioubou, ed. 1967. *Hikayat Maharaja Marakarma* [The Saga of Emperor Marakarma]. Manuscript C 1967, Saint-Petersburg Branch of the Institute of Oriental Studies, Russian Academy of Sciences. Malay Concordance Project, <http://mcp.anu.edu.au>.

Gouda, Frances. 1995. *Dutch Culture Overseas: Colonial Practice in the Netherlands Indies, 1900–1942*. Amsterdam: Amsterdam University Press.

Government of Malaysia. 2000. *Buku Tahunan Perangkaan Malaysia* [Yearbook of Statistics Malaysia]. Kuala Lumpur: Jabatan Perangkaan Malaysia [Department of Statistics, Malaysia].

Graham, Penelope. 1987. *Iban Shamanism: An Analysis of the Ethnographic Literature*. Occasional Paper of the Department of Anthropology, Research School of Pacific Studies, Australian National University.

Graham, Sharyn. 2001. "Negotiating Gender: Calalai in Bugis Society." *Intersections: Gender, History, and Culture in the Asian Context* 6:1–17. <http://www.sshe.murdoch.edu.au/intersections/issue6/graham.html>.

——. 2003. *Hunters, Wedding Mothers, and Androgynous Priests: Conceptualising Gender Among Bugis in South Sulawesi, Indonesia*. Ph.D. dissertation, University of Western Australia.

Gramsci, Antonio. 1971. *Selections from the Prison Notebooks of Antonio Gramsci*, trans. and ed. Quintin Hoare and Geoffrey N. Smith. New York: International Publishers.

Greenberg, David F. 1988. *The Construction of Homosexuality*. Chicago: University of Chicago Press.

Gregor, Thomas. 1985. *Anxious Pleasures: The Sexual Lives of an Amazonian People*. Chicago: University of Chicago Press.

Grewal, Inderpal and Caren Kaplan. 1994. "Introduction." In *Scattered Hegemonies: Postmodernity and Transnational Feminist Practices*, ed. Inderpal Grewal and Caren Kaplan, 1–33. Minneapolis: University of Minnesota Press.

——. 2001. "Global Identities: Theorizing Transnational Studies of Sexuality". *QLQ* 7(4):663–79.

Haensel, John Godfried. 1812. *Letters on the Nicobar Islands, Their Natural Productions, and the Manners, Customs, and Superstitions of the Natives, With an Account of an Attempt Made by the Church of the United Brethren to Convert them to Christianity.* London: W.M'Dowall, Pemberton Row.

Hamilton, Alexander. 1727 [1930]. *A New Account of the East Indies*, 2 vols, ed. W. Foster. London: Argonaut Press.

Hamonic, Gilbert. 1975. "Travestissement et Bisexualité Chez les 'Bissu' Du Pays Bugis." *Archipel* 10:121–134.

——. 1977. "Les 'Fausses-Femmes' du Pays Bugis (Célèbes-Sud)." *Objets et Mondes* 17(1):39–46.

Hardeland, Aug. 1859. *Dajaksch-Deutsches Wörterbuch*. Amsterdam.

Harding, Susan F. 2000. *The Book of Jerry Falwell: Fundamentalist Language and Politics.* Princeton: Princeton University Press.

Hart, Donn V. 1968. "Homosexuality and Transvestism in the Philippines." *Behavior Science Notes* 3:211–248.

Harvey, Barbara S. 1974. *Tradition, Islam, and Rebellion: South Sulawesi 1950-1965*. Ph.D dissertation, Cornell University.

Hatley, Barbara. 1990. "Theatrical Imagery and Gender Ideology in Java." In *Power and Difference: Gender in Island Southeast Asia*, ed. Jane M. Atkinson and Shelly Errington, 177-207. Stanford: Stanford University Press.

Hefner, Robert W. 1985. *Hindu Javanese*. Princeton: Princeton University Press.

——. 1998. "On the History and Cross-Cultural Possibility of a Democratic Ideal." In *Democratic Civility: The History and Cross-Cultural Possibility of a Modern Ideal*, ed. Robert W. Hefner, 3–49. Brunswick, NJ: Transaction Publishers.

——. 2000. *Civil Islam: Muslims and Democratization in Indonesia*. Princeton: Princeton University Press.

——. 2002. "Global Violence and Indonesian Muslim Politics." *American Anthropologist* 104(3):754–765.

——. 2009. "Islamic Schools, Social Movements, and Democracy in Indonesia." In *Making Modern Muslims: The Politics of Islamic Education in Southeast Asia*, ed. Robert W. Hefner, 55–105. Honolulu: University of Hawaii Press.

——, ed. 2005. *Remaking Muslim Politics: Pluralism, Contestation, Democratization.* Princeton: Princeton University Press.

Hefner, Robert W. and Patricia Horvatich, eds. 1997. *Islam in an Era of Nation-States: Politics and Religious Renewal in Muslim Southeast Asia*. Honolulu: University of Hawaii Press.

Heiman, Elliot M. and Cao Van Le. 1975. "Transsexualism in Vietnam." *Archives of Sexual Behavior* 4(1):89–95.

Heine-Geldern, Robert. 1956. *Conceptions of State and Kinship in Southeast Asia*. Data Paper No. 18. Ithaca: Cornell University Southeast Asia Program.

Hekma, Gert. 1993. "'A Female Soul in a Male Body': Sexual Inversion as Gender Inversion in Nineteenth-Century Sexology." In *Third Sex, Third Gender: Beyond Sexual Dimorphism in Culture and History*, ed. Gilbert Herdt, 213–239. New York: Zone Books.

Herdt, Gilbert. 1993a. "Introduction." In *Third Sex, Third Gender: Beyond Sexual Dimorphism in Culture and History*, ed. Gilbert Herdt, 21–81. New York: Zone Books.

——, ed. 1993b. *Third Sex, Third Gender: Beyond Sexual Dimorphism in Culture and History*. New York: Zone Press.

——, ed. 1993c. *Ritualized Homosexuality in Melanesia*, rev. ed. Berkeley: University of California Press.

Higham, Charles. 1989. *The Archaeology of Mainland Southeast Asia*. Cambridge: Cambridge University Press.

——. 2001. *The Civilization of Angkor*. Berkeley: University of California Press.

Hilley, John. 2001. *Malaysia: Mahathirism, Hegemony, and the New Opposition*. London: Zed.

Hirschfeld, Magnus. 1935. *Men and Women: The World Journey of a Sexologist*. New York: G.P. Putnam's Sons.

Hocart, A.M. 1927. *Kingship*. London: Oxford University Press.

Holt, Claire. 1939. *Dance Quest in Celebes*. Paris: Les Archives Internationales de la Dance.

Hoskins, Janet. 1990. "Doubling Deities, Descent, and Personhood: An Exploration of Kodi Gender Categories." In *Power and Difference: Gender in Island Southeast Asia*, ed. Jane Atkinson and Shelly Errington, 273–306. Stanford: Stanford University Press.

——. 1998. *Biographical Objects: How Things Tell the Stories of People's Lives*. New York: Routledge.

Houtman, Gustaaf. 2005. "Sacralizing or Demonizing Democracy? Aung San Suu Kyi's 'Personality Cult'." In *Burma at the Turn of the Twenty-First Century*, ed. Monique Skidmore, 133–153. Honolulu: University of Hawaii Press.

Hupe, Carl. 1846. "Korte Verhandeling over de Godsdienst, Zeden, enz. der Dajakkers." *Tijdschrift voor Nederlandsch-Indie* 8(3):127–172, 245–280.

Husin Mutalib. 1993. *Islam in Malaysia: From Revivalism to Islamic State?* Singapore: Singapore University Press.

Hyam, Ronald. 1990. *Empire and Sexuality: The British Experience*. Manchester: Manchester University Press.

Ileto, Reynaldo. 1979. *Payson and Revolution: Popular Movements in the Philippines, 1840–1910*. Quezon City: Ateneo de Manila University Press.

Ingraham, Chrys. 2002. "Heterosexuality: It's Just Not Natural!" In *Handbook of Lesbian and Gay Studies*, ed. Diane Richardson and Steven Seidman, 73–82. London: Sage.

Ishihara, Shintaro. 1990. *The Japan That Can Say No*. Trans. Frank Baldwin. New York: Simon and Schuster.

Jackson, Peter A. 1997. "Kathoey < > Gay > < Man: The Historical Emergence of Gay Male Identity in Thailand." In *Sites of Desire, Economies of Pleasure: Sexualities in Asia and the Pacific*, ed. L. Manderson and M. Jolly, 166–90. Chicago: University of Chicago Press.

——. 1998. "Male Homosexuality and Transgenderism in the Thai Buddhist Tradition." In *Queer Dharma: Voices of Gay Buddhists*, ed. Winston Leyland, 55–89. San Francisco: Gay Sunshine Press.

——. 2003. "Gay Capitals in Global Gay History: Cities, Local Markets, and the Origins of Bangkok's Same-Sex Cultures." In *Postcolonial Urbanism: Southeast Asian Cities and Global Processes*, ed. Ryan Bishop, John Phillips, and Wei Wei Yeo, 151–163. New York: Routledge.

——. 2004. "The Tapestry of Language and Theory: Reading Rosalind Morris on Post-Structuralism and Thai Modernity." *South East Asia Research* 12(3):337–377.

Jackson, Peter A. and Gerard Sullivan, eds. 1999. *Lady Boys, Tom Boys, Rent Boys: Male and Female Homosexualities in Contemporary Thailand*. Binghamton, NY: Harrington Park Press.

Jacobs, Hubert. 1966. "The First Locally Demonstrable Christianity in Celebes, 1544." *Studia* 17:251–305.

Jardine, John. 1893. "Introduction." In *The Burmese Empire a Hundred Years Ago as Described by Father Sangermano*, vii–xxix. Westminster: Archibald Constable and Co.

Jaspan, M.A. 1969. *Traditional Medical Theory in Southeast Asia*. Hull: University of Hull.

Jay, Sian. 1993. "Canoes for the Spirits: Two Types of Spirit Mediumship in Central Kalimantan." In *The Seen and the Unseen: Shamanism, Mediumship, and Spirit Possession in Borneo*, ed. Robert Winzeler, 151–168. Borneo Research Council Monographs, No. 2. Shanghai, VA: Ashley.

Jensen, Erik. 1974. *The Iban and their Religion*. London: Oxford University Press.

Jewell, Elizabeth J. and Frank Abate, eds. 2001. *The New Oxford American Dictionary*. New York: Oxford University Press.

Johnson, Mark. 1997. *Beauty and Power: Transgendering and Cultural Transformation in the Southern Philippines*. London: Berg.

———. 2006. "Comment." *Current Anthropology* 47(2):328.

Johnson, Mark, Peter Jackson and Gilbert Herdt. 2000. "Critical Regionalities and the Study of Gender and Sexual Diversity in South East and East Asia." *Culture, Health, and Sexuality* 2(4):361–5.

Jolly, Margaret and Lenore Manderson. 1997. "Introduction: Sites of Desire/Economies of Pleasure in Asia and the Pacific." In *Sites of Desire/Economies of Pleasures: Sexualities in Asia and the Pacific*, ed. Lenore Manderson and Margaret Jolly, 1–26. Chicago: University of Chicago Press.

Jordan, Mark D. 1997. *The Invention of Sodomy in Christian Theology*. Chicago: University of Chicago Press.

Jordt, Ingrid. 2005. "Women's Practices of Renunciation in the Age of Sasana Revival." In *Burma at the Turn of the Twenty-First Century*, ed. Monique Skidmore, 41–64. Honolulu: University of Hawaii Press.

Jost, John and Brenda Major, eds. 2001. *The Psychology of Legitimacy: Emerging Perspectives on Ideology, Justice, and Intergroup Relations*. Cambridge: Cambridge University Press.

Karp, Ivan and Steven Lavine, eds. 1991. *Exhibiting Cultures: The Poetics and Politics of Museum Display*. Washington, D.C.: Smithsonian Institution Press.

Keeler, Ward. 1987. *Javanese Shadow Plays, Javanese Selves*. Princeton: Princeton University Press.

———. 1990. "Speaking of Gender in Java." In *Power and Difference*, ed. Jane Atkinson and Shelly Errington, 127–152. Stanford: Stanford University Press.

———. 2005. "'But Princes Jump!': Performing Masculinity in Mandalay." In *Burma at the Turn of the Twenty-First Century*, ed. Monique Skidmore, 206–228. Honolulu: University of Hawaii Press.

Kelly, Raymond C. 1993. *Constructing Inequality: The Fabrication of a Hierarchy of Virtue Among the Etoro*. Ann Arbor: University of Michigan Press.

Kessler, Clive. 1999. "The Abdication of the Intellectuals: Sociology, Anthropology, and the Asian Values Debate—Or, What Everybody Needed to Know About 'Asian Values' That Social Scientists Failed to Point Out." *Sojourn* 14(2):295–312.

Keyes, Charles. 1984. "Mother or Mistress But Never a Monk: Buddhist Notions of Female Gender in Rural Thailand." *American Ethnologist* 11(2):223–241.

——. 1986. "Ambiguous Gender: Male Initiation in Northern Thai Buddhist Society." In *Gender and Religion: On the Complexity of Symbols*, ed. Caroline Bynum, Stevan Harrell, and Paula Richman, 66–96. Boston: Beacon Press.

Khoo Gaik Cheng. 2006. *Reclaiming Adat: Contemporary Malaysian Film and Literature*. Vancouver: University of British Columbia Press.

Kiernan, Ben. 1996. *The Pol Pot Regime: Race, Power, and Genocide Under the Khmer Rouge, 1975–1979*. New Haven: Yale University Press.

Kirch, Patrick. 1984. *The Evolution of the Polynesian Chiefdoms*. Cambridge: Cambridge University Press.

Kirsch, Thomas. 1982. "Buddhism, Sex Roles, and the Thai Economy." In *Women of Southeast Asia*, ed. Penny Van Esterik, 16–41. DeKalb, IL: Center for Southeast Asian Studies, Northern Illinois University.

——. 1985. "Text and Context: Buddhist Sex Roles/Culture of Gender Revisited." *American Ethnologist* 12(2):302–320.

Knauft, Bruce M. 1999. *From Primitive to Postcolonial in Melanesia and Anthropology*. Ann Arbor, MI: University of Michigan Press.

——. 2003. "What Ever Happened to Ritualized Homosexuality? Modern Sexual Subjects in Melanesia and Elsewhere." *Annual Review of Sex Research* 14:137–159.

——. 2005. *The Gebusi: Lives Transformed in a Rainforest World*. Boston: McGraw Hill.

——, ed. 2002. *Critically Modern: Alternatives, Alterities, Anthropologies*. Bloomington: Indiana University Press.

Komanyi, M.I. 1972. *The Real and Ideal Participation in Decision-Making of Iban Women: A Study of a Longhouse Community in Sarawak, East Malaysia*. Ph.D dissertation, New York University.

Krasner, Stephen. 1999. *Sovereignty: Organized Hypocrisy*. Princeton: Princeton University Press.

Kulick, Don. 1998. *Travesti: Sex, Gender, and Culture Among Brazilian Transgendered Prostitutes*. Chicago: University of Chicago Press.

Kuper, Leo and M.G. Smith, eds. 1969. *Pluralism in Africa*. Berkeley: University of California Press.

Lach, Donald. 1965. *Asia in the Making of Europe*, Vol 1. *The Century of Discovery*. Book 2. Chicago: University of Chicago Press.

Lal, Ruby. 2005. *Domesticity and Power in the Early Mughal World*. Cambridge: Cambridge University Press.

La Loubère, Simon De. 1693 [1969]. *A New Historical Relation of the Kingdom of Siam*. Rpt. Kuala Lumpur: Oxford University Press.

Law, Lisa. 1997. "A Matter of 'Choice': Discourses on Prostitution in the Philippines." In *Sites of Desire, Economies of Pleasure*, ed. Lenore Manderson and Margaret Jolly, 233–261. Chicago: University of Chicago Press.

Leach, Edmund. 1954 [1965]. *Political Systems of Highland Burma: A Study of Kachin Social Structure*. Rpt. Boston: Beacon Press.

Ledgerwood, Judy. 1994. "Gender Symbolism and Culture Change: Viewing the Virtuous Woman in the Khmer Story 'Mea Yoeng.'" In *Cambodian Culture Since 1975: Homeland and Exile*, ed. May Ebihara, Carol Mortland, and Judy Ledgerwood, 119–128. Ithaca: Cornell University Press.

Lee, Martin. 1998. "Testing Asian Values." *New York Times*, January 18.

Lev, Daniel. 1990. "Human Rights NGOs in Indonesia and Malaysia." In *Asian Perspectives on Human Rights*, ed. Claude Welch and Virginia Leary, 142–161. Boulder: Westview Press.

Lévi-Strauss, Claude. 1967. "The Effectiveness of Symbols." In *Structural Anthropology*, 181–201. New York: Anchor/Doubleday.

Lieberman, Victor. 1984. *Burmese Administrative Cycles: Anarchy and Conquest, c. 1580–1760*. Princeton: Princeton University Press.

——. 2003. *Strange Parallels: Southeast Asia in Global Context, c. 800–1300*. Vol I. *Integration on the Mainland*. Cambridge: Cambridge University Press.

Lim, Lin Lean. 1998. "The Economic and Social Bases of Prostitution in Southeast Asia." In *The Sex Sector: The Economic and Social Bases of Prostitution in Southeast Asia*, ed. Lin Lean Lim, 1–28. Geneva: International Labour Organization.

Loong Meng Yee and Elan Perumal. 2001. "Transvestites Gather for Thanksgiving." *The Star*, July 5.

Loos, Tamara. 2005. "Sex in the Inner City: The Fidelity Between Sex and Politics in Siam." *Journal of Asian Studies* 64(4):881–909.

——. 2006. *Subject Siam: Family, Law, and Colonial Modernity in Thailand*. Ithaca: Cornell University Press.

Louie, Kam. 2002. *Theorising Chinese Masculinity: Society and Gender in China*. Cambridge: Cambridge University Press.

Low, Hugh. 1848 [1968]. *Sarawak: Its Inhabitants and Productions, Being Notes During a Residence in that Country with His Excellency Mr. Brooke*. Rpt. London: Frank Cass and Co., Ltd.

Low, Hugh Brooke. n.d. "The Natives of Sarawak and British North Borneo." In *The Natives of Sarawak and British North Borneo*, 2 vols, ed. H.L. Roth 1896 [1980]. Rpt. Kuala Lumpur: University of Malaya Press.

Mabbett, Ian. 1977. "Varnas in Angkor and the Indian Caste System." *Journal of Asian Studies* 36(3):429–442.

Mabbett, Ian and David Chandler. 1995. *The Khmers*. Oxford: Blackwell.

Mahathir Mohamad. 1970. *The Malay Dilemma*. Singapore: Donald Moore/Asia Pacific Press.

——. 1976. *Menghadapi Cabaran* [*Meeting the Challenge*]. Kuala Lumpur: Pustaka Antara.

——. 1999. *A New Deal for Asia*. Kuala Lumpur: Pelanduk Publications.

Mahathir Mohamad and Shintaro Ishihara. 1995. *The Voice of Asia: Two Asian Leaders Discuss the Coming Century*. Tokyo: Kodansha International.

Manalansan, Martin. 1995. "Speaking of AIDS: Language and the Filipino 'Gay' Experience in America." In *Discrepant Histories: Translocal Essays on Filipino Cultures*, ed. Vicente Rafael, 193–220. Philadelphia: Temple University Press.

——. 2003. *Global Divas: Filipino Gay Men in the Diaspora*. Durham: Duke University Press.

——. 2006. "Comment." *Current Anthropology* 47(2):329–330.

Manderson, Lenore. 1996. *Sickness and the State: Health and Illness in Colonial Malaya, 1870–1940*. Cambridge: Cambridge University Press.

Marina Mahathir. 1997. *In Liberal Doses*. Kuala Lumpur: Archipelago Press.

Marmon, Shaun. 1995. *Eunuchs and Sacred Boundaries in Islamic Society*. New York: Oxford University Press.

Marre, Jeremy. 1992. *Lady Boys*. London: Harcourt Films.

Maung Htin Aung. 1962. *Folk Elements in Burmese Buddhism*. Westport, CT: Greenwood Press.

Maxwell, Sir George. 1907 [1982]. *In Malay Forests*. Singapore: Eastern University Press.

Maybury-Lewis, David, ed. 1982. *The Prospects for Plural Societies*. The 1982 Proceedings of the American Ethnological Society. Washington, D.C.: American Ethnological Society.

McCargo, Duncan. 2008. *Tearing Apart the Land: Islam and Legitimacy in Southern Thailand*. Ithaca: Cornell University Press.

Mead, Margaret. 1928 [1968]. *Coming of Age in Samoa: A Psychological Study of Primitive Youth for Western Civilisation*. Rpt. New York: Dell.

———. 1977. *Letters From the Field, 1925–1975*. New York: Harper and Row.

Merrison, Lindsey. 2001. *Friends in High Places: The Art of Survival in Modern Day Burma*. Berlin: Lindsey Merrison Film.

Merry, Sally Engle. 2000. *Colonizing Hawai'i: The Cultural Power of Law*. Princeton: Princeton University Press.

Meyerowitz, Joanne. 2002. *How Sex Changed: A History of Transsexuality in the United States*. Cambridge: Harvard University Press.

Mi Mi Khaing. 1962. *Burmese Family*. Bloomington: University of Indiana Press.

———. 1984. *The World of Burmese Women*. London: Zed Books.

Miksic, John. 1990. *Borobudur: Golden Tales of the Buddhas*. Boston: Shambhala.

Miles, Douglas. 1964. "The Ngadju Longhouse." *Oceania* 35(1):45–57.

———. 1966. "Shamanism and the Conversion of Ngadju Dayaks." *Oceania* 37(1):1–12.

———. 1971. "Ngadju Kinship and Social Change on the Upper Mentaya." In *Anthropology in Oceania: Essays Presented to Ian Hogbin*, ed. L.R. Hiatt and C. Jayawardena, 211–230. San Francisco: Chandler Publishing Co.

———. 1976. *Cutlass and Crescent Moon: A Case Study of Social and Political Change in Outer Indonesia*. Sydney: Center for Southeast Asian Studies, University of Sydney.

Millar, Susan B. 1989. *Bugis Weddings: Rituals of Social Location in Modern Indonesia*. Monograph No. 29, Monograph Series, Center for South and Southeast Asian Studies, University of California, Berkeley.

Milne, R.S., and Diane Mauzy. 1999. *Malaysian Politics Under Mahathir*. London: Routledge.

Ming, Hanneke. 1983. "Barracks-Concubinage in the Indies, 1887–1920." *Indonesia* 35:65–93.

Mohammad Hashim Kamali. 2000. *Islamic Law in Malaysia: Issues and Developments*. Kuala Lumpur: Ilmiah Publishers.

Mohd. Chouse Nasuruddin. 1995. *The Malay Dance*. Kuala Lumpur: Dewan Bahasa dan Pustaka.

Moore, Henrietta. 1994. *A Passion for Difference: Essays in Anthropology and Gender*. Bloomington: Indiana University Press.

Morris, Rosalind. 1994. "Three Sexes and Four Sexualities: Redressing the Discourses on Gender and Sexuality in Contemporary Thailand." *Positions* 2(1):15–43.

———. 2000. *In the Place of Origins: Modernity and Its Mediums in Northern Thailand*. Durham: Duke University Press.

Muhammad Abu Bakar. 1987. *Penghayatan Sebuah Ideal: Suatu Tafsiran Tentang Islam Semasa* [Appreciation of an Ideal: An Interpretation of Contemporary Islam]. Kuala Lumpur: Dewan Bahasa dan Pustaka.

Murdock, George, ed. 1960. *Social Structure in Southeast Asia*. Viking Fund Publications in Anthropology 29. Chicago: Quadrangle Books.

Murphey, Rhoads. 1996. *A History of Asia*, 2nd ed. New York: Harper Collins.

Murray, Allison. 1999. "Let Them Take Ecstasy: Class and Jakarta Lesbians." In *Female Desires*, ed. Evelyn Blackwood and Saskia Wieringa, 139–156. New York: Columbia University Press.

Mydans, Seth. 2005. "Looking for the Burmese Junta? Sorry, It's Gone Into Hiding." *New York Times*, November 14.

Nadiah Bamadhaj. 1999. "The Hot Potato: Sexual Rights Advocacy in Malaysia." *Saksi* 3, <http://www.saksi.com/jan99/nadiahb.htm>.

Nagata, Judith. 1984. *The Reflowering of Malaysian Islam: Modern Religious Radicals and Their Roots*. Vancouver: University of British Columbia Press.

Najmabadi, Afsaneh. 2005. *Women with Mustaches and Men without Beards: Gender and Sexual Anxieties of Iranian Modernity*. Berkeley: University of California Press.

Nanda, Serena. 1990. *Neither Man Nor Woman: The Hijras of India*. Belmont: Wadsworth.

———. 1993. "Hijras: An Alternative Sex and Gender Role in India." In *Third Sex, Third Gender: Beyond Sexual Dimorphism in Culture and History*, ed. Gilbert Herdt, 373–417. New York: Zone Books.

Napat Sirisambhand and Alec Gordon. 1999. "Thai Women in Late Ayutthaya Style Paintings." *Journal of the Siam Society* 87(1&2):1–16.

Nash, Manning. 1965. *The Golden Road to Modernity: Village Life in Contemporary Burma*. New York: John Wiley.

Newbold, T.J. 1839. *Political and Statistical Account of the British Settlements in the Straits of Malacca*, 2 vols. London: John Murray.

Ng, Cecilia, Maznah Mohamad, and Tan Beng Hui. 2006. *Feminism and the Women's Movement in Malaysia: An Unsung (R)evolution*. London: Routledge.

Nguyen, H.T. 2003. "Spirit Mediums (Ong Dong Ba Dong): Unwitting Bearers of Viet Culture." Paper presented at Conference on Vietnam in the Twenty-First Century. American Museum of Natural History, New York, March 22–23.

Noorhaidi Hasan. 2006. *Laskar Jihad: Islam, Militancy, and the Quest for Identity in Post-New Order Indonesia*. Ithaca: Southeast Asia Program, Cornell University.

Norodom Sihanouk. 2004. "Mon 2ème Texte Pour le 20 Février 2004, Drôleries, par Norodom Sihanouk" [My Second Text for 20 February 2004, Curiosities, by Norodom Sihanouk], <http://www.norodomsihanouk.info/mes%2004fev%2002txt2.htm>.

Oetomo, Dede. 1996. "Gender and Sexual Orientation in Indonesia." In *Fantasizing the Feminine in Indonesia*, ed. Laurie Sears, 259–269. Durham: Duke University Press.

———. 2006. "Comment." *Current Anthropology* 47(2):330–331.

O'Flaherty, Wendy Doniger. 1980. *Women, Androgynes, and Other Mythical Beasts*. Chicago: University of Chicago Press.

Ong, Aihwa. 1987. *Spirits of Resistance and Capitalist Discipline: Factory Women in Malaysia*. Albany: State University of New York Press.

———. 1999. *Flexible Citizenship: The Cultural Logics of Transnationality*. Durham: Duke University Press.

———. 2003. *Buddha is Hiding: Refugees, Citizenship, the New America*. Berkeley: University of California Press.

———. 2006. *Neoliberalism as Exception: Mutations in Citizenship and Sovereignty*. Durham: Duke University Press.

Ong, Aihwa and Michael G. Peletz, eds. 1995. *Bewitching Women, Pious Men: Gender and Body Politics in Southeast Asia*. Berkeley: University of California Press.

Oommen, T.K. 2002. *Pluralism, Equality, and Identity: Comparative Studies*. New Delhi: Oxford University Press.

Ortner, Sherry B. 1978. *Sherpas Through Their Rituals*. Cambridge: Cambridge University Press.

——. 1989. *High Religion: A Cultural and Political History of Sherpa Buddhism*. Princeton: Princeton University Press.

——. 1995. "Resistance and the Problem of Ethnographic Refusal." *Comparative Studies in Society and History* 37(1):173–193.

——. 1996. "Gender Hegemonies." In *Making Gender: The Politics and Erotics of Culture*, 139–172. Boston: Beacon Press.

Ortner, Sherry B. and Harriet Whitehead, eds. 1981. *Sexual Meanings: The Cultural Construction of Gender and Sexuality*. Cambridge: Cambridge University Press.

Orwell, George. 1934 [1962]. *Burmese Days*. San Diego: Harcourt.

Osborne, Milton. 1994. *Sihanouk: Prince of Light, Prince of Darkness*. Honolulu: University of Hawaii Press.

Pandey, Gyanendra. 2006. *Routine Violence: Nations, Fragments, Histories*. Stanford: Stanford University Press.

Peacock, James. 1968. *Rites of Modernization: Symbols and Social Aspects of Indonesian Proletarian Drama*. Chicago: University of Chicago Press.

——. 1978. *Muslim Puritans: Reformist Psychology in Southeast Asian Islam*. Berkeley: University of California Press.

Peirce, Leslie. 1993. *The Imperial Harem: Women and Sovereignty in the Ottoman Empire*. New York: Oxford University Press.

Peletz, Michael G. 1988. *A Share of the Harvest: Kinship, Property, and Social History Among the Malays of Rembau*: Berkeley: University of California Press.

——. 1993a. "Knowledge, Power, and Personal Misfortune in a Malay Context." In *Understanding Witchcraft and Sorcery in Southeast Asia*, ed. C.W. Watson and Roy Ellen, 149–177. Honolulu: University of Hawaii Press.

——. 1993b. "Sacred Texts and Dangerous Words: The Politics of Law and Cultural Rationalization in Malaysia." *Comparative Studies in Society and History* 25(1):66–109.

——. 1994. "Comparative Perspectives on Kinship and Cultural Identity in Negeri Sembilan." *Sojourn: Journal of Social Issues in Southeast Asia* 9(1):1–53.

——. 1995. "Neither Reasonable Nor Responsible: Contrasting Representations of Masculinity in a Malay Society." In *Bewitching Women, Pious Men: Gender and Body Politics in Southeast Asia*, ed. Aihwa Ong and Michael G. Peletz, 76–123. Berkeley: University of California Press.

——. 1996. *Reason and Passion: Representations of Gender in a Malay Society*. Berkeley: University of California Press.

——. 1997. "'Ordinary Muslims' and Muslim Resurgents in Contemporary Malaysia: Notes on an Ambivalent Relationship." In *Islam in an Era of Nation-States: Politics and Religious Renewal in Muslim Southeast Asia*, ed. Robert W. Hefner, 231–273. Honolulu: University of Hawaii Press.

——. 2002. *Islamic Modern: Religious Courts and Cultural Politics in Malaysia*. Princeton: Princeton University Press.

——. 2005. "Islam and the Cultural Politics of Legitimacy: Malaysia in the Aftermath of September 11." In *Remaking Muslim Politics: Pluralism, Contestation, Democratization*, ed. Robert W. Hefner, 240–272. Princeton: Princeton University Press.

——. 2006. "Transgenderism and Gender Pluralism in Southeast Asia Since Early Modern Times." *Current Anthropology* 47(2):309–325, 333–340.

——. 2007. *Gender, Sexuality, and Body Politics in Modern Asia*. Ann Arbor: Association for Asian Studies.

Pelras, Christian. 1996. *The Bugis*. Oxford: Blackwell.

Perelaer, M.T.H. 1870. *Ethnographische Beschriving der Dajaks*. Zalt-Bommel.

Pflugfelder, Gregory. 1999. *Cartographies of Desire: Male-Male Sexualities in Japanese Discourse, 1600–1950*. Berkeley: University of California Press.

Pires, Tomé. 1515 [1944]. *The Suma Oriental of Tomé Pires*. 2 vols. Trans. A. Cortesao. London: Hakluyt Society.

Pratt, Mary-Louise. 1992. *Imperial Eyes: Travel Writing and Transculturation*. London: Routledge.

Pringle, Robert. 1970. *Rajahs and Rebels: The Ibans of Sarawak Under Brooke Rule, 1841–1941*. Ithaca: Cornell University Press.

Proschan, Frank. 1998. "Filial Piety and Non-Procreative Male-to-Male Sex Among Vietnamese." Paper presented at the Annual Meeting of the American Anthropological Association.

——. 2002a. "Eunuch Mandarins, *Soldats Mamzelles*, Effeminate Boys, and Graceless Women: French Colonial Constructions of Vietnamese Genders." *GLQ* 8(4):435–467.

——. 2002b. "Syphilis, Opiomania, and Pederasty: Colonial Constructions of Vietnamese (and French) Social Diseases." *Journal of the History of Sexuality* 11(4):610–636.

Proudfoot, Ian, ed. and compiler. n.d. *Malay Concordance Project* [A Digital Corpus of Malay Texts], <http://mcp.anu.edu.au>.

Purcell, Victor. 1965. *The Memoirs of a Malayan Official*. London: Cassell.

Putnam, Robert D. 1993. *Making Democracy Work: Civic Traditions in Modern Italy*. Princeton: Princeton University Press.

——. 1995. "Bowling Alone: America's Declining Social Capital." *Journal of Democracy* 6(1):65–78.

Quintiliani, Karen. 1995. *One of the Girls: The Social and Cultural Context of a Cambodian American 'Gay' Group*. MA thesis, California State University, Long Beach.

Rafael, Vicente. 1988. *Contracting Colonialism: Translation and Christian Conversion in Tagalog Society Under Spanish Rule*. Ithaca: Cornell University Press.

——. 1993. "Preface to the Paperback Edition." In *Contracting Colonialism: Translation and Christian Conversion in Tagalog Society Under Early Spanish Rule*, ix–xvi. Durham: Duke University Press.

——. 2000. *White Love and Other Essays in Filipino History*. Durham: Duke University Press.

Raffles, Sir Thomas Stamford. 1817 [1830]. *The History of Java*, 2 vols, 2nd ed. London: John Murray.

Rais Nur and A.R. 1996. "Queering the State: Towards a Lesbian Movement in Malaysia." In *From Amazon to Zami: Towards a Global Lesbian Feminism*, ed. Monika Reinfelder, 70–85. London: Caswell.

Raja Chulan bin Hamid, ed. 1991. *Misa Melayu* [Malay Champion]. Kuala Lumpur: Pustaka Antara. Malay Concordance Project, <http://mcp.anu.edu.au>.

Ramji-Nogales, Jaya, Andrew Schoenholtz, and Philip Schrag. 2007. "Refugee Roulette: Disparities in Asylum Adjudication." *Stanford Law Review* 60(2):295–411.

Rappaport, Roy. 1999. *Ritual and Religion in the Making of Humanity*. New York: Cambridge University Press.

Raybeck, Douglas. 1986. "The Elastic Rule: Conformity and Deviance in Kelantan Village Life." In *Cultural Identity in Northern Peninsular Malaysia*, ed. Sharon Carstens, 55–74. Ohio University Monographs in International Studies, Southeast Asia Series, 63.

Reddy, Gayatri. 2005. *With Respect to Sex: Negotiating Hijra Identity in South India*. Chicago: University of Chicago Press.

Reid, Anthony. 1988. *Southeast Asia in the Age of Commerce, 1450–1680, Vol. I: The Land Below the Winds*. New Haven: Yale University Press.

———. 1993a. "Introduction: A Time and a Place." In *Southeast Asia in the Early Modern Era: Trade, Power, and Belief*, ed. Anthony Reid, 1–19. Ithaca: Cornell University Press.

———. 1993b. *Southeast Asia in the Age of Commerce, 1450-1680, Vol. II: Expansion and Crisis*. New Haven: Yale University Press.

Reinfelder, Monika, ed. 1996. *Amazon to Zami: Towards a Global Lesbian Feminism*. London: Cassell.

Reno, Janet. 1994. "Memorandum for Mary Maguire Dunne, Acting Chair, Board of Immigration Appeals." [Attorney General Order Designating Board of Immigration Appeals Case as Precedent], <http://www.qrd.org/qrd/world/immigration/us.gay.asylum.policy>.

Richardson, Diane and Steven Seidman, eds. 2002. *The Handbook of Gay and Lesbian Studies*. Thousand Oaks, CA: Sage Publications.

Ricklefs, M.C. 1998. *The Seen and Unseen Worlds in Java: History, Literature, and Islam in the Court of Pakubuwana II*. Honolulu: University of Hawaii Press.

Ritchie, Anne T. and Richardson Evans. 1894. *Lord Amherst and the British Advance Eastwards to Burma*. Oxford: Clarendon Press.

Robertson, Jennifer, 1998. *Takarazuka: Sexual Politics and Popular Culture in Modern Japan*. Berkeley: University of California Press.

Rofel, Lisa. 1999. *Other Modernities: Gendered Yearnings in China After Socialism*. Berkeley: University of California Press.

Roff, William. 1967. *The Origins of Malay Nationalism*. Kuala Lumpur: University of Malaya Press.

Roscoe, Will. 1996. "Priests of the Goddess: Gender Transgression in Ancient Religion." *History of Religions* 35(3):195–230.

Rose Ismail, ed. 1995. *Hudud in Malaysia: The Issues at Stake*. Kuala Lumpur: SIS Forum (Malaysia) Berhad.

Rosenthal, A.M. 1997. "On My Mind: Lessons of the Asian Collapse." *New York Times*, December 23.

Roth, Henry Ling. 1896 [1980]. *The Natives of Sarawak and British North Borneo*, 2 vols. Rpt. Kuala Lumpur: University of Malaya Press.

Rubin, Gayle. 1984. "Thinking Sex: Notes for a Radical Theory of the Politics of Sexuality." In *Pleasure and Danger: Exploring Female Sexuality*, ed. Carole Vance, 67–319. Boston: Routledge and Kegan Paul.

Rubin, Gayle with Judith Butler. 1994. "Sexual Traffic." *Differences: A Journal of Feminist Cultural Studies* 6(2&3):62–99.

Sachs, Susan. 1999. "Conference Confronts the Difficulties of Being Muslim and Gay." *New York Times*, May 30.

Sadan, Mandy. 2005. "Respected Grandfather, Bless This Nissan: Benevolent and Politically Neutral Bo Bo Gyi." In *Burma at the Turn of the Twenty-First Century*, ed. Monique Skidmore, 90–111. Honolulu: University of Hawaii Press.

Sahlins, Marshall. 1981. *Historical Metaphors and Mythical Realities: Structure in the Early History of the Sandwich Islands Kingdom*. Ann Arbor, MI: University of Michigan Press.

———. 2004. *Apologies to Thucydides: History as Culture and Vice Versa*. Chicago: University of Chicago Press.

Said, Edward. 1978. *Orientalism*. New York: Vintage.

——. 1993. *Culture and Imperialism*. New York: Vintage.

Sanday, Peggy. 1990. *Fraternity Gang Rape: Sex, Brotherhood, and Privilege on Campus*. New York: New York University Press.

Sandhu, Kernial Singh and Paul Wheatley, eds. 1983. *Melaka: The Transformation of a Malay Capital, c. 1400–1980*, Vol 1. Kuala Lumpur: Oxford University Press.

Sandin, Benedict. 1957. "Salang Changed His Sex." *The Sarawak Museum Journal* 8:146–152.

——. 1983. "Mythological Origins of Iban Shamanism." *The Sarawak Museum Journal* 32:235–250.

Sang, Tze-Ian D. 2003. *The Emerging Lesbian: Female Same-Sex Desire in Modern China*. Chicago: University of Chicago Press.

Sangermano, Vincentius. 1818 [1893]. *The Burmese Empire A Hundred Years Ago*. Rpt. Westminster: Archibald Constable and Co.

Sankar, Andrea. 1986. "Sisters and Brothers, Lovers and Enemies: Marriage Resistance in Southern Kwangtung." In *The Many Faces of Homosexuality: Anthropological Approaches to Homosexual Behavior*, ed. Evelyn Blackwood, 69–81. New York: Harrington Park Press.

Sassen, Saskia. 1996. *Losing Control? Sovereignty in an Age of Globalization*. New York: Columbia University Press.

——. 1998. *Globalization and Its Discontents*. Cambridge, MA: Harvard University Press.

Scharer, Hans. 1946 [1963]. *Ngaju Religion: The Conception of God Among a South Borneo People*. Trans. Rodney Needham. The Hague: Martinus Nijhoff.

Schiller, Anne. 1991. "On 'The Watersnake Which Is Also a Hornbill': Male and Female in Ngaju Dyak Mortuary Symbology." In *Female and Male in Borneo: Contributions and Challenges to Gender Studies*, ed. Vinson Sutlive, 415–433. Shanghai, VA: Borneo Research Council.

——. 1997a. *Small Sacrifices: Religious Change and Cultural Identity Among the Ngaju of Indonesia*. New York: Oxford University Press.

——. 1997b. "Religion and Identity in Central Kalimantan: The Case of the Ngaju Dayaks." In *Indigenous People and the State: Politics, Land, and Ethnicity in the Malayan Peninsula and Borneo*, ed. Robert Winzeler, 180–200. New Haven: Yale University Southeast Asia Studies. Monograph 46.

Schopen, Gregory. 1991. "Archaeology and Protestant Suppositions in the Study of Indian Buddhism." *History of Religions* 31(1):1–23.

Schwaner, C. 1853–54 [1896/1980]. "Ethnographical Notes by Dr. Schwaner." In *The Natives of Sarawak and North Borneo*, Vol. II, ed. H. Roth, clxi–ccvii. Kuala Lumpur: University of Malaya Press.

Scott, James C. 1976. *The Moral Economy of the Peasant: Subsistence and Rebellion in Southeast Asia*. New Haven: Yale University Press.

——. 1985. *Weapons of the Weak: Everyday Forms of Peasant Resistance*. New Haven: Yale University Press.

——. 1990. *Domination and the Arts of Resistance: Hidden Transcripts*. New Haven: Yale University Press.

——. 1998. *Seeing Like a State: How Certain Schemes to Improve the Human Condition Have Failed*. New Haven: Yale University Press.

Scott, Joan W. 1999. *Gender and the Politics of History*, rev. ed. New York: Columbia University Press.

Sears, Laurie, ed. 1996. *Fantasizing the Feminine in Indonesia*. Durham: Duke University Press.

Sen, Krishna and Maila Stivens, eds. 1998. *Gender and Power in Affluent Asia*. London: Routledge.

Shaikh Taha Jabir Al-Alwani. 2000. *Pendirian Syari'at Terhadap Hukuman Bersalah Ke Atas Dato' Seri Anwar Ibrahim* [*Syariah Review of the Guilty Verdict Passed on Dato' Seri Anwar Ibrahim*].

Shamsul, A.B. 1983. "A Revival in the Study of Islam in Malaysia." *Man* 18:399–404.

———. 1999. "From Orang Kayu Baru to Melayu Baru: Cultural Constructions of the Malay New Rich." In *Culture and Privilege in Capitalist Asia*, ed. Michael Pinche, 86–100. London: Routledge.

———. 2000. "Making Sense of Politics in Contemporary Malaysia: Resisting Popular Interpretation." *Trends and Issues in East Asia 2000*, ed. Ng Chee Yuen and Charla Griffy-Brown, 227–248. Tokyo: Idrus and Fasid.

Sharifah Zaleha Syed Hassan. 1989. "Versions of Eternal Truth: *Ulama* and Religious Dissenters in Kedah Malay Society." *Contributions to Southeast Asian Ethnography* 8:43–69.

Silverblatt, Irene. 1987. *Moon, Sun, and Witches: Gender Ideologies and Class in Inca and Colonial Peru*. Princeton: Princeton University Press.

———. 1991. "Interpreting Women in States: New Feminist Ethnohistories." In *Gender at the Crossroads of Knowledge: Feminist Anthropology in the Postmodern Era*, ed. Micaela di Leonardo, 140–171. Berkeley: University of California Press.

Sinnott, Megan. 2004. *Toms and Dees: Transgender Identity and Female Same-Sex Relationships in Thailand*. Honolulu: University of Hawaii Press.

Skidmore, Monique. 2004. *Karaoke Fascism: Burma and the Politics of Fear*. Philadelphia: University of Pennsylvania Press.

———, ed. 2005. *Burma at the Turn of the Twenty-First Century*. Honolulu: University of Hawaii Press.

Smith, M.G. 1965. *The Plural Society in the British West Indies*. Berkeley: University of California Press.

Smith-Hefner, Nancy. 1988. "Women and Politeness: The Javanese Example." *Language in Society* 17:535–554.

———. 1999. *Khmer American: Identity and Moral Education in a Diasporic Community*. Berkeley: University of California Press.

Snouck Hurgronje, Christiaan. 1906. *The Achehnese*, 2 vols. Trans. A.W.S. O'Sullivan. Leiden: E.J. Brill.

Spiro, Melford. 1967. *Burmese Supernaturalism*. Englewood Cliffs: Prentice-Hall.

———. 1970. *Buddhism and Society: A Great Tradition and Its Burmese Vicissitudes*. New York: Harper and Row.

———. 1977. *Kinship and Marriage in Burma*. Berkeley: University of California Press.

———. 1997. *Gender Ideology and Psychological Reality: An Essay on Cultural Reproduction*. New Haven: Yale University Press.

Spurr, David. 1993. *The Rhetoric of Empire: Colonial Discourse in Journalism, Travel Writing, and Imperial Administration*. Durham: Duke University Press.

St. John, Spencer. 1862. *Life in the Forests of the Far East*, 2 vols. London: Smith, Elder and Co.

Stallybrass, Peter, and Allon White. 1986. *The Politics and Poetics of Transgression*. Ithaca: Cornell University Press.

Steedly, Mary. 1999a. Comments on "Southeast Asian Studies—Wherefrom?" In

Weighing the Balance: Southeast Asian Studies Ten Years After, 13–14. Proceedings of Meetings held in New York City on November 15 and December 10. New York: Southeast Asia Program, Social Science Research Council.

——. 1999b. "The State of Culture Theory in the Anthropology of Southeast Asia." *Annual Review of Anthropology* 28:431–454.

Stepan, Nancy L. 1986. "Race and Gender: The Role of Analogy in Science." *Isis* 77:261–277.

Stivens, Maila. 1998. "Sex, Gender, and the Making of the New Malay Middle Classes." In *Gender and Power in Affluent Asia*, ed. Krishna Sen and Maila Stivens, 87–126. London: Routledge.

——. 2002. "The Hope of the Nation: Moral Panics and Constructions of Teenagerhood in Contemporary Malaysia." In *Coming of Age in South and Southeast Asia: Youth, Courtship, and Sexuality*, ed. Lenore Manderson and Pranee Liamputtong, 188–206. Richmond: Curzon.

Stoler, Ann. 1985. *Capitalism and Confrontation in Sumatra's Plantation Belt, 1870–1979*. New Haven: Yale University Press.

——. 1995. *Race and the Education of Desire: Foucault's History of Sexuality and the Colonial Order of Things*. Durham: Duke University Press.

——. 2002. *Carnal Knowledge and Imperial Power: Race and the Intimate in Colonial Rule*. Berkeley: University of California Press.

Strathern, Marilyn. 1988. *The Gender of the Gift: Problems with Women and Problems with Society in Melanesia*. Berkeley: University of California Press.

——. 1992. *Reproducing the Future: Anthropology, Kinship, and the New Reproductive Technologies*. New York: Routledge.

Stryker, Susan. 2006. "(De)Subjugated Knowledges: An Introduction to Transgender Studies." In *The Transgender Studies Reader*, ed. Susan Stryker and Stephen Whittle, 1–17. New York: Routledge.

Sutlive, Vinson H. 1978 [1988]. *The Iban of Sarawak: Chronicle of a Changing World*. Prospect Heights, IL: Waveland Press.

——. 1991. "Keling and Kumang in Town: Urban Migration and Differential Effects on Men and Women." In *Female and Male in Borneo: Contributions and Challenges to Gender Studies*, ed. Vinson H. Sutlive, 489–515. Shanghai, VA: Borneo Research Council Monograph Series, Vol. 1.

Swettenham, Sir Frank. 1895 [1984]. *Malay Sketches*. Rpt. Singapore: Graham Brash.

Syed Husin Alatas. 1977. *The Myth of the Lazy Native*. New York: Frank Cass.

Symes, Michael. 1827. *An Account of an Embassy to the Kingdom of Ava, in the Year 1795, To Which is Now Added a Narrative of the Late Military and Political Operations in the Birmese Empire*. 2 vols. Edinburgh: Constable and Co.

Takaki, Ronald. 1998. *Strangers From a Different Shore: A History of Asian Americans*, rev. ed. Boston: Little, Brown, and Co.

Talikowski, Luke and Sue Gillieatt. 2005. "Female Sex Work in Yangon, Myanmar." *Sexual Health* 2(3):193–202.

Tambiah, S.J. 1970. *Buddhism and the Spirit Cults in North-East Thailand*. Cambridge: Cambridge University Press.

——. 1976. *World Conqueror and World Renouncer: A Study of Buddhism and Polity Against a Historical Background*. Cambridge: Cambridge University Press.

Tan Beng Hui. 1999. "Women's Sexuality and the Discourse on Asian Values." In *Female Desires*, ed. Evelyn Blackwood and Saskia Wieringa, 281–307. New York: Columbia University Press.

Tan, Kok Kee. 2006. "From Nation to IndigNation: The Cultural Politics of Gay Parties in Singapore." Paper presented at the Annual Meeting of the American Anthropological Association, San Jose, CA.

Taylor, Robert. 2004. "Myanmar: Roadmap to Where?" *Southeast Asian Affairs 2004*, 171–184. Singapore: Institute of Southeast Asian Studies.

Teh Yik Koon. 1998. "Understanding the Problems of Mak Nyahs (Male Transsexuals) in Malaysia." *South East Asia Research* 6(2):165–180.

———. 2002. *The Mak Nyahs: Malaysian Male to Female Transsexuals*. Singapore: Eastern Universities Press.

Than Win Htut. 2005. "Aung Myo Min: A Burmese Gay with a Human Rights Cause." <http://www.mizzima.com/archives/news-in-2005/news-in-feb/20-February %2005-25.htm>

Thomas, Nicholas. 1994. *Colonialism's Culture: Anthropology, Travel and Government*. Princeton: Princeton University Press.

Thompson, Ashley. 1996. *The Calling of the Souls: A Study of the Khmer Ritual Hau Bralin*. Monash University Centre of Southeast Asian Studies Working Paper #98. Clayton, AU: Monash University.

Thompson, Eric. 2006. "Comment." *Current Anthropology* 47(2):332–333.

Thongchai Winichakul. 1994. *Siam Mapped: A History of the Geo-Body of a Nation*. Honolulu: University of Hawaii Press.

Tocqueville, Alexis de. 1835–1840 [2004]. *Democracy in America*, 2 vols. Trans. Arthur Goldhammer. New York: Library of America.

Topley, Marjorie. 1954. "Chinese Women's Vegetarian Houses in Singapore." *Journal of the Malayan Branch of the Royal Asiatic Society* 27(1):51–67.

———. 1956. "Chinese Religion and Religious Institutions in Singapore." *Journal of the Malayan Branch of the Royal Asiatic Society* 29(1):70–118.

———. 1959. "Immigrant Chinese Female Servants and their Hostels in Singapore." *Man* 59:213–215.

———. 1975. "Marriage Resistance in Rural Kwangtung." In *Women in Chinese Society*, ed. Margery Wolf and Roxane Witke, 67–88. Stanford: Stanford University Press.

Totman, Richard. 2003. *The Third Sex: Kathoey—Thailand's Lady Boys*. London: Souvenir Press.

Towle, Evan B. and Lynne M. Morgan. 2002. "Romancing the Transgender Native: Rethinking the Use of the 'Third Gender' Concept." *GLQ* 8(4):469–497.

Trawick, Margaret. 1990. *Notes on Love in a Tamil Family*. Berkeley: University of California Press.

Trocki, Carl A. 1990. *Opium and Empire: Chinese Society in Colonial Singapore*. Ithaca: Cornell University Press.

Trumbach, Randolph. 1993. "London's Sapphists: From Three Sexes to Four Genders in the Making of Modern Culture." In *Third Sex, Third Gender*, ed. Gilbert Herdt, 111–136. New York: Zone Books.

Tsing, Anna. 1993. *In the Realm of the Diamond Queen: Marginality in an Out-of-the-Way Place*. Princeton: Princeton University Press.

———. 2005. *Friction: An Ethnography of Global Connection*. Princeton: Princeton University Press.

Turner, Bryan S. 1996. *The Body and Society*, 2nd ed. London: Sage.

Turner, Victor. 1967. *The Forest of Symbols: Aspects of Ndembu Ritual*. Ithaca: Cornell University Press.

UNAIDS [Joint United Nations Program on HIV/AIDS]. 1999. "Drug User Programme, Ikhlas Community Centre, Pink Triangle, Malaysia." In *Comfort and Hope: Six Cases Studies on Mobilizing Family and Community Care for and by People with HIV/AIDS*, ed. UNAIDS, 37–51. Geneva: UNAIDS.

UNAIDS [Joint United Nations Program on HIV/AIDS]. 2008. "UNAIDS/WHO Epidemiological Fact Sheet on HIV and AIDS and Sexually Transmitted Infections, 2008 Update, for Myanmar." <http://www.who.int/globalatlas/default.asp>.

Van der Kroef, J.M. 1956. "Transvestitism and the Religious Hermaphrodite.". In *Indonesia and the Modern World*, Part II, 183–197. Bandung: Masa Baru.

Van der Meer, Theo. 1991. "Tribades on Trial: Female Same-Sex Offenders in Late Eighteenth-Century Amsterdam." *Journal of the History of Sexuality* 1(3):424–445.

——. 1993. "Sodomy and the Pursuit of a Third Sex in the Early Modern Period." In *Third Sex, Third Gender*, ed. Gilbert Herdt, 137–212. New York: Zone.

Van Driem, George. 1996. "Lexical Categories of Homosexual Behaviour in Modern Burmese." *Maledicta* 12:91–110.

Van Esterik, Penny. 2000. *Materializing Thailand*. Oxford: Berg.

Vaughan, J.D. 1857. "Notes on the Malays of Pinang and Province Wellesley." *Journal of the Indian Archipelago and Eastern Asia* N.S. II(2):115–175.

Vaughn, James C. 2006. "The Culture of the Bohemian Grove: The Dramaturgy of Power." *Michigan Sociological Review* 20:85–123.

Volkman, Toby. 1985. *Feasts of Honor: Ritual and Change in the Toraja Highlands*. Urbana: University of Illinois Press.

Walker, J.H. 1998. "'This Peculiar Acuteness of Feeling': James Brooke and the Enactment of Desire." *Borneo Research Bulletin* 29:148–222.

Walzer, Michael. 1983. *Spheres of Justice: A Defense of Pluralism and Equality*. New York: Basic Books.

——. 1997. *On Toleration*. New Haven: Yale University Press.

——. 2004a. *Arguing About War*. New Haven: Yale University Press.

——. 2004b. *Politics and Passion: Toward a More Egalitarian Liberalism*. New Haven: Yale University Press.

Warren, James. 1993. *Ah Ku and Karayuki-San: Prostitution in Singapore 1870–1940*. Singapore: Oxford University Press.

Waterson, Roxana. 1990. *The Living House: An Anthropology of Architecture in Southeast Asia*. Singapore: Oxford University Press.

Watson, C.W. and Roy Ellen, eds. 1993. *Understanding Witchcraft and Sorcery in Southeast Asia*. Honolulu: University of Hawaii.

Weber, Max. 1918 [1968]. *Economy and Society: An Outline of Interpretive Sociology*, 2 vols, ed. Guenther Roth and Claus Wittich. Berkeley: University of California Press.

——. 1922 [1963]. *The Sociology of Religion*. Boston: Beacon.

Weiner, Annette. 1976. *Women of Value, Men of Renown: New Perspectives in Trobriand Exchange*. Austin: University of Texas Press.

Weston, Kath. 1991. *Families We Choose: Lesbians, Gays, Kinship*. New York: Columbia University Press.

——. 1998. *Long Slow Burn: Sexuality and Social Science*. New York: Routledge.

White, David Gordon. 2003. *Kiss of the Yogini: "Tantric Sex" in Its South Asian Context*. Chicago: University of Chicago Press.

Wiener, Margaret. 1995. *Visible and Invisible Realms: Power, Magic, and Colonial Conquest in Bali*. Chicago: University of Chicago Press.

Wieringa, Saskia. 1999. "Desiring Bodies or Defiant Cultures: Butch-Femme Lesbians in

Jakarta and Lima." In *Female Desires*, ed. Evelyn Blackwood and Saskia Wieringa, 206–231. New York: Columbia University Press.

Wieringa, Saskia, Evelyn Blackwood, and Abha Bhaiya, eds. 2007. *Women's Sexualities and Masculinities in a Globalizing Asia*. New York: Palgrave Macmillan.

Wikan, Unni. 1990. *Managing Turbulent Hearts: A Balinese Formula for Living*. Chicago: University of Chicago Press.

Wilchins, Riki. 1997. *Read My Lips: Sexual Subversion and the End of Gender*. Ithaca: Firebrand Books.

Willford, Andrew C. 2006. *Cage of Freedom: Tamil Identity and the Ethnic Fetish in Malaysia*. Ann Arbor: University of Michigan Press.

Williams, Brackette. 1989. "A Class Act: Anthropology and the Race Across Ethnic Terrain." *Annual Review of Anthropology* 18:401–444.

Winstedt, Richard. 1961. *The Malay Magician, Being Shaman, Shaiva, and Sufi*, rev. ed. Singapore: Oxford University Press.

——. 1969. *Start from Alif: Count from One: An Autobiographical Memoir*. Kuala Lumpur: Oxford University Press.

Wolf, Eric. 1982. *Europe and the People Without History*. Berkeley: University of California Press.

Wolters, O.W. 1970. *The Fall of Srivijaya in Malay History*. Kuala Lumpur: Oxford University Press.

——. 1999. *History, Culture, and Region in Southeast Asian Perspectives*, rev. ed. Ithaca: Southeast Asia Program, Cornell University.

Wood, W.A.R. 1935. *Land of Smiles*. Bangkok: Krungdebarnagar Press.

Woodward, Mark. 1989. *Islam in Java: Normative Piety and Mysticism in the Sultantate of Yogyakarta*. Tucson: University of Arizona Press.

World Health Organization. 2007. *Global Health Atlas*, <http://www.who.int/globalatlas/default.asp>.

Worth, Robert F. 2002. "Duality of Gay Muslims is Tougher After Sept. 11." *New York Times*, January 13.

Wulff, Inger. 1960. "The So-Called Priests of Ngaju Dayak." *Folk* 2:121–132.

Wyatt, David K. 1994. *Studies in Thai History: Collected Articles*. Chiangmai: Silkworm Books.

——. 2002. *Siam in Mind*. Chiangmai: Silkworm Books.

——. 2003. *Thailand: A Short History*, 2nd ed. New Haven: Yale University Press.

Yanagisako, Sylvia. 1995. "Transforming Orientalism: Gender, Nationality, and Class in Asian American Studies." In *Natural Symbols: Essays in Feminist Cultural Analysis*, ed. Sylvia Yanagisako and Carol Delaney, 275–298. New York: Routledge.

Yengoyan, Aram A. 1983. "Transvestitism and the Ideology of Gender: Southeast Asia and Beyond." In *Feminist re-Visions: What Has Been and What Might Be*, ed. Vivian Patraka and Louise Tilly, 135–148. Ann Arbor: Women's Studies Program, University of Michigan.

Zainah Anwar. 1987. *Islamic Revivalism in Malaysia: Dakwah Among the Students*. Kuala Lumpur: Pelanduk Publications.

——. 2001. "What Islam? Whose Islam? Sisters in Islam and the Struggle for Women's Rights." In *The Politics of Multiculturalism: Pluralism and Citizenship in Malaysia, Singapore, and Indonesia*, ed. Robert W. Hefner, 227–252. Honolulu: University of Hawaii Press.

Zelditch, Morris. 2001. "Theories of Legitimacy." In *The Psychology of Legitimacy: Emerging Perspectives on Ideology, Justice, and Intergroup Relations*, ed. John Jost and Brenda Major, 33–53. New York: Cambridge University Press.

Newspapers

New Straits Times (Kuala Lumpur)
New York Times (New York)
News Planet (San Francisco)
Sunday Metro (Kuala Lumpur)
Sydney Star Observer (Sydney)
The Advocate (Los Angeles)
The Star (Kuala Lumpur)
The Straits Times (Singapore)
The Sun (Kuala Lumpur)
The Washington Blade (Washington D.C.)

Index